Springer Series on
Comparative Treatments for Psychological Disorders

Series Editor: Arthur Freeman, EdD, ABPP

1999   **Comparative Treatments for Substance Abuse**
edited by *E. Thomas Dowd, PhD,* and *Loreen Rugle, PhD*

2000   **Comparative Treatments for Relationship Dysfunction**
edited by *Frank M. Dattilio, PhD, ABPP,* and *Louis J. Bevilacqua, MEd*

2000   **Comparative Treatments for Eating Disorders**
edited by *Katherine J. Miller, PhD,* and *J. Scott Mizes, PhD*

Frank M. Dattilio, Ph.D., ABPP, is Clinical Associate in Psychiatry at the Center for Cognitive Therapy, University of Pennsylvania School of Medicine, and is the Clinical Director of the Center for Integrative Psychotherapy in Allentown, Pennsylvania. He is a licensed psychologist and is listed in the National Register of Health Service Providers in Psychology. He is also a clinical member and approved supervisor of the American Association of Marriage and Family Therapy and is a Diplomate in behavioral and clinical psychology with the American Board of Professional Psychology. Dr. Dattilio serves as a full Professor (Adjunct) at Lehigh University in Bethlehem, Pennsylvania. He has also served as a guest lecturer at Harvard School of Medicine and is visiting faculty at several major universities throughout the world.

Dr. Dattilio trained in behavior therapy through the Department of Psychiatry at Temple University School of Medicine under the direction of the late Joseph Wolpe, M.D., and was awarded a postdoctoral fellowship through the Center for Cognitive Therapy, University of Pennsylvania School of Medicine, under the direction of Aaron T. Beck, M.D. He has more than 100 professional publications in the areas of anxiety disorders, behavioral problems, and marital and family discord and has also presented extensively throughout the world. His works have been translated into more than one dozen languages. Among his many publications, Dr. Dattilio is coauthor of *Cognitive Therapy with Couples* (1990), *Panic Disorder: Assessment and Treatment through a Wide Angle Lens* (1999), *The Family Psychotherapy Treatment Planner* (2000); coeditor of *Comprehensive Casebook of Cognitive Therapy* (1992), *Cognitive-Behavioral Strategies in Crisis Intervention* (1994) *and 2nd edition* (2000), *Cognitive Therapy with Children and Adolescents: A Casebook for Clinical Practice* (1995); and editor of *Case Studies in Couple and Family Therapy: Systemic and Cognitive Perspectives* (1998). Dr. Dattilio has also filmed several professional videotapes and audiotapes and is on the editorial board of numerous professional journals.

Louis J. Bevilacqua, M.Ed. is a Doctoral candidate in Clinical Psychology at the Philadelphia College of Osteopathic Medicine and is the Clinical Director of Connections Adolescent and Family Care, a private psychotherapy practice in Exton, PA that specializes in adolescent and family therapy. He is a National Board Certified Counselor, who has been treating at-risk children and their families since 1986. Mr. Bevilacqua has presented numerous workshops on treating depressed and behaviorally disordered adolescents and their families and has published in the area of suicide. He has also been a Guest Lecturer for Immaculate College. His research interests include the treatment of families and couples. His academic interests include teaching comparative therapies, cognitive-behavioral family therapy, and providing clinical supervision to graduate students.

Comparative Treatments for Relationship Dysfunction

Frank M. Dattilio, PhD, ABPP
Louis J. Bevilacqua, MEd
Editors

Springer Series on
Comparative Treatments for
Psychological Disorders

Springer Publishing Company, Inc.
536 Broadway
New York, NY 10012-3955

Acquisitions Editor: Bill Tucker
Production Editor: Helen Song
Cover design by James Scotto-Lavino

00 01 02 03 04 / 5 4 3 2 1

Library of Congress Cataloging-in-Publication Data

Comparative treatments for relationship dysfunction / Frank M.
    Dattilio and Louis Bevilacqua, editors
        p.cm. — (Springer series on comparative treatments for
    psychological disorders)
        Includes bibliographical references and index.
        ISBN 0-8261-1324-9
        1. Marital psychotherapy—Case studies.   2. Family
    psychotherapy—Case studies.   I. Dattilio, Frank M.
    II. Bevilacqua, Louis.   III. Series.
    RC488.5.C634 2000
    616.89'156—dc21   99-088867
                                                                        CIP

Printed in the United States of America

In Memoriam

This book is dedicated to our distinguished colleague and dear friend, Dr. Neil S. Jacobson, whose passing came during the final stages of production of this volume. Jacobson was a giant not only in marital therapy, but also in research on domestic violence and depression. His keen intellect, his indefatigable energy, and his sharp sense of humor were an inspiration to those around him. His absence will be intensely felt by many.

Contents

Contributors   ix
Foreword   xi
Preface   xiii
Acknowledgments   xvii

1   Overview of Couples Therapy   1
    Louis J. Bevilacqua and Frank M. Dattilio
2   Introduction and Case Conceptualization of Mike and Jan   13
    Louis J. Bevilacqua and Frank M. Dattilio

Part I   Systems Theories

3   Bowen Systems Theory   25
    Daniel V. Papero
4   Structural Theory   45
    Harry J. Aponte and Edward J. DiCesare
5   Strategic Therapy   58
    James Keim

Part II Psychodynamic Theories

6   Object Relations Therapy   81
    Jill Savege Scharff and Yolanda de Varela
7   Adlerian Therapy   102
    Jon Carlson and Len Sperry
8   Imago Relationship Therapy   116
    Wade Luquet

Part III Cognitive-Behavioral Theories

  9 A Cognitive-Behavioral Approach   137
     Frank M. Dattilio and Louis J. Bevilacqua

Part IV Integrative Theories

 10 Emotionally Focused Couples Therapy   163
     Susan Johnson
 11 Integrative Behavioral Couple Therapy   186
     Janice Jones, Andrew Christensen, and Neil Jacobson
 12 Integrative Marital Therapy   210
     William C. Nichols
 13 The Intersystem Model   229
     April Westfall
 14 Conflict Resolution Therapy   247
     Susan Heitler
 15 Relationship Enhancement Couples Therapy   273
     Barry G. Ginsberg

Part V Postmodern Theories

 16 Recasting the Therapeutic Drama: A Client-Directed,   301
     Outcome-Informed Approach
     Barry L. Duncan, Jacueline A. Sparks, and Scott D. Miller
 17 Feminist Couples Therapy   325
     Cheryl Rampage
 18 Narrative Therapy with Couples   342
     Jill Freedman and Gene Combs

     Epilogue   362
     Frank M. Dattilio and Louis J. Bevilacqua

Index   *399*

Contributors

Harry J. Aponte, L.S.W., A.C.S.W.
Private practice
Philadelphia
Associate Clinical Professor
MCP Hahnemann University and
Director
Family Therapy Training Program of
  Philadelphia

Jon Carlson, Psy.D., Ed.D., ABPP, ABFamP
Professor of Psychology and
  Counseling
Governors State University
Illinois and
Psychologist
Lake Geneva Wellness Clinic
Lake Geneva, Wisconsin

Andrew Christensen, Ph.D.
Professor
Department of Psychology
University of California, Los Angeles

Gene Combs, M.D.
Codirector
Evanston Family Therapy Center and
Faculty Member
Chicago Center for Family Health

Edward J. DiCesare, Ph.D.
Private practice of psychology and
Consulting Psychologist
Counseling Department
Harcum College
Bryn Mawr, Pennsylvania

Barry L. Duncan, Psy.D.
Psychologist and Family Therapist
and Associate Professor
Department of Family Therapy
Nova Southeastern University
Fort Lauderdale, Florida

Jill H. Freedman, M.S.W.
Codirector
Evanston Family Therapy Center, and
Faculty Member
Chicago Center for Family Health

Barry G. Ginsberg, Ph.D.
Executive Director
Center of Relationship Enhancement
and
Ginsberg Associates
Doylestown, Pennsylvania

Susan Heitler, Ph.D.
Clinical Psychologist
Private practice and
President
TherapyHelp.com
Denver, Colorado

Neil S. Jacobson, Ph.D.*
Professor
University of Washington
Seattle, Washington

---

*deceased

Susan Johnson, Ed.D.
Professor of Psychology and
  Psychiatry
Center for Psychological Services
University of Ottawa
11 Marie Curie
Ottawa, K1N 6N5
Canada [soo@magna.ca] and
Director
Marital and Family Clinic
Ottawa Civic Hospital

Janice Jones, M.A.A.
Doctoral Candidate
Clinical Psychology Program
University of California, Los Angeles

James Keim, M.S.W., LCSW-C
Private practice
Fort Collins, Colorado
[oppositional.com]

Wade Luquet, M.S.W.
Instructor and Coordinator
Marriage and Family Therapy
Graduate Counseling Program
Eastern College
St. Davids, Pennsylvania

Scott D. Miller, Ph.D.
Cofounder
Institute for the Study of Therapeutic
  Change
Chicago, Illinois

William C. Nichols, Ed.D., ABPP
Adjunct Professor
Child and Family Development and
Graduate Faculty Member
University of Georgia

Daniel V. Papero, Ph.D., M.S.S.W.
Clinician
Georgetown Family Center
Washington, D.C.

Cheryl Rampage, Ph.D.
Senior Therapist
Family Institute
Northwestern University
Evanston, Illinois

Jill Savege Scharff, M.D.
Codirector International Institute of
  Object Relations Therapy
Washington, D.C. and
Clinical Professor of Psychiatry
Georgetown University Medical
  School

Jacqueline A. Sparks, M.S.
Marriage and Family Therapist and
Doctoral Candidate in Family
  Therapy
Nova Southeastern University
Fort Lauderdale, Flordia

Len Sperry, M.D., Ph.D.
Vice-Chair and Professor
Department of Psychiatry and
  Behavioral Medicine
Medical College of Wisconsin

Yolanda de Varela, M.Ed.
Psychologist
Satellite program of the International
  Institute of Object Relations
  Therapy
Panama City, Panama

April Westfall, Ph.D.
Clinical Assistant Professor of
  Psychiatry and Human Behavior
Jefferson Medical College and
Director of Clinical Services
PENN Council for Relationships
Phildadelphia, Pennsylvania

Foreword

One of the most important articles ever written by a clinical psychologist was a piece by Paul Meehl published many years ago and entitled "Why I Never Attend Case Conferences." In addition to the many other collegial turnoffs frequently observed by Meehl at such gatherings, he noted the regularity with which mental health professionals seem to turn these conferences into soapboxes for proselytizing, and arenas for competing for their colleagues' admiration and approbation.

Comparative Treatments for Relationship Dysfunction gets as close to a case conference format as could any printed presentation of multiple views of the same stimulus material, but, very fortunately, without the kind of conference-induced narcissism scorned by Meehl. Indeed, while the authors in this volume are certainly aware of the presence of their next door chapter-neighbors, there is a uniform respectfulness toward alternative views that makes this book very user-friendly and encouraging to read.

Not that this work is a multi-authored lovefest—it is never quite certain just how strenuously these talented contributors might have taken each other to task for some of their views, had this been an actual, face-to-face discussion of the case material. But what emerges from reading their various points of view is just that—that there *are* varied points of view about effective couple therapy. In my view, reading this volume also makes clear just how often we use different language to refer to the same underlying principles of human behavior change.

This book captures a good deal of the conceptual tension in the field of couple therapy today. As an integratively oriented therapist, I was very comfortable with, and even appreciative of, this implicit tension. But, as I read this manuscript, I frequently found myself assuming the role of the student reader, and wondered how this text would be absorbed by a relative neophyte in the field.

When I was in graduate school in the late 1960s, this book could never have appeared. Why? Because there weren't 16 theories of couples therapy! An important publication of that decade by Gerald Manus fittingly referred to couples therapy as a "technique in search of a theory." Some loosely patched together ideas from psychoanalytic therapy were as close to a coherent "theory" of conjoint couples therapy as one could find.

While it was not very challenging to master "the literature" of couples therapy in those days, it was also intellectually quite unsatisfying to do so. On the other hand, the student of couples therapy in the new millennium might wish for a return to such simplicity, when he or she now faces the daunting task of trying to make sense of so many competing theories. But, as they say in sports training, "No pain, no gain." I think this kind of varied panorama of perspectives is just what is needed by student therapists (and by more seasoned "veterans" trying to "stay in shape"—to stretch the athletic metaphor).

Why do I say this? Do I want therapists to suffer and drive themselves mad from doing all the comparative study of different theories that the very undertaking of this volume so strongly endorses? Well, maybe a qualified "yes." Because, in the end, good therapists, couple or otherwise, must, as some wise person once said, "make a theory one's own." That doesn't mean making up one's own theory (with over 400 extant theories of psychotherapy, we have quite enough!). It means finding a theory and a way of working therapeutically that really fits the therapist. While I am a moderately rabid empiricist, and certainly favor therapy methods that have some research grounding, I do not believe that therapists typically choose (or switch to alternative) modes of treatment on strictly scientific grounds. We choose therapies (or they choose us) because we identify with significant teachers, or because we find some way of thinking aesthetically or intellectually appealing.

Student therapists and more experienced therapists alike require numerous theories and methods to bump up against in order to define themselves clearly. As Robin Skynner once put the matter, we need "different thinks for different shrinks." So, if reading about 16 different approaches to the same clinical case material makes you, the reader, even just a bit disoriented, then *Comparative Treatments for Relationship Dysfunction* will have achieved its purpose. It will have helped us take several large steps forward in the field's evolving quest to enhance therapeutic effectiveness, not only through the expansion of therapeutic methods, but through the expansion of therapists' minds.

Alan S. Gurman, Ph.D.
University of Wisconsin Medical School

Preface

It is both an exciting and exhilarating time to compose a text on comparative psychotherapy. This work is being released not only at the turn of the century, but at the advent of a new millennium. What better time is there to share all that we know about couples treatment for the future?

At the turn of the last century, psychotherapy was only percolating in a stage of conceptualization. The concept of couples therapy at that time was nonexistent, and would only make its debut midway through the 20th century.

Despite its infancy, however, the field of couples therapy has grown exponentially within the past 50 years, to the point that several dozen theories now exist on the treatment of relationship dysfunction. What is more, serious attention has been given not only to the expansion of various modalities of couples treatment, but also to the concept of the integration of various models of couples and family therapy.

This book provides the reader with a comparative look at the contemporary models of couples treatment. The particular case of Mike and Jan was selected because we believe that it is a representation of the typical case that most clinicians are likely to encounter in clinical practice. With this type of comparison, it is our hope that we can fortify our search for what works and what does not with difficult couples. This text was designed to provide students, researchers, and practitioners with a comparison of how different modalities approach the same case from clinical specialists' respective therapeutic domains. In this regard, readers are able to compare and contrast various modalities, in an attempt to draw their own conclusions as to what may prove to be most efficacious for them as therapists.

This book also comes in the wake of several other works that have attempted to compare and contrast various modalities of treatment (Dattilio, 1998; Gurman, 1985). In addition, several video series have been produced, such as the famous Hillcrest Series, in which several pioneers interviewed the same families (Friedlander & Highlen, 1984; Friedlander, Highlen, & Lassiter, 1985). More recently, the film series "Five Approaches to Linda" included one-session interviews with the same patient by prominent therapists of varying modalities (Goldfried, Lazarus, Dattilio, Glasser, & Masterson, 1996).

With the presence of a well-established repertoire of therapeutic tools and modalities, mental health practitioners have the luxury of being able to select various combinations of approaches to address the broad spectrum of cases that are encountered in the field.

It is our belief that we have selected some of the finest names in the field of couples therapy to accomplish our goal: Providing a broad comparison for readers that will enable them to infer the similarities and differences in treating challenging cases.

Each chapter provides a brief update and overview of the respective modality along with each contributor's first-hand impressions of the case of Mike and Jan. We have divided the chapters into sections that best reflect the grouping of modalities. For example, several chapters fall into the division of the Systems Approach. A straight-forward chapter on Bowen Systems Therapy by Papero sets the stage for the Strategic chapter by Keim and a Structural Approach by Aponte and DiCesare. These chapters are followed by the psychodynamic approach, which includes work by Scharff and de Varela, Carlson & Sperry, and Luquet.

Only one chapter, contributed by the editors, represents the cognitive-behavioral approach, even though behavioral and cognitive therapy is integrated within a number of the other theories represented in this text.

The largest grouping of approaches is contrasted by the integrative theories, which portray a number of blended hybrids by Jones, Christensen, and Jacobson; Nichols; Westfall; Heitler; and Ginsberg.

Included among the postmodern theories are the works of Combs and Freedman on narrative therapy, Rampage on feminist therapy, and Duncan, Sparks, and Miller on client-directed, outcome-informed therapy.

It is our hope that we simulate an atmosphere in which the reader can "sit in" on the master therapists at work, maintaining consistency by using the same case study. In this manner, the reader may come to be more familiar with this case, which will hopefully help with the conceptualization and digestion of each of the respective approaches to treatment.

Each chapter also follows with a list of suggested readings and an epilogue of what may be concluded from this exercise of comparison.

In some instances, the information contained in the case of Mike and Jan was not enough to allow for every diverse approach and unique set of questions. As with any case, one can never have enough information. Therefore, some contributors were limited in how they could respond, despite our efforts to make the case as comprehensive as possible.

We are confident that this text will prove to be extremely useful to those who wish to compare and contrast contemporary theories of couples therapy. What's more, it may lend itself nicely to those also wishing to construct a base for integrating various theories in an attempt to find the right fit in treatment.

Frank M. Dattilio
Louis J. Bevilacqua

REFERENCES

Dattilio, F. M. (Ed.). (1998). *Case Studies in Couple and Family Therapy: Systemic and Cognitive Perspectives.* New York: Guilford Press.

Friedlander, M. L., & Highlen, P. S. (1984). A spatial view of interpersonal structure of family interviews: Similarities and differences across counselors. *Journal of Counseling Psychology, 31,* 477–487.

Friedlander, M. L., Highlen, P. S., & Lassiter, W. L. (1985). Content analytic comparison of four expert counselors' approaches to family treatment: Ackerman, Bowen, Jackson, and Whitaker. *Journal of Counseling Psychology, 32,* 171–180.

Goldfried, M., Lazarus, A. A., Dattilio, F. M., Glasser, W., & Masterson, J. F. (1996). Videotape: *Five Approaches to Linda* (Five - 50-minute cassettes). Bethlehem, PA: Lehigh University Media.

Gurman, A. (1985). (Ed.). *Casebook of marital therapy.* New York: Guilford Press.

Acknowledgments

An edited work such as this is not possible without the assistance of a number of individuals. We would like to thank the many colleagues who provided us with valuable input into the refinement of the case of Mike and Jan. These individuals include Maryann T. Dattilio, Joan M. Doherty, Norman B. Epstein, Francis S. Gaal, and Roberta Penn.

Many thanks are expressed to Michael P. Nichols, who provided us with excellent consultation on the overview chapter, as well as recommendations on how to group the various chapters in the text.

Michael Hoyt was also extremely helpful as a resource for soliciting contributors as well as providing his verbal support for the project.

Art Freeman has also been of great support to us, not only as the series editor, but as a trusted colleague and good friend.

We also thank our secretary, Carol Jaskolka, for her expertise in typing and assembling of the entire manuscript, as well as our editors at Springer Publishing Company, Bill Tucker and Helen Song, for their patience and untiring support during the development of this project.

Many thanks to Mike and Jan for serving as the model for which to compare against the many different therapeutic approaches.

Lastly, we would like to thank our spouses and families, Maryann and Michael Dattilio, Debbie, Rachael, and Amanda Leigh Bevilacqua, for their patience and understanding with our absences during the preparation of this manuscript. They have truly taught us to realize and appreciate the value of salubrious family life.

1

Overview of Couples Therapy

Louis J. Bevilacqua and Frank M. Dattilio

The roots of couples therapy extend almost as far back as individual psychotherapy. Until recently, however, couples therapy has had little effect on the field of therapy in general. In fact, quite the opposite is true. Couples therapy, or what used to be referred to as marriage counseling, was generally practiced outside of the therapeutic mainstream, which prior to the 1960s was predominantly psychiatry or psychoanalysis. This was due largely to the fact that the psychiatric community tended to follow Freud's belief that contact with a patient's family was taboo. Another reason for this was the influence of the medical community, which viewed problems within a marriage less seriously and not necessarily requiring psychotherapy. Despite this majority rule, there were several individuals who disagreed. For instance, Clarence Oberdorf, a psychoanalyst, was the first to present the psychoanalysis of married couples at the American Psychiatric Association Convention in 1931 (Nichols & Schwartz, 1998). In 1948, another psychoanalyst, Bela Mittleman, described how it could be beneficial for the same analyst to see a husband and wife, so that the irrational perceptions of each could be reexamined (Nichols & Schwartz, 1998).

In the 1950s, as the family therapy movement began to take hold, the focus began to broaden even more to all the members of the family unit. Framo (1996) writes of the remarkable shifts that became evident when family members began to be included in sessions and were viewed as needing help and as possible keys to creating changes, as opposed to noxious intruders. Framo (1996) analogizes the invention of seeing families to the discovery of the microscope, greatly magnifying the observer's scope of vision. For example, in family therapy it was often observed that as the identified patient began to improve, someone else in the family began to develop symptoms. This led to the conceptualization of the family as a system opening an entirely new perspective on treatment.

It wasn't until the 1960s and 1970s that the behavioral approach gained initial recognition among couples and family therapists. Although behavioral therapies were not considered systems therapies, they did take into consideration the effects of interactions among individuals. As a result, the couple was seen as a unit, in which each partner's behavior reinforced the other's behavior reciprocally. Consequently, as one partner became more critical the other partner tended to respond in a similar fashion, creating a circular pattern of interaction. Thus, the behavioral approach aimed to increase the amount and frequency of positive interactions between partners. A technique often utilized to achieve this goal was the use of behavioral contracts.

From the 1950s and up through the early 1980s, numerous individuals were conducting couples therapy. However, up to that point, there remained no central theoretical foundation from which a therapist could draw upon. In fact, histori-cally, couples therapists have generally borrowed ideas and interventions from various schools of individual psychology. This led Manus (1966) to write his article, "Marriage Counseling: A Technique in Search of a Theory." It is comfort-ing to report that 30 years after the publication of this article, couples therapy has finally earned the respect and acceptance it has long deserved. It is puzzling to note, however, why couples therapy took so long to have an impact on the field of therapy. In order to shed some light on this, the present chapter will provide a brief review of some of the contributing factors that led to the development of couples therapy.

One of the contributing factors was the various social movements that devel-oped in response to many of society's ills. One of these ills involved the family unit. Throughout the early 1900s, as well as in contemporary society, the rates of divorce and the increase of incidents of delinquency among juveniles was of great concern. The marriage-counseling field was one movement that responded to such concerns. As is true today, many parents turned to helping professionals to gain advice on issues ranging from child-rearing to sexual intimacy matters. Providing advice and counseling to couples was more of a part-time second profession for many physicians, particularly gynecologists, as well as for social workers, psychologists, ministers, lawyers, and educators. No one discipline claimed a monopoly on such services. As an artifact, couples therapy grew out of various fields and schools of thought on individual dynamics.

One field in particular was the psychiatric community. Prior to the 1950s, Freud's psychoanalysis was the dominant ideology among practitioners. Ac-cording to the psychoanalytic perspective, family relationships were viewed as contributive to the development of the individuals' personality structure. Many followers of Freud, however, eventually questioned the validity of this perspec-tive, and eventually disengaged from Freud to form new schools of thought. One such individual was Alfred Adler. A main idea that Adler stressed was the importance of social factors. In particular, Adler stressed the need to achieve adequacy and power and to overcome feelings of inferiority as the central driving force of one's life. In many respects, Adler's view of the individual struggling for power can be seen in most family therapy theories, which attempt to explain an individual's pathology as rooted in family conflict. In the 1930s, although psychoanalysis continued to be the primary theoretical approach, many analysts were leaving Europe and migrating to America to escape the Nazi invasion. It was around this time that the influence of sociology and anthropology began to take hold within the American community of analysts. An example of this can be found in Erich Fromm's emphasis on individuality, which foreshadowed the emphasis by Bowen and others on the individual differentiating from the family. Another example is Harry Stack Sullivan's work in treating patients with schizophrenia, which was emulated by many of the early family therapists such as Bowen, Haley, and Bateson who also began their work with patients diagnosed with schizophrenia (Broderick & Schrader, 1981).

Another influential movement that effected the field of couples therapy was that of the sexologists. Havelock Ellis and Magnus Hirschfeld are typically credited with being the two most influential sexologists. As Broderick and Schrader (1981) have explained, Ellis and Hirschfeld "paved the way for working with couples in a practical way on the sexual problems of everyday life" (p. 9). Ellis worked with many individuals, mostly women, on overcoming their sexual fears. Ellis wrote several volumes describing various aspects of sexual behavior, and most of his writings included excerpts of the sexual histories of his patients. What was unique about these works was how Ellis remained free from moralizing, which was so common among other sexual scholars. One of Ellis' goals was to "spare others the ignorance and discomfort in sexual matters which he experienced as a young man" (Broderick & Schrader, 1981).

While Ellis was working in Great Britain, Hirschfeld founded the Institute of Sexual Science in Berlin. Perhaps one of Hirschfeld's greatest contributions was his five-volume work on sexual education. This work was based on the responses of 10,000 questionnaires completed by those men and women who came to him for advice (Broderick & Schrader, 1981). Another important contribution by Hirschfeld was the development of the first German Marriage Consultation Bureau. This inspired Karl Kautsky of Austria to establish the first "Center for Sexual Advice." Hundreds of additional centers soon emerged. In addition to discussing birth control methods and eugenics, psychological and relational matters were routinely discussed (Hoenig, 1978).

Two other noted individuals who had a tremendous impact on the field of sexology and couples therapy were William Masters and Virginia Johnson. In the 1950s and 1960s, Masters and Johnson discovered that the human sexual response cycle had three distinct stages. This led to enormous advances in the treatment of sexual inadequacy and revolutionized the treatment that sex counselors provided to couples. In particular, their conceptualization of a sexual dysfunction as a problem of the couple versus the individual, and their intense brief approach, was demonstrated to be highly effective. Soon, others began to adapt their own versions of the approach that Masters and Johnson had been researching and using to treat couples.

One final movement to mention is the Family Life Education Movement. It was within this movement that Ernest Groves created the first Marriage and Family Relations course offered for college credit (Broderick & Schrader, 1981). Groves' approach was different then the traditional approaches in that it was practical, eclectic and addressed not only methods for analyzing and describing relationships, but also how to improve the courtship and marriage of the students participating in the course. Ernest Groves went on to become one of the pioneers of the marriage counseling movement. In 1942, Groves, along with Abraham Stone, proposed the establishment of a professional organization for marriage counselors. This idea was further developed when Lester Dearborn and psychiatrist Robert Laidlaw invited Ernest and Gladys Groves, Emily Mudd, Abraham Stone, Robert L. Dickerson, and Valerie Parker to meet and discuss organizational plans. Such meetings continued over the next 3 years, until 1945, when the American Association of Marriage Counselors (AAMC) was officially formed and Dr. Ernest Groves was elected as the first president (Broderick & Schrader, 1981). Around the same time, David Mace founded the National Marriage Guidance Council of Great Britain. Whereas the AAMC was developed for professionals who met specific requirements, the National Marriage Guidance Council of Great Britain was comprised of lay persons who were trained to be marriage counselors. A primary interest of AAMC was to determine who could be a marriage counselor. As a result, many academic and professional standards were set. By 1956, there were three training centers recognized and accredited by AAMC. These included the Marriage Council of Philadelphia, The Merrill-Palmer School in Detroit, and the Menninger Clinic in Topeka, Kansas, all programs that currently remain in existence.

Another significant development in the movement of couples therapy took place in 1963, when California became the first state to institute a law for licensing marriage and family counselors. Many individuals in the field recognize this act as marking the initiation of the marriage counseling profession. Despite this recognition, marriage counselors continued to lack an identity. One of the ways the marriage-counseling field sought an identity was by trying to join forces with the family therapy field. This attempt was met with friction and concern. As Jay Haley (1984) described, "Marriage counseling did not really seem relevant to the developing family therapy field, and it is a puzzle as well as a matter of theoretical concern why that was so" (p. 6). One of the primary issues surrounding the friction was whether or not those trained as marriage counselors were capable of effectively treating families as well. Despite the differences and concerns, the two fields merged to form the American Association of Marriage and Counseling

(AAMC). In 1970 the name was changed to the American Associatio
and Family Counselors (AAMFC). Eight years later, the name
again to the American Association of Marriage and Family Therap
This was due partly to the negative connotations (i.e., advice-givei) ~~~~~~
uted to the term of "counselor." Throughout the 1960s and 1970s, the marriage
counselors, or couples therapists, were basically absorbed within the field of
family therapy. It is the family therapy arena within which most couples therapies
are based today.

One of the most common areas addressed in any type of relationship therapy
is the aspect of communication. One prominent individual who studied the communication process early on in the field of relationship therapy was Gregory
Bateson. Bateson, who studied anthropology and animal behavior as well as
cybernetics, is for initially circulating the ideas of information, control, and
feedback as it relates to the process of communicating among couples and families.
In 1952, Bateson received a grant from the Rockefeller Foundation to expand
on his study in the area of communication with couples and families. Bateson
invited Jay Haley, who had just earned his Masters degree in Communications,
to Palo Alto in order to work together on a study focusing on the nature of
communication. John Weakland, a chemical engineer who was interested in
cultural anthropology, was also invited to join the investigation team. The primary
interest of the Bateson Project was to develop a comprehensive theory of communication, rather than developing an approach to treatment. Unfortunately, no
cohesive and comprehensive theory ever developed from Batesons' endeavors
(Guerin & Chabot, 1997).

In 1954, Don Jackson, who had received clinical training from Harry Stack
Sullivan, was brought in as a consultant and supervisor to the Bateson project.
The study that resulted from this endeavor became a landmark in the investigation
of communication among schizophrenics and their families (see Bateson, Jackson,
Haley, & Weakland, 1956). It was from this study that the terms of logical levels
and symptom functionality emanated. Jackson's concept of homeostasis explained
how families resist change and proposed that when families are challenged,
members fight to keep the status quo regardless of the emotional cost to a family
member. This concept also led to further refinement of the communications
theory. Another key concept that grew out of this work was the double-bind
theory, which Jackson and his colleagues continued to refine. This developed
into a therapeutic intervention known as the therapeutic double-bind, and can be
seen in the techniques of paradoxical intervention and reframing as practiced by
most contemporary strategic therapists (Guerin & Chabot, 1997). In 1959, Jackson
founded the Mental Research Institute (MRI) and continued to focus his efforts
on treatment. The primary interest among the MRI group was not on power and
control in relationships but more on the interactional sequence that occurred
among family members.

Haley moved on to work with Salvador Minuchin and Braulio Montalvo at the Philadelphia Child Guidance Clinic. It was their collaboration that helped to develop the structural approach. In the structural approach, techniques such as reframing, restructuring, joining, and enactments are used to produce change among clients. Haley continued to refine his thinking and focused more on the issues of hierarchy, power, and strategic interventions. One of the most influential people evident in Haley's work was Milton Erickson. This is clearly seen in Haley's work on trance and paradoxical communication. Another significant contributor to this effort was Cloe Madanes, who worked along with Haley to develop the strategic approach. One specific approach that Haley and Madanes developed for working with couples is that of Ordeal Therapy. Couples would be instructed to experience an ordeal together. The classic example of this strategic move involves the couple with a history of a sadomasochistic and physically abusive relationship. The two were instructed to shave their heads and bury the hair far away from their home. They were to then visit the burial site on a regular basis. This ritual was intended to provide a shared experience, which would then activate various unused and more functional relationship patterns (Guerin & Chabot, 1997).

As previously mentioned, a characteristic of most couples therapies has been to borrow ideas from various other approaches. Keeping with this practice, the Milan group (Selvini-Palazzoli, Boscolo, Cecchin, and Prata) pulled together the works of various others, such as Bateson, Haley, Minuchin, Jackson, and Bowen, to develop their systemic approach. An example of how they borrowed ideas can be seen in this groups belief that therapy is more beneficial when it is less frequent (i.e., once a month). This was often reflected by Bowen. Another characteristic of the Milan group is the idea of circular questioning, in which each question is framed to address differences of perceptions about events and relationships (Guerin & Chabot, 1997). The ideas of the Milan group can also be seen in the works of Papp and Hoffman from the Ackerman Institute and Watzlawick, Weakland, and Fisch from the MRI group.

Another approach that was strongly influenced by the MRI group and Milton Erickson is Solution-Focused Therapy (Shoham, Rohrbaugh, & Patterson, 1995). This approach developed during the 1970s and 1980s. Some of the key figures often associated with this model are Steve de Shazer, Insoo Kim Berg, and their associates at the Brief Family Therapy Center in Milwaukee (Piercy, Sprenkle, Wetchler, and Associates, 1996). The focus of this approach is to address the exceptions to the identified problem and to develop solutions that work. For example, to find times when a couple is getting along and to do more of that behavior, which is referred to as solution behavior (Gale & Long, 1996). This approach is oftentimes brief and symptom-driven. Solutions are sought through behavioral changes. Many solution-focused therapists also refer to themselves as post-modernists and social constructionists. Many of their ideas are also present within the narrative approach. It is also important to point out that the approach developed from the MRI group (brief problem-focused therapy) is generally seen as the parent model to this Milwaukee model. One last point to note is that often times both of these therapy approaches treat couples problems separately, by seeing the partners individually (Shoham et al., 1995).

Approaches that are less brief and less focused on the solution tend to involve psychoanalytic principles. One psychoanalytic approach in particular is the Object Relations Model, which was strongly influenced by Melanie Klein, Ronald Fairbairn, Harry Dicks, Jill Scharff, David Scharff, and Donald Winnicott (Framo, 1981; Nichols & Schwartz, 1998). This model emphasizes how people's early experiences and expectations contribute to their conceptualizations of these relationships and later impact their relationships as adults. A primary focus is on the impact of the parent-infant attachment experience on the developmental process. Two other important psychoanalytic theorists are Ivan Boszormenyi-Nagy, a psychiatrist and James Framo. Framo combined Fairbairn and Dicks' object relations theory with an intergenerational approach (Framo, 1981, 1996). Framo is primarily interested in the relationship between intrapsychic and transactional influences. Specifically, Framo's intent is to understand how individuals internalize past family conflict; he believes that they are now living through these conflicts with their spouses and children. Two interventions that Framo emphasizes is couples group therapy (three couples per group) and families of origin treatment. Ivan Boszormenyi-Nagy and his colleagues created an integrated systems model, which became known as contextual therapy. A primary issue in contextual therapy is that of invisible loyalties, which influence family members' behavior. These loyalties of what has been given and what is owed are tracked on unconscious ledgers. These ledgers carry a belief of entitlement as well as indebtedness. One of the goals of contextual therapy is to loosen these chains of loyalty in order for the person to give up symptomatic behaviors (Piercy et al., 1996).

Another approach that focuses on intrapsychic processes is that of the various experiential therapies. One of the founders, and perhaps the most influential individual, among the experientialists, is Virginia Satir. Satir, who was more of a communications theorist, blended a variety of approaches including Gestalt therapy, psychodrama, logotherapy, client-centered therapy, and communications training into a dynamic family therapy approach, which is still influential today. Another charismatic and influential individual was Carl Whitaker, who has been described by Nichols as the most dynamic—and irreverent—founders of family therapy. He believed therapy to be more of an art than a theory. Whitaker contended that therapists would be most effective if they paid specific attention to their own growth. As with most therapy models, the notability of the experiential therapists has been strongly influenced by the personality of their founders. Since the deaths of Satir and Whitaker, experiential therapies have suffered a great loss (Wetchler & Piercy, 1996). The new wave, however, of experiential therapy is continued by the works of Augustus Napier and David Keith, as well as within the emotionally focused therapy (EFT). Some of the most noted individuals associated with EFT include Susan Johnson, Leslie Greenberg, and Jeremy Safran. EFT focuses on attachment problems and believes that people hide their "primary emotions" and, as a defense, exhibit "secondary reactive emotions." This leads to negative interactions with others. The goal of therapy is to access these primary emotions and to restructure the emotional bond between individuals in order to promote a more functional relationship. EFT highlights the primary role that emotion plays in the defining and redefining of a relationship (Johnson & Greenberg, 1995).

Among the postmodern approaches is narrative therapy. The narrative approach moves away from the traditional family therapy view of human behavior. It is based on the view that individuals construct stories to make sense of their daily lives and experiences. Such stories are facts of history from the client's perspective, which are partly truth and partly constructions created by that individual. By listening to and identifying an individual's stories, the narrative therapist works to help individuals construct alternative stories, or, as Michael White describes, "re-storying." Without being able to understand what that truth or story is, a therapist's work is futile. It is believed that when knowledge and understanding is considered constructed, rather than discovered, by the telling of a story, clients can then begin to externalize their problems and develop alternative empowering stories. Another important aspect of the narrative approach is how it externalizes "the problem" from not just the individual but also the family system. Instead, the problem is seen as stemming from cultural and societal practices (Nichols & Schwartz, 1998; Shoham et al., 1995).

Another approach is that of feminist therapy. In the late 1970s and early 1980s, gender and the issues of power in intimate relationships became more and more of a focus. Literature in this area began to mushroom, typified by articles such as "A Feminist Approach to Family Therapy" (1978) by Rachel Hare-Mustin and books like "Feminist Family Therapy: A Casebook" (1988) by Goodrich, Rampage, Ellman, and Halstead. A sensitivity to the issues of power and gender was and continues to be incorporated into the therapies of a very diverse group of practitioners. One of the ways such issues have been woven into treatment has been through the involvement of the dimensions of gender in the formulation of the problem definition as well as the solution. Some of the other leading women in the feminist movement and the family therapy field include Peggy Papp, Marianne Walters, Betty Carter, and Olga Silverstein.

Two other approaches that have come about within the last 20 years include Integrative Marital Therapy and Imago Relationship Therapy (IRT).

Among those primarily associated with the Integrative Marital Therapy approach are William Nichols (1998), Larry Feldman (1992), and Feldman and

Pinsof (1982). Within this approach, several theories are combined. Among them are family systems; psychodynamic theory—particularly object relations; and social learning theories (Nichols, 1998).

Harville Hendrix (1988) was the primary contributor to the development of the Imago Relationship Therapy approach. Luquet and Hannah (1998) have also contributed greatly to the expansion and recognition of IRT. IRT is another approach which combines various theories and schools of thought. These include self-psychology, behavioral theory, systems theory, psychoanalysis, and physics, as well as various Western spiritual traditions (Luquet & Hendrix, 1998). A primary focus of IRT couples therapy is on the communication process, which is addressed through the technique of the "couple's dialogue." Similarly, Relationship Enhancement Therapy outlines specific ways for couples to communicate. Bernard Guerney and his associates originated the Relationship Enhancement approach in the 1960s, pulling together psychodynamic, behavioral, communications, experiential, and systems theory perspectives (Ginsberg, 1997; Guerney, 1977). Within the Relationship Enhancement approach, couples are taught various skills through a didactic presentation. The role of the therapist is that of a facilitator or consultant. This is also true of the therapist role in the cognitive-behavioral approach. Cognitive-behavioral marital therapy (CBMT) has its roots in behavioral marital therapy, which focused on the principles of social exchange theory (Jacobson & Margolin, 1979). One of the pioneers of behavioral marital therapy is Richard Stuart. Stuart worked with distressed couples by helping them focus on positive patterns of interaction rather than on negative exchanges. The use of contingency contracts was a primary intervention used by Stuart, as well as "caring days," in which couples would schedule specific days to demonstrate how much they cared for each other (Stuart, 1969). Within distressed couples, there is a tendency for more negative exchanges. An example of this is, as one partner communicates in a negative manner the probability increases that the other partner will respond in a similar fashion. The behavioral approach targeted this factor and developed interventions to shift the ratio of displeasing behaviors to more pleasing interactions among couples. In the last 10 to 15 years, many behavioral theorists have incorporated the cognitive factors involved in marital distress (Bacoum & Epstein, 1990; Bacoum, Epstein, & Rankin, 1995; Dattilio, 1993, 1994, 1997, 1998; Epstein & Bacoum, 1998). In addition to learning how to act more positively with each other, couples must learn how to communicate more effectively. A strong component within the cognitive-behavioral approach involves teaching couples problem solving and communication skills. Overall, the cognitive-behavioral approach is designed to address the interrelations among the behavioral, cognitive, and emotional factors that influence the quality of a couple's relationship.

One of the most recent theories of couples treatment to be developed is Integrative Behavioral Couples Therapy (IBCT) (Christensen, Jacobson, & Babcock, 1995). In addition to the focus on behavioral changes, IBCT places an emphasis on emotional acceptance of each other's behavior. There is also a cognitive piece to IBCT. This is clearly evident in the reframing that is done to help each partner gain a new understanding of their partner's negative behavior. In doing so, a softening develops in how each partner responds to the other. This is characteristic of many experiential therapies, particularly Emotionally Focused Therapy.

From this brief overview, it is clear that couples therapy is no longer the hodgepodge it used to be. Rather, psychotherapy with couples now includes, as Gurman and Jacobson (1995) have described, some of the most significant advances in conceptual understanding, clinical application, and empirical support as can be found in any other branch of psychotherapy. As Gurman and Jacobson reported, couples therapy has now "come of age."

REFERENCES

Bacoum, D. H., & Epstein, N. (1990). *Cognitive-behavioral marital therapy.* New York: Brunner/Mazel.

Bacoum, D. H., Epstein, N., & Rankin, L. A. (1995). Cognitive aspects of cognitive-behavioral marital therapy. In N. S. Jacobson & A. S. Gurman (Eds.), *Clinical handbook of couple therapy* (pp. 65–90). New York: Guilford Press.

Bateson, G., Jackson, D., Haley, J., & Weakland, J. (1956). Toward a theory of schizophrenia. *Behavioral Science, 1,* 256–264.

Broderick, C., & Schrader, S. (1981). The history of professional marriage and family therapy. In A. S. Gurman & D. P. Kniskern (Eds.), *Handbook of family therapy* (pp. 5–35). New York: Brunner/Mazel.

Christensen, A., Jacobson, H., & Babcock, J. (1995). Integrative behavioral couple therapy. In N. S. Jacobson & A. S. Gurman (Eds.), *Clinical handbook of couple therapy* (pp. 31–64). New York: Guilford Press.

Dattilio, F. M. (1993). Cognitive techniques with couples and families. *The Family Journal, 1*(1), 51–56.

Dattilio, F. M. (1994). Families in crisis. In F. M. Dattilio & A. Freeman (Eds.), *Cognitive-behavioral strategies in crisis intervention* (pp. 278–301). New York: Guilford Press.

Dattilio, F. M. (1997). Family therapy. In R. L. Leahy (Ed.), *Practicing cognitive therapy: A guide to interventions* (pp. 409–450). Northvale, NJ: Jason Aronson.

Dattilio, F. M. (1998). *Case studies in couple and family therapy: Systemic and cognitive perspectives.* New York: Guilford Press.

Epstein, N., & Bacoum, D. H. (1998). Cognitive-behavioral couple therapy. In F. M. Dattilio (Ed.), *Case studies in couple and family therapy: Systemic and cognitive perspectives* (pp. 37–61). New York: Guilford Press.

Feldman, L. (1992). *Integrating individual and family therapy.* New York: Brunner/Mazel.

Feldman, L., & Pinsof, W. (1982). Problem maintenance in family systems: An integrative model. *Journal of Marital and Family Therapy, 8,* 295–308.

Framo, J. (1981). The integration of marital therapy with sessions with family of origin. In A. S. Gurman & D. P. Kniskern (Eds.), *Handbook of family therapy* (pp. 131–158). New York: Brunner/Mazel.

Framo, J. (1996). A personal retrospective of the family therapy field: Then and now. *Journal of Marital and Family Therapy, 22*(3), 289–316.

Gale, J., & Long, J. (1996). Theoretical foundations of family therapy. In F. Piercy, D. Sprenkle, J. Wetchler, and Associates (Eds.), *Family therapy sourcebook* (2nd ed.) (pp. 1–24). New York: Guilford Press.

Ginsberg, B. (1997). *Relationship enhancement family therapy.* New York: Wiley.

Goodrich, T., Rampage, C., Ellman, B., & Halstead, K. (1988). *Feminist family therapy: A casebook.* New York: Norton.

Guerin, P., & Chabot, D. (1997). Development of family systems theory. In P. L. Wachtel & S. B. Messer (Eds.), *Theories of psychotherapy: Origins and evolution* (pp. 181–225). Washington, DC: American Psychological Association.

Guerney, B. (1977). *Relationship enhancement.* San Francisco: Josey-Bass.

Gurman, A., & Jacobson, N. (1995). Therapy with couples: A coming of age. In N. Jacobson & A. Gurman (Eds.), *Clinical handbook of couple therapy* (pp. 1–10). New York: Guilford Press.

Haley, J. (1984). Marriage or family therapy. *The American Journal of Family Therapy, 12*(2), 3–14.

Hare-Mustin, R. (1978). A feminist approach to family therapy. *Family Process, 17,* 181–194.

Hendrix, H. (1988). *Getting the love you want: A guide for couples.* New York: Holt.

Hoenig, J. (1978). Dramatic personae: Selected biographical sketches of 19th century pioneers in sexology. In J. Money & H. Musaph (Eds.), *Handbook of sexology* (Vol. 1). New York: Elsevier.

Jacobson, N. S., & Margolin, G. (1979). *Marital therapy: Strategies based on social learning and behavior exchange principles.* New York: Brunner/Mazel.

Johnson, S., & Greenberg, L. (1995). The emotionally focused approach to problems in adult attachment. In N. Jacobson & A. Gurman (Eds.), *Clinical handbook of couple therapy* (pp. 121–141). New York: Guilford Press.

Luquet, W., & Hannah, M. (Eds.). (1998). *Healing in the relational paradigm: The imago relationship therapy casebook.* Philadelphia: Brunner/Mazel.

Luquet, W., & Hendrix, H. (1998). Imago relationship therapy. In F. M. Dattilio (Ed.), *Case studies in couple and family therapy: Systemic and cognitive perspectives* (pp. 401–426). New York: Guilford Press.

Manus, G. (1966). Marriage counseling: A technique in search of a theory. *Journal of Marriage and the Family, 28,* 449–453.

Nichols, M., & Schwartz, R. (1998). *Family therapy: Concepts and methods* (4th ed.). Needham Heights, MA: Allyn & Bacon.

Nichols, W. (1998). Integrative marital therapy. In F. M. Dattilio (Ed.), *Case studies in couple and family therapy: Systemic and cognitive perspectives* (pp. 233–256). New York: Guilford Press.

Piercy, F., Sprenkle, D., Wetchler, J., and Associates. (1996). *Family therapy sourcebook* (2nd ed.). New York: Guilford Press.

Shoham, V., Rohrbaugh, M., & Patterson, J. (1995). Problem- and solution-focused couple therapies: The MRI and Milwaukee models. In N. S. Jacobson & A. S. Gurman (Eds.), *Clinical handbook of couple therapy* (pp. 142–163). New York: Guilford Press.

Stuart, R. B. (1969). Operant interpersonal treatment for marital discord. *Journal of Consulting and Clinical Psychology, 33,* 675–682.

Wetchler, J., & Piercy, F. (1996). Transgenerational family therapies. In F. Piercy, D. Sprenkle, J. Wetchler, and Associates, *Family therapy sourcebook* (2nd ed., pp. 25–49). New York: Guilford Press.

2

Introduction and Case Conceptualization of Mike and Jan†

Louis J. Bevilacqua and Frank M. Dattilio

The following is a case study of a young married couple: Mike and Jan. A brief narrative containing basic information is provided, including data on psychiatric, medical and social history; and history of substance abuse, child abuse, and criminal involvement. A description of the presenting problem and a history of the couple's difficulties will also be explained in detail.

CASE STUDY

Jan and Mike are a middle-class Caucasian couple residing in a suburban neighborhood of the Northeast Central States. Jan is a 49-year-old sales associate for a pharmaceutical company. She has been a sales representative with the same company for the past 14 years. Prior to this career, Jan was employed as a receptionist for a dental office and was also working part-time as a salesperson in a major clothing department store. Jan enjoys reading mystery novels and taking care of her animals, which include three horses, two cats, and two birds. Jan has been married to Mike for the past 12 years. They have had no separations to date. They also do not have any children from this union. Jan was married

---

†Jan and Mike are a real couple whose names and identity have been changed significantly to protect their true identity.

once before for 3 years. Her marriage ended in divorce due to her husband's continued drug abuse and infidelity. There were no children from Jan's previous marriage.

Mike was also married one time prior. His marriage of 1 year ended in divorce due to his drug abuse. There were no children from this union. Mike is 44 and currently employed as a welder/fitter. He acquired this trade while in high school and has maintained various employment in this field for the past 25 years. He has been employed by four different companies overall, the longest period with his present employer, which has been for the past 10 years. Mike enjoys taking care of animals and working on computers.

Mike and Jan met through a mutual friend during a summer outing. They dated only 4 months before deciding to marry. They decided to skip the formalities and were united by a Justice of the Peace in a rather impromptu fashion. They described their courtship as a fun time that they will always remember. While dating, Mike and Jan enjoyed seeing new films, dining out, attending parties, skiing, and taking care of Jan's animals. When they initially met, Mike had relatively few friends. When they would go out together with other couples, Mike and Jan generally socialized with Jan's friends, whom, Mike claims, eventually became his friends as well. Rarely did they socialize with any of Mike's acquaintances.

PSYCHIATRIC HISTORY

There is no prior history of psychiatric treatment for Mike. He has never been prescribed psychotropic medication, nor has he been hospitalized for any mental health reasons. Mike reports that during his adolescence, his mother received individual treatment for depression after divorcing his father. She was not treated with any medication that he could recall. Mike's brother received individual therapy for "behavioral problems" as a teenager. His father viewed therapy as something that only "crazy" people needed and looked upon therapy with disdain. Mike states that he is interested in initiating therapy in order to reduce the tension that exists between himself and Jan, and denies maintaining any of the same type of biases that his father held about therapy.

Jan reports that she received individual therapy for depression approximately 20 years ago after undergoing a hysterectomy. She recalled this as being part of the aftercare plan recommended by her gynecologist. Jan attended approximately 12 sessions and viewed her time in therapy as being very helpful. She has never been prescribed psychotropic medication, nor has anyone in her family. Jan reports that no one in her family, including herself, has ever been hospitalized for mental illness, and is unaware of any psychiatric history with her extended family.

MEDICAL HISTORY

Mike has a history of hypertension and elevated cholesterol levels. He inconsistently follows a diet plan to address these two conditions under the care of his family physician. His father had one heart attack, 5 years ago, and is still living. There is a family history of cancer and glaucoma on his mother's side of the family. His mother is currently in good health.

Jan has no current medical problems. There is a family history of cancer and diabetes on both sides of Jan's parents' family. At the age of 29, Jan underwent a hysterectomy as a result of ovarian cancer. Her first reaction to the news of having cancer was devastation. She was scared of dying. She said that, fortunately, her friends and family were very supportive and the surgery was successful. She also reported that having a child was never something that she was really interested in doing, yet the idea of having a hysterectomy bothered her. Jan recounted, "I did my share of parenting when I was raising my younger brother John. I used to have occasional thoughts of what it might have been like to have a child, but not for the past 12 or 13 years." Jan said what really helped her was when she met Mike and he expressed his lack of interest in children. This was a big relief to Jan and was one of the characteristics that she found attractive about him.

SOCIAL HISTORY

Mike is the youngest of two boys. His older brother, 2 years his senior, received part-time special education classes due to weaknesses in reading and math. His brother also had "behavioral problems" which became a central focus in the family during his upbringing. While growing up, Mike and his older brother Mark were not very close. Mike tended to stay more to himself, while Mark had lots of friends, but tended to get in trouble for not doing his homework and being disrespectful to teachers. Mike was in regular classes and maintained a C average. He recalls not enjoying school very much. In fact, Mike reports that there was never anything he really liked to do.

One of the things his mom always complained of was that Mike rarely finished anything he started. He remembers taking piano lessons and drum lessons, but quitting each one after a few months. He also tried out for a local baseball league, but quit after the second practice. Throughout elementary school, he was often teased for being the biggest kid in his class and for not being very coordinated. Finally, as Mike entered high school, his father made the suggestion that he become involved with football. This altered his reputation with his peers somewhat, and enhanced his social skills. Mike states that he was teased less by the guys, but still felt very uncomfortable and somewhat afraid of females. He dated on and off throughout high school but never maintained any serious female relationship. His mother never approved of any of the girls that he expressed an interest in. He recalls one of his mother's typical responses being, "Don't get serious, Michael, it will never last."

Mike describes his parents as being supportive, but to a limited degree. His father attended every one of his football games, and was very lenient in disciplining the children. When Mike had a problem, however, his father's usual curt response was "Get over it." Mike's mother was always there to discuss any problems Mike encountered in life, but tended to be very critical of him in general. He said that no matter what problem he was experiencing, his mother always pointed out that it was somehow related to something that Mike did to cause it. This created a great deal of conflictual feelings toward his mother, whom he views as very controlling and maintaining the power in the family.

In describing discipline, Mike reports that his mother set the rules in the house and that everyone was expected to follow them, even his father. Mike remembers one time that the family was having company. His father spilled a drink on the living room carpet and his mom reacted by yelling at his father and calling him a slob in front of the guests. Mike said his father just left the room and walked out of the house. He did not return home until the next day.

The year Mike graduated from high school, he pursued his trade in welding—something that he trained for in vocational classes and has practiced ever since.

That same year Mike's mother filed for divorce after 20 years of marriage, due to her husband's numerous affairs. Mike described his parents' marriage as involving frequent arguments and several separations. Mike was aware of his father's affairs, and believed they were due to his mother's constant "nagging" and "put-downs." When Mike's mother decided on the divorce, his father moved out.

Mike was very surprised and angered by this decision, but never shared his feelings with anyone. Mike rarely saw his father after he moved out, although they did talk over the phone every couple of weeks. He described his mother as becoming more and more critical and demanding of him. Mike said 2 years later, his brother Mark moved out of the house to live with his girlfriend. Mike lived with his mother until he got married for the first time at 29 years of age.

Mike has maintained contact with both of his parents throughout the years. His father never remarried. The year before Mike married his first wife, his mother married her second husband, to whom she has been married for the last 20 years. Mike describes his mother's second marriage as good, and he currently maintains a fairly positive relationship with his stepfather.

Jan is the oldest of two children. Despite being 5 years his senior, Jan reports a close relationship with her brother, John, during their upbringing. Her parents both had careers, and had little time for Jan and her brother during their childhood. She describes her parents as very lenient and supportive in a remote sort of way. Her parents rarely denied her anything, and frequently bought her and her brother whatever they wanted. Her parents placed a great deal of responsibility on Jan, since she was 5 years older than John. As a result, Jan spent a large portion of her childhood as a caregiver to John. She recalls that often, after school, she would make a snack for her and her brother before they began their homework. Sometimes when her mother was running late, Jan would make dinner for the entire family. She reports having enjoyed this type of responsibility until John started high school and became involved with drugs. Jan had been experimenting with marijuana herself, but saw her brother's use as extensive and clearly destructive. This led to frequent heated arguments between herself and her brother. Her parents were quite liberal regarding the drug use, and saw experimentation as "normal." Jan remembers one time that she was expressing her concerns of John's drug use to her parents. Her parents responded by saying, "As long as he only smokes it on the weekends, we don't think he has a problem."

Throughout high school, Jan did well academically, and had a number of friends. She reports that her friends were her "real supports." Anytime she had a problem, it was her friends who she went to. After graduation, Jan attended college and received a bachelor's degree in philosophy, with a minor in marketing. Upon graduating from college, Jan began working full-time in a local clothing department store.

SUBSTANCE ABUSE HISTORY

Throughout his senior year in high school, Mike drank alcohol quite heavily on the weekends. At the age of 20, he was introduced to marijuana by a co-worker. His alcohol and marijuana use continued on and off for approximately 10 years. At one point during this time, Mike lost his job as a result of coming to work late and frequently hung-over. Unfortunately, his dismissal did not change his frequency or quantity of substance use, which continued. This did not change until Mike became involved in an auto accident due to his drug use. After running over and killing a dog, he crashed into a telephone pole, totally destroying his car. He was charged with driving under the influence and spent one night in jail. This also resulted in Mike's dismissal from his second job. That same year, Mike's first wife divorced him.

At that point, Mike began thinking that his drug use was becoming out of control. He decided to stop using all substances except alcohol. This lasted for 3 years, until one day a co-worker offered Mike some marijuana after work and he accepted it. He explained this relapse as a result of stress from work. In particular, Mike described experiencing difficulty getting along with a female co-worker with whom he was competing for a position. Mike claims that the last straw to this conflict was when his co-worker was finally chosen for this position over him and received a substantial raise. Mike believed that she was underqualified for this position, and consequently he resigned from his position 2 weeks later.

Mike continued to use alcohol and marijuana for another 10 years. One night, after using alcohol rather heavily, Mike was driving home from a friend's house when he passed out and remained unconscious for several hours. When he awoke, Mike realized that he was in the middle of a cornfield and could not remember how he got there. Following this blackout period, Mike went through a 28-day in-patient drug and alcohol treatment program. As a result he has been substance-free for the last 7 months, and has also been attending Narcotics Anonymous meetings on a weekly basis.

Jan experimented with marijuana and alcohol while in high school and college. After graduating from college, she stopped using controlled substances, except for an occasional glass of wine. During her first marriage, she began using marijuana again. She and her first husband used together frequently. One year prior to separating from her first husband, Jan stopped using and began attending Narcotics Anonymous meetings.

CHILD ABUSE

Mike was sexually molested between the ages of 7 and 9 by a paternal aunt. This involved her fondling and kissing Mike on a sporadic basis. He reports that this ended when his aunt moved away. He has not disclosed this information to anyone besides his wife, Jan, and the therapist.

Jan reports no history of any type of child physical or sexual abuse.

CRIMINAL HISTORY

Mike was arrested for driving while under the influence and spent one night in jail. His license was suspended for 6 months.

Jan has no criminal history.

PRESENTING PROBLEM

Jan made the initial call for an appointment for marital therapy. She stated that she and her husband were experiencing difficulty achieving emotional intimacy due to continual conflicts and lack of effective resolutions. Jan and Mike tend to avoid discussing conflicts with each other. When they do argue, Jan tends to criticize Mike, and he simply dismisses what Jan says as being trivial. At times, Mike will avoid being around the house, particularly when Jan is at home. He does this to avoid tension in the relationship. This conflict-avoidance pattern of interacting has led to a lack of trust and emotional distance between them, which has naturally affected their intimacy. There have been times when attending therapy was discussed, but neither followed through due to periodic improvements.

For the past 7 months, Jan and Mike reported, they were getting along fairly well. Mike was calling Jan and letting her know where he was and what time he was coming home. Jan felt that she had begun to trust Mike again. This trust was violated, however, when 2 weeks prior Mike came home at 2:30 AM. Mike said he went to Jennifer's house for a party. Jennifer has been a family friend for the past 20 years and the party was for those who helped her to relocate to her new residence. Jan did not want to go to the party and secretly wished that Mike would decline as well. Unfortunately, she never told Mike her true feelings, and Mike ended up going by himself. Mike said he had fallen asleep while at Jennifer's home and did not wake up until 1:00 AM. Jennifer lives an hour and a half away and Mike said that he drove straight home when he realized what had happened. Jan felt that Mike should have called her immediately and had erred in his judgement. Mike said he just wanted to get home as fast as he could, and knew in advance that Jan would be upset. This incident resulted in a heated argument, that included a discussion about divorce. Jan told Mike she was not willing to continue the relationship because she didn't feel as though she could trust him any longer. Mike felt this was totally unfair of Jan. Mike pointed out to Jan that in the last 6 weeks he has done everything he said he would and that Jan should still be able to trust him. Despite Mike's efforts, Jan said she still wanted to pursue a divorce. Mike angrily responded by saying "Fine, if you want a divorce, go for it. Let's do it tomorrow." The next day Jan reconsidered her position and apologized to Mike, but did admit that she was confused about her feelings. Mike acknowledged Jan's confusion and admitted to his own frustrations with the marriage. It was at that point that Jan suggested they begin couples therapy, and Mike agreed.

HISTORY OF PRESENTING PROBLEM

Throughout the marriage, Mike and Jan have avoided discussing any conflicts, and do not recall ever really resolving any of their disagreements completely. Usually, arguments would end with Mike leaving the house for several hours. When they would reconvene, they would avoid bringing up the issue of contention, and the matter would simply be dropped. The majority of their arguments involved Jan's complaints about Mike's being undependable, and especially concerning his drug abuse. Mike would rationalize that he continued to use substances because of Jan's "nagging." Whenever there would be disagreements, Mike would tell Jan to "just drop it." This tended to infuriate Jan, and she would yell and cry more profusely. Eventually, Mike would leave the room and, sometimes, the house. Unfortunately, the matters would never be resolved—and would only be tucked away until they resurfaced in another argument and continued to erode the relationship.

CRITICAL LIFE EVENTS TIMELINE

1948	—	Jan is born
1951	—	Mike's brother, Mark is born
	—	Mike's parents are married
1953	—	Mike is born
	—	Jan's brother, John is born
1966	—	Jan graduates high school
1970	—	Jan graduates college—B.A. in Philosophy
	—	Jan begins working at a clothing department store
1971	—	Mike graduates high school
	—	Mike's parents divorce
1973	—	Mark moves out of his mother's home
	—	Mike begins using marijuana
1977	—	Jan is diagnosed with cancer and has a hysterectomy
	—	Jan attends 12 sessions of therapy for depression
1980	—	Jan marries her first husband
1981	—	Mike's mother remarries
1982	—	Mike gets married for the first time
	—	Jan stops using marijuana and starts attending Narcotics Anonymous
1983	—	Mike is charged with a D.U.I. and loses his second job
	—	Jan divorces her first husband
	—	Mike separates from his first wife
1984	—	Mike and Jan meet through a mutual friend
1985	—	Mike and Jan get married
1986	—	Mike begins using marijuana again
	—	Mike quits his job
1987	—	Mike starts working at his fourth and current job
1997	—	Mike attends inpatient drug and alcohol treatment program
	—	Mike starts attending Narcotics Anonymous meetings
	—	Mike and Jan begin couples therapy

COMPARATIVE PSYCHOLOGICAL TREATMENT OF COUPLES

In order to provide continuity among the chapters, we have organized specific questions to be answered by each contributor(s) based on his or her respective theoretical approach. The following instructions were given to each contributor.

We would like you to organize your response to the case of Mike and Jan in the following manner:

I.   TREATMENT MODEL

Please list the title of your approach and describe your treatment model in 3–4 double-spaced, typewritten pages. Include a brief description of how the major concepts of your model apply to the concerning factors influencing couple relationship functioning. We encourage you to reference your work, but please keep your references to a minimum (e.g., 8–10).

II.   THE THERAPIST'S SKILLS AND ATTRIBUTES

Describe the clinical skills or personal attributes most essential to the success of therapy in your particular approach. Please limit this section to 1–2 double-spaced, typewritten pages.

III.   THE CASE OF MIKE AND JAN

It is important to the goals of this volume that you answer each of the following questions regarding the enclosed material. Please limit your response to each question to 1–3 typewritten pages. If, for some reason, your particular modality of treatment does not lend itself to your answering a specific question, then explain this in detail with specific rationale.

1. What specific instruments or assessment tools would you use, if any, to further assist you in structuring this couple's treatment? Please describe the tools in detail and provide the rationale for their use (e.g., written inventories, surveys, diagnostic psychological testing, clinical interviews, home evaluations).
2. Describe your conceptualization of Mike and Jan individually as well as a couple. Address your view of their personality, behavior, affective state,

cognitions, and functioning, based only on the material provided in the case presentation. Identify and describe the strengths of Mike and Jan and explain how you would incorporate these strengths into the treatment process.

3. What would be your goals in treating this couple? Please distinguish between short-term and long-term goals. How would you measure progress toward reaching each treatment goal? How would you determine whether or not therapy was successful? What type of measurement would you use?

4. Are there specific techniques or interventions that you would implement during the treatment process? If so, what would they be? When and how would you use them?

5. What potential pitfalls would you anticipate with Mike and Jan? What would be the sources of difficulties, and how would you address them? How would you address limits or boundaries with this couple?

6. Are there any areas that you would want to avoid addressing with Mike and Jan? If so, why?

7. Who else, if anyone, would you include in your sessions with Mike and Jan? Why? This could include significant others, as well as, any other treating professionals.

8. What role would homework play in the course of treatment? What type of assignments might you use during the course of treatment?

9. What would be your timeline for therapy, if any? How often would you expect to see Mike and Jan? Would you see either of them individually for any sessions? Please describe under what conditions you would either see Mike or Jan individually, or would refer them to another therapist for individual therapy.

10. How would termination and relapse prevention be structured? How would you see this couple functioning or coping at the conclusion of treatment?

Note: We realize that the information in this case example is limited, and that therefore you may find yourself wishing to know more details about specific aspects of the case. Please try to answer the questions with the information that you have, with the understanding that no additional information will be provided to you. Your are certainly free to address the fact that you need more information. Just be sure to state why you would need the additional information.

PART I

SYSTEMS THEORIES

3

Bowen Systems Theory

Daniel V. Papero

TREATMENT MODEL

The Bowen Family System theory, developed by Murray Bowen from his extensive observations of human family functioning in structured and unstructured settings, rests on the concept of differentiation of self. While a great deal can be said about the central concept, on a practical level it describes individual variation in terms of the person's ability to manage him- or herself in an anxiety field. As Bowen described it,

> A poorly differentiated person can appear "normal" in an anxiety-free field, but he is the first to develop his usual symptoms when the anxiety increases. Those with the best levels of differentiation are among the least reactive to anxiety and the least likely to develop symptoms in an anxiety field. (Bowen, 1978, p. 407)

Poorly differentiated individuals tend to be easily overwhelmed by anxiety, displaying the physiological markers, cognitive patterns, and fundamental behaviors associated with anxiety. Activation of the sympathetic nervous system and hypothalamic-pituitary-adrenal axis produces large-scale change in the condition or state of the organism, suppressing growth, reproductive, digestive, and immune functions while flooding the frontal lobes with catecholamines, affecting profoundly the cognitive functions of the individual and rendering behavior much more automatic or programmed and coordinated by the limbic system and lower brain processes. People with better degrees of differentiation correspondingly display greater resiliency in the face of anxiety, maintaining enhanced capacities for functioning that are simply not available to the less well-differentiated person. For the better-differentiated individual, cognitive abilities remain functional, particularly in the areas of threat and risk assessment, breadth of perspective, including awareness of interdependency, flexibility of perceptual frameworks, capacity to observe one's own behavior and that of others, ability to incorporate new information, and awareness of one's own degree of tension with corresponding capacity to manage tension through self-regulation of physiological and mental processes and reduction of the tendency to transmit anxiety to others.[1]

Better-differentiated people base decisions and behavior on well-developed sets of internal beliefs and principles that they have thought about carefully and tested in real situations in their lives. Their actions, therefore, tend to be more self-determined and less reflexively reactive to the actions of others. They display a capacity to remain in good contact with others in spite of the tension or anxiety in the relationship network. They possess a freedom of functioning that eludes less well-differentiated people. Their energy remains available to direct toward goals of their choosing, and they are less constrained and more intimate in the important emotional relationships of their lives.

Differentiation of self also affects the nature of relationships that people form. Less well-differentiated people form intense relationships with others, and their actions depend largely on the condition of the relationships at any given time. Bowen characterized such relationships as "fused"; the relationship partners appear to be tightly connected or attached to one another so that they act as a single person. He posited that two forces actively press upon people in relationships—a force toward being connected, and a force toward being separate and different from. Both are naturally occurring and form a part of the human's adaptive capabilities. Each emerges and recedes as the conditions that individuals face and their perceptions of those conditions changes. He called the first the "togetherness force" and described it as a pressure to be connected; to be alike in thought, word, deed and even appearance. The second force, the force toward differentiation, emerged as a pressure to be separate and different from other people. Less well-differentiated individuals display the effects of the togetherness pressure. Decisions depend on what others think and whether the decision will disturb the fusion of the existing relationships.

The emergence of differences among participants in a relationship system produces pressure on the one perceived as different to conform to the fusion, to give up whatever thought or action that is disturbing and to fit more comfortably with the others. Better-differentiated people also experience the pressures of

---

[1]Excellent discussions of the general impact of anxiety and its physiological companion stress, as well as a review of the history of research in this area, can be found in Robert Sapolsky's *Stress, the Aging Brain, and the Mechanisms of Neuron Death.* His book *Why Zebras Don't Get Ulcers* provides much of the same information in a format more friendly to the interested lay reader. An excellent review article by Bruce S. McEwen on the same subject can be found in the *New England Journal of Medicine* in its January 15, 1998, edition.

togetherness, but they are able to separate their own best thinking from the opinion of the other important people; they make their decisions on the basis of their best objective assessment of the facts and their own principles; and they tolerate differences in important others without as much reactive pressure. They are less likely to take the reactive behavior of important others personally, and they can continue to make their decisions and accept responsibility for the outcomes without blaming others or seeing themselves as victims.

The pressures toward togetherness and toward differentiation appear to be oppositional. An increase in one leads to a compensatory increase in the other. The togetherness force intensifies as anxiety increases, so that togetherness pressures increase with anxiety. When anxiety is low, families may display a tolerance for difference that disappears as the family becomes more anxious. Increasing togetherness pressures trigger the oppositional force reactively, so that rebellious attitudes, oppositional behavior, and the use of distance and avoidance can mark increasing anxiety and togetherness pressure in families.

Under the pressure of rising tension, two-person relationships become unstable. Initially, the pair may cope or absorb the tension in the development of a repetitive series of interactions, often called patterns, that both signal the rising tension and moderate its impact. Four general patterns are possible—distance, conflict, reciprocal shifts in functioning, and the focus of tension on a third (a process that Bowen referred to as the family projection process)—although any particular relationship's presentation of the series may show considerable variation in detail (Bowen, 1978; Kerr & Bowen, 1988).

When the activation of these patterns proves ineffective in containing the tension at a tolerable level and moderating the relationship instability, another predictable process emerges. One of the twosome involves a significant third person in the set of interactions. The original party of the twosome approaches the third person with a story about the unstable relationship and either directly or implicitly about the other member of the twosome. The Bowen theory refers to the process of expansion of the two-person system into a three-person system as "triangling."

In families, some of the triangles become fixed; that is, they emerge in a predictable fashion as tension mounts, often with the same issues serving as the vehicle around which the relationships display their characteristic patterns. As the triangle emerges, the single relationship of the original twosome expands to form a system or network of three relationships. If the tension in the triangle spills over to involve yet a fourth person, the number of relationships in the system increases even more. The triangle consists of an intensely involved twosome and an outsider. The intensity of the twosome can either be positive or negative. When it is positive, the outsider attempts to draw one or the other of the pair into a new relationship with him- or herself and leave the other in the less comfortable outsider position. When the twosome is negative, the outsider position is sought, and one of the pair moves to acquire the outside position and leave the former outsider in the intensity with the other person. The various movements that form these maneuvers are fairly obvious and can be observed.

Problems in two-person systems (for example, marriages, couples, friendships, workplace relationships) tend to present as complaints about distance and conflict. Occasionally the over- and underfunctioning reciprocity also becomes a part of the complaint. Bowen noted, consistent with the concept of differentiation of self, that some pairs are more vulnerable than others to the effects of rising tension, while others are more resilient, able to withstand periods of tension with little change in the relationship.

He theorized that the less resilient pairs are more intensely connected to one another, or *fused*, than are the others, and that in these pairs each relies heavily on the other for his or her own emotional stability and functioning. Subtle changes in one result in the other's reacting automatically and emotionally in some degree of intensity. The reactivity leads into chains of emotional reactivity, with each responding automatically to the other in an emotionally intense fashion. Similar chain reactions occur in positive interactions, but people view the chains of negatively charged exchanges as problematic. If the intensity of anxiety is sufficiently high, even better-differentiated people can become entangled in the negatively charged interactional sequences, marked by physiological arousal, shifts in mentation, and reactive behavior.

With time, often the negative chain reactions become repetitive, with individuals displaying the same emotions and behavior in response to one another whenever the tension levels surpass the pair's threshold of tolerance. Anticipation of the repetitive sequences adds further tension, so that individuals act in ways to avoid the uncomfortable interactional sequences. Fewer subjects can be discussed without triggering the reactivity, and the relationship becomes less open, less flexibly adaptive, and more guarded. Often, even when not engaged with the other, participants spend time and energy thinking about the other, usually critically. Energy and time thus spent is not available to the person to apply to attainment of self-determined goals and individual development.

The triangling process described previously tends to develop automatically as tension and reactivity in the relationship mount, and other people can be brought into the anxiety field, consuming further energy and resources and spreading anxiety and tension. The anxiety of the other people can seep back into the pair, triggering even more intense episodes of reactivity and disturbance. Individual sensitivities, patterns of mentation, and behavior in interaction with others can shift in a semi-permanent fashion, and one can accurately think of the individual, the relationship, and the broader network of relationships in which the pair function as chronically tense or anxious.

Bowen postulated that the basic level of differentiation of self, expressed in the individual's sensitivities, mental processes, anxious behaviors, and relationship expectations and postures, develops in one's family of origin, particularly in the context of relationship to one's own parents during important developmental stages or windows. The family could transmit to its offspring chronic levels of tension and repetitive behaviors that became part of the offspring's repertory for living and become a part of that individual's dilemmas in relationships. He realized that an individual could in fact utilize the extended family as a laboratory in which he or she could observe the various aspects of differentiation of self and emotional reactivity unfold; could learn more about his or her own piece of the dance; and could, if he or she desired, work to manage oneself differently in the original family. His clinical observations led him to believe that people who took on this project actually made faster and more lasting progress in addressing their current marital and relationship problems than did those who focused only on the immediate problems of the relationship. If an individual had become relatively distant and isolated from the original family relationships, often simply contact by itself, without any particular effort to change oneself, resulted in a decrease in anxiety that had a beneficial influence on current difficulties.

The Bowen theory, therefore, views relationship difficulties as emerging from the mixture of level of differentiation of self plus intensity of anxiety in the relationship field. Each person brings the basic sensitivities and physiological and behavioral reactivities from his or her own family systems and other intense relationship experiences and displays them as anxiety mounts in current relationship. Over time, the present relationship develops its own reactive patterns based on past and present experience. These unfold repetitively and can mark the waxing of tension in the relationship network as well as in the particular relationship. As anxiety wanes, symptoms decrease in intensity and severity, sometimes even disappearing, only to reemerge as tensions once again inevitably mount.

From a clinical perspective, then, two central tasks emerge for the pair reporting relationship difficulties: 1. decrease anxiety and 2. enhance degree of differentiation of self. Bowen made an important observation that tension between two could resolve itself if both could remain in viable emotional contact with a significant third who could remain emotionally neutral about the tension between the twosome. When a clinician can regulate his or her own emotional intensity, particularly his or her own anxiety, while remaining in good contact with the pair, the anxiety in the pair decreases in intensity. The effort the clinician makes to gain and maintain emotional neutrality is disciplined and constant. In an emotionally neutral position, the clinician manages his or her anxiety well as well as his or her tendency to react to the participants with positive or negative affect. He or she can see the dilemma from several different perspectives, and can comment seriously or with humor about virtually any aspect of the dilemma.

The treatment model stems from the basic theoretical framework outlined cursorily above. Partners can be seen together or individually, using a methodology that Bowen called family psychotherapy. The clinical process is guided by family theory. The effort toward anxiety reduction occurs from the initial contact with the individual or the unit. The clinician works to remain in viable contact with the participants while remaining emotionally neutral about the problem between them in accordance with the process described above.

The work toward enhanced differentiation of self begins as the anxiety decreases. In a general sense, people work to recognize and regulate their own emotional reactivity. This occurs on the physiological, cognitive, and behavioral levels. Bowen encouraged people to become better observers of themselves and others in the relationship network. What was predictable about one's own behavior and that of others, and under what conditions? Are one's own responses automatically emotional and reactive, or more thoughtful? Can one see one's own perceptual and cognitive frameworks that are a part of the reactive process? Can one modify one's own part of the process? Can one leave the other free to be him- or herself with the responsibility for addressing his or her own life dilemmas?

People also begin to observe their own difficulties staying in viable contact with important other people, particularly those in their own families of origin. They begin to see the patterns of distance and avoidance that they and their family members have developed over time to avoid the discomfort of togetherness pressures and the accompanying patterns of reactivity that tend to make relationships difficult. They work to observe the triangling process in themselves and others and the concomitant shifts in anxiety, perceptual frameworks, and cognition that accompany the process. When motivated, the individual can experiment with modifications of his or her own behaviors in an effort to learn more about the skills of staying in good contact with others when the relationship or the network experiences pressure.

Individuals also take on the challenge of developing a coherent and consistent structure of beliefs or principles that over time may come to guide their decision-making processes. Bowen referred to this structure as the "solid self" and described its creation and maintenance in the following manner.

> The solid self does not participate in the fusion phenomenon. The solid self says, "This is who I am, what I believe, what I stand for, and what I will do or will not do," in a given situation. The solid self is made up of clearly defined beliefs, opinions, convictions, and life principles. These are incorporated into self from one's own life experiences, by a process of intellectual reasoning and the careful consideration of the alternatives involved in the choice. In making the choice, one becomes responsible for self and the consequences. Each belief and life principle is consistent with all the others, and self will take action on the principles even in situations of high anxiety and duress. (Bowen, 1978, p. 365)

Even more specifically, people work to modify their own part of a relationship disturbance. Bowen described the effort in the following manner.

In broad terms, the concept is one of withdrawing psychic energy from the other and investing it in the poorly defined ego boundaries. It involves the idea of "getting off the back" of the other by reducing the "other directed" thinking, verbal, action energy which is designed to attack and change the other, and directing that energy to the changing of self. The changing of "self" involves finding a way to listen to the attacks of the other without responding, of finding a way to live with "what is" without trying to change it, of defining one's own beliefs and convictions without attacking those of the other, and in observing the part that self plays in the situation. (Bowen, 1978, p. 178)

In this process, the clinician participates as a consultant or coach. He or she does not aim to develop an intense relationship to the participants nor to provide a corrective emotional experience within the confines of the clinical hour. He or she is attempting first and foremost to employ the same skills of observation, self-management, the guidance of behavior with thought and reliance on beliefs, and the maintenance of viable contact with another that the participant(s) themselves will ultimately work on. He or she can provide knowledge about the nature of emotional reactivity and relationship processes that the participants can incorporate into their own efforts with the people important to them. And he or she can lend a hand to the participants' efforts to manage themselves effectively, as the relationship network reacts to modifications in participants' own behavior and functioning in the relationship network.

THERAPIST SKILLS AND ATTRIBUTES

A clinician practicing within the framework of the Bowen theory views him- or herself as a consultant or, in Bowen's terms, a "coach." Training in the clinical application of the Bowen theory addresses how the clinician thinks about the nature of the clinical process and his or her knowledge of how human systems operate. Most clinicians are trained to think in terms of the individual and his or her internal processes. A clinician working with the Bowen theory often has to think beyond tenets of the individual in order to observe the individual in the context of the turbulent or disturbed relationship and its connection to a broader network of relationships.

He or she works to reduce his or her own personal importance in the clinical process in the face of the anxious family's push to make the clinician the expert who can fix the problem. Instead, from the first contact the clinician attempts to maintain an attitude of inquiry, working alongside the motivated family members to specify ever more precisely the nature of the disturbance in the relationship system, their thinking about how the specified problem is to be addressed, and to coach or supervise their efforts to modify their functioning.

The clinician works first to manage his or her own emotional reactivity while staying in open contact with the anxious relationship system. Many clinicians working with the Bowen theory have done extensive training in self-regulation, including personal bio- and neurofeedback training, relaxation training, and disciplined efforts to manage their own cognitive processes in the presence of anxious others. Clinicians trained at the Georgetown Family Center, founded by Murray Bowen, all engage in supervised efforts to observe and modify their own reactive behavior in their own families. The extended family serves as a laboratory of sorts for the clinician to learn about him or herself and to experience first-hand, with an observing and interested mind, the challenges of working on differentiation in a family. Here the forces of togetherness and differentiation can be seen and experienced first-hand, and the clinician takes on the challenge of managing him- or herself with the people to whom he or she is typically most sensitive—parents, siblings, extended family members, and so forth. Here the clinician develops the skills required to be in contact with an emotional issue while remaining thoughtful and as emotionally neutral as possible. For most, the task is rigorous, as one learns to recognize emotional reactivity and grapple with its management and to respect the depth and force of emotion operating in relationship networks.

THE CASE OF MIKE AND JAN

Assessment

A clinician guiding his or her efforts with the Bowen theory would construct a multigenerational family diagram compiling the vital statistics of each family member to the degree that the informant(s) could provide verifiable factual information. The process is not a rigid one, and information might be collected over several sessions. Much of the information is provided as people tell their stories, and the clinician needs only ask about clarifying details. Dates of births and deaths, history of courtship, dates of marriages, separations, and divorces, course and outcome of illnesses, mental health or substance abuse treatment, dates and outcome of affairs, nature of employment, reasons for termination, dates and type of education, dates of geographical moves and the reasons for those moves, the breadth and frequency of contact to the extended family, and any other factual information are noted on the diagram next to the individual or to the relationship to which it pertains. The clinician might also construct a timeline placing the events or perhaps the symptoms in chronological order (see Figure 3.1).

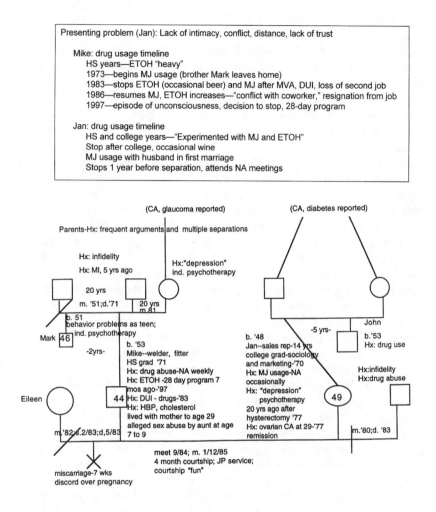

FIGURE 3.1 Timeline and family diagram for Mike and Jan.

   In addition to the factual information, the clinician asks each partner about more subjective information. The list of potential questions is limitless, but among the more common one finds the following. What attracted each to the other, how does each think about the relationship and, if married, about the nature of marriage? What was the early relationship like, and when, if at all, did either notice a shift? How has each thought about children and the nature of parenting? How has each responded to the birth of children, and how has the relationship changed as each child has entered the family? What's been the nature of relationships to ex-spouses and children from former marriages? How do people think about these relationships? How has each responded to death, birth, marriage, and illness in the family, if it has occurred? How has each reacted, and how has the family or the relationship been affected? How does each assess the impact of geographical moves and changes in employment on the family or the relationship? How do people think about and account for changes in the relationship or the family? What principles or values does each call upon to guide decision making? And so on.

For the clinician trained in Bowenian theory, the family diagram serves a number of functions. In a general sense, its construction with the informants expands the breadth of perspective from the intense relationship to the broader network of which it is a part. The process asks people to think about their situation as well as to respond emotionally. It reveals patterns of thinking about the relationship and the family that may be a part of the dilemma. The diagram also reveals to the clinician the nature of relationships in the broader family system, and suggests directions that the individual might pursue in order to learn more about his or her difficulties in relationships. It can identify antecedents and even current shifts in the relationship network that may be influencing the pair's present difficulties. It establishes from the outset the attitude of inquiry and learning that forms the basis of the clinical process.

The family diagram for Mike and Jan precedes (see Figure 3.1). It has been compiled on the basis of the information presented in the case summary, and it includes only the factual data as reported there. In the actual clinical situation, the more subjective information would be added and identified as such. It includes a timeline for the substance usage history of each. The reader will note that the diagram lacks much of the information that would usually be collected. For example, no information on the grandparents of either person has been provided, nor any information about siblings of their parents, other than Mike's allegation of being sexually molested by an aunt, who remains unidentified. Were there disturbances in the broader family that correlated in time with the emergence of the various manifestations of distress that have been included in the report? What have marital relationships been like in the broader family? No information is provided on the current status of Mike's or Jan's relationships to their larger extended families. Is either actively connected to a larger network, or does their relationship represent a relatively isolated fragment, with little viable connection to a broader family network? The absence of specific dates makes it difficult to ascertain the relationship of events to one another in time. For example, did Mike's DUI in 1983 precede or follow his separation from Eileen? No information is provided about the current relationship of each to his or her former spouse. Has contact been maintained, are the former partners deeply estranged, and does either have contact with the families of his or her former spouse? And so on.

The clinical process would address these gaps in the informational record. The working hypothesis would be that the current marital dilemma does not occur in a vacuum. The nature of connections in the family relationship network, via the triangling process, influence the marital pair's functioning, and they in turn contribute to the climate and reactivity of the broader system. Shifts in tension levels in the family system may play out in the marital pair, and relationships may be available in the system that might help stabilize the pair during a time of disruption. This cannot be determined on the basis of the information available.

In addition, relatively more detail is available for Mike and his family than for Jan and her family. While significant information is missing for both, the relative paucity of information about Jan and her family seems striking. Does this represent a tendency for the collector or reporter of the information to view Mike as the problem in the relationship? If so, does this bias or focus represent a mindset or perceptual framework that is active in the pair and in the people that surround them? If so, does this framework comprise a part of the difficulty they face? None of these questions can be answered without further follow-up with the pair and relevant others.

Conceptualization of Mike and Jan

One can comment only very generally based on the written case presentation and without personal contact and interaction with each member of the pair. A clinician employing Bowen theory to guide his or her approach to a symptom would avoid interpretations of the individual's intrapsychic mechanisms, personality, and affective state. Inferences would be treated as hypotheses subject to verification and amendment in light of emerging information and factual evidence. Instead, he or she would focus on factual information that can be characterized as the who, what, where, when, and how of the dilemma. Who is involved, what has taken place, where did it take place, when did it happen, and how did it occur (the process of the event)? The aim would be to assist participants to become observers and, ultimately, experts about their own relationship and its connection to a broader relationship system. With that knowledge, they could manage themselves within the relationship system and reduce the need for outside assistance in the future.

John Gottman has proposed a general cascade model of interactional process and of perceptual or cognitive frameworks that can serve as a general assumption about the nature of marital discord presenting as conflict distance (Gottman, 1994). The model of interactional process he refers to is the Four Horsemen of the Apocalypse, and he proposes, based on his research, that complaining criticism leads to contempt that leads to defensiveness that leads to withdrawal from the interaction. Additionally, he proposes a general set of individual perceptual frameworks that also form a cascade indexing distance and isolation. One partner initiates the cascade when he or she overwhelms the other with the intense expression of negative affect (anger, frustration, fear, etc.), a process Gottman and others have called "flooding."

> First, Ekman (1984) recently introduced the concept of flooding, by which he meant that through emotional conditioning a wide range of stimuli eventually become capable of eliciting blends of anger, fear and sadness. I add that the term flooding also suggests that the emotional state becomes disregulating in that a person can attend to or do little else when flood. In this manner, flooding may be highly disruptive of organized behavior. (Gottman, 1994, p. 75)

The cascade then moves to a perceptual framework that the individual will have to work the difficulties out alone. This framework leads into a perception of the problems in the relationship as severe and, ultimately, loneliness in the relationship.

A clinician could infer that some version of these models presents itself in Jan's and Mike's dilemma. That inference would serve as the basis for a process of investigation and observation about the nature and progression of the conflictive and distancing episodes that mark the course of the relationship. One could also infer that a degree of chronic tension pervades the relationship, and that the tension is based in sympathetic nervous system (SNS) and hypothalamic-pituitary-adrenal axis (H-P-A axis) tuning and activation. Each person would be reacting to subtle and overt stimuli presented by the other, leading to the activation of the stress system. As a consequence, each would in fact be developing greater sensitivity to one another. Accompanying that sensitivity would be cognitive frameworks that explain and justify the sensitivity and the tension, and each would have increasing difficulty recognizing, managing, and incorporating information that challenged or even contradicted those frameworks. As tension mounted, behavior would become much more stereotypic and predictable as well as more automatic and less thoughtful. To some degree, these emotionally reactive, tension-based cognitive frameworks and behaviors would reflect processes and patterns developed initially in the family of origin and reinforced with superficial modification in the first marriages of each. Mike's reported childhood relationship with his aunt could be included in the investigation of earlier relationship experiences and their role in the present difficulty. Typically, each would be relatively unaware of the pervasiveness of these processes carried over from earlier life experiences.

One could also infer that the tension in the pair was both responding to and influencing the tension levels in the relationship network around the pair. While the case presentation does not present adequate information to address this inference, the clinician would investigate this possibility. Could this sort of tension in the network or system be contributing to the apparently increasing social isolation of the pair alluded to in the case presentation? Is the nature of their contacts with friends and family reinforcing the tension and the patterns of behavior? How is Mike's involvement in Narcotics Anonymous (NA) influencing the situation? How does Jan's view of NA, based on her own prior experience and experiences with Mike, influence the situation? How does contact with friends affect either or both of the partners? How is each reacting to the other's contacts?

Both Mike and Jan have displayed relatively lengthy periods of stable functioning as marked by their long-term employment, their relatively long-term relationship, and their relatively well-developed individual interests. Mike has demonstrated an ability to address his own functioning in his decision to treat his difficulties with substances and his current 7-month period of abstinence. He and Jan both have recognized and appear to be willing to take a look at their own marital difficulty to the point of involving a stranger (the clinician) in their dilemma. This sort of stability and willingness to engage such a difficulty represent a reservoir of ability that each can draw upon to counteract the current tension and inferred emotional reactivity that each experiences in the relationship. Each clearly had the capacity, at least some of the time, to govern behavior by thought rather than automatic reactivity. From the perspective of the Bowen theory, the entire clinical process is based upon that ability to engage difficulties thoughtfully to the best of one's ability. The participants work to observe the reactive components of their own and the other's functioning, to think about one's own beliefs and values, to see clearly one's own part of the dilemma, and to modify one's own behavior while leaving the other relatively free of the emotional pressure to "be the way I want you to be."

Additionally, there is some indication that the relationship network retains a degree of stability and functioning. All parents and siblings are alive, apparently in good health and available to one degree or another to Jan and Mike. One presumes that broader family relationships are also available, although the presentation does not report that information. The availability of these relationships provides an arena for learning about the nature of relationships with other important individuals that each can address when things have bogged down with the spouse, should either begin to see the value of the broader network to the regulation of his or her own functioning.

Treatment Goals

One of the continual tasks in the clinical process requires that clinician and participants define ever more precisely what the nature of the problem is and what the participants want to do about it. From this perspective, the responsibility for the determination of the particular goal(s) of the process lies with the participants. The general format for the clinical hour comes to revolve, therefore, around three or four general questions: What are you working on, how are you working on it, what successes (failures) have you experienced, and how have these successes or failures influenced how you see the problem and how you are working on it? In a general sense, however, the short-term goal of the clinical process is the reduction of the intensity of anxiety, the longer-range goal involves the efforts of one or more individuals to enhance differentiation of self.

Decreases in the frequency and intensity of the particular symptom seem to be a reasonably accurate measurement of reduction of anxiety. Participants themselves can track the flow of the symptom, sometimes formally, by charting it, and sometimes informally by recollection and corroborated self-report (the partner corroborates the facts of the report). The longer-range effort toward improved functioning in an anxiety field can also be tracked best by the particular individual who undertakes it. Among the factors that can be tracked and recorded are observations about one's own patterns of emotional reactivity and behavior, one's own part of a difficult, repetitive interactional sequence, one's own planning for the attempt to shift one's emotional reactivity and behavior, and the success of the effort.

Finally, the ultimate criteria for the success of the clinical process reside with the participants. Only they can decide how close they have come to achieving the goals that they have established and the degree to which the clinical process has contributed to that outcome. The clinician's notions of a good outcome may not at all match the participants' notions.

Techniques and Interventions

Bowen referred to the clinician as a coach, rather than a therapist, and spoke of the clinical process as a "do it yourself process—almost." The coach did not assume responsibility for fixing the presenting problem, or for changing the family. He or she assumes the family has the capacity to address its own problems effectively, and the coach takes on the responsibility for maintaining a climate, structure, or atmosphere in the clinical sessions that allows participants to move toward their best objective thinking, planning, and implementing.

The clinician pursues a few general tasks. The first involves clarifying and defining the relationship between partners. The clinician explores with one partner his or her thoughts about the difficulties, the facts of the relationship, and how he or she views her own part of the problem while the other listens. In general, each person responds directly to the clinician, rather than to the other partner. If intense exchanges between the partners flare up, the clinician redirects the interaction away from the intensity with questions about fact and thinking, bringing the direction of interaction back to him- or herself. Each person is asked to produce his or her most objective thinking in as calm a way as possible.

Secondly the clinician works to keep him- or herself detriangled from the emotional system of the relationship and the family. This task is central to the maintenance of emotional neutrality. The clinician attempts to stay focused on the emotional process between the partners and to deemphasize or defocus the content of the exchange. He or she maintains an attitude that is neither critical nor judgmental, and he or she can respond seriously or with humor to the participants. When the clinician can remain fairly calm and casual in the presence of the anxious pair, they often can become more objective about their own situation.

In addition to establishing and maintaining a climate for the interaction, the coach provides information about how family systems function, where some of the minefields might be located, and some thinking about how a person navigates relatively safely through those difficult zones. He or she outlines the fundamentals of self-regulation and differentiation of self for the family and reviews with them their own skill development drills and their efforts toward performance under pressure. And finally, he or she demonstrates what Bowen referred to as I-positions as the situation requires. An I-position involves the person's defining what he or she can and cannot do; what he or she will and will not do about a particular situation. I-positions are not directed against others, but present clearly the parameters of one's own responsibility, direction, and effort.

Bowen observed that tension between two could resolve itself, provided a third party was involved who remained emotionally neutral about the tension. He described the process in the following manner.

> Conflict between two people will resolve automatically if both remain in emotional contact with a third person who can relate actively to both without taking sides with either. This reaction is so predictable that it can be used in other areas of the family system and in social systems. (Bowen, 1978, p. 177)

Each element of this description—emotional contact, relate actively without taking sides—requires much of the clinician. He or she must have awareness of and some ability to regulate his or her emotional reactivity. The clinician's emotional reactivity can block the contact with the participants and shift the tension to the relationship between coach and participant. Each clinician develops his or her own techniques for managing his or her own emotional reactivity, particularly anxiety.

Relating actively to each also requires discipline on the part of the clinician. He or she attempts to maintain an attitude of inquiry or research with the participants. The clinician asks about factual occurrences, about how each perceives the events, about the thinking that accompanies behavior, about patterns of interaction, and about one's assessment of one's own role in the interactional sequences. What are people thinking about the situation, what are they working on, what success or difficulty are they encountering, and how are they planning to address the difficulty? In the early stages of the clinical process, when anxiety may still be high and participants have not yet developed much ability to regulate their own emotional responsiveness, the clinician rarely asks about the feelings the person experiences. The expression of intense feeling tends to activate the emotional chain reaction in the clinical session, to interfere with participants' ability to think clearly about the situation, and to reinforce the very processes and patterns the participants find troublesome. Later on in the process, when a person has developed some ability to observe his or her own emotional reactivity and to regulate him- or herself, participants can talk thoughtfully about their feelings without adding the affective charge or edge that initiates the chain reaction.

Often, participants embark on their own efforts to learn the basics of self-regulation in a field of anxiety. Some explore biofeedback training, using both conventional measurements of muscle tension, peripheral body temperature, electrodermal response and cardiovascular responsiveness, as well as EEG training, using the newer techniques of neurofeedback. Some pursue various forms of disciplined meditation, with or without a spiritual component. Classical relaxation training also appears useful to some. Some pursue desensitization training, linking their efforts to specific situations and stimuli. The clinician makes suggestions, but does not pressure people to engage these techniques. Many individuals work effectively on their own functioning without these additional efforts.

The clinical effort can proceed when only one person displays motivation to address the difficulties. In addition to the tasks described briefly earlier, the clinician lends a hand more directly to the person's effort in his or her own extended family. The initial efforts resemble those when both partners are involved: learning about how relationship systems function, observing to discover one's own part in the system, and modifying one's own part of the dilemma. Sometimes, if the person is able to manage his or her own emotional reactivity more effectively, the other partner becomes interested in the process and joins the effort. The motivated person can also begin an effort toward resolving emotional impasses in his or her own extended family. Bowen observed that progress made in these relationships in the extended family translated automatically into better self-regulation and clearer definition of oneself in a marital relationship.

Areas to Avoid

Since the participants in a clinical process actually set their own agenda, they would determine what should be addressed or not. Inevitably, the process touches upon areas that people have not thought about or have not wished to address. Sometimes, particularly in conflictive relationships, one or the other openly attacks what he or she believes to be the other's problem. Sometimes, the natural course of the process of inquiry, observation, and reflection leads a person into sensitive areas. When sensitive areas become the focus of discussion, the clinician works to manage his or her own reactivity, to stay in contact with the participants, and to lend a hand to their efforts to think as clearly and objectively as they can about the sensitivity. When emotionally based chain reactions begin, the clinician diverts the participants away from the intensity by a series of questions about the process, leading the interaction away from the chain reaction and back into the three-way process described earlier.

Inclusion of Other Family Members

A clinician guiding his or her efforts with the Bowen theory would see anyone in a relationship network who was motivated to work on his or her own part of the dilemma in the relationship system. This could include other family members and members of a broader system that surrounds the relationship. The basic system principle—that a small, sustained modification in any portion of a relationship network can result in a modification of the entire system—is the basis for this position.

Increasingly, families and relationships appear to have more than one treating professional attached to them. A family physician, chiropractor, acupuncturist, massage therapist, spiritual advisor, individual psychotherapist, pastor or pastoral counselor, and psychic are but a few of the helpers who may be advising people about their life dilemmas, frequently at the same time. This simply becomes the reality that a clinician must address. There is little research into the impact of multiple treating professionals on a family or a relationship, but the effect does not invariably appear to be favorable. The complex effects of multiple interactive transferences can create a climate or set of circumstances that make progress for a person or a pair extremely difficult. There appears to be no simple, clear guideline for the involvement of multiple helpers in the relationship network's dilemma. The clinician must make his or her best decision based on his or her own understanding of theory, knowledge of the facts of the situation, his or her own experience, and what he or she is willing to take on in the clinical process.

Homework

Clinicians working with the Bowen theory vary on this matter. Few would actually assign tasks to people, but some might make suggestions that the individuals could follow up on or not as they saw fit. In general, the clinical process aims to assist people to define for themselves what they must work on if they are to attain the goals they have specified. The clinician may, as a coach, suggest skill drills that might be useful in their efforts.

Aside from the general suggestions to become better observers of themselves and their relationship systems and to modify their own part of the system, the coach might suggest various training regimens in self-regulation and individual discipline. He or she might assist participants to design their own drills in effective listening, recognizing the difference between emotionally based mental process and that which is more objective and less reactive. Together, the clinician and the participants might develop some exercises in behavioral modification. In short, many kinds of techniques might be developed collaboratively by the coach and the participants, but the responsibility for the implementation of those techniques, for assessing their effectiveness, and for modifying them when indicated would rest primarily with the participants.

Timeline for Therapy

As with other aspects of the clinical process, the time frame for the activity would in essence be specified by the participants. Basically, the goal would be for them to progress towards their goals with as much speed as possible for them. Many families and individuals end the clinical process when the anxiety has been reduced to levels that participants find tolerable and/or comfortable. This can often take place rapidly. Longer-range efforts toward enhanced differentiation of self may take significantly longer.

Once again, the participants have the responsibility to determine the frequency of appointments. Essentially, they have the task of determining what is useful to them in moving toward their goals. When people are highly anxious, the clinician might suggest that weekly appointments could be helpful in managing the anxiety, although the participants retain the responsibility for the decision. After an initial period of weekly sessions, commonly people spread the appointments out to once every 2 to 4 weeks. These people appear to progress as well as those coming more frequently.

As noted above, motivated individuals are seen by themselves when the partner does not wish to participate. In addition, people might be seen individually when the emotional reactivity between them is so strong that they cannot sit in a clinical session without automatically participating in the emotional chain reaction with the other. Most people begin to manage the reactivity better after a few visits, and can be seen together. Occasionally, participants ask to come alone so that they can think something through without the other listening and reacting to their efforts.

Termination and Relapse Prevention

Bowen described the anticipated outcome of the clinical process in the following manner.

> The overall goal was to help family members become "system experts" who could know the family system so well that the family could readjust itself without the help of an outside expert, if and when the family system was again stressed. (Bowen, 1978, p. 7)

Frequently people extend the interval between appointments further and further apart, sometimes even to one or two a year. Some supplement the actual clinical process with reading and educational programs that expand their knowledge of family systems and provide an arena to continue their development of skills after the conclusion of the clinical process. Some people choose to come in once a year for a while, as a way of checking their own progress and stability. The clinician remains available for consultation if and when anxiety again produces the various symptoms in the relationship that served as the initial reason for consultation.

There is no way to know how Mike and Jan would fare if they chose to engage in the clinical process as described. Much would depend on their own efforts to learn and employ the skills of self-management and the maintenance of viable contact with the other. As noted, people move at their own pace, and up to their own degree of motivation. Based on the case description of their relatively short-term involvement in clinical processes, one could speculate that Mike and Jan might well stop the clinical process once anxiety had decreased and they were in somewhat better contact with one another. However, one or both might find a degree of assistance in the process that could motivate them to a sustained effort.

REFERENCES

*Bowen, M. (1978). *Family therapy in clinical practice*. New York: Jason Aaronson.
Gottman, J. M. (1994). *What predicts divorce?* Hillsdale, NJ: Erlbaum.
*Kerr, M. E., & Bowen, M. (1988). *Family evaluation: An approach based on Bowen theory*. New York: Norton.
McEwen, B. S. (1998). Protective and damaging effects of stress mediators. *The New England Journal of Medicine, 338*(3), 171–179.
Sapolsky, R. (1992). *Stress, the aging brain, and the mechanisms of neuron death*. Cambridge, MA: MIT Press.

*Suggested reading.

Sapolsky, R. (1994). *Why zebras don't get ulcers: A guide to stress, stress-related diseases, and coping.* New York: W. H. Freeman.

SUGGESTED READINGS

Gilbert, R. (1992). *Extraordinary relationships: A new way of thinking about human interactions.* Minneapolis: Chronimed.

Papero, D. V. (1990). *Bowen Family Systems Theory.* Needham Heights, MA: Allyn and Bacon.

Sapolsky, R. M. (1994). *Why zebras don't get ulcers: A guide to stress, stress-related diseases, and coping.* New York: Freeman.

4

Structural Theory

Harry J. Aponte and Edward J. DiCesare

TREATMENT MODEL

The Traditional View

Structural Family Therapy (SFT) has been with us for over three decades. It is one of the early family therapy models, introduced in the sixties by Minuchin, Montalvo, and their colleagues with the publication of *Families of the Slums* (Minuchin, Montalvo, Guerney, Rosman, & Schumer, 1967). The structural approach was a dynamic approach to therapy. The model functioned as a tool for change more than as a theory about family development or family pathology. It grew out of the discovery of some very effective approaches to helping disadvantaged families that had traditionally been neglected by most therapeutic approaches. The structural model aimed less at analyzing their problems than at creating experiences in session to achieve quick, palpable results.

Structural family therapy made two particularly notable contributions to family therapy. One was the demonstration that poor families living in America's most chaotic "slums" could make good use of therapy. The second was a perspective on structure in family relationships that offered a new, powerful portal through which to treat family dysfunction. The model worked particularly well with people who not only had difficult family conflicts, but whose families because of serious social hardships were also often fragmented and underorganized (Aponte, 1976a). Restructuring family relationships was a prerequisite for solving the problems family members faced. From the work with the poor, SFT was able to give to the field a well articulated method of addressing underlying relationship structure with all populations.

The signature character of the approach became its focus on very precise dynamics (the boundaries, alignments and power distribution in people's current interactions) of the structure in relationships. By looking for structure, therapists could see beyond the content of families' problems into the relationship patterns that supported the shape conflicts were taking. By actively directing or joining in families' interactions, therapists could alter patterns even as they emerged and give families the immediate experience of different and better outcomes.

Today's View

Structural family therapy, over time, has evolved in different directions for different therapists. From this corner, it seems to us that SFT today needs to be not another insulated, self-contained model of therapy. It has become an approach that contributes a perspective to other models, and can comfortably utilize contributions from others. Today's model explicitly addresses both community and the individual along with family. It highlights more directly the personal involvement of the therapist. It also calls for an understanding of the spiritual dimension of life, recently much in the eye of the broad therapeutic field.

Behavioral and strategic techniques have comfortably fit into the present orientation of the model. Moreover, today, structural therapists routinely go beyond the here and now into the family of origin of people they work with. Working with the individual with a family perspective also fits into the model's special attention to subsystems in family.

With respect to community, SFT did indeed grow out of work with families who, by definition, had social problems. The model was always comfortable including larger systems and the contributions of those who worked with multiple systems (Auerswald, 1968; Aponte, 1976b). It has grown to consider not only more complex social systems, but also the social factors such as culture, race, and socioeconomic status that flavor our society at all levels (Boyd-Franklin, 1989; Aponte, 1994; McGoldrick, Giordano, & Pearce, 1996).

Another intriguing development has been the consideration of the therapist as a person in the context of SFT. The structural approach has depended heavily on *therapist* activity. Nevertheless, there was traditionally a reluctance in the early years to look too closely at what the therapist personally brought to the interaction. Today, SFT's contribution to this personal component of the therapist's activity (Aponte, 1992) has been to deepen training in the therapists' active use of self in the current interaction with clients.

Finally, as an outgrowth of SFT's special connection to clients' social context, it became apparent, that the model needed to address explicitly clients' underlying morals, values, and spiritual outlooks on life, as well as their religious affiliations and practices (Aponte, 1985; Aponte, 1996). Students of the model have long been aware that the active posture of structural therapists disposed them to intervening with families from their own notions of what is good for families. This required an awakening to the values inherent to the model and what values its practitioners personally brought to their work. The initial emphasis on addressing family structure in relation to family functioning was not enough. In a society undergoing a revolutionary upheaval of values, families needed to consider how they function in the light of the values and spirituality by which they chose to meet life's challenges. Values set the standards and religion provides a formal context for living by these values. Moreover, for people in therapy, religion offers the support of church communities, rituals, and their relationship with the Deity as defined by their beliefs.

With couples in particular, SFT has the advantage of taking into consideration by its eco systemic perspective the individual, the couple, and their social context. It relates the dynamics of this complex ecosystem to the issues at hand. The here-and-now focus draws couples into interacting in vivo around the issues in their lives that are at the heart of their couple's struggles. The intensity of the enactment powerfully brings into the room aspects of their individual selves, relationship, and social context that impinge on the issue at hand. The complex forces of a multilayered ecosystem can be observed as they converge in the couple's issue of the moment. The thinking, emotions, and patterns of interaction all come to life. Because the model essentially aims to resolve more than to explain, this convergence of forces is an opportunity now to mobilize people to engage fully with what ails them. The couplehood, for example, is seen as serving not only the relationship, but also the individuals *within* the relationship. The broader social context serves both to help understanding and as a resource for change.

THERAPIST'S SKILLS AND ATTRIBUTES

Focused thinking—identifying the issue, developing hypotheses, and formulating here-and-now specific interventions that will also address the family's underlying structure and dynamics.

Structural therapy has always required a precision of thinking behind interventions that are tailored to a particular moment in a patterned transaction. The focus is not on an abstract interaction, but on its link to the family's issue as dramatized in a real life personal struggle.

Therapists must have in their minds clearly articulated hypotheses about the nature of the issue and the underlying relationship structure. They must commit not only to the ultimate goals of the therapy, but to the changes they are aiming for in family members' interaction in their presence. Therapists must be prepared to evaluate the effectiveness of their intervention even as it is implemented in order to determine how to engage with the family in the very next transaction. The validity of this evaluation depends upon the clarity of the hypotheses and the precision of the intervention. Assessment and intervention are inextricably linked.

Active use of self—knowing and having access to self, and the ability to use the self intentionally with clients in ways that are integrated with the technical interventions.

Structural therapists observe and direct families to interact in new ways to better accomplish their goals. However, underlying this kind of interaction is also the therapist's manner of relating to the family members that furthers the personal impact of the therapist's words. More often than not, the main impact of the intervention will come from how the therapist relates to the family members so that words and actions are part of a relationship the therapist builds with the family. The intervention is technical in the sense that it is calculated, but is also personal in that it is delivered in a genuinely human connection with the people in the family.

This personal use of self includes what therapists bring of themselves to the therapy which embraces their personal psychology, family life experience, and cultural, ethnic, socioeconomic, and spiritual backgrounds. All this calls for a high degree of self mastery within the therapeutic relationship. This mastery assumes an awareness of all these aspects of the self. It presupposes the therapist having access to memories, emotions, and motivations while in the therapeutic transaction with the client. Finally, this mastery implies having the knowledge, skill, and freedom to use the richness of the self creatively and with discipline in the service of the therapy.

THE CASE OF MIKE AND JAN

Assessment

The principle assessment tool for the structural family therapist is the observation of family interactions and transactions between therapist and family members. Structural therapists do use history to develop hypotheses, but especially attend to the interactions that take place in the session be they spontaneous or strategically instigated by the therapist.

Structural therapists generate both "structural" and "functional" hypotheses. Structural hypotheses bear on the patterns of interaction that maintain the problems engaging the family today. Functional hypotheses look for the "why's" behind what spawned these problems. Functional hypotheses posit historical explanations as well as motives that drive the current family conflicts and difficulties.

History is solicited in relation to what is being transacted in a session. The inquiries about history and motivation are attached to the experiences the family members are living out in the session. These experiences are likely to spring old memories and emotions propelling current behavior. Clients have better access to accurate memories and true motives when bestirred by the experience of the moment.

However, that quest for information is not just for information. It serves as an opportunity to intervene in what is then taking place in session. Who, when, and what is asked becomes a way of influencing the interactions in the room. The genogram and structural diagraming can serve as instruments of assessment/ intervention. Assessment and therapeutic action are two sides of every intervention of the therapist.

An expanded structural approach to couple's therapy focuses on the individual not only as a subsystem of a larger relational field but as a differentiated entity. To this end, specific assessment instruments serve on an as needed basis along with history gathering, genograms, and structural mapping. For instance, if a client, like Mike, evidences signs of ADHD, a conclusive diagnosis may help to explain some of his behavior with Jan. The need for an individual assessment holds true in other diagnostic areas, such as in Jan's emotional nonresponsiveness, which can mean a number of different things, including certain types of depression. Traditional psychological instruments for individual assessment are compatible with SFT when their results are considered within the context of a couple's and family's relationships.

Meaning, morals, and, at a supernatural level, spiritual values also inform the notion of "structure supporting the pursuit of what?" Early on, family therapy pioneers often engaged in "reality chopping" their new contributions into perspectives about systemic pathology. Traditional family therapy models respectively laid claim to what made family systems go wrong, such as dysfunctional transgenerational legacies, double binding messages, or disabling relationship structures. Today, we see a new emphasis on spirituality in therapy (Walsh, 1999). Therapy represents philosophical perspectives, such as post-modern theory, and sociopolitical outlooks, such as feminism. Therapy is speaking to moral standards or the lack of, that are adversely affecting families. Our therapies also may reflect religious views, such as Buddhist and Christian (Aponte, 1999, p. 87).

We are in a society where philosophy and social values are strongly influencing trends and approaches to therapy. Therapists give much more importance to the sociopolitical values of society and the cultural and personal values of clients to explain human failure and its solutions. Today's SFT will also need to explore spirituality to understand dysfunction in clients' lives, optimize goals for therapy, and determine acceptable means to pursue those goals (Aponte, 1998).

Moreover, in an increasingly rootless society, today's structural therapists may well look to the spiritual for social supports and resources in their clients' lives.

As with other resources in people's lives, a thorough assessment of strengths would require a look into what moral values and religious practices serve as supports to clients contending with the issues they face. Formal religion and the social organization of church or temple may well be a resource for people and are ever more important today because of the dilution of the influence and power of family. Today, structural therapists intending a full ecosystemic evaluation are likely to ask about the spiritual in the natural context of people's lives rather than through formal instruments. However, again, for the structural therapist these inquiries will be made in direct relation to the issues being addressed and to the interactions in evidence at the moment in session.

From the information we have, however, we do not know how articulate are Mike's or Jan's values and spiritual life. Along with their ethnicity and race, we know nothing about their religions. These are all potential sources of strength for them, personal resources for solving life's problems.

Conceptualization of Mike and Jan

The structural therapist looks to identify the issue that activated the couple's looking for help, and the structure of the underlying relationship that brought them to this point. With Mike and Jan the immediate issue is the threat of divorce initiated by Jan. Basically, their avoidance of conflict has led to emotional and physical alienation. This is not a couple that has lost intimacy as much as a couple with developmental deficits that precluded intimacy from ever getting a start.

They seem to lack the ability to trust enough to be vulnerable with each other. Jan criticizes and Mike runs away. They cannot share their respective pains and fears with each other. They have learned to manage independently of one another, and have shut down to one another emotionally. In those circumstances, it takes little to destroy trust completely. However, that they both claim to still love one another holds out hope for therapy. That they acknowledge their respective difficulties with intimacy also allows for a potential sharing of responsibility for the marital failure and for sharing the effort to heal.

In technical structural terms, the lack of intimacy reflects a hardening of *boundaries* between them. The conflicts that arise from this lack of trust can be formulated as a negative *alignment*. The lack of trust fuels their *power* struggle about whose way will prevail. We do not know their ideals (values) about intimacy, love, and marriage, which we would need to understand to better negotiate the goals of couples work.

While SFT focuses on the current structure of relating between a couple in the here and now, there continues to be a need to be acquainted with each individual contextually. To be contextually informed means to have insight into the individual within the couple, but also into the events and circumstances that produced and partially maintain their situation. The avenue of change, however, is not through a pursuit of insight into the past, but through the challenge to action about the present.

A contextual understanding of the couple and the individual requires information from a number of domains. The therapist must gain an experiential perspective on the psychological, biological, familial, social, and spiritual aspects of their world that relate most directly to the circumstances that bring them in for help at this time. The entire personal ecology of the clients is context, but in SFT what is relevant is what life forces most directly converge into the issues calling for solution.

Evaluation of Mike

Mike has known little emotional intimacy and safety in relationships. His mother was critical and father was distant. He tried pleasing his parents to compensate for his brother's rebellion. As a result, he avoided conflict at home, but at the price of having to keep his anxieties, insecurities, and emotional needs to himself. He seems to have abused substances to avoid the chronic stress and anxiety with which he lived. He was very much alone emotionally, and socialized only superficially. He was not prepared for the intimacy and commitment of marriage.

There are other important factors which have a bearing on Mike's present relational difficulties. There is history indicative of impulsivity and difficulty finishing things. There is also evidence of short attention span, a predilection for concrete activities requiring motor skills and difficulty focusing on abstract, intellectual pursuits. These are strong indications that Mike may have ADD, which could help explain some of his behavior both to him and to Jan.

Another area of importance is Mike's family history of depression with his mother having been diagnosed with that disorder when he was a child. Mike seems rather out of touch with his own internal affective experience. Yet, there are some indications that he may have experienced the tip of an underlying depression.

Historically, it helps to understand the models of intimacy, relating, communicating, and conflict resolution Mike learned from and responded to. He was exposed to a mother who was powerful, and critical, not only of Mike but of his father. Father was disengaged and peripheral allowing mother control of the home by withdrawing and rebelling into his affairs. Mike's primary view of women is that they are controlling. From his identification with his father, he learned passivity and withdrawal rather than active engagement with a woman. A further factor complicating Mike's relations with women is the sexual abuse by his aunt between the ages of seven and nine. Mike maintains rigid boundaries with women generally. With a woman, Mike can be dependent while also withdrawn and self protective. Moreover, Mike's patterns have been supported and maintained by complementary patterns inherent in his wife, Jan.

Evaluation of Jan

In looking at the family factors that shaped Jan, we find a number of elements similar to Mike's background. With personal boundaries relatively impermeable to the children, her parents were disengaged from their children. While there is no evidence of the self-esteem destroying criticism Mike received from his mother, there are violations of boundary and hierarchy in Jan's being assigned too much parental responsibility for her younger brother, John. Jan seems to have had little genuine intimacy with either parent, but was enmeshed with her brother because of the responsibility she had for him. Because her parents did not support her authority over him, however, she learned to nag to influence his behavior. She recapitulated this pattern in her relationship with her husband, who interestingly is five years younger than she as is her brother, John. Nonetheless, Jan did learn responsibility and persistence in relationships.

Jan's family history may have impacted her choice of the men. In Mike, she chose a younger, potentially dependent man. Like her brother, he was prone to be irresponsible and to abuse substances. She powerlessly nagged him, and, with him, was unable to have her emotional needs met. Jan has not been able to communicate effectively with Mike. She never had an opportunity to talk honestly with her parents and today cannot be emotionally honest with Mike. With both husband and parents, Jan shows little faith that she will be heard, and only pushes her concerns when driven to desperation. In spite of all her disappointments, she has maintained relative integrity about fidelity and drugs.

Treatment Goals

A perspective one could assume for the structural model is that all people struggle with issues particular to themselves. They develop psychological and relationship structures to cope with these life challenges. Conditions, whether within themselves or in their relationships to people and events, draw out these issues. People then face making life choices and grow through their struggle with today's personal challenges.

Consequently, therapeutic work must take aim at the choices and decisions people face in today's challenge. However, it must also target the underlying long-term dynamics as they roil in the individuals involved and in their relationships. Today's solution for today's problem should also connote progress in resolving the long-term pain, conflicts, and dysfunctional patterns that are the form and substance of the underlying long-term dynamics.

The immediate goal for Mike and Jan is a readiness to work on the relationship, putting off talk of a divorce. It will require some ability to confront conflict and negotiate mutually satisfying solutions. Long term, we would be aiming for trust and intimacy in the relationship. Steps toward those goals are that each take responsibility for and claim personal power for his and her part of the relationship. Each has personal choices that affect the relationship. They then try sharing their vulnerabilities in safety and reciprocal understanding, opening up the potential for intimacy. Finally, they attempt to create space and build structures in the relationship within which they can share conversation, responsibility, and love.

Techniques and Interventions

The therapist using the today's structural approach is attempting to aid this couple to realize their relational goals to work at both levels, the relational and the individual. The influence of the couple or family system on the individual is a carry over from traditional systemic thinking. The new emphasis for the individual is on personal moral responsibility, that is, the power and freedom to make a choice between what that person considers right or wrong for self and the relationship. Much of this therapy hinges on focusing on and facilitating the free moral choices people make in their family and social interactions.

It is a crucial part of the therapeutic alliance that the therapist and the members of the couple be united in their view of the origin and present nature of the problem. This negotiation of reality does not imply a solipsistic reality leading to situational ethics and revisionist history. Today's structural therapy posits an objective reality that, while experienced subjectively, is also weighed as independently real.

The life of a couple, for example, has a reality of its own. The individuals in the relationship have decisions to make about their participation in the relationship that affects them as individuals and the life of the couple. This concept of treatment goes beyond the classic systemic model that views individual behavior as a manifestation of a system's dynamics. In couples' treatment SFT speaks to each participant's responsibility for the present relational problems. In this way they have the opportunity to exercise control of their individual destinies and, jointly, the course of their relationship.

When a couple is in trouble, but still relatively well connected, that is, still able to share responsibility for their marital problems, they are addressed as a couple. Treating them as sharing responsibility for the problem suggests they are also able to solve the problem jointly. However, in Mike and Jan's case, they are quite disconnected and view each other as the problem. In such a case, a standard beginning technique is to ask each one, "Tell me, putting aside your partner's contribution, what are you doing to cocreate the marital problem?" Each member of the couple is individually queried in the presence of the other, encouraging personal differentiation within an intimate relationship.

Personal empowerment through personal ownership is of special importance in this model. Another special value underlying the model is to encourage intimacy, the sharing of identity as a couple, as well as responsibility and aspirations for the relationship. It is probable, for instance, in the case of Jan and Mike that they will begin therapy complaining about each other. The therapist's appeal for each to acknowledge some personal responsibility in the other's presence invites a lowering of defenses for the sake of the relationship. Taking the risk of confessing guilt to the partner becomes an act of love. Mike and Jan need to share vulnerability so that the therapist can move to the ultimate step of eliciting a shared responsibility for solutions in the marriage.

These interventions do not obviate the use of other techniques with the enactment. However, whatever the technique, the underlying effort is to manage successfully the oscillating patterns of the differentiated boundaries of the individual and the shared boundaries of intimacy.

Pitfalls with Mike and Jan

Jan feels safe and needed when in charge and taking care of Mike. He feels safe and valued when avoiding criticism and receiving her approval. Neither is personally secure. Protecting either from the perils of self disclosure or conflict risks, at best, establishes the fragile pseudo harmony of their past. Encouraging to confront conflict may induce the anxious nagging of Jan and panicky flight of Mike.

Given how scared each one is and at the same time how unable to reassure one another they are, the safety will need to come from the strength of the therapist's personal connection with each. At the same time, the therapist will be the one to push the difficult questions of how Jan can ask for closeness without controlling, and Mike the appreciation he craves without denying Jan the chance to criticize legitimately. To give this safety and strength will demand much personally of the therapist.

Areas to Avoid

Quite the opposite—for them to feel safe in the relationship would mean that there is nothing they cannot address and no areas to avoid. They should come to believe that they can speak of anything and expect understanding and caring from each other. The possibility of solutions to difficult issues emanates from the shared wish to make the relationship a loving refuge and resource. The therapist would need to be prepared to put enough caring, structure, and challenge into the relationship with them for them to be willing to risk these efforts with each other.

Inclusion of Other Family Members

Who else to include? They have few people in their lives, and no one directly involved in their marital relationship. This does not mean that it would not benefit them to share more of life with others outside the therapy. Because they do not share a connection with their respective parents—their relationship could stand more of a shared community life to create a social ecosystem that would support their marriage. The "other" to include is the therapist investing much of the personal self as a bridge to their mutual trust and intimacy.

Homework

Homework assignments in the structural model grow out of the work done in session. They extend the therapeutic experience into the home. In the early stages of the therapy, Mike and Jan may profit from limited periods at home where they mutually volunteer their respective insecurities. The task for the listener in his or her turn is to understand the other without analyzing or suggesting fixes.

In later stages, the assignment could be to negotiate conflicts. After listening intently to the other, they could try offering ways to meet the other's needs without referring back to their own needs until both felt understood and taken care of.

In the last stage of treatment, they plan to address conflicts without special structure. This would begin in session. It should then happen spontaneously at home. Resolution that led to deeper closeness signals the end of treatment.

Timeline and Frequency

In this therapy there would be no timeline. The effort would be to generate understanding and resolution in a therapeutic context encouraging experience, which intensifies and shortens therapy. The exploration of mutual vulnerability would take place in exercises demonstrating mutual support. The effort would also be engaged with them as with active agents empowered to choose and act on their own behalf. Soliciting their values and framing courses of action as questions of personal choice for them places them in charge of their changes and hastens their independence from the therapy.

As far as couples versus individual work is concerned, the preference is to do all couples work. However, if the therapy starts with a couple too distant and distrustful to risk honest engagement, the therapist may need to meet individually with each around specific issues even as the couples work continues. Mike and Jan, for example, may each be too fearful at the start to expose their insecurities to each other. Some individual time for each with the therapist may allow them to reframe their respective vulnerabilities from faults to personal wounds that need loving healing more than punishment and fixing. If they can be more understanding and sympathetic with themselves, they may be able to communicate what they are struggling with in ways that elicit more empathy and antipathy. At the core stage of therapy, they may be able to engage exclusively in couples work increasingly looking to each other more than to the therapist as the source of understanding and support they need.

Termination and Relapse Prevention

The answer to (10) was ensconced in (9). Termination is the time when the couple has taken charge of solving their problems because they have accepted responsibility for their respective difficulties, have understood and want to understand the struggles of their partners, and have in place the ways to work together on their life's challenges. In the therapy, they have experienced enough success as a couple to believe they can go on without the therapist. They have accepted the complexity of their journey and their respective human vulnerability so that they expect to trip on the way, but will not be fatally discouraged by temporary reversals. They have faith that they can rebound and have the means within themselves as individuals and within the relationship with whatever supports they have in family, community, and spirituality to meet tomorrow's challenges.

REFERENCES

Aponte, H. J. (1976a). Underorganization in the poor family. In P. J. Guerin (Ed.), *Family therapy: Theory and practice* (pp. 432–448). New York: Gardner.

Aponte, H. J. (1976b). The family-school interview: An eco-structural approach. *Family Process, 15*(3), 303–311.

Aponte, H. J. (1985). The negotiation of values in therapy. *Family Process, 25*(4), 531–548.

Aponte, H. J. (1999). Stresses of poverty and comfort of spirituality. In F. Walsh (Ed.), *Spiritual resources in family therapy* (pp. 76–89). New York: Guilford Press.

*Aponte, H. J. (1992). Training the person of the therapist in structural family therapy. *Journal of Marital and Family Therapy, 18*(3), 269–281.

*Aponte, H. J. (1994). *Bread & spirit: Therapy with the new poor.* New York: Norton.

Aponte, H. J. (1996). Political bias, moral values, and spirituality in the training of psychotherapists. *Bulletin of the Menninger Clinic, 60*(4), 488–502.

Aponte, H. J. (1998). Love, the spiritual wellspring of forgiveness: An example of spirituality in therapy. *Journal of Family Therapy* (UK), *20*(1), 37–58.

Auerswald, E. H. (1968). Interdisciplinary versus ecological approach. *Family Process, 7,* 202–215.

Boyd-Franklin, N. (1989). *Black families in therapy.* New York: Guilford Press.

McGoldrick, M., Giordano, J., & Pearce, J. K. (1996). *Ethnicity & family therapy* (2nd ed.). New York: Guilford Press.

Minuchin, S., Montalvo, B., Guerney, Jr., Rosman, B., & Schumer, F. (1967). *Families of the slums.* New York: Basic Books.

SUGGESTED READINGS

Aponte, H. J. (1981). Structural family therapy. In A. S. Gurman & D. P. Kniskern (Eds.), *Handbook of family therapy* (pp. 310–360). New York: Brunner/Mazel.

Minuchin, S. (1974). *Families and family therapy.* Cambridge, MA: Harvard University Press.

Minuchin, S., & Fishman, H. C. (1981). *Family therapy techniques.* Cambridge, MA: Harvard University Press.

---

*Suggested reading.

5

Strategic Therapy

James Keim

TREATMENT MODEL

This chapter describes marital therapy from the perspective of the Washington School of Strategic Therapy, an approach developed by Jay Haley and Cloe Madanes in the 1970s. Rooted in the work of Milton Erickson, magnetic resource imaging (MRI; especially the work of Don Jackson), and of structural therapists such as Salvador Minuchin and Braulio Montalvo, the Washington School has been one of the more influential approaches in family therapy (Nichols & Schwartz, 1997).

The goal of strategic therapy is the solution of the presenting problem in the most efficient and ethical way possible. The therapist is expected to create two constructs of the presenting problem, one describing the client's view, and another describing the clinician's separate perspective. One of the central challenges of therapy is weaving the two constructs into a coherent plan for change. The case of Mike and Jan is a good example of the need to engage the client's world view without the therapist's losing his or her own perspective.

The directive, defined as any encouragement by a therapist to behave in a certain manner, is viewed as the central means of intervention. The success of directives is, with some exceptions, dependent upon the strength of the therapeutic relationship. Washington School clinicians need to be skilled at developing and maintaining a cooperative relationship, listening to clients, asking questions which reveal the clients' views, goal-setting and -contracting, initiating conversations and moods within the session, and in maintaining the focus and course of the therapy.

WASHINGTON SCHOOL DIAGNOSIS

Diagnosis may be described as the clinician's defining his or her own construct of the problem in relation to the clients' perspectives. It is viewed as a matter of respect and efficacy that the clinician works as much as possible within the client's world view and language. Yet change, both in and out of the context of therapy, necessarily involves a challenge to and shift in the client's world view. Washington School addresses this conflict by seeking change only as indicated by the therapeutic contract and by sensitivity to personal agendas which might inappropriately motivate a clinician to move beyond that contract.

THE THERAPIST'S CONSTRUCTIONS: DIAGNOSIS/ PROBLEM DESCRIPTION

In 1971, Haley wrote that a "diagnosis indicates ways of bringing about change . . . and by the third session an experienced therapist would have begun change rather than dwell on diagnosis" (Haley, 1971, p. 233). This quote exemplifies strategic problem description; it is a way of directing the therapist to the best way to facilitate change. Diagnosis is usually worded in a way that informs the clinician as to how to treat the problem.

Washington School problem conceptualization is informed by a constructivist view, therapeutic optimism, and the family life cycle. The therapist's construction of the presenting problem is achieved in terms of protection, unit, sequence, and hierarchy (the acronym PUSH, developed by Jay Haley, is used to describe this method of problem description). (We discuss PUSH in more detail later.)

THE CONSTRUCTIVIST VIEW

In the tradition of the Washington School, clinical theory is considered to be a collection of oversimplifications which help to solve problems. An MRI tradition is to compare theory to an interstate road map. The map is a practical oversimplification; roads aren't actually blue or red lines almost as thick as the cities they intersect; but a map is a great tool for getting from one spot to another. Similarly, clinical theory is viewed as a practical necessity that greatly oversimplifies human behavior. Remembering that it is just a tool, one must bend clinical theory to meet the needs of clients, or one will end up bending clients to meet the needs of theory.

CLINICAL OPTIMISM: A FOCUS ON CLIENT STRENGTHS

In the tradition of Milton Erickson and Don Jackson, strategic problem formulation emphasizes a focus on client strengths, and the potential of the client is approached with optimism. A clinician's view of human potential becomes a self-fulfilling prophecy. Therapeutic optimism involves remaining open-minded to the possibility of change and involves allowing clients to safely and constructively find their own limits; it is not about being judgmental or setting unrealistic goals.

FAMILY LIFE CYCLE THEORY

In *Uncommon Therapy* (Haley, 1973), Haley organized chapters on interventions according to the family life cycle, and this orientation has remained central to strategic thinking. A therapist is expected to have a solid understanding of what is normal at different ages and stages. A family life cycle orientation helps to avoid pathologizing problems that are better viewed as painful, but inevitable, transitions for individuals and families.

Some human problems are viewed as being inevitable based on the way a family develops over time (Haley, 1973). Stages described in *Uncommon Therapy* include courtship, marriage, childbirth and raising children, middle marriage, weaning parents from children, and retirement and old age. Each of these stages has a different influence on the therapy and on the process of problem-solving. The goals of therapy are often conceptualized as helping clients move from one stage of life to another.

PUSH: A WASHINGTON SCHOOL MAP

Although a therapist may believe that there are dozens of significant variables involved in the creation, maintenance, or solution of a presenting problem, the context of therapy demands that we focus on just a few. Clinical theory can thus be thought of as an acknowledged oversimplification. The oversimplification PUSH used by the Washington School is not on what creates problems but, rather, on what facilitates their solution. Solutions may have nothing to do with causes.

Protection

Problem behavior is often viewed as being motivated at some level by a desire to help loved ones. In other words, many problems brought to therapy are thought of as cases of "love gone wrong." They are efforts at protection of loved ones that are problematic (Haley, 1976; Madanes, 1981). The concept of protection is a construct that is often, but not always, useful. It is not applied, for example, to abuse.

The clinician's view of client motivation has an important impact on therapy. When therapists start from a position that problems involve inappropriate expressions of love and protection (while allowing themselves to change their minds if the case specifically warrants), the interventions tend to have a humanistic orientation. When clinicians start with the belief that human behavior is driven by negative motivations, the interventions tend to be authoritarian and vindictive.

Unit

The Washington School emphasizes describing problems in an interactional context involving at least three people or parties. A unit of three is the minimum number required for coalition theory (a coalition is when two support each other in relation to a third party). But imagining interactions between groups larger than three parties is very difficult; multiple sets of triangles are used to describe a social system.

Not only are problems conceived of in triangles, but it is additionally important for therapists to see themselves as a new point of triangulation for the couple (Haley, 1976). The therapist's ability to help or harm a marital relationship is a further reminder of the influence that other third parties may have.

Sequences of Interaction

Problems and solutions are viewed as involving a series of interactions between people. The therapist maps out the clients' stories not only into sequential form (A led to B led to C) but, more specifically, into an interactional sequence of events. Change is defined in part as the adaptation of new and preferred interactional sequences.

Focusing on interactional sequences leads to greater sensitivity to the interrelationship of problems within a system. The interactional view inspires a therapist to think that solving one problem sequence may result in a change in other sequences as well. For example, a couple that learns to deal with a problem behavior of a child may apply the same collaboration to handle an in-law problem.

The general tendency is for escalating sequences to be converted into soothing sequences. For example, a discussion between a parent and an adolescent that previously led to an all-out shouting match might convert to the adult's attempting to soothe the angry adolescent instead. Whether or not the adolescent is receptive to the soothing, the attempt by the parent would constitute an important sequence change.

Hierarchy

It is important for the therapist to focus not only on the marital hierarchy, but also on the hierarchy of the larger social system. We are interested not only in the balance of influence between the spouses, but also in the influence of other levels of hierarchy, such as in-laws, bosses, and children, on the couple.

The "marital hierarchy" is defined as the perceived balance of influence and contribution between spouses. In other words, it is the perceptions of each spouse of whether each is contributing equivalently to love and maintenance and whether each is appropriately open to each other's influence. The work of Schwartz (1995) is often used in Washington School training because of its illustrations of what leads couples to perceive balance or imbalance in relationships.

When viewing the hierarchy of the larger system, the Washington School therapist is particularly interested in "cross-generational coalitions" (Haley, 1976). A cross-generational coalition occurs when a) a person seeks to exert influence over a spouse by gaining the active involvement of another generation of the family, such as a child or in-law, or b) a spouse enters a coalition with a member of another generation of the family to deal with responsibilities that were previously the responsibility of the other spouse.

Cross-generational coalitions are not necessarily pathological; in fact, they may at times be highly adaptive. However, this type of coalition and the situations that produce it are associated with great amounts of stress for all in the family system. Furthermore, recognizing cross-generational coalitions is important because they require greater sensitivity and diplomatic skills on the part of the clinician.

INTERVENTION

Intervention is essentially the process whereby the clients move from a maladaptive sequence to their preferred sequence of interaction around an issue. The new sequence tends to emphasize a greater congruity between the role and functioning of the clients. The therapist's efforts to catalyze this change often take the form of directives.

The Washington School conceives of clinical influence in terms of directives. Directives tend to fall into two major categories: Urging clients to try ideas that the clients have introduced, and urging the clients to try ideas that the therapist has introduced. The most commonly employed technique in marital therapy is the coaching of negotiation. Washington School intervention involves the full range of human emotion and often employs humor, novelty, and even absurdity.

The success of directives is usually dependent upon the strength of the therapeutic relationship. Directives used in the context of warmth and understanding promote change, but their ultimate success is dependent upon the clients' continuing that change process beyond the therapy. Washington School intervention is viewed as being similar to knocking down a domino; it does not impact much unless the change develops its own momentum within the system.

THERAPIST SKILLS AND ATTRIBUTES

The strategic therapist depends upon the same generic set of skills employed by most other models of psychotherapy, but some skills are emphasized more than others. Washington School therapists need to be highly competent at developing and maintaining the therapeutic relationship and in catalyzing change.

One of the most challenging skills to develop is the art of discussing difficult topics in individual and group sessions. Problems that are brought to therapy usually involve issues that the clients are unable to discuss in a constructive manner. This is primarily an issue of training, as almost all clinicians begin their careers with both strengths and weaknesses in their ability to negotiate painful discussions with and between clients. Unless the therapist learns to initiate change in how discussions are handled, the previous pattern of failure will continue uninterrupted.

The therapist must be comfortable with the appropriate expression of the full range of human emotion during therapy. It is the responsibility of the therapist to create an environment which best facilitates open and honest communication, and sometimes this means that the clinician must directly or indirectly change the emotional tempo of the session. The Washington School is known for its use of humor and playfulness, as well as for highly emotional sessions, such as those involving apologies for abuse (Madanes, 1990). A central tenet of the Washington School is that the emotions of a session should equal the topic at hand.

The therapist must also be able to ask questions in a neutral manner. Interviews address a wide range of personal information, and this requires that the clinician develop the ability to ask questions without implying unwanted characterizations or criticisms. For example, a therapist should be able to ask about sexual abuse without mistakenly implying suspicion that the client has been victimized.

Perhaps one of the more characteristic skill sets of strategic therapists relates to giving directives. Directives require sensitivity to the degree of motivation of the clients. Directives which over- or underutilize client motivation are less likely to succeed. The Washington School also requires that therapists be skilled at inspiring the motivation required to address the therapeutic contract.

A strategic therapist must be sensitive to the degree of clinical influence called for by the therapeutic contract. For various reasons, some contracts do not require the clinician to work at being influential. Other contracts require the careful establishment of strong therapeutic influence.

Clinicians must be able to work with clients of varied ethnic and social backgrounds. Therapists must seek cultural competence, must be able to state ignorance, and must be comfortable with requesting that the clients educate them on issues relevant to therapy. In the tradition of the Washington School, therapy with the economically and socially dispossessed also requires an increased ability to connect clinical work to the other concerns in the clients' lives. A therapist might, for example, increase client participation by contracting to help with a lost Social Security check; while this kind of assistance might be a damaging distraction in the therapy of a middle-class family, it could be central to the success of a case involving clients whose lives are buffeted by such issues.

THE CASE OF MIKE AND JAN

Assessment

After the first session, the couple would be given an eight-page questionnaire asking about the individual and family history of the clients. It is used to conduct research and to collect information easily missed by the clinician.

The questionnaire is given after the first session so that clients do not read more into the questions than is intended. Often people begin therapy in great pain and in a state of exhaustion, and it is not difficult in such states to project motive into even the most neutral of questionnaires. Such projections appear to be reduced by the therapist's using the questionnaire after the establishment of a therapeutic relationship.

In this particular case, Mike would be referred for an extensive physical that would include a neuropsychological evaluation, electroencephalograph, and endocrine work-up, given his history of blackouts, car accidents, and health problems, as well as his long history of substance abuse. The Institute's preferred clinic for comprehensive physicals is the Mayo Clinic Executive Health Program, which is especially effective because it completes testing quickly and effectively. Some clinics tend to schedule appointments and testing in such a drawn-out manner that many clients drop out before completion.

Treatment Goals

For the Washington School, therapy ideally addresses that which clients want most in the world. When clinical work is wrapped around the issue of greatest motivation, it clarifies for the clients their own motivations in coming to therapy and creates clear, easily understood goals.Clear goals serve to organize the therapist as well as the therapy, and they are so central to strategic work that I have taken liberty of placing this section before the conceptualization discussion.

The presenting problem as described by Jan on the telephone is that "she and her husband were experiencing difficulty in achieving emotional intimacy due to continual conflicts and lack of effective resolutions. When they do argue, Jan tends to criticize Mike and he simply dismisses what Jan says as being trivial. At times, Mike will avoid being around the house." The lack of intimacy and trust is serious enough that the couple discussed divorce, but decided instead to pursue marital therapy.

Each spouse would be asked both individually and in each other's presence about their goals for therapy. Let us assume that Mike agrees that the above issues are the central problems (if he did not, we would add his goals to the ones above). One would expect that Mike would give a bit more emphasis to his pain over not being trusted and in feeling picked-on and overwhelmed by his wife's complaints. The initial therapeutic contract might look like this:

Mike and Jan agree to hire James Keim, LCSW, to work on the following issues:

1. Jan and Mike want a return of intimacy and trust. Jan would feel secure in issues of Mike's dependability and drug use, and Mike would need to feel that Jan trusts him and that their discussions will not overwhelm him.
2. Mike and Jan want to be able to solve conflicts and disagreements in an emotionally safe and complete way.
3. Mike and Jan want to feel positive, safe, and committed in their marriage.

To work on these goals, Jan and Mike agree to:

1. Participate in couples therapy until their problems improve or until it is determined that therapy is not helping
2. To seek a balance between acceptance and change
3. To take the following steps (to be filled out as therapy progresses)

Conceptualization of Mike and Jan

For the strategic therapist, there are separate conceptualization issues; the clients' views of their situation, the therapist's view of the situation, and the agreed-upon conceptualization that the therapist and clients must create in order to organize the therapy.

The constructs which most empower clients need not be similar to those which most empower therapists. In other words, a therapist may think in terms of hierarchy and sequence, but the client may be most empowered by constructing these same principles within the concepts of "getting along" and "having good communication." It is therefore noted that the observations below might or might not be shared with the clients (this will be addressed later in the chapter). It is additionally noted that strengths and weaknesses are often different manifestations of the same qualities.

The Washington School would start the description of the couple by using the constructs of protection, unit, sequence, and hierarchy.

Protection

The clinician would start therapy from the point of view that the efforts of Mike and Jan to change one another may not be working, but at least are motivated by love and caring. For example, if Jan is perceived as being overly optimistic in her stated belief that Mike is past his substance abuse problems, it is suspected not that she is trying to deceive the therapist, but, rather, that Jan believes that such optimism will help Mike to stay sober. The therapist's starting conceptualization of problems as being "love gone wrong" results in the clinician's communicating stronger empathy to the clients, and this strengthens the therapeutic relationship.

Unit

Triangles worth exploring include those of Mike, Jan, and

a. Jan's parents
b. Mike's parents
c. friends and coworkers of both spouses (including friends that Mike may be chatting with only by computer)
d. Jan's brother

Exploration involves finding competing aspects of relationships or perceptions of either spouse that the relationship with the triangulating party is harming the marriage.

From the information gathered from Mike and Jan, one would want to explore whether Mike still perceives his mother's belief to be that a romantic partner will eventually abandon him. Perhaps the mother's current involvement in a successful marriage is resulting in Mike's perceiving positive messages. The therapist would also want to explore the basis for Jan's visiting with her parents often on weekends. If perceptions of triangulation are present, the Washington School therapist would try to change those through direct involvement in the therapy of that third party.

Sequence

The sequence of the presenting problem appears to be:

1. Instead of spending time together, Mike and Jan go their separate ways.
2. When they try to discuss problems, Jan complains and Mike withdraws.
3. Mike and Jan have fallen out of the healthy habits of their earlier relationship.

The preferred sequence:

1. Mike and Jan find ways to request and receive desired time, attention, affection, and support from one another.
2. When they try to discuss problems, Jan and Mike will employ a structure which will allow them to solve their difficulties in a win-win context. Mike will not withdraw in a conflict-avoidant fashion, and he will ask for change from Jan, which balances Jan's requests for change from him. Jan will approach difficult conversations with Mike with an optimistic attitude that comes from an expectation that problems will actually get solved in a collaborative and positive fashion.
3. Mike and Jan would complete sufficient relationship-maintenance activities (such as dating—going to movies, etc.).

Hierarchy

This addresses the issue of whether there is a healthy balance of influence and contribution in the relationship. In the view of Jan, Mike is intimidated by her earning more money from her regular job, and Mike tries to make up for this by working on weekends. This is a nice example of an attempt to equalize the hierarchy, which hurts the relationship (because Jan then feels neglected on weekends).

Some of Jan's Strengths

1. Jan displayed great emotional strength in surviving cancer, not only physically, but emotionally as well.
2. She has demonstrated dedication and stability in her work, having maintained quality employment with the same company for 14 years.
3. Jan enjoys her work, and this demonstrates an ability to create fulfillment.
4. Jan is able to enjoy time by herself and enjoys reading and other activities. Her desire for companionship is not based on an inability to be happy while alone.

5. Jan is highly responsible towards others, as noted in her raising her younger brother John.
6. Although neglected emotionally by her parents, Jan has a history of organizing support from peers.
7. Jan succeeded in life, despite neglect from parents.
8. Nurturing tendencies are evident in her care for her younger brother while growing up, and currently in her enjoyment of nurturing animals.

Some of Mike's Strengths

1. Mike has proven that he has the quality of dedication: He has been able to maintain the same job for the last 10 years and his marriage for 12 years, despite difficulties.
2. Mike loves his work; this suggests an ability to organize his context to create fulfillment.
3. He has apparently been able to remain sober for the last 7 months, despite a long history of substance abuse. This demonstrates the ability to change long-held bad habits.
4. Mike values marriage, despite difficulties in his family of origin.
5. He is good at entertaining himself, and is not dependent upon others for amusement.
6. He enjoys socializing, and appears to have been compatible with his wife's friends.
7. Mike has proven that he has the ability to competently date, court, and in general have fun with his wife.
8. Mike enjoys nurturing animals.
9. Mike came to therapy even though he is embarrassed by it.

Some Couples Strengths

1. They have been able to maintain their marriage for 12 years without separations despite relationship difficulties.
2. Mike and Jan have proven that they can effectively date, enjoy each other's company inside and outside the home, and have in the past enjoyed an excellent sex life.
3. The two are compatible over the important issue of children.
4. Jan and Mike enjoy a nurturing activity together—taking care of animals.
5. They have no reported history of violence.
6. They seem to be able to handle their finances.

Concerns of the Therapist

Current Issues

1. The couple have slipped into a state of severely decreased intimacy. Jan and Mike appear to desire to return to the fun and intimacy that they have been able to achieve in the past, but seem unable to make the change. The couple has withdrawn from those activities which created a successful context for the earlier success of their relationship.

2. Jan appears to be conflict-avoidant, and demonstrates an inability to engage Mike in low-anxiety negotiations. Mike also appears to be conflict-avoidant, and reacts to complaints maladaptively. The style of conflict resolution needs changing, as there is a poor history of successful problem resolution or negotiation.

3. Mike has a history of severe and chronic substance abuse. Although it appears that Mike has not been drinking for 7 months, the issue weighs heavily in the therapist's conceptualization of the client context.

4. It appears that the couple have not yet developed new interactional patterns to replace those related to substance abuse.

5. The incident at Jennifer's party may represent a return to substance abuse or infidelity, two issues with tremendous ability to damage the marriage.

6. The couple seemed to have a history of tremendous tolerance for their dysfunctional relationship, and this speaks to the need for a good "early warning system" to address future difficulties.

7. Though Jan has positive associations with therapy, Mike does not.

8. Mike's self-care is not good (substance abuse, not keeping to diet, for example), and Jan's self-care may have decreased as well.

9. Mike's tendency to interpret requests for change, especially emotional ones from his wife, as being "controlling" is cause for concern.

10. The issues around money might reveal similar issues about power. Jan believes that Mike is afraid to earn less money than his wife, and this is worth exploring. Do Mike's issues about money and power relate to a desire for equality or for control?

Historical Issues

The following historical issues would be of importance to the degree that the clients believe they need to be addressed in therapy. In other words, these issues may have to be addressed if the clients feel they are important and would feel that the therapist is unempathic or uninformed if the issues were not explored. Change often needs to be justified in relation to the clients' view of change.

1. The modeling of Mike's father may be having a negative effect on the marriage. Mike's father's pattern of disappearing when things got rough, and of substance abuse, may be repeated in Mike's first and current marriage. Mike used the words "just drop it" as a way of trying avoid conflict, just as his father did.

2. Mike has a history as child of being a loner/self-soother, which may contribute to lowered expectation of good treatment from others in the here and now.

3. Jan has a history of caretaking relationships with drug-abusing males (her brother, first husband, and second husband all had drug problems). Mike has a history of being tolerated by his wife and mother while abusing alcohol and drugs.

4. Mike's negative views of his mother may have been generalized to his wife.

5. Jan may feel that her infertility and/or history of cancer may prevent other men from wanting to be in a romantic relationship with her; this may create an unhealthy reason for not leaving, which would then need to be replaced in therapy with a healthy reason for staying.

6. Mike and Jan would be asked in the most neutral of ways if they believe that Mike's sexual abuse has any bearing on the current problem.

Techniques and Interventions

A Win-Win Negotiation Exercise

Described below is a therapeutic exercise designed to playfully help a couple return to win-win negotiations. One goal of this negotiation is for the therapist to triangulate with the spouses in a fashion that helps the couple strike a benevolent balance of influence. The therapist begins by requesting agreement from the clients to pursue an intervention that will improve their ability to gain each other's cooperation. The therapist then hands each partner a copy of the negotiation rules and asks them to take turns reading each of the rules out loud to one another. A playful atmosphere that still respects the serious nature of the couple's problems is best. The therapist then explains the thinking behind this approach. After answering any questions clients may have, the therapist explains that these steps are meant only as a corrective step, and are not necessarily to be used forever. Also worth explaining is that the assignment of this negotiating program is not meant to imply that poor negotiating skills caused the clients' problems. The therapist might add that usually couples grow beyond these steps and create their own superior set of rules. Before proceeding further, the therapist asks for a solid commitment from each partner in the couple to attempt to improve their communication by trying this negotiating approach for two months.

The therapist, after receiving a commitment to try this approach, then gives the clients the homework assignment to write down lists of items to be negotiated:

a "want" list. When placed in the position of the responding partner, initially, some clients have difficulty coming up with items for counterproposal; it is thus more important for some clients to write down and keep the "want" list accessible. The therapist next coaches the clients through an easy negotiation involving participation in a fun or entertaining activity. This negotiating of fun is an important step because it creates a positive association with this particular type of negotiating, and clients are often scared of negotiations at the start of therapy because of painful recent failures to gain cooperation. The therapist then suggests that it will take about three therapy sessions of coaching before the couple can complete negotiations without having the therapist as an intermediary. However, the therapist states, if the clients wish, they may want to at least start a negotiation at home to be completed in the clinic office. It is important to add this bit of restraint lest the couple become frustrated at their initial lack of success at explicit negotiation. For a minority of couples, this attempt at restraint inadvertently and paradoxically encourages them to successfully use these steps to complete negotiations the first week after the introduction of the system.

Frequently during the start of negotiations, the therapist needs to take sides with one spouse or another. Actively shifting coalitions in a manner which is traditional in strategic and structural approaches, the therapist uses the agreed-upon rules as a vehicle for siding with each spouse at different times (Haley, 1976; Minuchin, 1974). Without active coalition-shifting during the first two or three coached negotiating sessions, the couple will usually revert back to their previous, unsuccessful style. Through the shifting of coalitions, the therapist becomes a more integral part of the negotiating triangle of a couple. Therapists should think of themselves as replacing another party whose involvement in the couple's negotiations is not presently helpful (Haley, 1976). For example, the success that a therapist may have in helping a couple negotiate a family vacation should not make the clinician blind to the degree that the parents of the spouses may be involved in the disagreement. Negotiating difficulties that are serious enough to be brought to therapy should be viewed as indications that the spouses are caught in conflicting coalitions. Coaching negotiation offers the therapist the opportunity to lessen the influence of unhelpful third parties, as will be later discussed in more detail.

Rules to Be Given to Clients

The following rules are given in written form to clients. The information given in the "therapist's explanation" is for the comprehension of the therapist and, according to the clinician's judgment, may be communicated to the clients.

1. Spouses need to begin negotiations with some degree of recently created good will. If the couple has not recently had fun together and enjoyed each

other's company outside the household, negotiation tends not to work. This is why good business negotiators are often big spenders when it comes to entertaining those they plan to do business with.

[*Therapist's explanation:* Couples' homes are so habitually distracting that often partners are unable to give each other the attention they need. This is especially true if there are children in the house. It is therefore recommended for most couples that they get out of the house.]

2. Some negotiations take one discussion, others five, and others 200. Have a style which allows negotiations to start, break, and restart easily. If one ends a negotiating session nicely, one can come back to it nicely.

3. Never say no to a request made during negotiations. The closest one should come to saying "no" is "I will seriously consider that."

[*Therapist's explanation:* In our culture, "no" simultaneously denies a request and blocks future discussion. Blocking future discussion is contrary to the spirit of cooperative negotiation. A phrase borrowed from Japanese business negotiating, "I will seriously consider," is understood to momentarily deny a request while leaving open the possibility of discussing the request again in the future.]

4. Negotiating is only about the present and future. Avoid bringing up the past except as an example of what is being requested.

[*Therapist's explanation:* This is one of the most important rules in many communication courses. One of the leading causes of failure in negotiation is getting sidetracked. Talking about the past is the best way to avoid completion of a negotiation.]

5. Avoid explanations as to why one wants the package being negotiated. These will only sidetrack conversation.

[*Therapist's explanation:* Requesting an explanation not only sidetracks the negotiation, but also may be perceived as patronizing.]

6. In negotiation, assume that one knows only what is best for oneself, and not for others.

[*Therapist's explanation:* This type of discussion sidetracks negotiation. Additionally, no matter how well-intended, questioning the validity of another's request is usually received as being patronizing.]

7. Each party owes the other a "price" for the request in negotiation, as long as what is being requested is moral.

8. Avoid only doing those activities that both enjoy. Use negotiation to get one's partner to try something that she or he have not experienced, and be prepared to do the same in return.

9. Each party in a healthy romantic relationship is benevolently trying to change 2% of one another while accepting the other 98%. If one is trying to change much more than 2%, the relationship is one characterized by nagging. If one is not trying to change the other at all, the partners grow apart over time, and do not feel an adequate amount of intimacy.

[*Therapist's explanation:* Oddly enough, the perception that one's spouse is interested in changing one is part of the perception of intimacy. The research of Neil Jacobson (1998) has emphasized the importance of acceptance to successful marital therapy.]

10. Define time parameters of what is being requested. Be very specific about terms.

[*Therapist's explanation:* Couples should start by only negotiating for time segments of one week at a time and slowly build up the amount of time involved in transactions. Also, requests should be described in very behavioral terms, especially early in the therapy. For example, "Be more loving" is too general a request, whereas "hugging and cuddling" are appropriately specific requests. Global requests for change must be broken down into simple behaviors.]

11. Hold hands continuously through difficult or emotional negotiations. The physical closeness is a reminder of the love that underlies all discussions.

[*Therapist's explanation:* This is an especially effective approach for a couple whose arguments quickly spiral out of control even in the therapist's office. Negotiation is not a time for couples to fight, and such unproductive disagreements must be quickly blocked. Therapists know that they should intervene quickly to stop an argument if the couple, in the midst of a disagreement, disengage their hands.]

12. Seal all negotiations with a kiss. Write all negotiations down in a specific place, such as a blank book of the type often sold as a diary.

[*Therapist's explanation:* With emotional negotiations, couples tend to later confuse the memory of their starting position with the final agreed-upon compromise. Spouses tend to confuse where they started in a negotiation with where they ended. Writing negotiations down addresses this almost inevitable problem.]

13. The negotiation should not end until each partner feels that a "win-win" situation exists whereby each is happy with the negotiated arrangement.

14. When a couple learns to negotiate explicitly, it is at first more troublesome than helpful. Have patience!

Pitfalls

One of the most common mistakes made in therapy is failure to pace the therapy according to the needs and situation of the clients. Sometimes couples will leave an initial session with unrealistic expectations of how quickly or evenly change will come. What makes such expectations all the more dangerous is that coming to therapy leads spouses to shed the protective numbness with which they have enveloped their relationship; they feel the pain of even small failures all the more powerfully after the start of therapy. Open discussion with couples as to these pitfalls is the best preparation.

Another pitfall might be a return to substance abuse by Mike. Many successful cessation of substance abuse involve some "slips," or isolated returns to substance abuse. Mentioning this to Jan during individual discussion and helping her plan ahead about how she would react are helpful steps to take.

An additional problem might be the powerful influence of a third party on the relationship. The best defense against this is the questioning which evokes the perception of third-party influence on the marriage.

The most common reason for failure in Strategic Therapy is failure to establish a strong therapeutic relationship. One of the three major emphases in the 2- and 3-year training programs of the Washington School is establishing and maintaining the therapeutic relationship. Live supervision allows for correction of clinical mistakes of which the therapist is unaware, that damage the therapeutic relationship.

Areas to Avoid

An issue might be avoided for two reasons. First, the clients have explicitly and together asked that the issue not be addressed. If this could be done without risking harm and without interfering with the therapeutic contract, the issue would be avoided through direct and overt agreement with the clients that it was not to be discussed.

The second reason for temporarily avoiding an issue would be that the therapist was unable to bring it up in a professional and empathic manner. The therapist would, in this situation, seek immediate supervision to deal with this problem.

Inclusion of Other Family Members

An axiom for the Washington School is that if the therapy is not meeting with success, expand the unit. The goal of adding people is to increase the clinician's perspective with additional points of view, to add potential helpers, and to disengage the overinvolved. It would be hoped that Mike and Jan could address their problems on their own, but if they could not, their parents, siblings, and/or friends might be invited to join certain sessions.

For the Washington School, expanding the unit beyond the marital dyad is common with substance abuse, and usually required in domestic violence cases. If Mike's drinking returned, for example, his coworkers might be asked to join a session as well, if they could be of use in helping him to stay sober.

Homework

The negotiation exercise would be given as homework after three sessions in which the couple employed the process. A critical part of giving homework is that it must absolutely feel to the clients that the assignment is addressing the issue that they have hired the therapist to work on. The value of homework is that it initiates or continues the change process outside of therapy, and is thus more likely to be continued than a pattern which is dependent upon occurring in a clinician's office.

Homework can fail if the clients are not motivated proportionately. Clients who are unsure of their desire for change must not be given homework that is out of proportion with their motivation. The therapist in such a case must either create stronger motivation for change (for example, by truthfully noting the dangers of not changing), or must employ homework which does not require great motivation to complete.

One way to encourage homework participation is to employ humor or friendly competition. For example, one might begin negotiating homework by asking the clients to start by negotiating fun which does not last more than 5 minutes. Another example would be for the therapist to state that a small prize will be awarded to the spouse who initiates the "smallest" negotiation.

Proportionality may motivate the therapist to give homework that is particularly difficult or challenging. Clients with tremendous motivation to change may feel that the therapist does not understand their desperation if the homework is perceived as being unchallenging.

Timeline and Frequency of Therapy

The average marital therapy at the founding clinic of the Washington School is 8 to 10 sessions. The length of the therapy is sometimes determined by the presenting problem; severe violence usually results in a therapy which continues over a year. Outside of severe substance, physical, or sexual abuse or severe emotional disturbance, the length of therapy tends to be determined by the strength of the couple's family and community support network. Briefer therapies of four or five sessions are not uncommon with couples who are well connected to supportive social networks.

My best guess with Mike and Jan is that the therapy would be about 8 to 10 sessions. The first three or four sessions would occur on a weekly basis, and would then go to twice a month for the next three to four sessions, with the remainder occurring on a monthly or emergency basis. The Washington School has a family practice model which encourages clients to return every 6 months for a check-up. Often, especially in a therapy with quick change, clients are too embarrassed to return to therapy until their relationship has profoundly deteriorated. The framework of check-ups constructs returns as being normal and healthy.

The average session would start with my seeing the couple together for half the session and individually for another half (each spouse would receive a quarter-session). The individual interview achieves a joining that is sometimes difficult in front of the spouse because it may appear as coalition-building. Individual sessions also allow for revelation of information that the client is unable to discuss in front of the spouse. The confidentiality rule stated at the beginning of therapy is that there is no individual confidentiality for information unless specifically granted by the therapist; this prevents the individual session from becoming a tool with which to triangulate the therapist into secrets.

Termination

The goals of the Washington School, in order of importance and emphasis, are:

1. To do no harm by action or inaction to clients or others;
2. To keep the clients coming to therapy until the problem is solved, until a referral can be made elsewhere, or until it can be determined that therapy will not help;
3. To solve the presenting problem.

This hierarchy of goals requires that the therapist not pursue solving the presenting problem so energetically that it results in the client's dropping out of therapy. Pursuing a child protection issue would occur, even though it might destroy the therapy, because the greatest priority is avoiding harm. Therapy is not a race, and termination is very much an issue of when the client feels that the goals have been met or that the therapy is no longer helpful.

THE THERAPIST'S VIEW OF SUCCESS

The Washington School therapist is very dependent upon the client's perception of whether or not the therapeutic contract has been met. Therapy would be terminated in the sense of only scheduling a check-up in the future if the couple feel that their goals have been reached in and outside of the clinician's office and that they are ready to end it. However, the therapist has certain expectations of what success looks like. In the view of the Washington School, the average North American client feels successful when:

1. There is a return to previous levels of intimacy that allow each spouse to perceive strong emotional support from each other.
2. The couple is having enough fun, both together and individually, to provide a sense of quality of life, or at least to have a realistic plan for when such joy might reenter their lives.

3. The spouses find and perceive a fair balance of contribution and influence.
4. The spouses are at peace with what aspects of the marriage are worth working on, and which are best thought of as requiring acceptance.
5. Third parties identified as a source of stress have been dealt with in a way which both couples accept.
6. There is no dependence on the therapist; the clients and their support system have, in a healthy and less expensive fashion, taken over the role played by the clinician.

It is understood that the perception by clients that they have a happy marriage and no longer need therapy is also mediated by culture. For example, successful marital therapy with a fundamentalist Islamic couple from Iran might result in a very different sense of what a successful marriage looks like.

THE CLIENT'S VIEW OF SUCCESS

In the imagined therapeutic contract, Jan and Mike noted the following goals:

1. Jan and Mike want a return of intimacy and trust. Jan would feel secure in issues of Mike's dependability and drug use, and Mike would need to feel that Jan trusts him and that their discussions will not overwhelm him.
2. Mike and Jan want to be able to solve conflicts and disagreements in an emotionally safe and complete way.
3. Mike and Jan want to feel positive, safe, and committed in their marriage.

Therapy would be a success to the degree that Mike and Jan perceive that these goals have been reached.

CONCLUSION

The evolution of therapy in the last decade has been characterized by increasing efficiency in description of what we believe creates change. It is no longer acceptable in the eyes of most clinicians to describe an approach in language so stylized to a particular school that outsiders are unable to comprehend the literature.

The next step in the evolution of therapy is widespread comparative outcome research to determine the effectiveness of not only interventions and schools, but also of generic factors, such as strength of the therapeutic relationship. Before this next and very important step can be taken, a generic language is necessary to describe clinical intervention. Comparative literature such as this book is critical to the development of a common understanding of therapy.

REFERENCES

Erickson, E. H. (1959). Identity and the life cycle. *Psychological Issues, 1,* 1–17.

Haley, J. (1971). *Changing families.* New York: Grune and Stratton.

Haley, J. (1973). *Uncommon therapy.* New York: Norton.

*Haley, J. (1976). *Problem-solving therapy.* San Francisco: Jossey Bass.

Jacobson, N., & Christensen, A. (1998). *Acceptance and change in couple therapy: A therapist's guide to transforming relationships.* New York: Norton.

*Madanes, C. (1981). *Strategic family therapy.* San Francisco: Jossey-Bass.

Madanes, C. (1990). *Sex, love, and violence: Strategies for transformation.* New York: Norton.

Minuchin, S. (1974). *Families and family therapy.* Cambridge, MA: Harvard University Press.

Nichols, M., & Schwartz, R. (1995). *Family therapy: Concepts and methods.* Boston: Allyn and Bacon.

Schwartz, P. (1995). *Love between equals: How peer marriage really works.* New York: Free Press.

ADDITIONAL SUGGESTED READINGS

Gottman, J. (1994). *What predicts divorce? The relationship between marital process and marital outcomes.* Hillsdale, NJ: Erlbaum.

Jackson, D. D. (1965). Family rules: The marital quid pro quo. *Archives of General Psychiatry, 12,* 589–594.

Keim, J. (1998). Strategic family therapy. In F. M. Dattilio (Ed.), *Case studies in couple and family therapy* (pp. 132–157). New York: Guilford Press.

Keim, J. (1999). Brief strategic marital therapy. In J. M. Donovan (Ed.), *Short term couple therapy* (pp. 265–290). New York: Guilford Press.

---

*Suggested reading.

PART II

PSYCHODYNAMIC THEORIES

6

Object Relations Therapy

Jill Savege Scharff and Yolanda de Varela

THE TREATMENT MODEL

Object Relations couples therapy is a psychodynamically oriented way of working with couples (Scharff & Scharff, 1987, 1991). It derives its methods from the classical psychoanalytic principles of technique handed down from Freud, namely: following unconscious themes by listening to words, silence, and gesture; responding to unconscious material; developing insight; interpreting dreams and fantasies; and working with transference. However, Object Relations couples therapists do not function as a blank screen in the classical analytic way. Instead, they are interactive with the couple; yet, at the unconscious level, they are nondirective. This shift in stance from the classical analytic position is required by the therapeutic focus on the relationship, not on the individual, and is made possible by adopting, integrating, and applying the principles of various object relations theories, not classical Freudian theory.

These object relations theories have in common the view that a person's current relationships take shape from the structure and functioning of the unique pattern of internal relationships that were set down as the person interacted with and adapted to others early in life. Psychic structure is viewed as an internal system of relationships, an internal group that functions as a prototype, a working model of relationships, and a map of what to expect from others. This inner scape determines the choice of the partner and the nature of the couple relationship—for better or worse.

The couple is not simply a pair of individuals. The couple relationship is a tightly organized, closed system of interacting individual internal relationships which are experienced in the interpersonal arena of the couple relationship in ways unique to the couple at conscious and unconscious levels. The outward manifestations of these ways of being recur often enough that the couples therapist can detect the patterns of interaction and show how they embody old ways of feeling and behaving rooted in earlier experiences with the families of origin.

Object Relations couples therapists offer a therapeutic relationship that creates a psychological holding environment similar enough for old patterns of relating to important figures in the family of origin to be recreated, and yet different enough to allow for their detection. The couples therapist will have plenty of opportunity to identify patterns of interaction and, over time, to rework them. The therapist brings the capacity for listening and following, for sharing the couple's experience, for tolerating anxiety and loss, and for being different from the original figures in the life of each member of the couple. The gap between the couple's experience of the therapist as a re-edition of the early objects of their dependency, love and aggression, and their experience of the therapist as a new object in the here and now, provides space for understanding that allows room for the couple to grow and develop in healthier ways.

To understand Object Relations couples therapy further, we need to note the building blocks of object relations theory upon which this therapeutic method is based (Scharff & Scharff, 1992).

THE MAJOR CONCEPTS OF OBJECT RELATIONS THEORY AND THEIR APPLICATION TO COUPLES' RELATIONSHIP FUNCTIONING

Ronald Fairbairn (1952) challenged Freud's theory of human motivation based on instincts. Fairbairn believed that the infant is born with an ego capable of relatedness, and that there is no id full of undifferentiated impulses, as Freud had suggested. Fairbairn argued that the human infant is driven, not by sexual longing and aggressive drives, but by the need for attachment. As the infant develops a relationship, naturally there will be some frustration. A manageable amount of frustration can be coped with, and in that case, a relatively satisfying view of the experience is taken into the ego. Intolerable features of the relationship need to be repressed because they are too painfully rejecting or too exciting of need to be borne in consciousness.

The unbearable experience is controlled by being taken inside the central ego in the form of an internal object that has then to be rejected by consciousness because it is painful. Splitting of the object into rejecting and exciting objects and their repression into unconsciousness occurs together with splitting and repression of parts of the ego that have been in relation to them (called antilibidinal and libidinal egos, respectively), along with the appropriate affects of rage and longing. In this way, human experience is transformed into psychic structure through the action of introjection, splitting, and repression. Closest to consciousness lies the central internal object relationship, while the antilibidinal and libidinal internal object relationships are mostly in unconsciousness, the libidinal being the most deeply repressed of all. The resulting personality is then a system of parts of ego, object, and affect joined in these internal object relationships, all of them in dynamic relation.

Donald Winnicott (1958, 1965, 1971) used the image of the nursing couple as a guide to understanding child development. The mother has two basic functions: to safeguard or hold the environment for growth (the environmental mother) and to be the object of the child's love and hate (the object mother). Similarly, in couples therapy, the couples therapist offers a psychological holding environment in which he or she can be experienced as a representative of both the holding mother and the object mother. Winnicott also said that there had been a somatic partnership between the pregnant mother and her fetus, and that at the point of birth this partnership developed into a psychosomatic partnership that organized the infant's psyche, and also the psyche of the mother of that infant as she related to and learned about her child. In the transitional space between mother and infant, interpersonal interaction gives rise to experience and expectations that create internal structure. We find this concept helpful, particularly when we are considering the quality of the sexual relationship in the couple. Like the nursing couple, the romantic sexual couple has a partnership with psychological meaning, heightened physical sensation, interdependence, and commitment over time in which growth and development of both parties will occur. Husband and wife relate to each other and contribute to each other's growth through the life cycle.

Melanie Klein (1946, 1975) reconstructed the child's infantile fantasy about the earliest relationship during those anxious months of infantile dependency. She suggested that the infant imagines parts of its own feelings to reside in the caretaking person so as to protect itself, the loved and needed other person, and the relationship between them from the force of the death instinct that might otherwise overpower the life instinct. She went on to say that this mechanism of displacement, for which she borrowed Freud's term projection, would be followed by a more extensive process, for which she coined the term projective identification, in which the infant misidentifies parts of the self in the other person. In projective identification the child finds a part of the self in the parent and thinks that this self-state is emanating from the parent. For instance, when aggression has been projected from the child into the parent, the child experiences the parent as aggressive. This misperceived persecutory object is then introjected and identified with so that the child's aggression is reinforced. If the mother is also available to accept projections of positive, loving feelings, by which she is colored positively, this leads to an introjection of warmth and goodness that counteracts the introjection of a persecuting object.

It was Henry Dicks (1967) who first described the process of projective identification in the selection of a partner and the maintenance of the marital relationship. Dicks applied Fairbairn's concept of psychic structure and Klein's mechanism of projective identification to the marital couple. He found that each partner projects unwanted or endangered parts of the self into the spouse, leading to a system of mutual projective identification. The partners choose each other not just for conscious reasons of compatibility, but because they offer the possibility of unconscious connection to repressed parts of the self that can be discovered in the partner. Protection of the self and the relationship is intended, and in the healthy marriage it may work that way, at least for some time. But in the unhealthy marriage, deterioration of the couple relationship results when the projective identifications are too concretely cemented or when they are rejected.

Imagine a wife looking to her husband to meet her need. If he meets the need, then she learns that it is all right to express the needy part of herself (her libidinal internal object relationship). If she misidentifies him as nurturing at that moment, she meets a frosty response (emanating from his antilibidinal internal object relationship). She deals with this by introjective identification: She becomes like the rejecting object that she met in her interaction with him. She finds that it is better not to express her need, and this amplifies her internal rejecting object system. She then represses her internal libidinal object relationship as before. The projective-introjective identification system is always mutual. He has simultaneously misidentified his own needy self in his wife's approach and attacked it there to keep it from emerging to his conscious awareness. If he has less need to repress his needy self so thoroughly, he will be able to respond to the need that he finds in her. In homosexual couple relationships, the additional factor of gender similarity drives the projective-introjective identification system.

The partners (heterosexual or homosexual) must have a balance of unconscious communication that permits a degree of feeling of at-one-ness so that a joint personality can form from the fusion of the two intrapsychic structures, and at the same time enough separation and difference from the original objects that growth can occur in the couple context. Understanding and interpreting the mutual projective and introjective identificatory system of the couple relationship is the basis of the therapeutic action of object relations couples therapy.

Wilfred Bion (1959, 1962, 1967) applied Kleinian theory to his study of groups. He noted that projective identification occurs between the group and the leader, in which some individuals are drawn to create an unacknowledged subgroup operating not in pursuit of the group task, but in hopes of meeting shared unconscious needs which Bion named basic assumptions. Individuals take the leadership for expressing one or another basic assumption because of their valency to relate to others in this way—either to express a dependent relation to authority, a fight-or-flight reaction against authority, or a tendency to substitute magical pairing between two individuals as an alternative to the group's task of working out its relationship to the leader. Similarly, we find that in marriage, spouses are chosen because of their valencies to accept the projective identifications of their spouses. In the small group of two, they deal with dominance and submission, with leadership through the exercise of authority or the assumption of power, through depending one on the other, fighting, fleeing from the issues, and pairing. Pairing generally supports the task of the marital dyad, but it becomes a destructive defense when the pairing involves a lover, a parent, a child, or an unskilled therapist.

THERAPIST SKILLS AND ATTRIBUTES

The Object Relations couples therapist needs to learn the following skills (summarized in Table 6.1).

The primary skill is setting the frame. "Setting the frame" refers to the process of conducting the interview, establishing the fee schedule and the arrangements, managing the anxiety of the initial session, and establishing a working alliance. In an attitude of involved impartiality, we maintain friendly but nonintrusive interest and concern in the couple as a partnership, without taking sides or holding ambition about how they should change. We simply create a psychological space in which they can share thoughts and feelings that they could not do without our help, because we are trained to be able to bear pain and to think about feelings. We are in a state of negative capability which is to say that we are not bound by our memory of what has gone before or blinded by our desire for their relationship—or for us as therapists—to be a certain way. We are not trying to force things, or to guess at meanings prematurely. We remain open to whatever may transpire.

TABLE 6.1   Skills of the Object Relations Couples Therapist

Setting the frame

Maintaining a neutral, but not remote, position of involved impartiality

Creating a psychological space for sharing thoughts and feelings

Developing negative capability in the therapist's use of self

Interpreting defense, anxiety, fantasy and inner object relations using the "because clause"

Working with transference and countertransference

Working through to termination

We will recognize repeated patterns of interaction. Then we ask ourselves what protective purpose they serve. For this laborious work of excavating from surface to depth, we have found useful the "because clause," a concept borrowed from the group therapy work of Henry Ezriel (1952), who showed that the first level of defense is to involve the therapist in a particular type of relationship, the required relationship, that succeeds in covering over a feared and avoided relationship. This in turn covers over a calamitous relationship that is feared above all. We show the couple how they require each other to behave in a familiar way that hides their avoidance of true intimacy because they are afraid of catastrophe. The avoidance of intimacy shows up in various relationship problems, and the catastrophe is imagined in many different forms. Ultimately, the couple's deepest fear is that the relationship will die or will kill one or both partners. In short, the calamity is loss of the relationship, loss of the object, or loss of the self. This technique of the "because clause" enables us to interpret the couple's defenses and the underlying anxiety that makes them necessary.

However, we do not simply look at the behavior of the couple before us. We attend closely to how the couple perceives us and involves us in their experience (their transferences to us), and we observe our reaction to the being with them (our countertransference). The transference-countertransference dynamic depends on projective and introjective identificatory processes. Projective identification that occurs between the mother and her infant, or between the husband and his wife, also occurs between the couple and the therapist. Temporarily, we become part of the couple's projective and introjective identification system, and then we interpret the couple's transference from our experience in the countertransference.

We find that countertransference is of two major types, contextual and focused countertransference. The contextual countertransference occurs in response to the couple's attitude toward the treatment context and to us as the provider of help, where we are experienced as the environmental mother. The focused countertransference stems from the resonance between our internal objects and those of the members of the couple, where we are experienced as the object mother. In couples therapy, there is an oscillation between these two types. We aim to receive the couple's projective identifications of us, so as to understand their dilemmas from inside our experience of focused and contextual countertransference.

Working through involves repeating the work of detection and interpretation until the defenses and anxieties are understood and worked through. At that point, the couple has internalized the therapeutic space and can provide psychological holding, intimate relating, and understanding of each other.

The interpretive work of object relations couples therapy is not arrived at by intellectual formulation alone, but relies on the use of the therapist's self. We use our countertransference (our personal reactions) for the detection, understanding of, and conviction about the projective and introjective identificatory system of the couple. Therefore, therapists need to have undergone enough personal therapy, supervision, and peer supervision to be aware of their own internal object relations set so that they can observe its interaction with the couple's system. Even though self-revelation is not called for in this approach, the therapist's self is interacting and remains vulnerable to resonating with the full panoply of emotions. The therapist who wants to use the object relations approach with couples needs personal attributes of honesty, courage, insight, and commitment to ongoing reflection, process and review, and self analysis.

The following vignette from a couple consultation with Jill Scharff will illustrate the object relations way of working in the initial interview.

Case Vignette: Lynn and Denis

Lynn and Denis, a highly educated couple from intellectual, professional families, sought consultation shortly after their marriage. Both of them felt hesitant about sharing their thoughts with the therapist. They told me that they cared for each other greatly but Lynn felt lonely, ignored and resentful of his lateness and absence, while Denis felt tied down, controlled and puzzled by her neediness. She found him callous and oblivious, while he found her clinging. Her way of suffering in silence had begun to bother her and so she had suggested getting help. The conscious basis for their selecting each other was their intellect and their shared feeling of distance from the less intellectually well-endowed.

Denis had parents who were close as a couple and who put their need for behavior that conformed to bourgeois standards above any concern for him. Lynn had parents who stayed married to fulfill their responsibility to the children but who lived separate lives, sometimes in separate countries. In addition to being absent frequently on account of the location of his work, when present her father threatened absence by suicide.

In my countertransference I felt quite mystified by their abstruse language which had the effect of excluding me from their conversation. Both seemed oblivious to the difficulty I might have in understanding them. I felt ignored, stupid, inferior, and cloddish. I detected their defense of reassuring and aggrandizing themselves by projecting feared incompetence, low self esteem, inferiority, and envy of omniscience outside the couple. Illuminating this countertransference experience of them were details from Lynn and Denis's histories that led to the following view of their shared projective and introjective identificatory system.

Lynn had identified with her uncomplaining, unhappy mother who envied Lynn's father's freedom. Lynn carried an image of an internal couple as one that was split, or held together only by the wife accepting the husband's absence. Newly married, she had refound in her husband her rejecting internal object characterized by the callousness of her father. Because of Denis's similarity to her father and her identification with her mother, Lynn's internal couple was being expressed in the form of the new marriage where she had to struggle with it all over again. Denis's rejecting object relationship turned against his central ego so that, even though highly educated, he was working in a blue collar job, unlike his successful father. Lynn's preference for a close relationship reminded Denis of his parents' marriage from which he felt excluded, and so he rejected Lynn just as he had felt rejected by his parent, and also attacked his own marriage just as he attacked the internal couple inside himself.

In the consultation, this couple's contextual transference was one of initial suspicion, but they gradually came to trust the therapist's intentions and concern for them. They did not show focused transferences at this time. In couple therapy, recognition of repetitive patterns of interaction leads to awareness of the couple's internal object relationships and relationship to their internal couples projected into each other and into their couple relationship as they are expressed in their marriage. This is then followed by understanding, insight, owning one's projective identifications, and taking back those that otherwise spoil the couple's chance for creating their own gratifying relationship.

THE CASE OF MIKE AND JAN

Assessment

The case of Mike and Jan is rich in data concerning the history of the individual partners and their couple relationship, but it does not convey the affective tone of their relationship. It does not tell us how Mike and Jan related to the interviewer or how the interviewer felt about them. No session transcript is there to help us analyze the affective interaction of the couple. We can only guess at their resistance, defensive process, and underlying anxiety. There is not enough information to work with in developing a hypothesis about the transference and countertransference which is the major focus of the Object Relations approach, even in consultation. This case report does not give us material that demonstrates the technique of Object Relations therapy in action with Mike and Jan. The reader can get a better idea of technique from the brief report of work with Lynn and Denis and vignettes in earlier texts (D. Scharff and J. Scharff, 1991; J. and D. Scharff, 1992; J. Scharff, 1995). However, Mike and Jan certainly give us plenty to think about.

What we will do with Mike and Jan's material is use it to illustrate how we might gather more information from experience with the couple and begin to develop hypotheses about the case from the Object Relations perspective.

In order to get the information we need, we would arrange a series of clinical interviews to complete an extended assessment for this couple. We would study how Mike and Jan deal with the therapist and the entry into the treatment process, and how the therapist responds to each of them individually and as a couple. We would not tend to do a home evaluation, but would arrange to see them in the office setting. The office provides a controlled therapeutic space where the therapists are able to manage the frame of a treatment. Within this frame we create a safe environment in which the couple feels held and where the partners can enter a psychological space in which they can face their anxieties. We would set a fee and a time to meet, and we would start and stop the session on time. Then we would look at Mike and Jan's way of dealing with the frame of treatment. Were they compliant with our expectations, or did they seek to bend the frame, and if so, in what ways? These behaviors would give clues as to how they felt about the prospect of therapy with us.

We would be attentive to our own reactions to detect our contextual counter-transference to their contextual transference. We would look out for focused transferences to us which would help us understand from inside our own experience difficulties in how they related to each other. Speaking from inside our own experience gives us a better chance of connecting with the couple and getting through to them in a non-judgmental way.

During this assessment we would inquire more about the couple's sexual history (D. Scharff, 1982; J. Scharff, 1989). The information given so far suggests that their sexual relationship was entirely satisfactory; in fact, it was excellent. All the more peculiar, then, is the fact that it has virtually ceased. We would want to know why. How did each partner feel about its cessation, and how do they understand that a sexual relationship that was pleasurable has now gone into abeyance? If it turns out that the couple had a great deal of difficulty talking about sex, and that was why the information was so cryptic, then we might give them a sex questionnaire to discover their sexual histories and their attitudes toward sexuality in a shared situation, masturbation, sexual fantasies, and reaction to their own and their partner's nudity. It might be found at this point that the description of excellence in the sexual relationship was defensive, and that the couple requires adjunctive behavioral sex therapy. If it turns out that a good sexual relationship has been destroyed by marital conflict, then we would feel secure in going ahead to recommend couples therapy without specific behavioral sexual intervention.

Conceptualization of Mike and Jan Individually and as a Couple

Mike as an Individual

Mike's brother Mark was placed in special education classes because he had attention deficit disorder and difficulty with reading and math. Mike was in regular classes where he got Cs, felt dumb, and tended to quit things. Mike now asks whether he might also have attention deficit disorder.

On first reading of the case study, we mistakenly remembered that Mike, like Mark, had been in special education classes. This slip in comprehension may have been an attentional problem on our part due to other factors in our work or personal lives, but it may also be evidence of a specific countertransference response to Mike's depression and low self-esteem in the area of intellectual functioning. We might have identified with Mike's self-diagnosed attentional deficit disorder. We might be picking up a fusion in Mike's unconscious between Mike and his brother, a defense organized to eliminate Mike's guilt over being better endowed. We might have identified with a projection of Mike's ego that feels weak and dumb. We might have identified with a projection of his object that criticizes him and exaggerates his weak points. If we made an error like this in a session, we would look into its relevance for understanding at the unconscious level.

Mike's drug abuse history points to a search for heightened simulation that can be a marker for attention deficit disorder and for mood disorder. Diagnostic psychological tests of attentiveness are needed, but should be combined with testing of intelligence, personality, and cognitive style. It seems that Mike has good coordination of large motor functioning, as shown in his ability to play football and to do welding and blacksmith work. He has the fine motor coordination to manipulate the keyboard, but it is possible that his competence with the computer masks a difficulty with the hand-eye coordination needed for writing. Mike is bright enough to be of interest to an educated woman like Jan, but it seems quite likely that an attention deficit, perhaps complicated by a subtle specific learning disability, has seriously limited Mike's capacity to achieve his potential. The results of intelligence testing, projectives, attention deficit scales, and learning disability assessment tests, such as the Woodcock-Johnson, could be helpful.

It seems to us that Mike was depressed during school. He tended to quit activities, perhaps because he lost heart due to the effects of undiagnosed weaknesses less obvious than his brother's. He almost quit his marriage when he responded to Jan's suggestion of pursuing a divorce by saying "Fine, let's go for it, do it tomorrow," which did not reflect his true feelings at all. Here he shows counterphobic defenses in addition to hopeless responses.

We would ask for more reflection on Mike's early drug use and self-destructive behavior. What triggered the first drink? What events were happening in his family at that time? Was his self-destructive behavior an attempt to punish himself? Was he guilty about something? Even though he is now sober, he still seems to push himself in a self-mortifying way, as if only that will keep him free from the self-destructive impulses. After abusing alcohol and marijuana steadily for 20 years, Mike has been substance-free for 7 months and attends

Narcotics Anonymous meetings. We would continue to support his attendance there. He has made a major change in terms of accepting his addiction and working on his recovery. His recent absence from work for a 28-day hospital inpatient stay seems to have been acceptable to his employer. Apparently, substance abuse, or treatment for it, did not compromise his ability to maintain employment, but it probably did compromise his ability to branch out on his own and work for himself, which he would have preferred.

A related problem in the area of oral behavior is Mike's difficulty in managing his food intake. Despite having raised levels of cholesterol and high blood pressure like his father who has already had one heart attack, Mike is not following the diet his doctor recommended. He is wanting to add oral medication to his intake, instead of modifying his present intake. Mike wants his blood chemistry to be controlled by the doctor's prescription of medicine, rather than by Mike's taking control of himself. His self-destructiveness is evident in his negligence towards his physical condition.

Mike spends a lot of time working on his home computer, but it is not clear from the record what he does. We would want to know much more about his computing activities and the purposes that they serve. Is he exercising his intelligence in a private way, or is he playing games? Is he transferring his addictive behavior to the Internet? Does he have a secret sex life there? We have been told that in real time, Mike is not a particularly social person, and that he has been fairly quiet and keeps to himself. So we wonder if he is using his computer to provide a virtual social reality by joining discussions in chat rooms.

Mike seems to have been quite dependent on his parents. He maintained an attachment to his mother, staying at home until he was 29. As an adolescent, he was quite dependent on his father's approval through attendance at his football games. It is unclear how Mike responded to his parents' relationship, but he was certainly angry when they got divorced. Incidentally, it is notable that Mike did not marry for the first time until a year after his mother remarried, which raises the question of guilty inability to pursue his own needs if his mother's were not met. Could this be an underlying dynamic preventing him from being more successful in relation to Jan? Mike recognizes the value of the good marriage that his mother has had for the last 20 years, and has been able to form a relationship with his stepfather. His relationship with his father remains rather tenuous.

Mike's mother was critical of him. She was the disciplinarian, whereas his father was lenient and not particularly involved. He tended to deny problems and to leave when confronted. Mike has picked up his father's habit of avoiding confrontation, and he is identifying with this lost father when he emotionally abandons Jan. As far as we know, he has not picked up his father's habit of having affairs. Mike conceptualizes affairs as a response to nagging and belittlement. The story of Mike's coming home late from a party, which was the event that precipitated consultation, would need to be investigated further, to see whether Mike was acting on an affair fantasy.

We would want to know more about Mike's first marriage, during which his wife became unexpectedly pregnant, but miscarried before the couple's ambivalence about bearing a child could be worked through. We are told how the first wife felt about Mike's reluctance to have a child. But we do not learn enough about Mike's reaction to the miscarriage. We wonder whether his increased drug abuse and failing to sleep in the marital bed were responses to unhappiness in the relationship with his wife, or whether they were responses to his resentment regarding his ambivalence concerning the child. It is striking that they separated after 9 months, this being the duration of a pregnancy. We find that there is not enough material in the record to help us understand Mike's reluctance to have children in either marriage. Although he enjoys taking care of Jan's animals, Mike has not wanted children. Perhaps he felt that a pregnancy would ruin his marriage, and he might have got this idea from perceiving that his older brother's difficulties ruined his parents' marriage.

The record does not provide enough information about Mike's sexual molestation. Although we know that his aunt fondled and kissed him, we do not know what parts of his body she touched and kissed, or indeed what kind of requests she made of him. Nor do we know why he did not ask his parents for help in understanding or dealing with this situation. In further consultation interviews, we would want to open up this topic, because it could shed light on the couple's sexual difficulties and on Mike's fears of intimacy. If it was too difficult for Mike to talk about this topic with his wife present, we might agree to parallel individual interviews, where he could deal with this subject along with the possibility of affair behaviors and the effect of the child abuse on his sexual adjustment. Jan could use her individual session to talk more freely about her reproductive losses and her present feelings about her husband. The history of sexual abuse and the issue of intimacy would be evaluated in depth in ensuing couple sessions.

Jan as an Individual

Jan has a good work record. Her social development is much more satisfactory than Mike's. Her previous marriage lasted 3 years and ended because of her husband's drug abuse and infidelity. We would want to know much more about her first marriage. It is interesting to consider why her marriage to Mike did not also end over the issue of drug abuse. Perhaps this means that infidelity is the critical issue for her, as it was for Mike's mother. Like Mike, Jan has maintained strong attachments to her family. She uses the opportunity when Mike is busy at work to visit with her parents. Perhaps she is adapting to his unavailability, or perhaps his involvement in work is a response to her primary attachment remaining with her family.

As a young woman, Jan was successfully treated by hysterectomy for ovarian cancer, following which she had depression which responded to short-term psychotherapy. Jan is able to remember her fear of death at the time of her cancer diagnosis, but she is less able to talk about the loss of her fertility. It must have hurt to sustain such enormous damage to her young adult body that she could not create a child. Jan loves to care for animals, and seems to have no idea that they are a replacement for the children that she cannot have. She was glad to find a man like Mike, who did not want to have children and so did not face her with conflict over the damage to her reproductive system. She appears to take care of him as her child, just as she took care of her drug-abusing first husband, and before that her drug-addicted brother, who is the same age as Mike. Jan is repeating her history of taking care of a damaged boy. What else is she repeating in her relationship with Mike? We would inquire about feelings of loneliness, abandonment, and fear in her childhood to try to get in touch with her needy self which she splits off into her objects.

Perhaps Mike senses her need to take care of him and keeps his distance so as not to be totally inhabited by her projections. He keeps up a threat of imminent breakdown to keep her interested in curing him. When Mike makes a spontaneous, autonomous gesture, Jan panics. This suggests that she needs him to need her so that she can take care of her own needy self that she projects into him, while denying her own longings to be mothered and to have real babies to mother. She tries to heal him and repair his flaws, as if to prove that she can be creative and the damage to her maternality was not total. Nevertheless, she finds herself sadly unable to repair the damaged couple and create an atmosphere of sexual intimacy.

Jan was raised in a family whose parents were lenient, supportive, liberal, indulgent and denying of problem areas. At the same time, they expected a great deal of autonomy from their children, and especially from Jan, who was 5 years older than her brother. Jan seems to have been a parentified child who filled in for her mother as housekeeper, nurturer, and limit-setter. This arrangement guaranteed that Jan turn to her peer group for support and for company. Nevertheless, she remains close to her parents, and talks freely about her marital problems with them and with her best friend. Despite being fully informed, her parents deny the gravity of Jan's marital problems, just as they denied their son's drug abuse problem when he was a teenager. Jan feels emotionally abandoned by them, even if they are socially present in her life.

Jan and Mike as a Couple

The manner in which the case is presented puts most of the responsibility for the couple's difficulties on Mike. It does not give a clear take on Jan's contribution to the conflict. The report tells us that the majority of the arguments involve Jan's complaints about Mike not being dependable and especially about his drug abuse. In the past 7 months, however, he has become more trustworthy, and has stopped using substances. Whereas Mike is impulsive and shows addictive patterns that have led him into trouble, Jan has been able to control her addictive behavior.

Jan is clearly more confident in her intellectual achievements than is Mike, and yet she chose him because she found him fascinating. She feels comfortable being the bigger earner in the couple. We learn that Jan does tend to criticize Mike, a way in which she is like his mother, and Mike avoids dealing with her critical comments, which resembles the way his mother behaved towards his father. Mike's conflict-avoidance manner contains a passive/aggressive stance that supports his fragile sense of autonomy, but that leads to a serious breach in their intimate relating. Whereas Jan does raise conflictual issues, Mike ignores them and avoids dealing with her. She is unable to push through to resolution because his technique is successful in shutting her up. He also defends himself by leaving the scene until she stops bringing up the topic.

Mike and Jan's social life has deteriorated and has not recovered. Jan has been Mike's avenue to a couples' social group. It seems likely that substance abuse was his other, less desirable avenue to social relatedness. Although the presenting problem is said to be Jan's wish that she and Mike could discuss conflict and reach resolution, rebuild trust, and avoid divorce, it seems to us that the precipitant for Mike and Jan's seeking therapy is shared anxiety over the unfamiliar possibility of having a relationship that is not clouded by the use of substances and the repetitive interactive pattern of nagging and avoidance.

Mike always felt "dumb" compared to girls, who seemed smarter than he was. Yet he chose to marry Jan, who has a college degree. The report does not indicate any feeling of belittlement that Mike might feel in relation to Jan. The only mention of competition concerns his wish to make up the differential in their incomes by working extra on the weekends. We would want to know much more about this area.

Strengths to Build On

Mike and Jan have both had experience with substance abuse, and can empathize with each other in dealing with addiction. Both enjoy taking care of animals, which indicates a capacity for nurturing and a weakness in dealing with verbal confrontation. Both of them enjoy solo activity: Jan likes reading; Mike likes computing. In the past, they have enjoyed shared activities: going to the movies, going out to dinner, and going to parties, in addition to taking care of the animals. These shared activities could be revisited to rebuild social areas for mutual enjoyment. Their social life could be improved by reconnecting with Jan's couple friends. We need to know more about Mike's social group. Apparently his friends are single, rowdy and raucous, which suggests that they are a group of drinking buddies. He needs a different, independent social group, which he may find in Narcotics Anonymous.

The couple might rediscover some shared physical activity, such as skiing, walking, or horseback riding, and lastly they would need to make time to rebuild their sexual relationship. We have the impression that the blocks to sexual intimacy reside in history that predates the lack of trust in the marital relationship. We think that Jan has unresolved issues concerning her sexuality due to the assault on her reproductive tract, and that Mike has unresolved issues of intrusion by females due to the sexual abuse he sustained as a child.

Dynamic Formulation of Mike and Jan as a Couple

As a couple, Mike and Jan have developed a marital projective and introjective identificatory system based on Jan's projection into Mike of the needy part of herself that she formerly projected into her younger brother, and Mike's projection into Jan of the critical and controlling part of his mother to whom he remains attached. This sets up a dynamic where Mike is like a troublesome child over whom Jan helplessly frets and fusses, while Jan is like a nagging mother whom Mike avoids, tunes out, and frustrates. Jan feels abandoned by Mike the same way that she feels abandoned by her parents. In this way, she expresses her internal couple in her current marriage. The early fascination, enjoyable sex, shared physical activity, and leisure pursuits with friends operated at the level of adult equality during courtship, but this has been invaded by a regressive mother-child dynamic, exacerbated by the self-sustaining substance abuse problem.

Mike and Jan both struggle to repair something, but they do not know what it is. Jan works as a pharmaceutical sales associate who sells medicine to help sick people get well. In this way she can continue her efforts to help weak and damaged objects, like her brother, and her cancer-mutilated self. Mike works as a welder and blacksmith who puts together hard objects so that they will hold against force and not come apart. Symbolically, his work represents his attempt to keep his parents together inside him and not allow his disrupted internal couple to fall apart, like his parents did, and destroy his relationship with Jan.

Treatment Goals

In the short term, Mike and Jan would work toward restabilizing their social network and rebuilding their context of shared activities. Facing and analyzing their conflicts and reversing their sexual withdrawal would be medium-term goals. Rebuilding intimacy would be the ultimate goal. The goals of Object

Relations couples therapy are distinguished from the goals of short-term approaches to couples therapy in that we do not aim for symptom resolution. Our goals are to help the couple to face their conflicts, re-evaluate their choice of partner, consider whether to recommit to the marriage, or arrive at a decision to separate with concern for each other.

How would we know when Mike and Jan had done enough work in therapy to finish? The criteria that indicate readiness for termination are described in Table 6.2. Our goal is to effect a return to the appropriate developmental phase of family life, with improved capacity to master developmental stress, an improved ability for work as a team, and an improved ability to differentiate between, and to meet the needs of, husband and wife.

We tend not to use specific measurements to determine when these goals have been met. We have, however, participated in a research project in which a self-administered questionnaire, known as the Persons Relating to Each Other Questionnaire (Birtchnell, 1993), gives couples a score before and at the end of treatment in terms of their ways of relating along the dimensions of upperness, lowerness, closeness, and distance (Scharff & Scharff, 1998). When these goals are met, it then remains for the couple to consolidate their gains by engaging actively in the final piece of work, the process of the termination of therapy.

Techniques and Interventions

We do not use specific techniques and strategies, directives, homework, or paradoxical instructions. Our technique consists in maintaining an attitude of listening,

---

TABLE 6.2   Criteria for Termination

The partners have internalized the therapeutic space and now have a reasonably secure holding capacity.

Unconscious projective identifications have been recognized, owned, and taken back by each partner.

The capacity to love and work together as life partners is restored.

The sexual relationship is intimate and mutually gratifying.

The partners can envision their future development and provide a vital holding environment for each other and for their family.

The couple can differentiate between and meet the needs of each partner.

Alternatively, the couple recognizes the failure of the marital choice, understands the unconscious object relations incompatibility, and the partners separate with some grief work done and with a capacity to continue mourning the loss of the marriage individually.

following, recognizing patterns, observing our own feelings, and making interpretations. The use of countertransference to interpret transference is at the heart of the technique of Object Relations couple therapy, and yet it may be hard to understand in a single reading. Without burdening the couple with telling them how they make us feel, we use the information from our reactions (our countertransference) to arrive at an understanding of what it is like to be with each of them, and with them as a couple. Our technique is to enter a state of unconscious communication with them, note, and then analyze our feelings and associations. In countertransference, we receive the couple's projective identifications and feel affected by them. There is a resonance between the object relations set of the couple and our inner objects, especially including our internal couple when we are dealing with a couple in therapy.

The internal couple is a psychic structure that is based on our experience of the relationship between our father and mother as they cooperated together in their marital relationship and as they dealt with us as parents at various developmental stages. This original construction is then modified as we interact with other couples. Mike has a fractured internal couple that is partly intrusive and partly neglectful, and so arouses anger in him. Jan has a secure internal couple that is somewhat oblivious and leaves her feeling helpless and overlooked.

Our internal couple derives from our earliest, oral level experience of our parents as a couple whom we imagined to be enjoying an orgiastic feeding frenzy. In the toilet-training years, we saw them as a fighting, sadistic couple; in the oedipal phase we are aware of their romantic excitement at the genital level; and so on, until we are mature enough to detach from them as our primary pair of love objects. Becoming familiar with this internal structure in couples and in ourselves is important for the couple therapist. The therapist also has an internal couple which interacts with the couples being treated. Trouble in this area may lead the couple therapist to feel like quitting so as to avoid feeling excluded, guilty, envious, competitive, and rejected, like a child in relation to the parents who have each other. Alternatively, the couples therapist may use the defense of identifying with the omniscient parents so as not to reexperience painful childish feelings.

The couple's shared transference to us stems from the projection onto us of their difficulties in providing holding for each other, and is elicited in response to their expectations of the therapist. The contextual transference expresses attitudes toward the therapist's responsibility for the therapeutic context. In therapy, Mike and Jan might have a positive contextual transference if they trusted us, as Jan trusted her social worker, or a negative contextual transference if together they felt as uncertain of the value of therapy as Mike and his parents do. Individual focused object transferences stemming from the internal objects of husband or wife seek to experience early object relationships with the therapist in the here and now. The therapist becomes both a representative of the environmental mother, who will provide safety and continuity, and the object mother who is there for direct relating to expressed needs, wishes, and fears. The direct focused transference may attempt to substitute for the contextual transference when the couple cannot sustain confidence in the therapeutic context. In couples therapy, we expect oscillation between focused and contextual transference. For instance, Mike might have a focused transference in which he experienced one of us as critical and might wish to quit rather than discuss this, or Jan might feel critical of our approach, might express worry about our reliability, and feel that we are not addressing her concerns.

Pitfalls and Limits

Any unrecognized transference creates a potential pitfall. The best way to address these difficulties is to be on the lookout, ask for reactions, comment on our perceptions of the clients' views of us, and interpret their defenses against therapy. A major route of acting out could be substance abuse that went unrecognized.

We would make our support for sobriety clear. We set limits by meeting only at the agreed-upon times, and we expect prompt payment of the agreed-upon fee. Attempts to change the parameters of the treatment are quickly explored, related to underlying feelings, and made conscious, so that the couple can choose to exercise control over their choices.

Areas to Avoid

We cannot imagine any area as being off-limits for our work. Therapy has to deal with all aspects of a couple's life, including secrets. As always, tact and timing would determine when and how to bring up a sensitive topic for discussion or to confront difficult defenses and anxieties. We work with the clients' reluctance, embarrassment, ignorance, or shame. We try to understand why these defensive postures are still needed. This helps them to develop comfort when approaching their trigger points.

Inclusion of Other Family Members

We would not include other family members, friends, or therapists in the couples therapy, but we would respond to requests to collaborate with other treating professionals. We conceive of couples therapy as a private space for the couple to deal with each other and with the influence of their internal figures on their current relationship. On the other hand, there may be a good reason to deal with one of Jan's or Mike's actual family members whose support or input is regarded as essential. This, however, is not usual in our practice, since our focus is internal, not external.

Homework

We would not use homework or special assignments unless sex therapy exercises were found to be necessary. Our only suggestion is that the couple make time between sessions to talk to each other.

Timeline for Therapy

We would see Mike and Jan as a couple once a week, or twice a week if they wanted to intensify their commitment to therapy. Our sessions would be 45 minutes long unless Mike and Jan had to travel some distance to see us, in which case a longer session every other week might be more realistic. We would prefer not to see Mike and/or Jan individually unless they showed their need for individual privacy to discuss an issue that could not yet be raised with the other present. It would be our intention to use the individual session to prepare for shared discussion. A pitfall here is that the therapist may receive a piece of confidential information and be stymied in the next couple session. Better to make it clear that confidentiality pertains to the couple. A marriage with secrets cannot grow and develop in therapy. If one of them clearly had internalized problems that dominated the couple sessions, then referral to another individual therapist would be arranged.

Termination and Relapse Prevention

Mike and Jan have a good prognosis. They have already stayed together through hard times, and Mike has stopped using drugs. They are in agreement about wanting to avoid divorce. They have had a good sexual relationship to draw on to hold the center of their relationship together, if the sexual bond can be reawakened. It is not clear from the limited information presented how committed Mike and Jan are to facing their conflict. An extended four-session assessment in the Object Relations approach would let us see how they attempt to discuss their problems in the shared interview situation. But only a course of therapy would let us see if they could tolerate the anxiety of disagreement and the feelings of anger, hurt, and frustrated desire that would need to be worked through before the goals of therapy could be met. We use the criteria listed in Table 6.2 to determine when the couple is ready for termination.

We would not build in follow-up interviews, because we think that this might suggest that the couple would not manage by themselves. When Mike and Jan terminate, we want them to feel secure in the couple's ability to provide a good holding environment for each of them, and yet to feel that they could come back to see us if future experience led them to think that they needed more help. The best relapse prevention comes from the couple's continued practicing of the lesson learned in therapy: that they need to make time to communicate their feelings to each other, to listen respectfully, and to own their individual contributions to shared difficulties.

REFERENCES

Bion, W. (1959). *Experiences in groups*. New York: Basic Books.

Bion, W. (1962). *Learning from experience*. New York: Basic Books.

Bion, W. (1967). *Second thoughts*. London: Heinemann.

Birtchnell, J. (1993). *How humans relate*. Westport, CT: Praeger.

Dicks, H. V. (1967). *Marital tensions: Clinical studies towards a psychoanalytic theory of interaction*. London: Routledge and Kegan Paul.

Ezriel, H. (1952). Notes on psychoanalytic group therapy. II: Interpretation and research. *Psychiatry, 15,* 119–126.

Fairbairn, W. R. D. (1952). *Psychoanalytic studies of the personality*. London: Routledge and Kegan Paul.

Klein, M. (1946). Notes on some schizoid mechanisms. *International Journal of Psycho-Analysis, 27,* 99–110.

Klein, M. (1975). *Envy and gratitude and other works: 1946–1963*. London: Hogarth Press and the Institute of Psycho-Analysis.

*Scharff, D. E. (1982). *The sexual relationship: An object relations view of sex and the family*. London: Routledge and Kegan Paul. (Reprinted 1997, Northvale, NJ: Jason Aronson.)

Scharff, D. E. (1989). An object relations approach to sexuality in family life. In J. Scharff, *Foundations of object relations family therapy* (pp. 399–417). Northvale, NJ: Jason Aronson.

Scharff, D. E., & Scharff, J. S. (1987). Couples and couple therapy. In *Object relations family therapy* (pp. 227–254). Northvale, NJ: Jason Aronson.

*Scharff, D. E., & Scharff, J. S. (1991). *Object relations couple therapy*. Northvale, NJ: Jason Aronson.

Scharff, J. S., & Scharff, D. E. (1992). *A primer of object relations therapy*. Northvale, NJ: Jason Aronson.

---

*Suggested reading.

Scharff, J. S., & Scharff, D. E. (1998). *Object relations individual therapy.* Northvale, NJ: Jason Aronson.

Winnicott, D. (1958). *Collected papers: Through pediatrics to psycho-analysis.* London: Hogarth Press.

Winnicott, D. (1965). *The maturational processes and the facilitating environment.* London: Hogarth Press.

Winnicott, D. (1971). *Playing and reality.* London: Tavistock.

SUGGESTED READINGS

Scharff, D. E. (Ed.) (1995). *Object relations theory and practice.* Northvale, NJ: Jason Aronson.

Scharff, J. S. (1995). Psychoanalytic marital therapy. In N. S. Jacobson & A. S. Gurman (Eds.), *Clinical handbook of couple therapy* (pp. 164–193). New York: Guilford Press.

Scharff, J. S. (Ed.) (1989). *Foundations of object relations family therapy.* Northvale, NJ: Jason Aronson.

7

Adlerian Therapy

Jon Carlson and Len Sperry

TREATMENT MODEL

Adlerian Psychology, also called Individual Psychology, was developed by Alfred Adler. It is essentially a systems theory which is holistic, purposeful, cognitive, and social and focuses on the relationship or the patterns of interaction between partners. Adler realized that people are social beings and therefore that all problems are based in a context. He contended that couples issues and conflicts were less likely to reflect personality pathology and more likely to be problems of cooperation between the partners.

Adlerian psychotherapy is a constructivist therapy approach which provides a number of principles that serve as the basis for an integrated approach to couples therapy (Carlson & Sperry, 1998). The following principles underpin this therapeutic approach.

1. The couple relationship is understood as an interpersonal social system in which input from each partner either (a) improves the relationship or (b) stimulates dissonance and conflict.

2. "Trust only movement." The interaction, communication, and movement between the partners are purposive and goal-directed. The movement reveals intentions, feelings, and values that influence the system. It is essential to understand the psychological movement between the couple that creates cooperation or conflict.

3. Therapists must concentrate on observing and understanding what partners do instead of focusing on what they say. There has historically been too much interest on verbal communication between the couple. Although verbal communi-

cation is important, movement is more revealing. Recognizing movement that is cooperative and movement that is resistive is what attracts individuals to each other. This is also the basis for what causes relational conflict.

4. What attracts individuals to each other also is the basis for their relational conflict. Dreikurs (1946) was one of the first to observe that the qualities that initially attract two individuals to each other are basically the same factors that cause discord and divorce. Dreikurs noted that any human quality or trait can be perceived in a positive or a negative way. A person can be considered either kind or weak or strong or domineering, depending on a particular individual's point of view. Dreikurs suggested that one person does not like another for his or her virtues or dislike that person for his or her faults. Rather, an emphasis on a person's positive qualities grows out of affection for that person, just as an emphasis on weaknesses grows out of rejection. This emphasis on the individual's weakness or negative trait provides an excuse for having to communicate, to negotiate, and to resolve conflicts.

As Dreikurs (1946, 1967) noted, this process of relabeling—that is, of perceiving formerly "ideal" qualities as "despised" qualities—has much to do with cooperation. He stated that whatever two people do to and with each other is based on mutual agreement and full cooperation. No relationship is possible without both spouses communicating to each what they think and feel and without full cooperation, be it for the good or for the bad. Dreikurs noted that people are so accustomed to using the term "cooperation" for constructive interactions that they overlook the fact that one person cannot even fight without the other's full cooperation. Cooperation is an orderly, harmonious effort in which both work together toward a common objective. Positive cooperation is the expression of a sense of belonging together, a sense of self-confidence, a sense of confidence in each other, and the element of courage. Dreikurs believed that these four qualities are the sources of positive cooperative action, whereas hostility, distrust, inferiority feelings, and fear are the basis of negative cooperation (Dreikurs, 1946).

5. Each person is an individual, social, decisive human being whose actions have a purpose.

> The attitude of every individual towards marriage is one of the expressions of his (her) style of life: We can understand it if we understand the whole individual, not otherwise. (Ansbacher & Ansbacher, 1956, p. 434)

The communication and movement between partners serve to express the intentions and goals of each partner. There are some relationship-destroying goals that may include attention, power, vengeance, or displaying inadequacy in order to be excused (Dinkmeyer & Carlson, 1984; Huber & Baruth, 1981). These goals are diagnosed by observing the feelings expressed by each partner. The feelings that are experienced indicate the purpose of the transactions (i.e., feelings of annoyance may indicate attention; feelings of anger may indicate power; feelings of "wanting to get even" may indicate revenge; and feelings of "giving up" and discouragement may indicate displays of inadequacy). The therapist guides communication toward positive interaction, with the goal of increasing the potential for involvement, trust, and caring.

6. Each partner has the creative capacity to choose and to create his or her own perceptions and meaning. The couple is helped to see that their goals and the ensuing conflict are chosen. Choice is an essential component of all behavior, but is frequently denied in human relationships. Couples are helped to see that through their beliefs, behavior, and attitudes they can make new choices.

7. Each partner has the responsibility to decide. Each person is responsible for his or her own behavior. When each person is responsible, equilibrium and solutions exist instead of dysfunction and blaming.

8. Change in the relationship always begins with one's self, not with one's partner.

9. The beliefs, behavior, and feelings that exist in the system between the partners are the result of subjective perception. Behavior is a function of one's perception. We look at what certain experiences mean to a particular person. The therapist helps the partners understand the meaning they are giving to their experiences. Relationships have the potential for continuous miscommunication, because each partner anticipates or thinks he or she knows what the other will say and therefore decides that they need not wait to listen to their spouse.

10. Couples happiness is based on each person's self-esteem, social interest (capacity to give and to take), and sense of humor. These are the ingredients of a happy relationship. Self-esteem is the individual's sense of worth and acceptance. Social interest is the desire to cooperate, and sense of humor is the ability to see the relationship in perspective.

11. Relationships are also influenced strongly by the belief systems of the couple. The belief systems are related to priorities (Kern, 1997). Some of the priorities significant in the couple relationship include the following: control, perfection, pleasing, self-esteem, and expectation. The personality priorities are based on perceptions and reveal what people believe they must do to belong and be accepted (Dinkmeyer, 1991).

12. An important factor in understanding couple relationships is how the lifestyles of each partner fit together. This interaction, according to Dreikurs (1946), is evident with the choice of a partner. We choose a partner "who offers us an opportunity to realize our personal pattern, who responds to outlook and conceptions of life, who permits us to continue or to revive plans which we have carried with us since childhood" (Dreikurs, 1946, pp. 68–69).

Adlerians see this as complementary in the give and take of the lifestyles of two people. A couple relationship "is not merely one of a conscious choice and logical conclusions; it is based more profoundly upon the integration of the two personalities" (Dreikurs, 1946, p. 83). This involves fitting together both the similarities and differences of a couple.

COUPLE SYSTEM

A relationship system is created by the couple. The system and the partner constantly influence each other. Problems in the relationship often serve the purpose of maintaining a type of equilibrium. Problems or symptoms result when too much pressure for change is occurring. This is often viewed as discouragement about being valued or counting.

> When people feel their self-esteem threatened in any way, the energy they would spend in developing cooperation with their partner may be used to blame each other, make excuses, or defend themselves. None of this behavior brings them closer together or invites cooperation between them. (Bettner & Lew, 1993, p. 372)

The system is developed and influenced by choices. Behavior is always influenced by the subjective meanings assigned to an experience and the conclusions and beliefs that come from these experiences. What partners think and how partners feel influences both the choices they make and the kind of direction and behavior they pursue. These choices create the organization and pattern for relationships we call "the system." For example, one partner may decide to control the relationship, which can lead to a conflict over some issue. The conflict is not about the issue or symptom, but rather the real concern—which is control.

The goal of the system is to seek a relationship with communication and respect as equals. The system is a unified whole. The therapist understands the couple system by understanding each partner and how the partners influence the system and how in turn the couple system influences them.

The Adlerian system is organized by the purposes of behavior. There is an underlying private logic (rules) unique in each system that guides the system to organize and function in a particular fashion. Once the therapist understands the logic of the system, the behavior begins to make logical sense, even though it may be confusing to those outside the system.

Private logic is defined by the subjective perceptions of the couple and each partner. The logic may be, for example, "I must control"; I am right"; or "My partner should always please me."

Psychological movement is influenced by the goals and priorities of the system and by the cooperation and the competition between the partners and the consequences of their behavior. To be effective in couples therapy, it is necessary to understand and comprehend each partner. It is even more important, however, to recognize the significance and essential nature of understanding and fostering of the development of a healthy and cooperative system.

THE THERAPIST'S ACTIONS, SKILLS, AND ATTRIBUTES

Because of its phenomenological heritage, Adlerian psychology tends to view the client as a self in process and therefore views assessment as dynamic rather than static. This therapeutical approach favors technical eclecticism and utilizes a variety of techniques. The therapeutic relationship could be described as "collaborative empiricism" (Beck, 1976; Guidano & Liotti, 1983). Adlerians hold that the therapeutic relationship is optimal, when equality and mutuality between clinician and client are achieved (Dinkmeyer, Dinkmeyer, & Sperry, 1987). Encouragement and empowerment are both values and strategies for bringing about change. Establishing a mutual and collaborative relationship is the first important task in therapy. Achieving such a relationship means the clinician and client align or realign their goals for the outcome of the treatment process. The Adlerian clinician seeks to understand the client's lifestyle, since it is through this lifestyle that the client will relate to and safeguard against the clinician and therapeutic context (Dinkmeyer et al., 1987).

Through a solid therapeutic alliance, a secure base is often created. Adlerians believe that how the client relates to others will eventually surface in the therapeutic relationship. What transpires in therapy is an important process for understanding the client. Accordingly, the use of immediacy of thoughts, feelings, and intuitions becomes important in early sessions (Jones, 1995).

From an Adlerian couples therapy perspective, assessment is viewed as a dynamic process, rather than a static event, with the end point of establishing a clinical diagnosis and a diagnostic code. Assessment begins immediately and is always "in process." Adlerians perform a lifestyle analysis exploring family of origin issues, early recollections, and the influence of birth order rank (Dinkmeyer et al., 1987). Lifestyle assessment has traditionally been a part of Adlerian psychotherapy. Lifestyle assessment involves completing a family constellation and eliciting several early recollections from an individual. The assessment of the family constellation involves understanding how the individual found a sense of belonging in early life, particularly within the family context. Accordingly, information on early life dynamics is sought by examining childhood sibling relationships, the parent's relationship to each other and to the children, and the life tasks, as well as early school and social milieu and relevant biological and health factors of family members. This inquiry also includes the individual's response to the tasks of life which include work, family, and community. Psychological birth order, i.e., the dynamics of the first-, middle- or last-born child, is also noted. Early recollections are defining memories that reveal the individual's beliefs about themselves, other people, the world, sex-role identification, and their strategy for establishing and maintaining a sense of belonging and coherence in life. Typically, six or more early memories are elicited and amplified. Two to three hours is requested to adequately elicit, formulate, and feedback all these elements of the lifestyle assessment.

In traditional Adlerian couples therapy, a therapist would likely complete separate lifestyle assessment for each partner. The purpose of assessing both partners' lifestyles is to determine their mistaken or dysfunctional beliefs and convictions about themselves. Lifestyle assessments are conducted in the presence of both partners whenever possible. Since this process is quite time-intensive, practicing Adlerian couples therapy in the age of a managed care requires considerable modification. Today, an Adlerian couples therapist might complete an abridged lifestyle assessment on each partner, in addition to other assessment data (described later) within the first or second conjoint session.

An abridged lifestyle assessment begins with a brief, focused overview of the family constellation. The family constellation is diagramed for each partner, including brief descriptions of each member of the families of origin, with particular attention to all the parental figures who were influential in the formative years. Brief inquiries are made into physical, sexual, and social development, and education and occupational experience. Here, partners often learn significant new things about their spouse which had perhaps never been discussed before. This inquiry, in the presence of the partner, permits each to learn, usually for the first time, significant elements of the partner's childhood. In short, the couples' lifestyle formulation provides the therapist and the couple with overall patterns of relating.

Also, each partner's attitude toward oneself and the spouse is elicited with regard to the various life tasks: work, friendship, lover, spouse, relating to the other sex, getting along with oneself, search for meaning, relating to members of the same sex, parent, and player. This person is presented with a scale of 1 to 5 (1 being the highest and 5 the lowest rating) and asked to relate herself, for example, as a worker. The therapist asks, "How responsibly are you attending to the task of work at this point in your life?" After answering, the partner predicts how the spouse will rate him or her; then the process is reversed. This procedure can pinpoint trouble areas or areas that need to be explored more fully. The therapist evaluates how well the partners know themselves and each other. The results also provide a baseline to refer to later to evaluate the success of the treatment.

Next, two or three early childhood recollections are elicited and recorded verbatim. These reveal subjective themes in a person's self-view and further indicate how each partner found a sense of self-worth and belongingness. Both partners are also asked to recall memories of childhood. The description of what impressed them about the item is useful toward understanding the subjective beliefs about life and relationships. This method elucidates key basic themes involving relationship dynamics, and while not as complete as the traditional lifestyle formulation, is usually sufficient for most couples.

Juxtaposing two lifestyles together offers considerable insight into the origin and strategies of the couple's relational dynamics. This process makes it possible to discover areas of agreement. For instance, both partners may have incorporated into their personality styles what Adler called the "masculine protest." Masculine protest is a tendency to think that life is a man's world, that men have more privileges, are more important, have more power, and perhaps are more dangerous than women. The complementarity of another couple's relationship may be based on the "agreement" that life must be exciting and dramatic. On the other hand, it may become obvious that there are significant differences in how the partners view life and in what expectations they have of a spouse and other people. This process of comparing lifestyles and pointing out the differences clarifies for the first time why the partners see life so differently. These differences can add great richness to the relationship, or they can be a source of conflict. Ultimately, the goal of the couples therapy is of the couple to realize how much tolerance there is for individual differences within the relationship.

Additionally, instruments such as the Millon Clinical Multi-Axial Inventory (MCMI) are utilized. An interesting and effective assessment strategy popularized by constructivist family therapists is the use of therapeutic questions. Although popularized by Selvini-Palazzoli, Boscolo, Cecchin, and Prata (1980) and elaborated by others (e.g., Tomm [1987]), it appears that Adler first described this strategy over 70 years ago (Sperry, 1992). Therapeutic questioning is utilized to understand relationships among family members and difference among relationships. Besides a method of gathering information, this strategy is also a powerful intervention for provoking change in the identified client, as well as in the family. Perhaps the most well-known Adlerian example of therapeutic questioning is "the question" first described by Adler (1956) in the 1920s and popularized by Rudolph Dreikurs in the 1950s and 1960s. For example, Dreikurs (1954) would ask a patient, "Let us imagine I gave you a pill and you would be completely well as soon as you left this office. What would be different in your life? What would you do differently?" The answer to "the question" indicates against whom or against what condition the symptom is directed. If he were well, the patient might look for another job, do better on his present job, or get along better with his wife. These answers indicate why the patient is sick, if the illness is entirely "neurotic," or what use the patient may make of an actual physical ailment. A similar question, called the "miracle question" (deShazer, 1988) has become commonplace among brief therapists in the last few years.

THE CASE OF MIKE AND JAN

Assessment and Conceptualization of Jan

Jan is a 49-year-old married Caucasian female. She has been married to her second husband, Mike, for 12 years. She is 5 years older than him. She possesses a college degree and has worked 14 years for the same company. She enjoys animals, did well in school, and had many friends. She has no history of psychiatric problems. She reports having remotely supportive parents with whom she has some continued contact. It is likely that she maintains a critical outlook on life. This outlook seems similar to that of Mike's mother.

Her abridged lifestyle assessment yielded the following formulation. From the inquiry into Jan's family constellation we can formulate that while Jan was the first-born of two, she was also a parentified child. She found her place by being a caretaker and assuming responsibilities without having much authority. From one of her early recollections, it is apparent that Jan was stunned at the sudden revelation and realization of the flaw in her father's character. Another early recollection suggested how impressed she was with the goodness and importance of men. Accordingly, we can conjecture that Jan views herself as strong and decisive, but uncertain of her ability to influence others. She appears to view the world as both demanding and unpredictable. Therefore, her strategy is to exert control over circumstances, to be hardworking and decisive, and to be critical and suspicious of others' motivation. Parenthetically, her conflicting views of males, i.e., good but flawed, together with her critical attitude, seem to have been enacted in both her marriages, and need to be addressed in couples work.

Assessment and Conceptualization of Mike

Mike is a 44-year-old married Caucasian male. He has been married to his second wife, Jan, for 12 years. He is the second of two boys whose parents divorced when he graduated high school. He has a distant relationship with his father and a critical mother. He appears to be more of a loner with avoidant traits. He has a history of both drug and alcohol problems and subsequent treatment. He seems to have trouble following through on activities and verbally expressing his thoughts and feelings. When conflict occurs, he has a tendency to withdrawal. Mike reports that he has been substance-free for the past 7 months and has worked 10 years for his current employer. He describes himself as hard-working, having skills in the trades, and enjoying animals. Additionally, he enjoys computers, being a blacksmith, and welding furniture. His eventual goal is to be self-employed. Mike reports having an okay relationship with his parents. He describes never being a very social person and having a hard time handling criticism in which he tends to withdrawal. It is very likely he suffers from "inferiority feelings" due to an education and income level less than his wife's. He reports having few friends and not liking the tension he experiences when around other people. He has a history of hypertension and high cholesterol, however, inconsistently follows directions for its appropriate control. This seems to be a pattern in that Mike rarely finishes what he starts. It is very likely that he adheres to his mother's message "Don't get serious, it will never last." Mike has no significant history of mental health problems. His parents divorced when he was 18 years old. Mike's brother had learning and behavioral problems and had a lot of friends. Mike was the largest person in his class and did what he could to try to please his parents. He believed that girls are smarter than him and made him feel dumb. Additionally, he was sexually abused by an aunt at a young age. His mother discouraged dating and pointed out how it was his fault whenever things went wrong. His father's words of advice were, "Get over it." Mike had no role model in his life for handling conflict.

From the inquiry into Mike's family constellation, we can formulate that he was the last-born child who found a sense of belonging by attempting to please others and avoid conflict as well as involvement in family feuds, i.e., between his mother and older brother, and between mother and father. It appears that he modeled his father's avoidance and retaliation behaviors, i.e., stonewalling and escape in the face of relationship conflict, as well as infidelity. Mike probably perceived his mother's depressive symptoms—the results of her failure to control her husband's, as well as her older son's, acting-out behavior—as a failure to care for him and a rejection of his efforts to please his parents. It is noteworthy that Mike experienced considerable teasing from both his brother and his peers, and was sexually abused by an older female relative. From one of his early recollections, it is apparent that Mike recoiled in fear and anger when he observed older girls acting mean and condescending toward a small boy. Another early recollection suggested his lack of perseverance and fear of failure when attempting to complete a school project. It appears that he views himself as special but passive, incapable, and emotionally brittle, and sees the world as populated by demanding, hurtful, and inconsistent, with older women alternating between being cruel and loving, and men as emotionally distant. He appears to exhibit an avoidant personality style. Accordingly, his strategy in relationships is to avoid conflict, to negate in emotional stonewalling, and to passively express anger and rage.

Mike's abstinence from alcohol has been significant in the couple's relationship. Both are presently attending NA. Jan's first marriage ended in infidelity and drug use. The couple rarely ventures out socially and they have a detached relationship with one another. They do not spend much time together and have few common interests. Recently, their sexual contact has decreased significantly. Apparently Jan's parents were lenient and underinvolved, and Mike's parents were critical and overinvolved in their children's lives.

Couple Conceptualization

By juxtaposing both their lifestyles, some common themes emerge. First, there is a complementarity of birth order. Jan is a first born while Mike is a last-born, a very common pattern of couples pairing and marital dynamics. Thus, Jan has considerable experience in being a caregiver and decision maker, while Mike has considerable life experience being cared for and being a follower—albeit a reluctant one. Second, their self- and world-views have a complementary theme. Jan's lifestyle can be characterized as dutifulness, decisiveness, hard work, and limited spontaneity and life satisfaction, while Mike's lifestyle is more spontaneous, uncomplicated, and freer. Thus, it is not surprising that Jan's initial attraction to Mike was described in terms of being "fascinating" and "exciting." Presumably, Mike was attracted to the prospect of someone taking care of him, assuming responsibilities, making decisions, and doing all of those things which he was neither particularly predisposed to do nor effective in accomplishing. Third, there is a complementarity in the attraction and conflict/divorce of both their previous marriages. In other words, not only did both Jan and Mike marry a parental figure in their first marriages, but both re-enacted this dynamic in their second marriages. Processing this enactment dynamic must be a central feature of this couples therapy. Fourth, the family dynamic of substance use and infidelity are present in both family lines, as well as in their marital pairing. It appears that an abuse dynamic—emotional and sexual abuse involving Mike—will be complicating factors in this therapy, since these were perpetrated by women, and older women at that. Interestingly, Jan is older than Mike.

Goals

The couple specifically has problems with emotional intimacy along with continual conflicts. Additionally, they lack effective procedures for resolution of their conflicts. The treatment goals would involve:

1. Increase Mike's ability to handle tension.
2. Reduce Jan's critical nature and help her to learn how to express "softer" emotions. "Softer" emotions occur when the Four Horsemen of the Apocalypse—criticism, contempt, defensiveness, and stonewalling—are absent (Gottman & Silver, 1999).
3. Increase the amount of positive time together.
4. Maintain present level of control over addiction.
5. Help Mike adopt a healthier attitude toward women.
6. Continue to point out the strengths in the relationship, including the ability to maintain sobriety, ability to get along well when sobriety occurs, and the committed nature to their relationship and counseling.
7. Increase the type and amount of appreciation they show one another.

Short-term goals involve increasing the amount of time together, maintaining the present level of control over the addiction, and continuing to point out strengths and to increase appreciation. Mike's need to develop a healthier attitude toward women, as well as to increase his ability to handle tension, are long-term goals, as is Jan's need to reduce her criticism.

The actual sequencing of activities to reach the goals will be collaboratively determined. The Adlerian therapist will ask, "Where would you like to begin?" in order to address the most pressing concern for the couple. Failure to begin where the couple want help will result in dissatisfaction and recidivism. The goals are not mutually exclusive, and work in one area always influences others.

Techniques

The techniques and intervention strategies center around the therapeutic questions described earlier. Specifically, the couple needs to develop insight into the trans-generational nature of their relationship. It is likely that once they understand the goal of their actions, they will be able to consider changing them. The couple can benefit by understanding and creating a holding/accepting environment. It will be necessary for them to continue NA meetings to support the addiction-free lifestyle. The focus needs to be on solutions (rather than problems) and assisting the couple to see just how far they have come. A positive approach allows Jan and Mike to experience hope and to maintain a poise outlook. Couples that continually focus on what is wrong become discouraged and disheartened. A solution-focused approach looks at what works for them and just how they have made themselves healthier. It is important to address thinking patterns, including Jan's critical nature and Mike's attitude toward women. Strategies that help to increase appreciation, such as psychoeducational suggestions, will be implemented (Carlson & Slavik, 1997). Psychoeducational strategies help to make up for learning deficits for their families of origin. Skills such as congruent communication, encouragement, and problem-solving would be especially helpful to Jan and Mike. It is important that the couple begin dating one another and putting some life into the relationship.

Challenges

Challenges that relate to this couple center around Mike's inability to follow through on treatment plans. It is likely, however, that this has to do with his inability to handle tension. It is also possible that Jan could become extremely critical of the process. It would seem to be important that a male therapist be used. Mike has a negative view of women and might feel "dumb" and "inferior" with a female therapist.

We would avoid addressing Mike's feelings of inferiority and their decision about not having children. Mike's feelings of inferiority would probably only support something that we are attempting to remove, and the notion of children seems to have been successfully resolved.

Because of the circumstance, we would not involve anyone else in treatment such as family of origin, etc. This is typically not part of the process of Adlerian couples therapy.

Homework

Homework is tailored to the treatment process (Carlson, Sperry, & Lewis, 1997). Tailoring is the process of "fitting" or customizing a particular treatment/homework strategy to the couple. This protocol involves four steps:

1. Comprehensive assessment.
2. Matching of homework strategies based on the comprehensive assessment.
3. Tailoring the chosen homework strategy to the couples' needs, circumstances, treatment capacity, and response to the therapist and treatment.
4. Implementation, review, and revision of matching/tailoring efforts.

Homework activities for Jan and Mike would involve:

a. Controlled dialogue (Carlson & Dinkmeyer, 1984) in which one partner would talk for 5 minutes and the other will remain silent and then reverse roles.
b. Use of an encouragement meeting (Carlson & Dinkmeyer, 1984) to increase the number of positive exchanges.
c. Take turns dating.
d. Hold weekly business meeting (Carlson & Dinkmeyer, 1984) to handle business of their marital relationship.
e. Continue attendance at Narcotics Anonymous meetings.

Timeline

The timeline would be approximately 10–14 sessions over the next 6 months. The couple would initially be seen together, each partner alone for one meeting, and then together from then on. This therapist would see either person alone as needed during the course of therapy. Typically, this is done at the clients' request, the only condition being that it would be done with the other partner's knowledge.

Termination and Relapse Prevention

Termination and relapse would be structured by holding regular booster sessions at 3 months and then every 6 months for 2 years and then yearly thereafter. The likelihood of relapse is minimized due to the tailored nature of the treatment and the high level of functioning at the end of treatment. Adlerians see effective marriage/partnership not as a privilege, but as a responsibility. Traditional methods of therapy focus on the front end of change rather than on the maintenance of a successful intervention. We recommend the following strategies to prevent relapse and increase treatment adherence (Carlson et al., 1997):

1. Engage couples and involve them in homework assignments throughout therapy.
2. Match strategies to the couple's unique needs.
3. Use booster sessions and planned procedures to handle normal external stress.
4. Train couples in essential skill.
5. Gradually increase time between visits, allowing the couple to be gradually less dependent on therapy.

REFERENCES

Ansbacher, H. L., & Ansbacher, R. (Eds.). (1956). *The individual psychology of Alfred Adler: A systematic presentation in selections from his writings.* New York: Basic Books.

Beck, A. T. (1976). *Cognitive therapy and emotional disorders.* New York: International Universities Press.

Bettner, B. L., & Lew, A. (1993). The Connexions focusing technique for couple therapy: A model for understanding lifestyle and complementarity in couples. *Individual Psychology, 49,*(3/4), 372–391.

*Carlson, J., & Slavik, S. (Eds.) (1997). *Techniques of Adlerian psychotherapy.* Philadelphia: Taylor and Francis.

Carlson, J., Sperry, L., & Lewis, J. (1997). *Family therapy: Ensuring treatment efficacy.* Pacific Grove, CA: Brooks/Cole.

*Carlson, J., & Sperry, L. (1998). Adlerian psychotherapy as a Constructivist psychotherapy. In M. F. Hoyt (Ed.), *Handbook of constructivist therapies* (pp. 62–82). San Francisco: Jossey-Bass.

deShazer, S. (1988). *Clues: Investigating solutions in brief therapy.* New York: Norton.

Dinkmeyer, D. (1991). *The basics of understanding your lifestyle.* Coral Springs, FL: CMTI Press.

Dinkmeyer, D., & Carlson, J. (1984). *TIME for a better marriage.* Circle Pines, MN: American Guidance Service.

Dinkmeyer, D., Dinkmeyer, D., & Sperry, L. (1987). *Adlerian counseling and psychotherapy* (2nd ed.). Columbus, OH: Merrill.

*Suggested reading.

Dreikurs, R. (1946). *The challenge of marriage.* New York: Hawthorne.

Dreikurs, R. (1954). The psychological interview in medicine. *American Journal of Individual Psychology, 10,* 99–122.

Dreikurs, R. (1967). *Psychodynamic psychotherapy and counseling.* Chicago: Alfred Adler Institute.

Gottman, J., & Silver, N. (1999). *The seven principles for making marriage work.* New York: Crown.

Guidano, V. F., & Liotti, G. (1983). *Cognitive processes and the emotional disorders.* New York: Guilford Press.

Hoyt, M. (1998). *The handbook of constructivist therapy.* San Francisco: Jossey-Bass.

Huber, C. D., & Baruth, L. G. (1981). *Coping with marital conflict: An Adlerian approach to succeeding in marriage.* Champaign, IL: Stipes.

Jones, J. V. (1995). Constructivism and individual psychology: Connor ground for dialogue. *Individual Psychology, 51*(3), 231–243.

Kern, R. (1997). *Lifestyle scale.* Coral Springs, FL: CMTI Press.

Selvini-Palazzoli, M., Bosocolo, L., Cecchin, G., & Prata, G. (1980). Hypothesizing-circularity-neutrality. *Family Process, 19,* 3–12.

Sperry, L. (1992). The "rediscovery" of interventive interviewing. *North American Society of Adlerian Psychology Newsletter, 25*(1), 3–4.

*Sperry, L., & Carlson, J. (1991). *Marital therapy: Integrating theory and technique.* Denver, CO: Love Publishing.

Tomm, K. (1987). Interventive interviewing: Part II. *Family Process, 26,* 167–183.

8

Imago Relationship Therapy

Wade Luquet

TREATMENT MODEL

Imago Relationship Therapy (IRT) (Hendrix, 1988, 1992; Luquet, 1996; Luquet & Hannah, 1998) is a synthesis and expansion of various schools of thought, including psychoanalysis, Self psychology, behaviorism, systems theory, Western spiritual traditions, and modern physics. Together, these schools work synergistically to form a relational model of couples therapy that utilizes behavioral, cognitive, and affective interventions to facilitate understanding and change within the dyad. IRT utilizes its basic tool of "Couples Dialogue" to facilitate a desired state of connected differentiation within the couple's relationship. IRT's main objective is to foster empathic connection between the couple, while at the same time assisting each spouse in developing a strong sense of self through dialogue. When accomplished, couples have the necessary tools to solve relationship problems, receive and give empathy, develop individual goals, and feel heard and understood by each other.

IRT therapists are trained to become facilitators of a process that teaches couples about the healing nature of relationships. They give the couple an experience of healthy communication through couples dialogue which allows them to enhance their ability to understand their selves and their partner in a clearer, less adversarial manner. When couples are able to hear each other fully, they are better able to understand the meaning and nature of the frustrations they experience with their partner. To accomplish this, couples are first taught to calm and center themselves so they can listen without defensiveness. Defensiveness—aspects of fight, flight, freezing, hiding, or submission—is the nature of the reptilian portion of the brain as it tries to defend itself against death or harm. These defensive maneuvers are naturally, though erroneously (unless abuse is present), used by couples to win a fight and protect themselves from perceived danger. Couples are taught to self-soothe and tolerate their anxiety to fully hear what their partner has to say to them.

The way that each member of the couple listens to their partner is structured into a three-part dialogue process. The "now-centered" receiving partner mirrors back their partner's words in an effort to ensure that they understand what their partner said without distortion. Once they fully understand their partner's message, they validate what their partner said to them. Validation is not agreeing, nor is it giving a seal of approval, such as "Yes, I agree" or "You're smart to think that way." Rather, validation is saying to the partner, "I can see how *you* might see it that way. If I were looking at the world through *your* eyes, I could see how *you* would view it that way." There is no requirement for agreement, just an understanding that the sending partner may have their own way of seeing things.

The third part of the dialogue process involves the receiving partner offering empathy to what the sending partner has said. The word empathy is translated from the German word *Einfühlung*, meaning "in-feeling," and is described as an abstract noun (Shlein, 1997). Because it is an abstract noun that did not exist before 1910, there are many definitions for empathy, and it has also been extended to become a verb, such as in *to empathize*. Basically, empathy is an attempt to understand the inner world of the other, without crossing the line and taking on the others world as one's own. It is a cognitive and affective process. In the dialogue process, the receiving partner may say, "I imagine you might feel sad, frustrated, and confused." It is an attempt by the receiving partner to momentarily connect to the emotional world of the sending partner: a sense of empathic connection without fusion. When the sending partner feels fully heard and understood, the process can be switched, and the sending partner listens to the receiving partner. While the process is awkward at first, couples can become comfortable with the process through practice, and are able to listen to each other with less defensiveness and more authenticity.

Once the couple becomes comfortable with the dialogue process and creating a sense of safety in their communication, usually in two to four sessions, they can move more in depth with the Imago processes. Imago is a philosophy as well as a technique for helping couples. The word "Imago" is from the Greek word for "image." It implies that intimate partners carry an unconscious image of their early childhood caretakers that they use to pick each other as partners. One partner carries traits that frustrate the other (unknown during the romantic phase of the relationship), and it is within these frustrations that personal growth lies. It is not that one partner has what the other needs, but rather that what one needs is what the other partner most needs to grow into, to become whole and fully functioning. The opposite is also true: what the other partner needs is what the original partner need to grow into. When one partner gets what they need from the other partner, they become healed; and when the other partner gives their partner what they most need, they grow. However, to do so without understanding why partners need to give each other what they need would be coercion. To give freely takes a desire for growth, and empathy toward the partner's wounds that are causing the frustration.

The couple is shown how to deepen their empathy through two processes: the parent/child dialogue and the holding exercise. In the parent /child dialogue, the sending partner talks to the receiving partner as if they are one of their parents who has just asked, "I am your mother/father. What was it like to live with me?" and later "I am your mother/father. What did you need from me that you did not get?" The receiving partner is typically able to see their partner's wound clearly in this exercise as well as their contribution to the frustration through their behavior. The couple is also shown the holding exercise, in which the sending partner is held by the receiving partner across their chest. The sending partner talks in the present about their childhood, "When I was a little boy/ girl . . . " When one partner can see the reason behind the others behavior, they begin to see their partner in a different light. Imago calls these processes "reimaging" as the partner is reimaged from enemy to ally in the journey of growth.

Once empathy is established, the couple needs a safe forum to make behavior changes. The process of restructuring frustrations is done through Behavior Change Request (BCR). Imago assumes that a frustration is a desire stated negatively: "I hate when you are late" becomes "My desire is that you arrive on time." The reptilian brain of the individual processes frustrations as a threat and desires as neutral. Couples are taught to convert frustrations into desires and then desires into specific BCRs: "If you are going to be more than 15 minutes late, I would like for you to call me a half hour before you leave to tell me you will be late. I would like for you to do this three times this month." Request from one partner typically take aim at the other's growth area. To fulfill the request, the receiving partner will need to stretch into the new behavior and, thus, grow into a new area of self.

While the couple has now learned listening, empathy, and behavior change skills, it is important that they learn one of the most important aspects of the couples relationship—a process Imago calls "re-romanticizing." Gottman's research (1997) on couples showed that happy and stable marriages have five positive behaviors for every one negative behavior. Couples in Imago therapy spend several sessions discussing and making a list of behaviors that, if their partner did for them, would make them feel loved and cared for. They are encouraged to do these behaviors regularly, as well as surprising their partner with other caring behaviors (flowers, breakfast in bed, an overnight in a hotel) and to have regular belly laughs that promote well-being between the couple.

The final two Imago processes involve developing a vision for the marriage that both partners agree on if they were to design a perfect marriage: We are financially stable. We take walks together regularly. We are happy with our jobs. We have good communication skills. This vision serves as a guide for couples on their journey through their lives and reminds them that their relationship has purpose. The couple is also shown processes that help them deal with anger, such as the container process. Basically, this involves the receiving partner listening without comment to the other partner's anger to discover the hurt that has fueled the anger. This is the most difficult of Imago processes, and should be done for the first few times with a trained therapist.

The theory and processes of IRT work together to help the couple develop a new paradigm for their relationship. Frustrations possess the seeds of personal growth. Nature has set up the relationship to help individuals heal from wounds started by frustrations in childhood relationships and healed by positive interactions in adult relationships. Once the wounds begin to heal, couples are able to use their relationship for enjoyment and for spiritual adventure as they break the bounds of the impasses that have held them back. Though this is not an easy journey, couples are taught that toughing out the difficult parts of the marriage in dialogical process is valuable to their relationship and to each of them individually as they develop a stronger sense of self.

THERAPIST SKILLS AND ATTRIBUTES

The therapists who work with couples utilizing IRT should also be on their own path toward relational growth. While the therapist does not have to be married or in a committed relationship, a belief in the healing aspect of relationship is necessary. Pinsof (1995) stated that psychotherapy seems to be divided into two types: problem-centered—teaching skills and problem solving—and value-centered—having some norm or ideal to achieve. While IRT does have problem-solving skills for the couple, it also has a philosophy of self-growth-in-relationship and attaining wholeness. Therapists working with this model should have some knowledge of and "buy in" to the philosophy of relational healing. Though Imago theory would not be considered dogmatic, having this relational philosophy is not unlike individual therapists having a psychoanalytical or humanist philosophy—they serve as templates for the progression of treatment.

Therapists who become certified in Imago Relationship Therapy through the Institute for Imago Relationship Therapy must be licensed in their state, have 6 years of supervised post-master's practice, and complete a 96-hour training program. They must also participate in an Imago couples weekend with their partner or a significant friend in order to experience the work firsthand. They are encouraged to continue in supervision with a more experienced Imago Therapist or a trainer until they feel comfortable using the processes and philosophies of IRT.

THE CASE OF MIKE AND JAN

Instruments and Assessment Tools

There are several inventories and interviews IRT uses to access the developmental wounds of couples. More importantly, this information is utilized to educate the couple to the purpose of their relationship. The first inventory that I use is the Imago work up (see Luquet, 1996), first developed by Harville Hendrix for a study guide to the book *Getting the Love You Want: A Guide for Couples* (1988). The Imago workup asks the couple to answer several questions about their early childhood caretaker.

A. The positive traits of my male and female caretakers
B. The negative traits of my male and female caretakers
C. What I always wanted and needed in my childhood was . . .
D. My recurring frustrations and what I did when I was frustrated
E. My positive memories of childhood and how I felt

The couple is asked to write as much as they can remember from as far back in their childhoods as possible. This information is then transferred into a series of sentence stems about their partner.

I am trying to get a person who is (negative traits).

To always be (positive traits).

So that I can get (what I did not get as a child).

And feel (positive memories of childhood).

I stop myself from getting this sometimes by (what I did as a child when I was frustrated).

An example of how this might work for Jan and Mike, from the information in the case study, might be as follows for Mike:

> I am trying to get a person who is critical, shaming, lenient, and not there. To always be available, encouraging, and involved. So that I can get encouragement and to know that I am worthy. And I would feel encouraged and worthy. I stop myself from getting this sometimes by avoiding the discussion of problems, isolating myself, getting involved in a project.

This information was taken from information on Mike's childhood, but seems to apply to the present situation in Jan and Mike's marriage.

The Imago workup typically helps the couple see that they married someone who frustrates them in a similar way that they were frustrated during their childhood, and they are reacting in ways similar to the way they did as a child. IRT therapists use this information to teach the couple that they choose each other as part of an unconscious process, and that to have a mature relationship, they have to live above their unconscious reactions. Imago therapy helps couples work toward healing those wounds so they can live beyond them and end the impasses that grip couples in distress. The Imago workup is an excellent visual tool to help couples understand this process.

A second diagnostic process I use is a clinical lecture/interview that teaches couples the importance of their developmental wounding in their choice of mate and their subsequent desire to heal those wounds. It also expands on the knowledge obtained from the Imago workup. Keeping in mind that IRT is a philosophy and paradigm shift as well as a treatment approach, the couple needs several experiences of understanding the meaning behind the work they will do. This lecture/interview will provide both the therapist and the couple with valuable information about the relationship and IRT.

The lecture (see Luquet, 1996) educates the couple on the developmental stages of childhood as viewed by IRT in very simple terms. The stages include attachment (birth to about 1 1/2 years old), exploration (about 1 1/2 to 3 years old), identity (about 3 to 4 years old), power and competence (4 to 6 years old), and concern (6 to 9 years old). Through this lecture, the couple is able to understand that where their parents were not able to meet their developmental needs is where their partner's needs were not met as well. We fall in love with those who are developmentally wounded in the same phase. Because of this arrangement, what one partner needs is the most difficult for the other to give—the partner needing to be held is attracted to the partner who becomes anxious to hold. But, for one partner to stretch their range of behaviors to meet the other's needs (for example, to be held) meets the one partner's desires, and causes behavioral and functional growth for the partner making the change.

Following this lecture/interview, couples understand that IRT is hard work. It is more than a communication process; it is a change of behavior to meet needs, expand behaviors, and move relational impasses along. A basic goal of IRT is to move couples out of their reactive, dependent relationship and into a mature, interdependent relationship.

Conceptualization of Mike and Jan

Imago Relationship Therapy is far more concerned with Jan and Mike's process of relating than with the content of their discussions and actions. Certainly their personality, behavior, affect, and cognitions are important to their relationship, though IRT will view these aspects within the context of the relationship. Their ability to connect and fully understand each other cocreates Jan and Mike's personality, behaviors, affect, and cognitions. Their difficulties and resulting individual behaviors—sulking, angry, avoidant, ignoring, and critical—may well be a result of their relational dissatisfaction, and not a true picture of who they really are as individuals.

Jan and Mike's relationship resembles those of many couples. They began with romantic love—a chemically induced state that brings couples together and blinds them to the faults of the other—and evolved into their power struggle stage. While their marriage seems bleak right now, they do have some promising aspects that may make treatment successful.

One way of conceptualizing Jan and Mike's relationship is by using Gottman's Sound Marital House assessment (1997). Jan and Mike have good early memories of their early marriage, and have knowledge about each other's likes and dislikes—what Gottman calls "Love Maps." They have some fondness and admiration for each other, as evidenced by their desire to stay together, however, this can be increased in their day-to-day interactions. They seem to be drifting away from each other, so their emotional bank account is nearly drained, and they seem to be feeling negative about the relationship. Their problem-solving skills are poor, as evidenced by Mike's tendency to walk away and ignore problems. Jan and Mike do not seem to be supportive of each other's dreams and aspirations, which is witnessed by their emotional distance from each other. And, finally, they do not fully understand how each other's background affects their present relationship, and causes the annoying patterns of conflict and impasse they are experiencing. According to Gottman, these seven areas have to be functional for couples to enjoy a happy and stable marriage, and should be kept in the foreground of the treatment for Jan and Mike.

Developmentally, Mike seems to come from a somewhat rigid, traditional home in which shaming was used as a way of changing behavior. There was no doubt that he was important to the family, but Mike either could not do anything right, or what he did was ignored by his parents: his father was only available to him during football season, and his mother had many rules and was critical. This parenting style tends to develop a wound around having a sense of competence—that what one does is important and well-done—and seems to have led Mike to underestimate his abilities and self-worth. This fits well into Jan's complementary wound of receiving praise when she was doing things for the family. She became parentified, and learned that praise came with accomplishments. Because she developed an over-functioning competency, she responds to Mike's inadequacy with criticism. According to IRT, these individuals will often marry as a way to work through their past wounds: Mike needs praise and acknowledgment without shaming—a task difficult for Jan, since one must earn praise—and Jan needs recognition from the person who has the most difficulty giving it—Mike, who was shamed around accomplishments.

Mike and Jan have struggled in this relationship—their relationship impasse seems to be around competence. This has led to resentment and isolation in the marriage. They now rarely eat or socialize together, and they have little or no sex life. They rarely work out a problem anymore—Mike will leave for several hours and return as if nothing has happened. Such resentment has created a schema of marital dissatisfaction, misunderstanding, and fear between this couple. At this point, it seems that they look for ways to be apart to avoid any chance of confrontation, or repairing the relationship.

Treatment Goals

My short-term goals for Mike and Jan would be to help them learn and use skills that will help them in the long term. Consequently, my long-term goal would be for them to become so adept at the communication skills that they could handle any situation that came along comfortably and naturally—something that definitely has not occurred in the last 12 years. In the short term, Jan and Mike will learn skills that will seem awkward to them at first. They will learn new skills to communicate, solve problems, and make contact. They will also learn the importance of positive interactions in the relationship.

I would have four short-term goals for Jan and Mike. First, Jan and Mike need to increase their positive interactions and fun times with each other. Gottman reports that happy and stable marriages have a constant ratio of five positive behaviors for every one negative. In other words, happy couples act like friends and flood each other with positives. My first goal would be to educate Jan and Mike about this and have them begin the process of adding positive caring behaviors to their daily lives. Though there may be resentments that get in the way of providing caring behaviors, Jan and Mike will have to do something to bring back the good will that they enjoyed in their early marriage.

My second short-term goal would be for them to develop healthy communication skills by learning IRT's couples dialogue technique. Couples dialogue is designed to help them hear each other completely in an effort to understand the other. Jan and Mike's communication skills are poor, and they need training in communication that will keep Jan calm, keep Mike involved in the conversation, and help them both to be understood by each other.

My third short-term goal would be to teach Mike and Jan the purpose of relationships as viewed by IRT—to meet those needs not met in childhood, to heal those wounds, and learn to use their relationship for development of self and a deeper spiritual experience through relationship with the partner.

Finally, in the short term, Jan and Mike need to learn problem-solving skills that will help them with the problems they encounter from day to day in their marriage. Presently, Jan criticizes, complains, and screams while Mike ignores, minimizes, and walks away. The problems do not go away for Jan and Mike, and seem to be exacerbated by their typical approach to problem-solving. They will need to learn skills that will give them a structure that allows them to safely understand the problem and deal with it rationally. And, of course, some things they will have to learn how to accept as unchangeable and as a part of their partner's personality makeup.

If they can accomplish these short-term goals, Jan and Mike should be able to accomplish their long-term goals of maintaining contact through dialogue, encouraging each other in their personal and self-development, and having fun once again spontaneously as a couple. Because there is no such thing as "happily ever after," Jan and Mike will also learn how to solve problems as they arise, or know early when to return for more therapy to get them over the humps.

Techniques and Interventions

There are several interventions that I would use immediately to shore up this couple as well as to teach them IRT skills. First, Jan and Mike are in need of positive interactions with each other. They need to begin doing some of the things they once enjoyed—being with friends, going out to dinner, eating and talking at the dinner table, and going to movies. It may seem difficult to do these positive behaviors at first, since there is a lot of bitterness between them, but it will be necessary for them to build their relationship. They will have to start slow, and they may find it difficult, and sometimes impossible, to participate in the positive behaviors with each other. Yet, if they do not try or find that they can not participate in positive interactions with each other, they miss out on one of the most important aspects of a happy and stable marriage.

Because of the distance that has developed between Jan and Mike, I would have them do a daily reconnection ritual when they come home. Soon after they come home and before they get involved in any type of activity such as reading the mail, they are asked to hug each other for 2 minutes. Two minutes may not seem like much, but for disconnected couples, it feels quite long. Then, they are each to listen to the other about their day for 6 minutes, using the Couples dialogue process they will learn. Finally, they will end this process with another 2-minute hug. This simple process will aid in their reconnection and feeling of the importance of the relationship.

Within the first two sessions, Jan and Mike would also learn the couples dialogue process. As mentioned earlier, the couples dialogue is a three-part process wherein the receiving partner mirrors the sending partner's words, validates what they said from the sending partner's point of view, and offer empathy by guessing what the sending partner may be feeling. An example that could come from Jan and Mike may be Mike mirroring back Jan as follows:

Jan: I get really angry when you leave the house when we are trying to work things out.

Mike: If I hear you correctly, you get really mad when I leave the house when we are in the middle of a discussion trying to work things out. Did I get that? Is there more?

Jan: Yes, I hate when you run off to the bar and then come back as if nothing has happened. You leave me by myself to deal with how I'm feeling.

Mike: So you hate when I go to the bar, come back as if nothing has happened, and leave you to deal with your feelings by yourself. Did I get that? Is there more?

Jan: It reminds me of what my mother did to me when she put me in charge all the time. She thought I was big enough to handle things and I wasn't. I should not have been left by myself so much to handle things on my own. I needed someone to talk to.

Mike: So, if I'm getting it, this reminds you of when you were a kid and your mom would leave you in charge of your brother and your house and you had no one to talk to about your feelings. She thought you could handle it and you were just a kid and needed someone to talk to. That makes sense to me. I can see how when I leave in the middle of our discussion, you feel by yourself and left with your own feelings. It makes sense that you need someone there, namely me, to listen to you. I imagine you might feel lonely, sad, and abandoned.

This process would go on for several rounds until Mike fully understands why leaving during the discussion has such meaning to Jan. When he fully understands, Mike may request to talk and the sender/receiver roles are reversed. This process, though difficult because of our natural tendency to defend ourselves, will result in a deeper understanding between partners. Couples begin to understand the motivation and purpose of their impasses—Mike's leaving was abandoning, and needs to be changed. But the deeper sadness for Jan is how that abandonment reminds her of her relationship with her mother. If Mike can understand the pain it causes, he is likely to make a behavior change without feeling coerced and pressured.

Once Jan and Mike have fully learned the couples dialogue process and empathy has been established, they can learn the Behavior Change Request (BCR) process. This process teaches the couple to convert their frustrations into desires or wishes and then into specific, positive, doable, and measurable BCRs. To continue our example with Jan and Mike, Jan gets frustrated when Mike leaves during a discussion or argument. Her desire, therefore, would be, "I would like you to stay in the room with me during a discussion or argument, no matter how anxious you feel."

Jan would then convert that desire into one or more BCR. She might say, "Twice this week, I would like to have a discussion with you on serious issues. I would like for you to sit on the couch with me, stay in the room for 30 minutes, and preferably until the conversation is complete, and do this in the couples dialogue process." A request like this would satisfy Jan's need to be heard, and would promote growth in Mike, who needs to develop tolerance for his anxiety about problem-solving. The more Mike is able to tolerate the anxiety, the easier it will be to stay with Jan during conversations with substance.

Of course, Mike may later have another BCR that may sound counter to Jan's. Mike may get frustrated that when Jan wants to talk that it can go on for hours. Mike's desire may be that Jan get to her point quickly and tell him what he needs to do to make her feel better. He may make a request: "Twice this week, when you feel frustrated, I would like for you to approach me and say that you would like to have a 10-minute dialogue. I would like you to say what frustrates you and what you would like for me to do about it within the 10 minute time frame and let the subject go for the night." This request will teach Jan to keep things short, and that she has to learn how to self-soothe the additional anxiety she may be experiencing when the time is up.

There are additional skills taught in IRT; however, these are the basic skills needed by a couple to reestablish connection and problem-solve. Along with the new understanding of how their childhoods play a part in their struggles, Jan and Mike will have the necessary tools and knowledge to move their marriage forward.

Pitfalls and Limits

The biggest pitfall for Jan and Mike is that the intervention may be too late. From the Sound Marital House assessment (Gottman, 1997), Jan and Mike were definitely on their last legs of this marriage. The importance of an assessment tool like this is that it gives the therapist a quick picture of whether the marriage is worth saving, or is it better to help them to dissolve their relationship. A therapist aware of the signs can usually tell within a few sessions whether the therapy will work. If a couple like Mike and Jan came in and either one said something like, "I just do not have any feelings for him/her. It's more like we are brother and sister," this could be a strong indication that the marriage is over. This is often the case even if the other partner is pleading for the defeated partner to try "one more time." It is very difficult to restart intimate love, though it does occasionally happen and should be given a chance. Since Jan and Mike indicated they would like to make it work, they will have to make their marriage a priority and institute many pleasurable experiences and intimate discussions with each other.

There is also the possibility that either Jan or Mike will see themselves as "the right one" and will want all changes made their way. Because their wound seems to be in the competency stage, this possibility is less likely, because these couples will often do whatever it takes to make things work. This scenario is more likely to happen with identity-wounded couples whose rigid partner is sure they know the answers. They can usually convince their complementary diffuse partner that they know the answer and that the diffuse partner should just listen to them.

Another possible pitfall is that Mike and Jan will not buy into the IRT model of treatment. There are couples that make fun of the dialogue process—they say it is too hard, or too ridiculous to do with each other. As a therapist, I need to be prepared for these couples, and know other models of couples treatment, such as cognitive, PAIRS, PREP, or be ready to refer them to a therapist that is trained in these models. You can not squeeze a round peg into a square hole, so if Jan and Mike were not able to fully use IRT, I have to be prepared to help them in other ways than labeling their displeasure as "resistance."

Marriage therapy does not have the best track record when it comes to relapse. There is the possibility that 6 months after treatment this couple will return to their old patterns of relating and the marriage will end. It will be important during treatment that I check to make sure Jan and Mike are doing work at home, and not just waiting until the sessions to talk and practice the skills. During termination, they will have to be fully prepared to continue their work at home and be prepared to return to therapy for a checkup as needed.

Areas to Avoid

Imago therapy is not typically a therapist-directed therapy. Rather, the topics come from the couple with therapist guidance or set-up. Early in the therapy, it is probably not important for this couple to discuss Jan's hysterectomy and inability to have children, because there are so many immediate issues to deal with to stabilize the relationship. However, if they chose to stay in therapy for an extended period of time, the therapist might say to them during one of these later sessions, "You have not talked about not having children. I wonder if you could take a few minutes to dialogue about that now?" Jan and Mike may choose not to do it, but if they have the luxury of time, it may be beneficial for them to discuss their heartache, disappointment, sadness, or resentment about the cancer, the surgery, or not being able to have children.

The same might be said for Mike's substance abuse. While he seems to be in a good place now, Jan went through stress and uncertainty with Mike in his drug-abusing years. Perhaps she has some resentments to express to him, or some fears that he may relapse. Once this couple has skills in place and seem to be on a more positive path, they may choose to dialogue those issues that have defined whom each of them is individually and who they are as a couple.

Inclusion of Other Family Members

It is not typical for IRT to include others in the therapy sessions with the couple. IRT is a dyadic model of treatment, and therefore, the work tends to be exclusively with the couple. However, most of IRT's practitioners are systems and family therapists, and are well aware of the systemic forces that are important to the well-being and the shaping of the couple. As a family therapist, I always keep the broader system in mind, and will at times bring others into the sessions. This is especially true when young children or teenagers are involved.

Bringing others into IRT treatment would only occur after the couple is stabilized enough to listen to what the others had to say. If a couple was proficient at dialogue, I might consider bringing in their teenage children for them to express how they feel about the difficulties their parents are experiencing, and its effect on them. I would have the parents listen to the children in the dialogue process. Because IRT has a developmental philosophy, part of the work is to help parents stop the cycle of wounding that occurred to them in their childhood, and that tends to be passed on to the next generation. I teach parents of young children how to use dialogue processes and empathic connection to minimize wounding to the growing child and help them achieve developmental milestones.

In the case of Jan and Mike, they have no children, so I would not likely need any others present to work with this case. Had one of them been involved with an individual therapist, I would have made contact with the therapist to discuss the treatment. Sometimes, individual therapists can work counter to the goals of the couples treatment. There have been times when I have worked with couples on issues that involved a behavior change, only to have an individual therapist say to them, "Don't do it if you don't want to. Remember, you have to take care of yourself first." I can certainly understand the good intentions of the individual therapist taking care of their clients; however, relationships often require sacrifices that can be painful or uncomfortable as new behaviors are utilized. It is important that the couples therapist stay in touch with the individual therapist so they are both proceeding in the same direction.

I would also make use of other professionals as needed for medications or alternative treatments. If I suspected that Mike really had ADD, I would refer him for testing, and then for medication as needed. If Jan showed signs of depression during the course of treatment, I would recommend a physician for medication, or offer information on alternative methods of dealing with depression (i.e., cognitive therapy, St. John's Wort, meditation, or going out with friends). This will be a difficult time for Mike and Jan as they work to resurrect their marriage, so anxiety and depression might be expected. Having them discuss their anxiety and depression with each other in dialogue would also help.

Homework

Homework is a very important aspect of IRT. Jan and Mike will not improve if they only engage in this work an hour per week. The treatment will have to become a way of life to be successful, and to do that, it has to become habit. Each week, Jan and Mike will be assigned homework which they will be expected to accomplish by the next session.

IRT homework is specific and designed to help the couple practice and embody the skills learned each week. After the first week of learning couples dialogue, Jan and Mike would be asked to spend 2 days having fun with it by having all of their conversations in dialogue, "I heard you say you stopped and got gas on the way home. Did I get that? Is there more?" It may seem silly to them, but necessary to make it a permanent part of their lives. After two days of learning the parts of the dialogue, Jan and Mike will use the dialogue process every other night for one-half hour talking about more serious matters. This will provide them with the opportunity to practice on issues that they need to talk about before their next visit.

I would check their homework at that session by being somewhat interested in what they said in the dialogue, but more interested in how the dialogue process worked for them. In that session, I would ask them to dialogue for me, so I can see how they were doing it and correct anything they may be doing wrong in the dialogue process. These skills will only take hold if it becomes habit. Homework, and the checking of homework, is one way to begin the habit-making process. If they did not do the homework, I would give them the natural consequence: they have to do the homework in the session—and now they are paying for something they could have done for free at home. I would also point this out to the couple that we could be moving forward if they did the work, but instead we have to make sure they fully understand last week's processes. It usually does not take many of these sessions for the couple to understand that homework is serious to this work.

Because managed care has shortened the time that couples can spend in therapy under insurance coverage, any written work will be done at home, so that the sessions can be fully utilized for dialogue and reestablishing connection. For example, they will do their written work concerning their caretakers on the Imago workup at home, and bring their answers back to the next session. While I am filling out the Imago form for them, the couple will be dialoguing about one of their issues or concerns. This helps the couple to utilize their time well and keeps them working in the process at home and in the session.

Jan and Mike will also be given the task of writing down their frustrations with each other, converting them into desires, and then converting them into specific BCRs. They would bring that work into the session and I would check to make sure the BCRs are written in positive, doable, and measurable terms. I would next spend a session having them present the BCRs to each other using the dialogue process. This would teach Jan and Mike how to use this process at home after the therapy is complete.

As Jan and Mike progress, I would also give them the assignment to write down what their relationship would look like if they woke up tomorrow and had the perfect relationship. They would write it in terms of "We" and in the present—as if they have it now: We take long walks together. We are financially secure. We enjoy a satisfying sex life. We talk using dialogue. In a subsequent session, they would combine their list into their dream marriage list—one that can be posted in their home as a reminder of what they are striving for in their work.

Of course, since one of the goals in treatment is to increase positive behaviors, Jan and Mike would have to make a list of positive behaviors they would both enjoy and do several of these behaviors on a weekly basis. These behaviors may involve some activities that they already do—taking care of and riding their horse—or things they want to start to do—go to the theater or go to dinner once a week. To experience pleasure with each other, Jan and Mike have to do something—anything—that is pleasurable to them each week.

Timeline for Therapy

Typically, 10 to 12 sessions of IRT are sufficient to teach couples the Imago processes. Because Jan and Mike need time to practice the skills taught and understand the new ideas of the relational paradigm, I would see them for one-and-a-half hour sessions every other week. This format would give them time to complete their homework and practice the skills learned in the sessions. It also lessens the number of sessions they would have to attend, yet extends the number of months Jan and Mike will have contact with the process. It also gives them an extended time to have a therapist available to get them over the hurdles that are inevitable in couples therapy.

Because of the severity of Jan and Mike's relationship distress, there is the possibility that they will need extended treatment that will give them the opportunity to utilize their new skills in the presence of a therapist. I might also recommend a weekend couples workshop for Jan and Mike to improve their skills and give them the opportunity to see other couples in similar situations. IRT has an extensive workshop network internationally that conducts weekend *"Getting the Love You Want"* workshops. These weekends basically teach the same concepts and skills to which Jan and Mike would be exposed during their weekly therapy sessions; however, some couples report that it is helpful to learn the material in both settings, so they can meet other couples learning similar skills.

I would not typically see members of a couple in individual sessions. Though there is some value in connecting with each of them individually, there is a danger that they will reveal a secret in those meetings (affairs, a crime, financial indiscretions) that the other partner does not know about. Occasionally, I will get a request from one member of a couple to see them without their partner. In that case, I inform them that I will only see one of them if I also see the other at another time to balance the scales. I also tell them that they cannot divulge any secrets. If they want to tell me something they have not told their partner, it must be in the context of working toward revealing this to their spouse.

In the case of Jan and Mike, there appears no need to see them individually. It would seem that they can work well together. I am also seeing little need to refer them to an individual therapist. One exception may be Mike's question about Attention Deficit Disorder. If Mike were to truly have ADD, it would be important to have a definitive diagnosis and begin treatment. ADD has a great effect on the communications skills of a couple (Kelly & Luquet, 1998). Because ADD has become a popular syndrome that is subjected to self-diagnosis and overuse, I would first have Mike and Jan read books such as *Driven to Distraction* (Hallowell & Ratey, 1994) to see if the book feels "familiar" to the two of them. If it does feel familiar, I would send them for testing to a clinical psychologist. If the diagnosis was positive, it would be important to work with the consulting clinical psychologist and physician and to gear the couples therapy toward working with a couple in which ADD is present (Kelly & Luquet, 1998).

Termination and Relapse Prevention

Jan and Mike would complete therapy far from perfect. IRT views the journey of marriage as a lifetime process that facilitates continued developmental growth as the couple ages together. Jan and Mike would complete therapy when they have learned all of the Imago processes and have some ability to do them on their own. Typically, the couple decides when therapy ends, depending on the needs of the marriage. Some couples want to learn the skills and ideas of IRT and terminate treatment quickly, while others prefer to stay in contact with a therapist on an occasional basis to make sure that their relationship stays on course.

As I did at the beginning of treatment, I would use Gottman's Sound Marital House (1997) as an assessment for readiness to terminate treatment. First, Jan and Mike would have to have considerably more knowledge about each others' likes and dislikes, and they would have to considerably increase their fondness and admiration behaviors for each other. They would have to learn how to use each other to discuss their problems and stresses to build up their emotional bank account. They would have a noticeable positive shift in their perspective of the relationship—the glass is now half-full, rather than half-empty. They would also have good problem-solving skills that would be developed through couples dialogue and Behavior Change Requests.

Given these changes, I would also want to see Jan and Mike become more involved in each other's personal and career goals, and also have more interest in each other's early lives that have developed schemas that may have caused impasses in the relationship. In other words, I would like to see Jan and Mike less fearful of the relationship and its tensions, and more willing to understand where the tensions originate.

The Gottman assessment provides a perspective on how the relationship is progressing through the course of therapy. Conversely, if Jan and Mike were not able to progress beyond the early stages of this assessment, I would question whether the relationship has the ability and the energy to turn itself around. If I did not see progress after 10 weeks, I might have a conversation with Jan and Mike about the possibility of ending the marriage, or possibly trying a different approach (Along with Imago, Marriage Encounter, PAIRS, and Retrouvaille are several successful programs for the treatment of troubled marriages). While my bias is usually in favor of the marriage, there are times when ending the relationship may be the best alternative. If indicated, I would then work with Jan and Mike to end the marriage.

Relapse is a common problem in marital therapy. During the termination process, I would strongly emphasize to Jan and Mike that they are likely to experience problems in the marriage. It will feel discouraging, but they should not look toward ending the relationship every time a problem arises. I use the analogy that I first learned from John Gottman, who said that marital therapy is not like surgery, where the problem is removed, but more like going to the dentist, where the problem is repaired. It will mostly stay repaired if you floss regularly, but more than likely will develop a cavity that needs attention, no matter how careful you are. Appointments would be scheduled every 3 to 6 months for at least a couple of years as a check-up—whether or not the couple is having a problem. Relationships, like teeth, are something you want to last a lifetime.

I would anticipate that Jan and Mike would leave the course of therapy with a good possibility of a long-term stable marriage. My main reason for saying this is because they stated that "Deep down inside they truly love each other.

They want very much to be together and both want to avoid being divorced at age 50." To do so, they will need to have consistent contact with each other and deal with problems directly, fully, and quickly in the dialogue process. They will also have to learn to have fun with each other, develop a mutual friend network, and live as if they are a couple—rather than in the parallel marriage that has developed. Their long-term prognosis depends fully on what they do day to day.

REFERENCES

Gottman, J. (1997). *A scientifically-based marital therapy: A 12-hour video course with extensive notes and handouts.* Seattle, WA: Seattle Marital and Family Institute.

Hallowell, E. M., & Ratey, J. (1994). *Driven to distraction: Recognizing and coping with attention deficit disorder from childhood through adulthood.* New York: Pantheon.

*Hendrix, H. (1988). *Getting the love you want: A guide for couples.* New York: Holt.

Hendrix, H. (1992). *Keeping the love you find: A guide for singles.* New York: Pocket Books.

Kelly, K., & Luquet, M. P. (1998). The impact of attention deficit disorder on couples. In W. Luquet & M. T. Hannah (Eds.), *Healing in the relational paradigm: The Imago relationship therapy casebook* (pp. 183–211). Philadelphia: Brunner/Mazel.

*Luquet, W. (1996). *Short-term couples therapy: The Imago model in action.* New York: Brunner/Mazel.

*Luquet, W., & Hannah, M. T. (Eds.). (1998). *Healing in the relational paradigm: The Imago relationship therapy casebook.* Philadelphia: Brunner/Mazel.

Pinsof, W. (1995). *Integrative problem-solving therapy.* New York: Basic Books.

Shlien, J. (1997). Empathy in psychotherapy: A vital mechanism? Yes. Therapist conceit? All too often. By itself enough? No. In A. Bohart & L. Greenberg (Eds.), *Empathy reconsidered* (pp. 63–80). Washington, DC: APA Press.

SUGGESTED READING

Gottman, J. M. (1994). *Why marriages succeed or fail.* New York: Simon and Schuster.

Hendrix, H. (1996). The evolution of Imago Relationship Therapy: A personal and theoretical journey. *Journal of Imago Relationship Therapy, 1*(1), 1–18.

Hendrix, H. (1992). *Keeping the love you find: A guide for singles.* New York: Pocket Books.

Hendrix, H., & Hunt, H. (1997). *Giving the love that heals: A guide for parents.* New York: Pocket Books.

Luquet, W. J., & Hendrix, H. (1998). Imago Relationship Therapy. In F. Dattilio (Ed.), *Integrative cases in couples and family therapy: A cognitive behavioral approach* (pp. 401–426). New York: Guilford Press.

---

*Suggested reading.

PART **III**

COGNITIVE-BEHAVIORAL THEORIES

9

A Cognitive-Behavioral Approach

Frank M. Dattilio and Louis J. Bevilacqua

TREATMENT MODEL

During the past two decades, cognitive-behavior therapy has gained recognition among professionals in the mental health field as a mainstream approach to psychotherapy. This is due in part to the fact that cognitive-behavior therapy has generated more empirical research and resulted in more outcome studies than any other psychotherapeutic modality in existence (Beck, 1991). Moreover, the rapid growth of cognitive-behavioral therapies regarding their applications to couples and families has been based on practical as well as empirical grounds. Research has documented how a couple's behavioral interaction patterns, cognitions, and emotional responses have an important impact on the quality of their intimate relationships (Dattilio, 1998; Epstein & Baucom, 1993; Fincham, Bradbury, & Scott, 1990; Gottman, 1993; Weiss & Heyman, 1990).

Aside from the established validity and strong empirical basis, cognitive-behavioral therapy with couples provides a relatively short-term, structured approach that is consistent with demands for specific treatment plans and assessment of defined therapeutic attainment.

Cognitive-behavior therapy with couples emanated from the behavioral approach to relationship problems as presented first in the literature in the late 1960s and 1970s (Liberman, 1970; Stuart, 1969; Weiss, Hops, & Patterson, 1973). The specific focus placed emphasis on the association between marital satisfaction and the exchange of pleasing versus aversive behavior between partners. Early research studies confirmed the premise of social exchange theory first promoted by Thibaut and Kelley (1959) which postulated that the stressed partners exchanged more displeasing and less pleasing behaviors than members of non-distressed relationships. Later, longitudinal research studies would indicate that spouses' behavioral responses to each other during discussions of relationship problems were predictive of the relationship's stability, such that more stable couples exhibited higher ratios of positive to negative behavior than did unstable couples (Gottman, 1993a). Additional research supported the notion that behavioral exchanges between partners tended to be reciprocal, in that a negative communication from one spouse increases the probability that the other spouse will respond negatively (Baucom & Epstein, 1990). The real exchange of positive behaviors tend to be equal or greater in non-distressed than in distressed couples.

A large part of the cognitive-behavioral approach to working with couples involves interventions for shifting distressed couples toward more satisfying ratios of pleasing to displeasing behavior. These interventions include behavioral contracts—commonly written agreements for both partners to behave in ways that their mates identified as pleasing, and procedures for training couples in more constructive communication and problem-solving skills (Jacobson & Margolin, 1979; O'Leary & Turkewitz, 1978; Stuart, 1980; Weiss et al., 1973). More recently, research indicating that patterns of withdrawal and defensiveness are associated with marital distress and dissolution (Christensen, 1988; Gottman, 1993a, 1993b) has led behavioral couple therapists to pay more attention to these patterned responses.

There are a number of initial outcome studies that have demonstrated the efficacy of cognitive-behavioral couple therapy in modifying couples' negative relationship cognitions (Baucom & Epstein, 1990; Baucom, Epstein, Rankin, & Burnett, 1996a). The cognitive-behavioral approach with couples is primarily designed to address the interrelations among partner's behaviors, cognitions and affect, as they influence the quality of a couple's marriage and other intimate relationships.

It was only in the late 1970s that clinical researchers involving behavioral marital therapy began to add cognitive components to behavioral treatments in controlled outcome studies. Initial aspects of cognitions were introduced as auxiliary components of treatment within the behavioral approach (Margolin, Christensen, & Weiss, 1975). A study by Margolin and Weiss (1978) compared behavioral marital therapy with a treatment in which behavioral marital therapy was supplemented with cognitive restructuring techniques. The results suggested that cognitive restructuring significantly enhanced the effectiveness of traditional behavioral marital therapy on several outcome measures. During the 1980s, cognitive factors became more of a focus in the couples research and therapy literature (e.g., Baucom, 1987; Baucom, Epstein, Sayers, & Sher, 1989; Beck, 1988; Dattilio, 1989, 1998). This movement underscored the need for couple treatment procedures to include a focus on the partner's cognitions regarding each other's actions, and led to the application of an establishment of cognitive interventions in behavioral couple therapy.

The primary tenet of CBT as applied to couples involves: (a) the modification of unrealistic expectations in the relationship, (b) correction of faulty attributions in relationship interactions, and (c) the use of self-instructional procedures to decrease destructive interaction. A primary agenda of CBT is identifying partners' schemata or beliefs about relationships in general and, more specifically, their thoughts about their own relationship (Beck, 1988; Epstein, 1986) and how this affects their emotions and behaviors.

Basic beliefs about relationships and the nature of couple interaction are often learned early in life from primary sources such as parents, local cultural mores, the media, and early dating experiences. These schemata or dysfunctional beliefs about relationships are often not articulated clearly in an individual's mind, but may exist as vague concepts of what should be (Beck, 1988). These beliefs can, however, be uncovered by examining the logic and themes of one's automatic thoughts.

Automatic thoughts, as defined earlier, are "surface thoughts" or ideas, beliefs, or images that individuals have from moment to moment that are situation-specific (e.g., "My wife is late again; she doesn't care about my feelings.")

Automatic thoughts usually stem from the individual's schemata, which are underlying or more core beliefs that are inflexible and unconditional in character. Schemata constitute the basis for coding, categorizing, and evaluating experiences during the course of one's life.

The therapist working with couples from a cognitive-behavioral perspective must focus equally on each partner's expectations about the nature of an intimate relationship. In addition, the distortions in evaluations of experience derived from those expectations are critically important. Cognitive distortions may be evident in the automatic thoughts that couples report and may be uncovered by means of systematic or Socratic questioning regarding the meaning that a partner attaches to a specific event. Spouses' automatic thoughts about their interactions with one another commonly include inferences about the causes of pleasant and unpleasant events that occur between them. Below is a list of common cognitive distortions typically found among couples:

Arbitrary Inference. Conclusions are made in the absence of supporting sub-stantiating evidence. For example, a man whose wife arrives home a half-hour late from work concludes, "She must be having an affair."

Selective Abstractions. Information is taken out of context and certain details are highlighted while other important information is ignored. For example, a woman whose husband fails to answer her greeting the first thing in the morning concludes, "He must be angry at me again."

Overgeneralization. An isolated incident or two is allowed to serve as a representation of similar situations everywhere, related or unrelated. For example, after being turned down for an initial date, a young man concludes, "All women are alike, I'll always be rejected."

Magnification and Minimization. A case or circumstance is perceived in greater or lessor light than is appropriate. For example, an angry husband "blows his top" upon discovering that the checkbook is unreconciled and states to his wife, "We're financially doomed."

Personalization. External events are attributed to oneself when insufficient evidence exists to render a conclusion. For example, a woman finds her husband re-ironing an already pressed shirt and assumes, "He is dissatisfied with my preparation of his clothing."

Dichotomous Thinking. Experiences are codified as either black or white, a complete success or total failure. This is otherwise known as "polarized thinking." For example, upon soliciting his wife's opinion on a paperhanging job underway in the recreation room, the wife questions the seams, and the husband thinks to himself, "I can't do anything right."

Labeling and Mislabeling. One's identity is portrayed on the basis of imperfections and mistakes made in the past, and these are allowed to define oneself. For example, subsequent to continual mistakes in meal preparation, a spouse states, "I am worthless," as opposed to recognizing her error as being human.

Tunnel Vision. Sometimes spouses only see what they want to see or what fits their current state of mind. A gentleman who believes that his wife "does whatever she wants anyway" may accuse her of making a choice based purely on selfish reasons.

Biased Explanations. This is almost a suspicious type of thinking that partners develop during times of distress, in which they automatically assume that their spouse holds a negative alternative motive behind their intent. For example, a woman states to herself, "He's acting real 'lovey-dovey' because he'll later probably want me to do something that he knows I hate to do."

Mind Reading. This is the magical gift of being able to know what the other is thinking without the aid of verbal communication. Spouses end by ascribing unworthy intentions onto each other. For example, a gentleman thinks to himself, "I know what is going through her mind, she thinks that I am naive to her shenanigans."

Cognitive-behavior therapy with couples focuses on the cognitions and beliefs that are identified as components of relationship discord and as contributing to each partner's subjective dissatisfaction with the relationship. This approach moves to the core of relationship difficulty by focusing on hidden as well as obvious here-and-now problems, rather than by dwelling on early childhood traumas.

There are several major focal areas in the cognitive-behavioral model that are essential when addressing the issue of change in relationships. These include: beliefs about the relationship, unrealistic expectations, and causal attributions and misattributions. (For a detailed explanation of these concepts, refer to the following case study or to Dattilio, Epstein, and Baucom, 1998; Dattilio & Padesky, 1990).

THERAPIST SKILLS AND ATTRIBUTES

Since cognitive-behavior therapy tends to lean more towards an analytic perspective, the skills and attributes of the therapist involve a type of deductive reasoning that the therapist applies during the assessment phase. Even though the therapist works in some respects as a coach with couples, joining the marriage in a remote sense, the therapist's primary role is to indicate to the spouses how their specific perceptions and beliefs about themselves and each other impact their emotional and behavioral reactions, and identify specific distortions and adaptive behavior patterns that lead to conflict and relationship deterioration. In this regard, most therapists who practice in cognitive-behavior therapy need to be amenable to a more directive approach at times, to a point that may appear almost intrusive to therapists of different orientations. Cognitive-behavior therapy was designed to be a short-term act, an active and directive process of educating spouses on the specific aspects that contribute to their relationship dysfunction. The mode of treatment involves a structured and collaborative approach that serves to initiate the mechanism for change. This sets the stage for the later adaptation of both couples to employ the techniques and strategies to themselves with the goal of facilitating future change.

While it is desirable that the therapist maintain a somewhat humanistic posture of providing warmth, empathy, and positive regard for the spouses, at the same time, the approach is directive in its goal of facilitating change.

One of the most important aspects of the process of treatment is the accuracy and detail of the clinical assessment. The assessment phase is typically the initial stage in which the therapist builds a positive rapport with the spouses as well as "learns their dance," to quote the systems theorist.

The one aspect about the cognitive-behavioral approach that differs radically from many of the other current modalities for couples' therapy involves the specific use of assessment tools, in the form of questionnaires and inventories. These instruments are typically used after the initial conjoint interview which consist mostly of history-taking and time for the therapist to develop an initial impression of how the partners interact with each other. During the initial conjoint interview, which usually lasts approximately 90 minutes, the therapist gains an understanding of how each of the spouses view their problem in the relationship differently and the specific attributions that they make with regard to their conflict.

With regard to the case of Mike and Jan, specific questions would be asked regarding how and under what circumstances the couple met, specific aspects of their relationship that existed prior to their marriage, respective recollections of positive experiences, and negative events in the relationship that may or may not have contributed to the current state of relationship dysfunction.

There are a number of specific forms that have been developed for intake purposes. One of these forms was developed by the Center For Cognitive Therapy in Philadelphia and can be found in Dattilio and Padesky (1990).

At the end of the initial conjoint visit, the therapist may or may not decide to utilize specific questionnaires or inventories, which are then provided to each spouse to complete independently. These inventories are then brought separately to the second set of sessions, that involves an individual interview with each of the spouses separately.

These individual sessions are designed to gain greater insight into each spouse's individual perspective of the problem, but also allows for the therapist to investigate more into the specific family of origin of each partner, with the attempt of better understanding their thinking styles and beliefs they bring from their family of origin to the current relationship.

Because the intake process is usually limited by time, there are a host of written inventories and questionnaires that can be used to assess attitudes, beliefs and behaviors about the relationship. These instruments also allow couples to pinpoint the specific areas of their conflict and to mention additional information that they may have been reluctant or embarrassed to mention during the initial conjoint interview.

ASSESSMENT

The assessment stage of CBT usually starts with a conjoint interview with both partners, lasting approximately 60–90 minutes. The session is consumed with learning the partners' "dance" and listening to their joint conceptualization of the problem. At the end of the initial session, it is typical to provide each couple with some of the questionnaires/inventories listed below in order to gain greater information about their thinking and perception of themselves, their spouse, and the relationship. This is later followed by an individual visit with each of them separately, at which time we review their responses to the questionnaires/inventories. From this point, it is quite typical to continue to work with the couple in conjoint sessions. It is important to keep in mind that the assessment period may be continual even after treatment begins. It is our opinion that assessment is ongoing, since couples continue to change over time. We may also elect to administer some of the questionnaires/inventories repeatedly over time as a measure of assessing their progress.

There are a number of empirically related as well as nonempirical questionnaires and inventories that may be used in the cognitive-behavioral approach, the majority of which include self-report questionnaires.

Among the more common are Eidelson and Epstein's (1982) Relationship Belief Inventory. This inventory was developed to tap unrealistic beliefs about close relationships. It includes subscales assessing the assumptions that partners cannot change the relationship; that disagreement is always destructive; that heterosexual relationship problems are due to innate differences between men and women and standards; that partners should be able to mind-read each other's thoughts and emotions; and that one should be perfect sexual partners.

Another popular inventory is the Inventory of Specific Relationships Standards (ISRS) (Baucom, Epstein, Rankin, & Burnett, 1996a). This inventory assesses an individual's personal standards concerning major relationship themes, including the nature of boundaries between partners (autonomy versus sharing), distribution of control (equal versus skewed) and partner's level of instrumental and expressive investment in the relationship, as the individual applies the standards to his or her own relationship.

Several attribution scales have been developed for the use in clinical research, and these can be and are also applied in clinical practice as well. Pretzer, Epstein, and Fleming (1991) Model Attitude Survey (MAS) includes subscales assessing attributions for relationship problems to one's own behavior, one's own personality, the partner's behavior, the partner's personality, the partner's lack of love, and the partner's malicious intent.

Other popular scales include the following:

Dyadic Adjustment Scale (DAS) (Spainer, 1976): This is a self-report inventory of adjustment in relationships (couples). Thirteen consensus items in the areas of household tasks, finances, recreation, friends, religion, decision-making, and so on, are measured with regard to the degree that the spouse reports agreement or disagreement. This instrument assesses global marital distress and yields an overall score on the interrelated aspects of relationship adjustment.

Marital Happiness Scale (MHS) (Azrin, Naster, & Jones, 1973): The degree of happiness is assessed across 11 domains (e.g., childrearing, financial, communication, etc.). Spouses rate on a 10-point scale from "completely unhappy" to "completely happy" how they view each domain in the relationship. This inventory provides a rather quick overview of the couples' distress.

Marital Satisfaction Inventory (MSI) (Snyder, 1981): This is a dichotomous forced-choice (true/false) inventory constituting 280 items embedded in nine domain areas such as: childrearing, finances, sexual problems, communication, family history, and so on. A global distress scale is also included to provide the clinician with an overall rating of distress. The couples' score can than be plotted out on a profile sheet together in order to compare their perceptions of the difficulties in the relationship with each other.

In the specific case of Mike and Jan, we may decide to utilize some of the above inventories, as well as additional psychological measures, to assess the level of psychopathology. Of specific concern in this case is Mike's history of substance abuse, which may indicate issues of dependency in his personality. It would be very important to assess the potential for change with this aspect, particularly as it relates to its contribution to the relationship dysfunction. In addition, the factor of Mike's early sexual abuse by his aunt suggests an unaddressed trauma that occurred and clearly may be affecting his sexual performance in his relationship with Jan. His dependency issues may also be underscored by the short period of time that he remained single between his first marriage to Eileen and his marriage to Jan.

It would be our hope that the assessment instruments would provide us with additional information about this couple's specific thoughts and belief systems regarding their relationship, as well as relationships in general. This, combined with the clinical interviews, would hopefully allow us to investigate more into Mike and Jan's pattern of avoidance, as well as their inability to getting closure on incidences of conflict and tension in the relationship.

CONCEPTUALIZATION OF MIKE AND JAN

With regard to the conceptualization of this case, it strikes us that Mike and Jan are two individuals who found themselves during a period of neediness in their respective lives. Both had just come out of a failed marriage embarking on the decade of their 40s. We found ourselves wondering whether or not both Mike and Jan experienced enough of a significant period of dating prior to linking up with each other. Some of the more underlying dynamics of this relationship suggest that Mike was the more dependent and needy individual, and found Jan to be one who was good at caretaking. Because of Jan's history and upbringing, she was the responsible caretaker for her brother, and may have sought to continue identifying in this role in her relationship with Mike. This is also underscored by the fact that Mike remained at home with his mother until the age of 29, a relationship in which, in many ways, each probably served as a pseudo-spouse. Mike only left his mother's residence after marrying his first wife at age 29. In many respects, one must question whether or not Mike felt somewhat responsible for his parents' failed marriage. It was only after Mike moved out on his own that his mother remarried her second husband of 20 years.

It is also our impression that Mike and Jan never really got to know each other as intimately as they would have liked. It seems that they both remained superficial in their intimacy, and fell into a pattern of avoidance fairly early in their marriage. This was aided by the use of controlled substances as well as their respective social activities and hobbies in which they would immerse themselves. Mike and Jan are clearly a couple who, no doubt, would become enmeshed with their children, had they had any. The fact that they chose not to have children left them to become involved in other external activities in order to avoid certain aspects of their relationship. There is also some indication that they are both avoiding a deeper level of intimacy, since both have a significant history of having difficulty with intimate relationships.

With respect to Mike's background, it is obvious that his parents had marital difficulties, and that he wasn't bonded well with either of his parents. It was mentioned that he was a bit closer to his mother; however, the fact that she experienced depression suggests that this hampered the relationship that existed. Mike was also traumatized by the early sexual abuse by his relationship with his aunt, which made for a rather bad foundation for relationships with women. Jan's relationship with her brother was interrupted by her brother's drug use. The same happened with Jan's relationship with her first husband, who also used drugs. It appears that one of the only ways that Jan could relate to her first husband was through the use of drugs. It was not until her first marriage ended that she also discontinued her own use of controlled substances as well.

With regard to the conceptualization of Mike and Jan from a personality standpoint, Mike appears to be more of an antisocial personality, with some clear indication of law-breaking patterns in the past. While this is primarily due to his substance abuse, there is indication that Mike is more prone to taking social risks than Jan. Mike's behavior also is clearly, in our opinion, self-destructive. He is a very dependent type of individual whose dependency exacerbates when it involves intimate relationships. Michael strikes us as having been depressed for a significant portion of his life, and was likely to have begun self-medicating out of the pain that he experienced from his depression at a young age. Much of Mike's cognitions appear to be based on distortions that developed from his upbringing; this would be a very important aspect to pursue during an individual assessment. There is likely to be other schemas about self-protection and danger, as well as any shortcomings about relating to others on an intimate level.

With respect to Jan's personality, she appears to be more of the caretaker, and takes responsibility for others. She is likely to have low self-esteem, and compensates for her low sense of self-worth by being the responsible one in relationships and taking care of others (i.e., her brother, her husbands, etc.). This may also be the way she maintains power and control in relationships. Jan's behavioral response is likely to work harder when tensions mount and escalate, but in a sense may be prone to miss the fact that the harder she works, the less likely things will change in the relationship. In many respects, Jan's behaviors may tend to undermine trust, because of her tendency to take on too much responsibility in relationships. It is also likely that this has led to depression for her, for which she admits to having sought treatment 20 years ago.

With regard to Jan's cognitions, it is very likely that she struggles with her self-worth and self-esteem in relationships and the association with taking responsibility. There is probably a great deal of fear with regard to support systems falling apart in her life if she does not remain in control. There may also be some underlying need for her to subject herself to situations where she continues to be shortchanged (i.e., violated trust with fidelity, husband's relapse to substance abuse, etc.).

As with any relationship, there are always strengths that exist in a marriage, despite the condition of the relationship. With regard to this case, some of the perceived strengths have to do with Jan and Mike's desire to remain together. There appears to be a basic respect for the union of matrimony, as well as the needs that they do fulfill for each other. Mike and Jan report that during times that they are not arguing, they do get along well together, and participate in household chores and duties as a team. In cognitive-behavior therapy, one of the important questions that is asked of couples as well as families during the assessment period is, "What works well in your relationship?" It is our belief that by focusing on what does function well in any relationship, a therapist can learn about certain aspects that are causing dysfunction and what can be done to help the couple rectify their conflicts. In this particular case, we would be more pointed in our questioning with Mike and Jan about what works well in the relationship and their perceptions as to why certain aspects work well. We are of the belief that most successful relationships do not occur by accident, and that there are strengths that exist within every relationship. In the process of treatment, then we would incorporate some of the mechanisms of these strengths and attempt to reinforce them by interweaving them into other areas. For example, we would take the reported activity in which both claim to clear out the horse stalls together harmoniously and function as a good team with regard to chores around the house. Perhaps part of the reason they get along so well in these activities is that the focus is directed away from their relationship and onto something else. As cognitive-behavior therapists, we would begin to have Mike and Jan look at each other's perceptions about this issue and then deal with Jan's reported frustration with Mike being "undependable." Focusing on schemas and specific expectations of each other in the relationship is a cornerstone of the cognitive-behavioral approach.

Treatment Goals

It is our belief that goals of treatment always need to be made collaboratively with the couple. It is important that the therapist have input into this; however, the therapist must be cautious not to superimpose his or her own belief about what goals are important without the collaboration and consent of the couple. In this respect, some of the long-term goals may be to achieve relationship harmony, whereby both spouses can remain content with each other and develop the communication and problem-solving skills to deal effectively with the repeated issues that arise. One of the long-term goals in this case might be to educate

Mike and Jan to the notion that relationships are difficult and require a great deal of work. Somehow it comes across to us that this is something that they have fallen short to recognize, and that their expectations that the relationship should fly on its own is a faulty assumption under which they have operated for many years. In addition, some of the long-range goals would be to contain their substance use and help them maintain sobriety. Also, we would want to address some of the dependency issues in the relationship, as well as to address with each partner some of the issues that stem back to their respective families of origin (i.e., Mike's early sexual abuse, his relationship with his parents, Jan's family relationship and her need to assume responsibility).

It is here that some of the more specific schema work would occur. For example, we may help Jan examine her schema that she needs to maintain the role of the caretaker in order for the relationship to function adequately. This is clearly a belief system that developed during her earlier years with her family of origin. Much of our work would be to help Jan see how this schema is causing problems in her marriage to Mike and learn how to challenge the schema in order to restructure it.

Some of the short-term goals might be to better define some of the problems in the relationship as well as the stated objectives. Second of all, we would want to assess whether or not these objectives are realistic, and how both Mike and Jan assess their own capability to change and how much of the problem is unlikely to change. We strongly support the concept proposed by Jacobson and Christensen (1996) regarding acceptance in relationships. We are firm believers that couples need to accept that which is unlikely to change as a measure of mediation and learn how to cope with the situation as an "unchangeable" entity.

In addition, another short-term goal might be to help each partner become aware of their respective schemas about the relationship and address issues of expectations, attributions and identifying distortions in their thinking, as was done with Jan above. Intermixed with these short-term goals would be targeting difficulties in communication, problem-solving, and dealing with unrealistic expectations of each other.

One of the ways to measure progress is always to take the couple's emotional temperature with regard to their day-to-day activity. Cognitive-behavior therapists also use the same aforementioned inventories and questionnaires in order to track progress. For example, the Marital Attitude Survey (MAS) by Pretzer et al. (1991) can be used as a continuous measure of assessing attributions in Mike and Jan's own behaviors as well as each other's. A combination of additional inventories may include the Dyadic Adjustment Scale as well as the Marital Happiness Scale and the Marital Satisfaction Inventory (MSI) (Snyder, 1981). Couple scores can be plotted out on a profile sheet together in order to compare the perceptions of the difficulties and progress in the relationship as it progresses in treatment.

Treatment Success

Determining whether or not therapy is successful in many respects is always difficult. It is always not as easy as simply measuring it on self-report inventories, since sometimes these measures fail to capture the emotional tenure, and more importantly, whether or not the real meat of the issue has been resolved or whether the clinician is simply seeing a veneer that involves a honeymoon period of initial relief. Obviously, as with anything else, the "proof is in the pudding." The real indicator will be time and incidences of relapse of the initial problems reported. Therefore, aside from the aforementioned measures and inventories, the most important indicator is the feedback that the clinician receives from the couple. Clinicians need to develop an intuitive sense of feel that will allow them to often take the "pulse" of the couple and make a determination as to whether or not things are progressing in therapy. Oddly enough, oftentimes couples who drop out of treatment spontaneously sometimes do so for reasons of improvement. In a private survey that we took of couples that dropped out of treatment, more than 50% of them responded by saying that they decided to discontinue treatment because things were going well and they feared a backslide if they continued to "push the matter any further." Most times, however, success is defined by the couples' reporting that their life is being managed more smoothly without any major events to distract them from the issues.

For cognitive-behavior therapists, when we are able to determine that couples are examining their automatic thoughts and intervening with distorted belief systems to change maladaptive behavior, this is usually a very strong sign of success. This also provides us with a measure to improve communication and problem-solving, which is also an excellent indicator that progress has been made.

Techniques and Interventions

There are a number of techniques and interventions that are used with standard cognitive-behavior therapy. An extensive list can be found in a number of comprehensive works currently in the literature (Baucom & Epstein, 1990; Dattilio, 1998; Dattilio & Padesky, 1990). Below is a highlight of several of the more commonly used techniques.

Behavioral Interventions

The major forms of behavioral interventions include communications training, problem-solving training, and behavioral change agreements which are designed to increase exchanges of positive behaviors and decrease negative exchanges.

Communications Training

Communications training is probably one of the behavioral techniques most widely used by couples therapists, regardless of their psychotherapeutic orientation. This specific goal of communications training is to increase the couple's skills in expressing their thoughts and emotions clearly, listening to other's messages effectively, and sending constructive rather than aversive messages. In the case of Mike and Jan, clearly communications training is something that would eventually be addressed during the course of treatment. Such techniques may begin with minor clarification and reflective listening techniques and build more gradually to exercises that would allow them to express their emotions and thoughts more clearly to each other. It may also be prudent to teach Mike and Jan specific training in expressive listening skills as outlined by Guerney (1977) or those specific exercises outlined in Markman, Stanley, and Blumberg (1994).

In addition to reducing misunderstanding between Mike and Jan, the use of expressive listening skills would also aid in reducing the emotional intensity of conflict during their discussions, thus broadening the scope of their perceptions with each other.

Problem-Solving Training

This technique usually constitutes a special type of communication that couples can use to identify specific problems in their relationship that require a solution. The problem-solving training helps couples both to generate a potential solution that is feasible and attractive to both parties, and to implement a designated solution. An example of this might be used with regard to the incident where Mike fell asleep while attending a party at his friend's home. Helping both partners go back, in a nonemotional fashion, to review the situation and take a look at some of the steps that Mike may have considered in solving the problem may help them apply the same to situations that would occur in the future.

Typically, specific steps in problem-solving training include 1) achieving a clear and specific definition of the problem in terms of behaviors that are not occurring, 2) generating one or more specific behavioral solutions to the problem, using a creative brainstorming strategy without evaluating one's own ideas, and 3) evaluating each alternative solution that has been proposed and identifying advantages and disadvantages to the solution. A final step, 4) usually involves agreeing on a trial period for implementing this solution and evaluating its effectiveness (Dattilio et al., 1998).

Behavior Change Agreements

Formal behavioral contracts were more prominent in behavioral couples therapy during the early introduction in the 1960–1970s. This included devising homework assignments that couples agreed to carry out between sessions as a measure to incur change. Even though such behavioral contracts are not so rigidly adhered to in contemporary cognitive-behavior therapy, it is not uncommon to end therapy sessions with an agreement specifying what behaviors will be addressed in enacting change during the therapeutic sessions.

With Mike and Jan, contract agreements may be more verbal than written, and may be accessed to help each other target specific behavioral changes that need to occur. For example, one assignment may include having Mike and Jan agree to be more conscientious about engaging in behaviors that would be less inclined to exclude each other in their day-to-day routines.

Another type of behavioral change agreement may involve focus on increasing the couple's positive shared activities. It is well documented in the literature that distressed couples commonly complain of a lack of intimacy and little positive time together. Whether or not the current lack of shared time and activities is a result of the couple's negative feelings towards each other, or to competing demands on their time due to job or social activities, the therapist may want to discuss these issues and the role that continued behavioral disengagement would have on maintaining their lack of intimacy.

Cognitive Interventions

Cognitive restructuring techniques are equally utilized for changing dysfunctional interaction patterns between couples. Cognitive interventions are designed to specifically increase family members' skills at monitoring and testing the validity and appropriateness of their own cognitions. The issue of appropriateness is often relevant when one individual holds a standard to which the other will probably not be able to relate in the manner that the individual will find satisfactory. Cognitive interventions are usually blended with behavioral interventions, but may also be the primary focus of all of the therapy sessions, depending on the specific situation.

With Mike and Jan, it may be necessary to shift temporarily to sole cognitive exploration and intervention from a primary focus on behavior when it appears that their interactions are being affected by their cognitive responses. A perfect example of this is situations in which Mike may be engaging in certain behaviors that appear accidental when, in fact, they are a means of passive-aggressive expression of his anger. Thus, more than a focus on simple behaviors, the therapist may want to specifically zero in on any specific schemas that Mike may have with regard to his anger or resentment for Jan.

Identifying Automatic Thoughts

Increasing a couple's ability to monitor their automatic thoughts is a prerequisite for modifying distorted or inappropriate cognitions. Automatic thoughts are typically defined as thoughts that occur spontaneously about certain life circumstances which include the relationship interaction. They are often stereotyped and biased, and may either be negative or positive, but in most conflictual situations, they are negative. One of the early objectives of cognitive interventions is to help couples to develop skills that identify automatic thoughts (including visual images) that may spontaneously flash through their minds. These are other cognitions that can trigger charged emotional responses and negative behaviors towards each other. Thus, Mike and Jan may be encouraged to keep track of their automatic thoughts, particularly during times of conflict. One method used for maintaining a track of automatic thoughts is the use of the Dysfunctional Thought Record (Beck, Rush, Shaw, & Emery, 1979). This specific form was designed to help individuals link their automatic thoughts to their emotion and distortions in which they may be engaging, so that they may weigh the evidence that substantiates their current thought and consider whether or not an alternative explanation may be used. This would set the prelude to help Jan and Mike begin to restructure their thinking, particularly in situations in which they are engaging in cognitive distortions.

The following is an example of both Jan and Mike's potential automatic thoughts:

Automatic Thought	Emotion	Cognitive Distortion
Jan's automatic thought Mike only gives a damn about his computers. I have no place in his life.	Angry, rejected	Arbitrary inference and all-or-nothing thinking
Mike's automatic thought Jan is so condescending she makes me feel like a child.	Depressed, resentful	Personalization and selective abstraction

This sets the prelude for Mike and Jan to begin to weigh the evidence that exists, and see whether or not it is insufficient to support any strong conclusions about the way they feel. This will set the pace for them to later weigh and question the evidence, and gather either more or new evidence in the process of reframing their views and responding in a different fashion. It is important, when helping couples to engage in cognitive restructuring, that they learn to rely on solid evidence to support the correction of distorted or inappropriate cognitions. What's more, it is important for them to see the link between their cognitions and their emotions and how this affects the way in which they behave. By collecting substantial evidence and reframing the situation, it allows individuals to weigh contrasting information against both their current thoughts and their longstanding schemas. This typically takes a great deal of coaching, which would probably constitute a great deal of the course of treatment with Mike and Jan.

Pitfalls and Limits

Some of the potential pitfalls that may occur in a case such as Mike and Jan's would most likely be substance relapse. We are fairly convinced that Mike's substance dependency is very strong, and that there are a number of enabling behaviors in which Jan is engaging that may contribute to Mike's relapse, in addition to Mike's own issues.

It would be very important for us to be able to identify some of those issues, since they are likely to be very subtle and perhaps even unconscious to some respect. This would require looking more closely at some of the patterns of interaction, particularly Mike's prior history of relapse and what distortions and automatic thoughts were involved. Another area that would need to be addressed would center around what happens with Jan, and how she changes in the relationship when Mike is experiencing periods of sobriety. As mentioned before, we suspect that both of these individuals have difficulty with intimacy, so the question remains whether or not in some way part of Mike's relapse to substance use may be an inadvertent way of dealing with or avoiding intimacy in the relationship. Certainly this would need to be addressed or continued relapse may occur.

Another potential pitfall is the issues of limits and boundaries with this couple. This is an area that has not been defined very well in this relationship. For example, the issue involving Mike's decision to attend Jennifer's party alone and then falling asleep and not calling Jan ahead of time suggests a major problem with boundaries and basic respect for each other. Once again, this may also have its roots in passive-aggressive behavior on Mike's part, which would need to be explored more in detail. The use of a technique known as Socratic Questioning may lead to Mike's underlying anger or resentment for Jan.

Areas to avoid addressing in treatment initially might be Mike's early sexual abuse by his aunt. While this is something that certainly needs to be addressed at some point in the treatment process, the question remains as to whether or not it is best to address this in conjoint or individual psychotherapy. As a rule of thumb, we like to avoid separating couples after the initial assessment, since it can prove to have some negative effect on the clinician's role in dealing with the couple. It is important that the couple perceive the therapist as remaining balanced throughout the treatment process; to split off and work with one on more than an individual basis sometimes causes questions of loyalty on the part of each spouse. There is also an issue as to what extent the limits of confidentiality exist, particularly if Mike or Jan request that specific issues not be addressed in conjoint sessions.

Inclusion of Other Family Members

With regard to the question of who else would be included in the particular sessions, that depends on whether or not any family-of-origin work would be utilized. For the most part, sessions would include Mike and Jan exclusively in conjoint sessions. However, on occasions when issues regarding family of origin are paramount and directly affecting the relationship, we often consider conducting family-of-origin meetings. The way this works follows closely along with the specific modality of transgeneration therapy (Framo, 1992). In this respect, separate sessions with Mike and Jan and their respective families of origin would be held, but would only include those members of the family of origin. For example, if some issues needed to be addressed in Jan's family of origin, separate visits would be held with Jan, her brother, and her two parents. In these sessions, Mike would not be present, nor would any other individuals, such as Jan's brothers' wives or any paramours. The intention of these visits would be to address some of the unfinished business that each partner experienced with regard to their family of origin and then later providing for some food for discussion in the relationship. In this particular case, it appears that Mike would be the individual who might require some family-of-origin meetings, particularly with respect to some of his anger and unmet dependency needs that occurred during his upbringing. This would be something that would need to be addressed with both Mike and Jan, and agreed upon in advance. Likewise, the same would also be offered to Jan and her family of origin as well if needed.

Homework

Homework is a very important part of cognitive-behavior therapy, since the skills that are acquired in treatment need to be ingrained through learning assignments. Research on cognitive-behavior therapy has indicated that clients who engaged in homework learning tasks displayed greater and faster improvement than those who did not (Persons, Burns, & Perloff, 1988; Primakoff, Epstein, & Covi, 1986).

The rationale for assigning homework is that individuals learn best by doing. Homework assignments can facilitate small changes in one or more of the areas discussed above in order to lead to some of the larger changes that may need to occur.

Basically, there are two types of homework assignments in cognitive-behavior therapy. The first is observational assignments, which include noticing and writing down feelings and automatic thoughts and beliefs and keeping track of positive gains or problem behaviors. It may also involve observing one's spouse to notice similarities or differences in behavioral speaking patterns, and keeping a timed journal to see if patterns exist and if they are tied to times of the day, specific activities, or moods.

Experimental learning tasks, on the other hand, are as varied as couples' problems themselves. These include such assignments as trying out new behaviors or communication styles and recording the outcome. It may also involve completing an automatic thought record and seeing whether this reduces the distressing emotion; changing the time of the day or conditions under which a certain interaction occurs; and asking the couple to try out new problem-solving strategies.

Homework assignments may be given individually or to the couple conjointly, and they involve thoughts, feelings, behaviors, biology, or involvement. Whatever the assignment, however, it should be collaboratively designed to relevant issues with the couples' problems, and be assigned in the majority of the therapy sessions.

Homework assignments are critical for achieving the goals of changing beliefs and building new skills. It is important for the therapist and client to be aware that it may require continued practice or experimentation over a period of time before any reliable change is observed.

In the case of Mike and Jan, one of the homework assignments may be to have the couple practice listening to each other without interrupting prematurely and take note of how they feel after they receive some indication that the other has heard what they had to say.

At times, homework assignments are not completed by the couple for various reasons. Time compliance is usually an indication that there is some resistance or difficulty with the specific assignment. Therapists can also contribute to homework noncompliance by either assigning too much homework, or not choosing homework that is relevant to the couple's primary concerns.

Despite the fact that homework may be appropriately chosen and integrated with the treatment process, the couple may still not complete it. In such cases, it is important for the therapist and clients to understand what may be precluding the homework's completion and addressing these issues directly. This is also "grist for the mill" in the sense that the thoughts and beliefs about homework assignments can be processed during the course of treatment.

Timeline for Therapy

Timelines always vary, of course, depending on the couple and the nature of the problem. With a case such as Mike and Jan's, we would expect that therapy would last for at least a 6-month period. This would include seeing them on a weekly basis for the first 2 months and then, depending on the progress obtained, tapering the visits off to every 10 days to 2-week intervals. By the end of treatment, monthly meetings are typically planned, with a follow-up session 2 months later which may be conducted on the telephone or in person.

In addition, some individual sessions may be conducted; however, once again this is only true in a case where a matter of confidentiality exists. More importantly, we like to refer spouses of couples to their own individual therapy if needed, since we never know when we are going to need to resume our position as a couples therapist, and want to avoid any kind of side relationship that may affect the course of couples treatment.

In our opinion, it is extremely important for the therapist to remain in a neutral role. Anything that can and may be perceived as a bias or siding with a particular partner is something that should be avoided. This also goes for telephone calls that we receive in between sessions from one spouse with the request of not divulging the content of the call to the other spouse. In order to avoid such complications, we make it a standard practice to initially review a set of guidelines with couples. One of these guidelines includes not receiving any telephone calls outside of the therapeutic session from the spouses unless their mate is on the other end of the extension. We explain in the initial assessment that it is important that we maintain a balance in treatment and that accepting telephone calls outside of context may disrupt that balance. We also state that telephone calls will be received jointly if in the case of an emergency; however, we prefer that couples wait until the conjoint session to bring the issue into treatment.

Termination and Relapse Prevention

We consider termination and relapse prevention to be one of the most important aspects of treatment. If termination or some type of inoculation to prevent a relapse from occurring is not addressed, there is a good chance that the relationship will once again deteriorate. Termination is an aspect of treatment that is usually collaborative between the couple and the therapist. Even though the therapist may recommend against premature termination, the couple obviously still has the power to terminate if they so desire. Typically, we address issues of termination very early in the treatment process, in order to prepare couples for the time when the close of treatment is near. This is done with the attempt to avoid any premature termination which often occurs when couples feel that they are doing quite well. We usually explain to couples that it is extremely important to follow through with the treatment process, even if they think that they don't need to continue. This is particularly true with respect to discussing how to prevent any relapse and instilling the idea that both will follow the regime that they have learned during the course of treatment. We often explain that it is a natural occurrence for individuals to become remiss over time, in employing the many strategies and techniques that they have learned for keeping the relationship alive. Most of the prevention relapse is centered around how to avoid slipping back into old dysfunctional thought and behavioral patterns, and how each partner can monitor and take their own emotional temperature in the relationship.

With regard to Mike and Jan, there is some indication that they could prematurely discontinue treatment once their situation has improved. Periodically, throughout the case history, there was indication that at times Mike and Jan felt that they didn't need treatment when things were going well and it was only after a most recent crisis that the two of them jointly decided to seek help. Therefore, it would be extremely important with Mike and Jan to be very concrete with them in the beginning and almost request that they sign a behavioral contract dissuading them from prematurely terminating treatment and following through with all of the relapse-prevention techniques planned. A contract, of course, is never any guarantee; however, it is an important aspect of the cognitive-behavioral repertoire.

Relapse prevention has been a major focus of research in clinical practice in the last several decades (Marlatt & Gordon, 1985). This is particularly so where addictive behaviors are involved.

Because it provides structured learning, the cognitive-behavioral approach is ideally suited to help prevent relapse. In the final phase of therapy, the therapist and couple can review the strategies, learning new problem-solving steps for handling future difficulties. This may involve providing them with a variety of problem scenarios similar to the ones handled in therapy and ask the couple to demonstrate how they would manage these issues should they arise in the future. This type of brainstorming and foresight has been proven to be very successful in the course of couples treatment.

An additional step to help maintain treatment gains is to schedule follow-up booster sessions. The couple can be invited to make one or more appointments for 6 months following the end of regularly scheduled therapy. This is regardless of whether or not the couple continues to do well during the course of treatment. Such reinforcement and reviewing skills and patterns maintain the relationship's success and serve to avoid any potential toward relapse.

REFERENCES

Azrin, N. H., Naster, B. J., & Jones, R. (1973). A rapid learning based procedure for marital counseling. *Behavior Research and Therapy, 11,* 365–382.

Baucom, D. H. (1987). Attributions in distressed relations: How can we explain them? In S. Duck & D. Perlman (Eds.), *Heterosexual relations, marriage and divorce* (pp. 177–206). London: Sage.

*Baucom, D. H., & Epstein, N. (1990). *Cognitive-behavioral marital therapy*. New York: Brunner/Mazel.

Baucom, D. H., Epstein, N., Rankin, L. A., & Burnett, C. K. (1996a). Assessing relationship standards: The Inventory of Specific Relationship Standards. *Journal of Family Psychology, 10,* 209–222.

Baucom, D. H., Epstein, N., Rankin, L. A., & Burnett, C. K. (1996b). Understanding and treating marital distress from a cognitive-behavioral orientation. In K. S. Dobson & K. D. Craig (Eds.), *Advances in cognitive-behavioral therapy* (pp. 210–236). Thousand Oaks, CA: Sage.

Baucom, D. H., Epstein, N., Sayers, S., & Sher, T. G. (1989). The role of cognitions in marital relationships: Definitional, methodological, and conceptual issues. *Journal of Consulting and Clinical Psychology, 57,* 31–38.

Beck, A. T. (1988). *Love is never enough*. New York: Harper & Row.

Beck, A. T. (1991). Cognitive therapy: A 30 year retrospective. *American Psychologist, 46,* 368–375.

Beck, A. T., Rush, J. A., Shaw, B. F., & Emery, G. (1979). *Cognitive therapy of depression*. New York: Guilford Press.

Christensen, A. (1988). Dysfunctional interaction patterns in couples. In P. Noller & M. A. Fitzpatrick (Eds.), *Perspectives on marital interaction* (pp. 31–52). Clevedon, England: Multilingual Matters.

Dattilio, F. M. (1989). A guide to cognitive marital therapy. In P. A. Keller & S. R. Heyman (Eds.), *Innovations in clinical practice: A source book* (Vol. 8, pp. 27–42). Sarasota, FL: Professional Resource Press.

*Dattilio, F. M. (1998). (Ed.). *Case studies in couples and family therapy: Systemic and cognitive perspectives*. New York: Guilford Press.

*Dattilio, F. M., & Padesky, C. A. (1990). *Cognitive therapy with couples*. Sarasota, FL: Professional Resource Press.

Dattilio, F. M., Epstein, N. B., & Baucom, D. H. (1998). An introduction to cognitive behavioral therapy with couples and families. In F. M. Dattilio (Ed.), *Case studies in couple & family therapy: Systemic and cognitive perspectives* (pp. 1–36). New York: Guilford Press.

Eidelson, R. J., & Epstein, N. (1982). Cognition and relationship maladjustment: Development of a measure of dysfunctional relationship beliefs. *Journal of Consulting and Clinical Psychology, 50,* 715–720.

Epstein, N. (1986). Cognitive marital therapy: Multilevel assessment and intervention. *Journal of Rational-Emotive Therapy, 4,* 68–81.

Epstein, N., & Baucom, D. H. (1993). Cognitive factors in marital disturbance. In K. S. Dobson & P. C. Kendell (Eds.), *Psychology and cognition* (pp. 351–385). San Diego: Academic Press.

Fincham, F. D., Bradbury, T. N., & Scott, C. K. (1990). Cognition in marriage. In F. D. Fincham & T. N. Bradbury (Eds.), *The psychology of marriage: Basic issues and applications* (pp. 118–149). New York: Guilford Press.

Framo, J. (1992). *Family-of-Origin Therapy: An Intergenerational Approach*. New York: Brunner/Mazel.

*Suggested reading.

Gottman, J. M. (1993b). *What predicts divorce? The relationship between marital processes and marital outcomes.* Hillsdale, NJ: Erlbaum.

Gottman, J. M. (1993a). The roles of conflict engagement, escalation, and avoidance in marital interaction: A longitudinal view of five types of couples. *Journal of Consulting and Clinical Psychology, 61,* 6–15.

Guerney, B. G., Jr. (1977). *Relationship enhancement.* San Francisco: Jossey-Bass.

Jacobson, N. S., & Christensen, A. (1996). *Integrative couple therapy.* New York: Norton.

Jacobson, N. S., & Margolin, G. (1979). *Marital therapy: Strategies based on social learning and behavior exchange principles.* New York: Brunner/Mazel.

Liberman, R. P. (1970). Behavioral approaches to couple and family therapy. *American Journal of Orthopsychiatry, 40,* 106–118.

Margolin, G., Christensen, A., & Weiss, R. L. (1975). Contracts, cognition and change: A behavioral approach to marriage therapy. *Counseling Psychologist, 5,* 15–25.

Margolin, G., & Weiss, R. L. (1978). Comparative evaluation of therapeutic components associated with behavioral marital treatments. *Journal of Consulting and Clinical Psychology, 4b,* 1476–1486.

Markman, H. J., Stanley, S., & Blumberg, S. L. (1994). *Fighting for your marriage.* San Francisco: Jossey-Bass.

Marlatt, A., & Gordon, J. (Eds.). (1985). *Relapse prevention: Maintenance strategies in addictive behavior change.* New York: Guilford Press.

O'Leary, K. D., & Turkewitz, H. (1978). Marital therapy from a behavioral perspective. In T. J. Paolino & B. S. McCrady (Eds.), *Marriage and marital therapy: Psychoanalytic, behavioral and systems theory perspectives* (pp. 240–297). New York: Brunner/Mazel.

Persons, J. B., Burns, D. D., & Perloff, J. M. (1988). Predictors of dropout and outcome in cognitive therapy for depression in a private practice setting. *Cognitive Therapy and Research, 12,* 557–575.

Pretzer, J. L., Epstein, N., & Fleming, B. (1991). The Marital Attitude Survey: A measure of dysfunctional attributions and expectancies. *Journal of Cognitive Psychotherapy, 5,* 131–148.

Primakoff, L., Epstein, N., & Covi, L. (1986). Homework compliance: An uncontrolled variable in cognitive therapy outcome research. *Behavior Therapy, 17,* 443–446.

Snyder, D. K. (1981). *Marital Satisfaction Inventory (MSI) Manual.* Los Angeles: Western Psychological Services.

Spanier, G. B. (1976). Measuring dyadic adjustment: New scales for assessing the quality of marriage and similar dyads. *Journal of Marriage and the Family, 38,* 15–28.

Stuart, R. B. (1969). Operant-interpersonal treatment for marital discord. *Journal of Consulting and Clinical Psychology, 33,* 675–682.

Stuart, R. B. (1980). *Helping couples change: A social learning approach to marital therapy.* New York: Guilford Press.

Thibaut, J. W., & Kelley, H. H. (1959). *The social psychology of groups.* New York: Wiley.

Weiss, R. L., & Heyman, R. E. (1990). Observation of marital interaction. In F. D. Fincham & T. N. Bradbury (Eds.), *The psychology of marriage* (pp. 87–117). New York: Guilford Press.

Weiss, R. L., Hops, H., & Patterson, G. R. (1973). A framework for conceptualizing marital conflict, a technology for altering it, some data for evaluating it. In L. A.

Hamerlynck, L. L. C. Handy, & E. J. Mash (Eds.), *Behavior change: Methodology, concepts, and practice* (pp. 309–342). Champaign, IL: Research Press.

SUGGESTED READING

Epstein, N., & Schlesinger, S. E. (1994). Couples problems. In F. M. Dattilio & A. Freeman (Eds.), *Cognitive-behavioral strategies in crisis intervention* (pp. 258–277). New York: Guilford Press.

PART IV

INTEGRATIVE THEORIES

10

Emotionally Focused Couples Therapy

Susan Johnson

TREATMENT MODEL

In the last decade the landscape of couples therapy has changed dramatically. Emotionally Focused Couples Therapy (EFT) has reflected and been part of that change. The key landmarks in the present landscape are:

- A new understanding of the nature of marital distress that stresses the importance of emotional responses and particular negative cycles of interaction. As John Gottman, the main contributor to this new understanding, has pointed out, EFT is entirely consonant with this new research (Gottman, Coan, Carrere, & Swanson, 1998). A central strength of EFT is, then, that it is on target in terms of contemporary thinking in couples theory and research. It appears to address the factors that determine whether a relationship will be satisfying and durable.
- In the recent couples literature, there is a new interest in and respect for emotion as a positive organizing force in human functioning (LeDoux, 1994) and in systemic therapies (Johnson & Greenberg, 1998). EFT was named to reflect the traditional humanistic belief in the power of emotion in the change process. At that time, in the early 1980s, specified interventions in couples therapy seemed to be almost entirely concerned with changing behavior or creating cognitive insight. Emotion is now receiving more attention and being viewed as a guide to adaptive behavior, rather than as inherently irrational and problematic (Damasio, 1994; Greenberg & Safran, 1987; Johnson & Greenberg, 1994).

- A major focus on brief, systematic interventions and a continuing need to be able to substantiate the effects of therapy with empirical data. Interventions in EFT are specified, and are also placed in the context of the stages of change and the nine steps in the therapeutic process (Johnson, 1996; Greenberg & Johnson, 1988). There is considerable evidence for the effectiveness of EFT, both subsequent to treatment and at follow-up, the longest follow-up being 2 years. These effects are superior to improvement rates quoted in the general couples therapy literature (Johnson, Hunsley, Greenberg, & Schindler, 1999).

- Another key landmark involves the continuing recognition of the need for a theory that will provide the "conceptual coherence one would expect from an advancing discipline" (Bergin & Garfield, 1994, p. 822). Although postmodern theorists have suggested (Hoffman, 1998) that couples and family therapists do not need a model to guide their interventions, therapists continue to seek maps for the territory of human relationships and to struggle to explain the patterns they observe in close relationships in some systematic way. EFT uses attachment theory as a frame for understanding adult love relationships (Bowlby, 1969, 1988; Johnson, 1986; Johnson & Whiffen, 1999). This theory suggests that although close relationships can vary widely according to culture and context, there are certain universals wired into human beings, and the need for safe contact with responsive others is one of them. This theory has a rich and expanding research base to support it, linking the quality of attachment to other variables of current interest, such as resilience and physical and mental health (Lyons-Ruth, 1996; Mikulincer, Florian, & Weller, 1993). Attachment is the most promising map we have of couples and family relationships, and one that has concrete applications to couple and family therapy (Diamond & Siqueland, 1995; Johnson, 1999; Kobak, Ruckdeschel, & Hazan, 1994).

Attachment theory also parallels the feminist literature in that it depathologises dependency needs and validates the desire for emotional responsiveness that is often of particular concern to female partners. Attachment theory includes a focus on the pivotal role of emotion in close relationships and is compatible with systems theory. (Marvin & Stewart, 1990)

- A new awareness of the need for a collaborative alliance with partners in intimate relationships, an alliance where the therapist walks with clients rather than providing "treatment" from an expert distance. Kierkegaard's maxim (1948) that to help someone it is necessary to "make sure one finds where the other is and start there," and his belief that is necessary to let clients teach helpers about his or her own reality, fits well with the stance of the therapist in EFT. The present zeitgeist to "give back therapy to the people you serve" (Reimers & Treacher, 1995) echoes the principles of Rogers (1951) and the humanistic movement of which EFT is a part. New postmodern approaches to therapy (Anderson, 1997) echo Rogers' belief in the power of validation and the necessity of showing respect for how clients construe their world.

The basic premises of EFT have been discussed elsewhere (Johnson, 1998; Johnson & Greenberg, 1995; Johnson, 1996). Briefly, they are that:

1. The therapist moves between inner and outer realities that are seen as providing the context for and generating each other; so a client's sense of helplessness spurs his withdrawal from his wife and the cycle of his withdrawal and his wife's aggressive response then feeds his helplessness
2. Emotion organizes interactions between intimates and is an essential feature in the process of change
3. Couples who come for therapy are involved in a struggle for secure attachment and are caught in the protest, clinging, and depression that characterize separation distress

The focus of this chapter will be on what EFT looks like in practice.

A fly on the wall of an EFT therapy session would see the therapist following and leading, reflecting and expanding emotional experiences with both partners, and setting up interactive tasks that invite the couple into new kinds of conversations. These conversations move partners, step by step, from their rigid interactive stances, for example pursue/withdraw, and enable them to become more accessible and responsive to each other. Accessibility and responsiveness are the two building blocks of secure attachment. The therapist is a process consultant who joins the partners dance and moves with the partners to foster safe emotional engagement and secure attachment. EFT is usually completed in 12 to 15 sessions; more sessions may be necessary if relationship distress is complicated by factors such as depression or post-traumatic stress issues (Johnson & Williams-Keeler, 1998). The major contraindication for the practice of EFT is physical abuse (Johnson, 1996).

Stages of Change

1. *De-escalation of the negative cycle that maintains attachment insecurity.* This stage has four treatment steps: joining and assessment; formulating the negative cycle; linking underlying emotions to each person's stance in the cycle; and framing the problem in terms of the cycle that traps both partners in their insecurities. Step by step, the couple become more open and less reactive to each

other. They may begin to spend more time together and to make love. However, there are still unresolved issues and specific attachment injuries and sensitivities (Johnson & Whiffen, 1999) that sway the couple's interactions in a negative direction.

2. *Helping both partners to shift their interactional positions to facilitate secure attachment.* During the second stage, withdrawn partners are supported to clarify and articulate their reluctance to engage and to become more active in defining the relationship. As these partners explore their emotional experience, they are able to formulate what they need to become more accessible and responsive. A spouse might be able to tell his partner, "I am lonely too, but I cannot face your rage. It takes my skin off. It makes me raw. I want you to stop trying to nuke me. I want you to give me a chance to stand beside you." More aggressive blaming partners are able to risk expressing vulnerabilities and attachment needs in a way that pulls the other towards them and helps him/her respond. The treatment steps here involve the elaboration of attachment needs and hurts, helping the partner to respond to these needs and hurts, and helping spouses express these needs in a manner that creates safety and emotional engagement for both partners. This process culminates in identifiable change events, withdrawer reengagement, and blamer softening. Both spouses are then able to respond to each other in a manner that redefines the relationship as a safe haven and a secure base (Bowlby, 1969). The process of change has been examined empirically (Greenberg, Ford, Alden, & Johnson, 1995; Johnson & Greenberg, 1988) and change events specifically described and illustrated in the literature (Johnson 1996, 1999; Johnson & Greenberg, 1995).

3. *The treatment process is summarized in a manner that empowers the couple and consolidates the new responses that structure a more secure bond.* In this final stage of treatment, the couple now experience negative cycles as background rather than figure, as blips in the cycle of secure responsiveness that defines the relationship.

In terms of factors that predict success in therapy, engagement in the therapy process appears to be more predictive of outcome in EFT than initial distress level. EFT appears to be effective with inexpressive men, particularly older men (over 35), who are perhaps more aware of attachment issues. The quality of the therapeutic alliance and the female partner's initial trust level are important predictors of success in EFT (Johnson & Talitman, 1997). Emotional disengagement, particularly by the female partner, may be especially hard to deal with in couples therapy in general (Gottman, 1994).

THERAPIST SKILLS AND ATTRIBUTES

The EFT therapist has, above all, to be able to create safety, to empathically attune to both partners. This involves being able to inhabit each client's world for a moment and to suspend judgement. This is easier if one's model of therapy espouses a positive view of human nature and a belief in people's ability to change and grow. This stance of respect and acceptance allows partners to face, with the therapist standing beside them, what they could not face alone, or reveal to the other partner. Acceptance is one of the cornerstones of humanistic therapies, as is the genuineness and transparency of the therapist (Rogers, 1951). The therapist asks clients to teach him/her about their experience. The expertise of the therapist is that of a process consultant who has a meta-perspective on relationship patterns and therapy processes. The therapist and both partners collaborate together, leading and following in a process of mutual discovery. The culture of EFT parallels that of the newer postmodern approaches to therapy (Anderson, 1997) where therapy is a "shared inquiry" rather than a technology implemented by an all-knowing expert. The therapist has to be able to monitor the safety of the alliance and to openly and genuinely invite and respond to client challenges, corrections, questions, or comments. To help the couple create accessibility and responsiveness, the therapist has to also reflect these qualities. Therapy is then a genuine personal encounter. To stay responsive, the therapist must also be able to deal with the strong emotions that arise in attachment relationships and be comfortable allowing them to unfold in the session. In EFT training, this comfort is enhanced by a positive focus on emotion and an understanding of its role in change. As a student remarked, "Strong emotions are not so scary when I understand them and know what to do with them."

The therapist skills in EFT involve the tracking and expansion of experience, with a particular emphasis on emotion, and the restructuring of interactions (Johnson, 1996). Emotional responses are viewed as organizing perceptions and meaning schemas, and priming key responses to our partners. Emotion is the music of the attachment dance. The therapist reflects and validates emotional responses; often, in the beginning, these are secondary reactive responses, such as anger. By tracking a series of evocative questions, the therapist also expands this experience, accessing more primary emotions that are often unattended to or disowned, such as the hurt underlying rage. The therapist goes with the client to the leading edge of his/her experience, where this experience is perhaps difficult to formulate, and helps the client differentiate and articulate it. So anger unfolds into hopelessness and hopelessness unfolds into grief; an interaction centered around the expression of grief tends to be very different than an interaction centered around anger; grief also pulls for different responses from the partner. The therapist also heightens particular responses, bringing them into the limelight so that they add new elements to the dialogue. For example, heightening a partner's fear can create a new context for this partner's withdrawal which the other partner has seen as indifference or hostility. Heightening usually involves the use of repetition, images, metaphors, or enactments. The therapist also makes interpretations to clarify or formulate new meanings. These conjectures are as close to the client's experience as possible and made tentatively, with the client's help. So "dislike" may be formulated as "wanting to escape," which the client will then expand into "wanting to hide" and a sense of shame. The therapist invites each partner to direct clarified or expanded responses to his/her spouse, so shaping new interactions.

When shaping interactions, the EFT therapist tracks and reflects negative steps and sequences. The couple and the therapist identify the patterns that characterize their dance and any exceptions to those patterns. The therapist clarifies and heightens interactional sequences that defeat the couple's attempts at contact and caring. This allows for the perspective that "Both of us are caught in this cycle," rather than a "You are doing this to me" perspective. Partners begin to see how they unwittingly help create the other's distress and resulting negative responses. The therapist also restructures and shapes new interactions based upon expanded emotional responses; for example, encouraging a spouse to talk directly to his partner about the newly acknowledged fears that precede his distancing responses. At particular points in therapy, the therapist also choreographs particular change events, such as a softening, that redefine relationships. In the case of a softening, the therapist will support a partner to risk being vulnerable and to ask for a response to his/her attachment needs. These skills are presented in more detail, together with examples, elsewhere (Johnson, 1996, 1998).

THE CASE OF MIKE AND JAN

Instruments and Assessment Tools

I would ask Mike and Jan to complete the Dyadic Adjustment Scale (DAS, Spanier, 1976) to obtain a general sense of how they rate their level of distress compared to other couples and to each other. However, clinical interviews with the couple and an interview with each partner alone are the main assessment tool in EFT.

Mike and Jan describe the classic pattern of one partner criticizing and complaining while the other defends and distances. Gottman (1994) describes this pattern as apocalyptic for marriages. They now seem to be at the point where the pattern is changing into mutual withdrawal. This is usually the point at which many couples ask for help; perhaps because when the pursuing partner begins to withdraw and stop investing, the threat to the relationship becomes real and obvious to both partners. At this point, the pressure to find a way to reconnect or to move on to the next step of separation, namely detachment (Bowlby, 1969), tends to be obvious and compelling.

An EFT therapist like myself would begin by asking each partner to describe the problems in the relationship from his/her point of view. Reflection and validation would be used to structure the dialogue and create safety. With the couple's help, I would then piece together the patterns of Jan and Mike's interaction with each other and the moves of each partner in the relational dance. The effects of the pattern, in this case criticize/withdraw, on each of them and the connection between them would be explored. I would also discuss with Jan and Mike their goals for therapy; in this case, it appears that they have compatible goals and do not show any contraindications for EFT. For example, their relationship has never included violence or abuse. I would explicitly ask about this, especially since higher educational or job status in the wife and addiction in the husband are risk factors for physical abuse. I would also listen for landmark incidents, particularly disappointments and betrayals, such as Mike's not calling from the party, that impact how the relationship is defined. I would be interested, for example, in Jan's response to Mike's car accident and how they interacted around this incident. I would wonder what it is like for her to love someone who is so careless with his life.

I would also focus on the problems they have faced and the strengths they have found, as individuals and together, to overcome them. Both have been previously disappointed in relationships, yet they found the courage to try again. Both have struggled with addiction, and Jan has faced cancer. The EFT therapist deliberately creates an environment where both partners sense that they are seen and respected. From the first moment the concern is to create the therapy session as, to use John Bowlby's terms (1969), a safe haven and a secure base from which to explore the relationship. The creation of safety and the collaborative nature of the alliance may explain the exceeding low dropout rate that is found in studies of EFT and in clinical practice.

As Mike and Jan tell their story, respond to questions and, at my request, interact around specific issues, I gauge the reactivity of their responses, the rigidity of the positions they take with each other, and how open each one is to the therapists suggestions and inquiries. As an EFT therapist, I would also begin to elicit each partner's emotional experience of the relationship, and make hypotheses about how each has experienced the attachment between them. For example, evocative questions would be used to elicit what happens to Mike when Jan "nags" him. As the underlying emotions are articulated, the models of self and other and coping strategies also become clear. So, Mike might say, "I just feel battered. There is nothing I can do. I hear echoes of my relationship with my mum and I feel dumb. Like I'm never going to make it here; there is something wrong with me. I'll never get it right. I just give up and numb out." Even in the first session, if the therapist can create enough safety, partners can begin to clarify their experience in a new way and begin to put this experience in the context of the interactional cycle. Often, partners have been so absorbed with the external struggle with their spouse that they have not recognized key elements in their own experience of the relationship. This couple also appear to be typical of the kinds of couples we see in that Mike is concerned with lessening conflict, where he probably feels out of control and experiences a sense of failure or inadequacy, while the female partner, Jan, is concerned with connectedness, and most likely experiences loneliness and abandonment. When they are distressed, it is natural therefore for Mike to go to activities where he feels competent—his computer and his metalworking—and for Jan to seek connection with friends and her animals.

Using an attachment framework, I might ask Jan how she experiences the patterns in the relationship, and how she becomes caught in the position of critical blamer. EFT assumes that attachment needs are universal, albeit they can be expressed differently by different people, so I might ask Jan how she attempts to get close to Mike, and explore her experience of Mike's withdrawal from her and his relationship with alcohol. I would also be interested in Jan painting a picture of the times when she did feel close and supported and how Mike helped her trust him in the beginning of the relationship. A very brief attachment history is usually elicited from both partners, often in the form of questions about how each partner sought and received comfort in their family of origin and how they learned to cope with lack of responsiveness on the part of their attachment figures. Individual history is used in EFT to contextualize and validate partners' present responses; the therapist's primary focus, however, is on the present relationship.

The couple are also invited to interact around attachment-oriented issues in the initial sessions (usually, the first two couple sessions are designated as assessment). I might explore Jan's distress that Mike is so busy on weekends and ask her to help Mike understand this distress. Depending on the couple's response to this, I might, even in the first sessions, see if the couple could step beyond their usual way of relating and experiment with a different kind of contact. So if Jan, generally cool and critical, mentioned how lonely she was in a tearful voice, I might ask her to share this with Mike. If she cannot, or she changes the message, or if Mike responds negatively, I then have more of a sense of the pattern between them and the blocks to responsive open communication that exist in their relationship.

I would also see each partner for one individual session. This allows me to foster the alliance with each partner and to elicit information that may be difficult to discuss in the couple sessions. This includes information about how each perceives the other, competing relationships, and levels of commitment. These sessions also allow me to refine and elaborate on each partner's underlying emotions and attachment insecurities. In this case, I would like to explore with Jan her experience of being vulnerable when she was sick and if particular sensitivities remain that triggered in interactions with Mike. I would also explore Mike's experience of abuse and his relationship with his mother. The latter may be particularly salient in light of the fact that I am a female therapist. I would be particularly sensitive to any echoes of the abuse that occur for Mike in his relationship with Jan and any feelings of fear or shame. Neither partner gives the impression that they have experienced a secure attachment where they could depend on others. Jan gives the impression that to feel connected in her family she had to take care of others rather than be taken care of, and Mike's experience of attachment figures seems to be that he had to protect himself against his mother's criticalness and could not count on support from his father, who expected him to "get over" any distress. This couple resemble many of the couples in our research projects and clinical practice, and I would expect them to make good progress in EFT and to be able to repair their relationship to the point where they were no longer distressed.

Conceptualization of Mike and Jan

The EFT therapist might articulate the strengths of this couple in the following ways:

a. Mike has taken his addiction in hand and, a few years ago, Jan had been able to do the same. Now they have made the decision to take control of their relationship and learn how to create a better one. They obviously know how to fight for the kind of life and relationship they want.
b. After negative attachment experiences at home and with first marriages, they are still willing to risk and try for a new kind of relationship.
c. Mike knows how to work hard. He is a good welder and metalsmith. He has also dealt with the secret of being abused for many years and is still willing to risk a relationship.
d. Jan has dealt with having cancer and the results of that—not being able to have children—with courage. She is also able to articulate her needs and goals for therapy.

It is important that these strengths are not referred to in a formulaic superficial way. The most basic principle in EFT, arising from its roots in the Rogerian humanistic tradition, is a genuine regard for and acceptance of clients. At various points in the process of therapy, partners may access parts of themselves that they are ashamed of or do not accept. They may believe that to really need another human being is immature or weak, or they may have specific sources of shame or feelings of unworthiness, particularly if they have been sexually abused. The therapist goes to where each partner lives and attempts to honor and prize aspects of self that they may not be able to accept. Therapy is a genuine encounter and one from which both the clients and the therapist learn.

If we are to consider personality, including behavior, affect, and cognition, the Sullivanian notion that personality is the recurring interpersonal situations a person creates in his/her life is pertinent. Attachment theory is also a theory of personality that addresses affect, cognition, and behavior and how these are formed in relationships with significant others. Apart from positing a wired-in need for a particular kind of connection with a few significant others, and a process of separation distress that inevitably occurs when this connection is threatened, attachment theory outlines particular individual differences that may occur when attachment figures are less than available and responsive. A large body of research has outlined attachment styles, or ways of processing attachment information (Bartholomew & Perlman, 1994; Shaver & Hazan, 1993). These styles, which are predispositions that are confirmed or modified by present relationships, may be viewed as answers to the question "Can I count on this person to be there for me when I need them?" Possible responses to a stable biologically based need and its frustrations are finite. Although there are different versions of attachment styles, there is consensus that attachment can be secure or hyperaroused, as in anxious or preoccupied attachment, or it can be hypo-aroused, as in avoidant attachment. From the case data offered here, I would hypothesize that Jan was characterized by an anxious or preoccupied style and Mike by a fearful avoidant style. These styles offer therapists clues as to how partners process information in close relationships, ascribe meaning to events and so organize their responses.

Partners who have developed an anxious style are vigilant to loss and threat, and tend to aggressively demand reassurance. Partners who have had little or no reason to hope for security and responsiveness tend to deny their need for attachment and focus on activities and tasks. Styles have been associated with adjustment in relationships (Simpson, 1990), different responses to conflict (Simpson, Rholes, & Phillips, 1996) and to seeking and giving support (Simpson, Rholes, & Nelligan, 1992). Abuse survivors tend to exhibit fearful avoidant styles, where they view others as dangerous and undependable and the self as unlovable. These styles have been found to predict interpersonal behavior better than personality traits (Shaver & Brennen, 1992).

Attachment theory suggests that it is not enough for the couples therapist to teach communication skills or help the couple modify a set of problem behaviors. Effective couples therapy has to offer couples a corrective emotional experience that addresses attachment insecurities and allows partners to revise working models of self and other. The more secure partners become, the more they will rely on new information when making social judgements. They will also tend to be more curious and will tolerate ambiguity better (Mikulincer, 1997). A corrective emotional experience occurs most often in loaded attachment situations, where old models of self and other and habitual emotional responses will automatically arise. An emotional experience of secure attachment allows partners to use the relationship as a source of affect regulation and to communicate more effectively, particularly in times of crisis and emotional distress (Johnson & Whiffen, 1999). Attachment security enhances the ability to communicate openly, to take a balanced assertive stance, and to respond empathically to the other (Kobak & Hazan, 1991; Kobak & Sceery, 1988).

It is useful for the therapist to adjust interventions to partners' attachment styles. I would expect to help Jan to differentiate and clarify her expressions of negative emotion and help Mike hear her fear rather than just her frustration at him. I would also expect to offer Mike extra help in touching and accepting the emotions that he usually masks and avoids. Partners with avoidant styles tend to exit or become unresponsive, particularly when they or their partners experience vulnerability (Simpson et al., 1992), that is, when the other partner needs supportive contact most. Mike will need support to stay engaged at those moments.

The many implications of attachment theory for couples therapy are summarized elsewhere (Johnson & Whiffen, 1999). It is perhaps worth mentioning just a few of them in relation to this case:

- Partners with avoidant styles are more likely to be skeptical about therapy and wary of the therapist. It is necessary to be particularly sensitive to Mike's concerns and reservations, not just at the beginning, but throughout the therapy process.
- Anxious attached partners tend to become absorbed in their own affect, particularly reactive anger, and lose sight of the impact of their responses on their spouse. Jan will need help in articulating her loneliness on the weekend, rather than her formulation that Mike is working weekends to compete with her around money. Jan's former marriage, in which her husband turned to other women and drugs, will likely also have left her with particular sensitivities and fears.
- Often, partners like Mike see dependency and vulnerability as despicable weakness or a sign of inadequacy. Mike will then need to create some new positive frames for his attachment needs and sensitivities, and he will need support to stay engaged with his emotions.
- The lack of fit between working models of self and other and new, evolving relational realities has to be extremely apparent for change to occur. New kinds of interactions can be qualified and discounted in favor of old familiar ways of seeing. The therapist has then to highlight and help partners process the meaning of new events in therapy. For example, when Jan expresses attachment needs and longings, optimally Mike, with the therapist's help, is able to conclude: "She needs me. I'm important to her, that's why she is often so angry, not just because she's just trying to control me or make me feel like a failure. Maybe I can do something here."

Treatment Goals

The EFT therapist's goal in treating this couple would be first to help them de-escalate their cycle of criticize/distance. This cycle does not necessarily disappear after treatment, but it is less significant in the definition of the relationship, and the couple can exit from it more easily when it occurs. The second goal involves creating more general emotional engagement and inviting both partners to expand their interactional positions. Mike would be invited to become more actively involved in the relationship, and Jan to soften her stance and ask for her attachment needs to be met. These specific change events are easily discernable in the process of therapy and have been documented in process research (Greenberg et al., 1993; Johnson & Greenberg, 1988). Once these shifts in position have occurred, the therapist fosters secure bonding interactions that create a new cycle of accessibility and responsiveness and help to heal old relationship wounds. At the end of therapy, this new cycle becomes self-reinforcing and promotes resilience in both partners, allowing them to deal with problems such as depression or post-traumatic stress disorder more effectively.

Since EFT is set out in nine steps with identified change events, the change process is relatively easy to monitor, chart, and measure. Concretely, the therapist invites the partners to engage in particular tasks and interactions, and can measure progress by how the couple respond to these tasks. For example, can Mike begin to share his sense of failure or his fear that, as his mother said, his relationships are doomed and will "never last"? Can he also begin to insist that Jan not put him down when she becomes anxious? Can he then ask for her support and commit himself to risking with her and helping her deal with her insecurities? If he can complete these tasks, which of course will vary in specific form and content with different couples, he is in an engaged stance, rather than his usual "head down and avoid" position.

The short-term goals of EFT will depend on the stage of therapy and which step in the change process the couple are presently negotiating. For example, in Step 3, the goal is to help each partner articulate and explore the primary emotions underlying the interactional cycle in a manner that expands this cycle and creates new kinds of interaction. This is not about ventilation, catharsis, or simply new information. When a distant partner such as Mike is able to express a sense of helplessness and intimidation to his wife, he invites her into a new dance. He also experiences himself in a different way, and becomes aware of new goals for himself; rather than wanting to be left alone and not harassed, he begins to ask for her understanding and the space to learn how to come close. He begins to formulate his needs in the relationship. He presents a new side of himself to his wife, who sees that he withdraws out of desperation and fear, not out of indifference. His sharing also pulls for new responses from Jan. She is less angry. When he can talk about his insecurities, she begins to see that he, like her, is in pain. She is then more able to share her own fears, rather than standing back and criticizing him. The steps and stages of change in EFT act as reference points and process goals for the therapist.

How does the therapist know that EFT has been successful? First, the couple can unlatch from their negative cycle at home and in the session. They are less reactive, more emotionally engaged, and more responsive to each other. They describe their relationship and their problems in a different way, and they can talk clearly about their attachment needs and desires. Since the relationship is defined as a place of safety, they can now solve pragmatic problems together relatively easily. At the end of therapy, they are spending more time together, confiding in each other more, and making love more often. They speak of their relationship in terms of being a safe haven and a secure base for each of them. In this kind of relationship, both the male partner's need for less tension and disagreements and the female partner's need for more intimacy have been addressed and are no longer problematic.

For the researcher or therapist who wishes to corroborate the changes observed in the couple's interactions, the measures most commonly used in recent EFT outcome research are:

1. *The Dyadic Adjustment Scale (DAS) by Spanier (1976).* The items in this scale are divided into four subscales: Consensus, Satisfaction, Affection Expression and Cohesion. It is perhaps the most commonly used scale in couples research and has demonstrated good reliability (.96) and validity. Most items involve a five- to six-point Likert-type scale defining the amount of agreement or frequency of an event.

2. *The Miller Social Intimacy Scale (Miller & Lefcourt, 1982).* This is a 17-item self-report measure of the level of intimacy in a relationship. Items are rated on 10-point scales and it also has good reliability (.91) and validity.

3. *The Relationship Trust Scale (Holmes, Boon, & Adams, 1990).* This is a 30-item self-report inventory designed to assess interpersonal trust. There are five subscales: Responsiveness of Partner, Reliability, Faith in Partner's Caring, Conflict Efficacy, and Dependability Concerns. Partners respond to items on a 7-point scale, and the scale has good reliability.

An Implementation Checklist has also been used in all EFT research (Johnson & Greenberg, 1985) to ensure that EFT was faithfully implemented. The therapeutic alliance is also measured by the Couples Therapy Alliance Scale (Pinsof & Catherall, 1986). This scale measures the bond with the therapist, agreement as to therapeutic goals, and the perceived relevance of tasks. The partners respond to 28 items on a Likert 5-point scale. In EFT research, the perceived relevance of therapeutic tasks factor was highly predictive of treatment outcome (Johnson & Talitman, 1997). This seems to reflect our clinical experience that couples find an attachment framework meaningful and relevant. The Structural Analysis of Social Behavior (Benjamin, 1993) has also been used in process studies to code observed responses on the dimensions of affiliation and control.

The research on EFT has found that 70 to 73% of couples receiving 10–12 sessions of EFT are recovered from relationship distress at follow-up assessment; that is, they score over 100 on the DAS, which is the cut-off point for distress. Obviously, a couple can improve their relationship considerably and still not meet this stringent criterion. The effect size for EFT has been calculated at 1.3 (Johnson et al., in press). This is a significant improvement over the effect sizes reported as typical of couples therapy in recent meta-analytic reviews, which ranged between .60 and .90 (Dunn & Schwebel, 1995; Shadish et al., 1993). We have not found evidence of the relapse phenomena reported in recent reviews of couples therapy (Jacobson & Addis, 1993). The longest follow-up study of EFT (2 years after therapy) found that all the results of therapy were stable (Walker, Manion, & Clouthier, 1998). Although the need for a model of distress and change in couple and family therapy has been questioned (Hoffman, 1998), one of the many advantages of having such a model is that the therapist has clear goals, clear markers for change, and a clear sense of when the couple have arrived.

Techniques and Interventions

Apart from the interventions that are an integral part of EFT and are summarized in detail elsewhere (Johnson, 1996), are there interventions that might be particularly useful at particular times in therapy with this couple?

In general, the therapist is most active in the middle stage of therapy (Steps 5–7) when he/she is shaping change events. However, in the first stage of therapy, de-escalation, it would be particularly important to help Mike explore his responses when he feels criticized by Jan. He copes by dismissing her comments and avoiding her, which then exacerbates her need to be heard and responded to. An EFT therapist would replay moments when this occurs in the session and ask Mike, "What happens to you as Jan says . . . ?" The therapist might use Mike's past experience with his mother, or with other women with whom he felt "dumb" or "controlled," to validate his sensitivity to Jan's comments, but would generally stay focused on the present relationship (unless abuse issues became central). The therapist would need to track Mike's experience closely, use his language whenever possible, and slowly expand this experience with him. Often, partners such as Mike begin to talk about how they can never win or get their spouse's approval or acceptance. Hiding out or denying the other's frustration then seem to be the only recourse. The therapist would heighten his experience and help him focus at the leading edge of his awareness. As he is able to articulate his underlying emotions, these emotions help clarify what he needs to be able to stay engaged with Jan. He may be able to tell her, "I need you to give me a chance. Give me the benefit of the doubt sometimes. I want you to see I'm trying and let me know what it is you want."

As an EFT therapist, I would expect that as Jan moved into the middle stage of therapy (Step 5), she might access hurts from her first marriage that have created particular trigger points for her and also a sense of betrayal, for example, about Mike's staying at the party. Depending on how significant this last event was to Jan, it may be what is termed in EFT an attachment injury. This is a particular event that defines the relationship as insecure and the other as untrustworthy at a particularly crucial time. For the injured person, this is often a time of particular vulnerability or questioning of the relationship. Anxiously attached parties will bring up these incidents again and again, especially when a potential new risk arises. The other spouse, not knowing how to resolve the issue, attempts to discount it, which exacerbates the injured one's anxiety. I might use evocative questions to help Jan articulate her attachment fears and hurts connected with this incident. I would help Mike to hear her by framing this incident in terms of how important it is for Jan to feel safe and receive reassurance from him. He is so important to her that she will continue to struggle for this. I would use heightening to clarify Jan's attachment fears and I would structure interactions where she can begin to ask for what she needs in this particular kind of situation. If this incident is typical of their relationship and Mike is already re-engaged, exploring the incident further may become a way into a general change event, a softening, for Jan.

If and when impasses occur, the first step for the therapist is to simply follow the resistance. So the dialogue might sound like,

Jan:	I can't tell him how hurt I was that night. It's too hard.
Therapist:	That's too hard ? Can you help me understand. Is it that you feel too exposed, you have mentioned that, perhaps it seems like too much of a risk?
Jan:	Yes, I can't tell him. I know he's listening to me as I talk to you, but . . .
Therapist:	So could you tell him, I won't risk right now, it's too hard to show you my hurt.

As Jan does this, the dialogue opens out into how hurt she has been and how hard it is for her to let Mike see this. Mike will then begin (with the therapist's help if necessary) to see her as vulnerable, rather than simply as controlling and angry. In this kind of dialogue, Jan stays with the emotion, in this case, fear. This new music then begins a new attachment dance, one in which each person's sense of self and sense of the other evolves.

If Jan could not take this step—if she changed the subject, found exits and returned to blaming Mike in a cool detached manner—I might use a disquisition (Johnson, 1996). A disquisition is a story told from a distance that reflects the dance between the couple that is occurring in front of the therapist. It is a reflection and heightening of the interaction, but with no pressure that the couple own the reflection. The story also adds a particular perspective, or expands the description to include elements omitted by the couple that the therapist conjectures are salient. I might say, "For some reason, and this may not be relevant for you at all, I keep remembering a couple where one of the partners had just never experienced anyone really taking care of her, really responding to her hurt. Part of her just couldn't even let herself long for that any more. It just felt too hopeless. So she just tried not to feel the need, to act like it wasn't there and indeed her partner didn't see it. He didn't know it was there." This is the most indirect and least transparent intervention in EFT, and is based on the therapist's empathic attunement to the partners. It can be very short, or have the quality of a simple fairy tale. Our experience is that partners become caught by the story and follow it, using it to open up their own awareness. So Jan might then comment, "I promised myself after my first marriage, never again. I don't want to feel that longing." This then opens up a new level of dialogue.

In impasses the EFT therapist also uses diagnostic pictures which he/she draws with the partners. This is a simple picture of the couples cycle, the process of therapy and where both they and the therapist are stuck. The therapist heightens the "stuckness" and invites the couple to formulate a new step. Occasionally the therapist will also invite each partner to come in for a single session to discuss specific obstacles or roadblocks in the therapy process without the audience of the spouse.

Pitfalls and Limits

If we assume that neither partner has experienced a secure close attachment bond, the process of therapy would then be slower. The process is then not about recreating a dance that you have danced before but lost touch with. It is about creating a dance that feels alien and dangerous and to which you have never even heard the music. The couple will then need more support from the therapist.

Mike was also victimized by a female relative and found it necessary to keep this from his family. This implies an isolation which may be as potentially damaging as the abuse. EFT is used with couples where partners have been abused (Johnson & Williams-Keeler, 1998). Mike may need to spend some time with an individual therapist talking about this issue and how it may have links to his drug abuse. Specifically, I would be concerned about the impact of this abuse on Mike's ability to trust Jan and also whether the abuse left him feeling unworthy, shameful, or degraded. However, the fact that he has told his wife about the abuse is positive, and, from our experience with abuse survivors, we know that the relationship with Jan can be a powerful part of his healing. As van der Kolk, Perry, and Herman (1991) point out, the most potent predictor of the effects of trauma is whether the victim can seek out and receive comfort from significant others. If Mike could do this with Jan, it would also be a powerful building block towards a more secure bond between him and his wife. Mike might need support to recognize the impact of the abuse, since this goes against his father's injunction to "get over it." The effects of this trauma, his mother's critical responses to him and her advice that his relationships will "never last" contextualize Mike's distance with Jan. A recognition of these elements can lessen any sense of failure Mike may have in this relationship and help Jan see his distancing in less threatening terms. Both Mike and Jan seem to have turned for comfort to sources other than close relationships (drugs, for Mike, animals, for Jan). However, Jan does seem to have experienced some significant friendships and found some support when she was facing the trauma of fighting cancer. She may also have learned lessons from that battle that help her understand Mike's struggles.

It would be important to explore whether specific cues in the interaction evoke a re-experiencing of Mike's trauma. Certainly detachment from his emotions, drug abuse and destructive behavior (while driving), and concentration on tasks and activities are coping mechanisms that survivors of abuse habitually use. These ways of coping and protecting himself prime his wife's insecurities and his own relationship distress. The point for the therapist here is not the creation of insight per se, but that Mike be able to take small steps towards building trust with his wife. If Mike is indeed still dealing with the aftereffects of his abuse, couples therapy is a place where he can learn to deal with his fear and shame in a positive way by turning to his spouse. This will give Mike a sense of mastery over his fear, and has the potential to be deeply rewarding to his wife as well as to himself. Proximity to a significant other is an inborn affect regulation device (Mikulincer, Florian, & Tolmacz, 1990) and one that offers more positive possibilities to Mike than his usual coping mechanisms.

Areas to Avoid and Including Others in the Session

There are no areas that I would particularly want to avoid addressing with Mike and Jan. Bearing in mind that my client is Mike and Jan's relationship, I would want to address Mike's addiction only as it reflected and impacted his relationship with Jan, although I would also refer to his recent ability to control this addiction as an indication of his strength. I would not include anyone else in my sessions with this couple; this is not part of the usual practice in EFT. If Mike were to see an individual therapist about his abuse and/or his trauma history, I would, with the couple's permission, make contact with that therapist and share my goals for the couple and the basic process of EFT. The couple and individual therapies can then inform and potentiate each other in a positive manner.

Homework

If homework is given in EFT, it is usually centered around awareness rather than practicing behaviors. The therapist might say to Mike, "Can you notice this week what happens to you when you try to open up to Jan and somehow it doesn't work, like when she goes off to call her friends? It might be interesting to talk in the next session about what you say to yourself, how you feel or how you respond." The therapist might ask Jan to be aware of times when she holds back and does not tell Mike about her concerns or desires (similar to the party incident) and what that's like for her. If Mike identifies moments in interactions with his wife when he feels hopeless, and finds himself agreeing with his mother that his relationships will never work, I might encourage him to notice these moments and how he responds to them.

In the middle stage of therapy, occasionally I might ask the couple to try an experiment at home. For example, I might ask Jan and Mike, "Can you take 10 minutes and discuss how each of you experienced this session and what you thought was particularly important? The other person doesn't have to agree, but maybe has to just understand your point of view." This kind of homework encourages the couple to experiment with a little of the kind of contact they have during sessions, and often provides material for the next session. There is no pressure for the couple to comply with these requests. Such pressure would potentially change the nature of the therapeutic alliance, and it is often just as useful to discuss how partners could not or did not wish to engage in the homework. These kinds of homework experiments in awareness or contact are not a large part of EFT.

One of the functions of homework is to create focus and continuity from session to session. EFT therapists foster this kind of continuity by referring back to the model and the steps of treatment. Most EFT therapists also tend to note and record the most powerful moments of emotional engagement, key images and affects, and attachment-relevant comments made by partners in a session. This allows the therapist and the couple to stay on track and move forward in the next session.

Timeline for Therapy

I would expect to see this couple once a week for approximately 15 weeks. The length of treatment would depend on factors such as how much of a role the sexual abuse plays in the relationship and how easy it is for the couple to engage in therapy. Our research suggests that engagement in the tasks of therapy predicts success in EFT better than factors like initial distress level (Johnson & Talitman, 1997) that are usually predictive of success in couples therapy. Clinical experience suggests that trauma survivors often take longer to build trust in their partner, and the process of couples therapy has to address trauma cues that arise in the relationship.

In addition to regular couple sessions, partners are sometimes offered individual sessions if an impasse occurs; for example, if a particular behavior consistently derails the therapy process and has not been impacted by other interventions. If Jan kept setting tests for Mike and not telling him what she wanted, I would have a session focused on this. I would also have a session with Mike to talk about his perceptions of being tested. The vast majority of couples do not need such sessions; if they are offered, we always see both partners for one, and, very occasionally, two sessions. As stated previously, depending on the nature and impact of the abuse on Mike, the EFT therapist might refer him for individual therapy. It may be that if the couple's relationship improves and he can confide in and be affirmed by his spouse, couples therapy would be sufficient.

Termination

Steps 8 and 9 of EFT facilitate the emergence of new solutions to old issues and consolidate new positions and new cycles of attachment behaviors. In Step 8, the couple are encouraged to discuss and resolve old problems that could not be explored or negotiated without the safety of a secure attachment. Pragmatic content issues are addressed after the process issues that define the relationship are resolved. This is in contrast to other models of couples therapy which begin by focusing on such content issues. There is research evidence that in secure attachment relationships people can meta-monitor the process of interaction, unlatch and change the direction of negative interactions, and consider alternative arguments and strategies. Secure attachment allows people to negotiate effectively (Kobak & Cole, 1991). Jan and Mike might discuss and resolve pragmatic problems, such as her need for companionship on weekends and his desire for sexual contact. Our experience is that, at this stage in therapy, couples access and display the communication skills necessary to solve problems, although, as Gottman and his colleagues (1998) point out, they may not use skills such as active listening per se. Gottman suggests that physiological soothing, the softening of "harder" emotions such as anger and hostility and, engagement and responsiveness are more crucial than skills for the stability and happiness of long-term relationships. We agree with him and suggest that he is talking about the security of the bond between partners. Our understanding is that standing with one's toes over the edge of a cliff, as Mike and Jan are in their relationship, elicits reactive self-absorbed responses and overrides most people's ability to listen to others, take the other's perspective, and consider alternative actions. Wired-in, survival-oriented fear responses take precedence. Standing together in a safe place, however, pulls for consideration, the ability to meta-communicate, and to confide in the other.

Step 9 involves the consolidation of the gains of therapy and new definitions of the relationship. The therapist and the couple summarize the gains of therapy and contrast old and new interaction patterns. The therapist heightens how the couple can help each other stay accessible and responsive and regain safety if they get stuck in their old cycle. Jan and Mike would then construct a clear unambiguous story of how and where they came to be stuck in a destructive dance, how they escaped from this dance, and how they can now maintain new cycles of caring and closeness. The therapist heightens the new definition of the relationship and validates the couple's struggles and achievements. Mike might now be able to discuss a time when he turned to Jan for reassurance. He might be able to describe a time when he became overwhelmed by feelings of inadequacy and shame and turned to her, rather than to alcohol. He could also be explicit about how Jan made this easier for him to do. The last sessions take a meta-perspective on the process of the relationship and how it has changed.

I would expect Jan and Mike to be functioning well at the end of therapy. I would also expect Mike to be dealing well with his addiction problem. This kind of couple, with a criticize/distance cycle and a history of disappointment and violation in relationships, is not at all unusual in EFT referrals. EFT may be particularly suited to such couples because of its focus on dealing with affect and attachment issues. If the reduction of fear is the most important basic goal in the treatment of post-traumatic stress disorder (Foa, Hearst-Ikeda, & Perry, 1995), nothing seems to reduce fear like a loved one standing beside us. I would also expect that Mike and Jan will experience less negative affect and use their relationship to regulate fears and insecurities as they arise. As a result, they will be able to maintain emotional engagement and experience more intimacy. On a behavioral level, they will be more responsive to their partner and will be able to ask for what they need in a way that helps their partner respond. They will also be able to problem-solve more effectively. On a cognitive level, the couple will perceive each other differently (Greenberg et al., 1993) and make more generous attributions about the other's behavior. They will have included new elements in their definitions of the other and have a new understanding of attachment relationships. On an interpersonal level, the couples dance will have expanded to include new comforting cycles of confiding and caring.

How do you know when the couple have arrived, when they have created a stable and happy relationship? If we have only theories of change in couple therapy, whether those theories be systemic or extensions of individual psychotherapy, it is hard to say which specific changes are significant or sufficient. The theory of intimate relationships espoused by EFT suggests that emotional engagement and responsiveness are the basis of a secure attachment bond; recent research into stable, happy marriages comes to the same conclusion (Gottman et al., 1998). When the couple have built a safe harbor, they no longer need a pilot; at the end of therapy Jan and Mike would be clear that the therapist is no longer needed; they have each other.

REFERENCES

Anderson, H. (1997). *Conversation, language and possibilities.* New York: Basic Books.

Bartholomew, K., & Perlman, D. (Eds.). (1994). Attachment processes in adulthood. *Advances in personal relationships* (Vol. 5). London, PA: Jessica Kingsley.

Benjamin, L. (1993). *Interpersonal diagnosis and treatment of personality disorders.* New York: Guilford Press.

Bergin, A., & Garfield, S. (1994). Overview, trends and future issues. In A. Bergin & S. Garfield (Eds.), *Handbook of psychotherapy and behavior change* (4th ed., pp. 821–830). New York: Wiley.

Bowlby, J. (1969). *Attachment & loss. Vol. 1: Attachment.* New York: Basic Books.

Bowlby, J. (1988). *A secure base.* New York: Basic Books.

Damasio, A. (1994). *Descartes' error: Emotion, reason and the human brain.* New York: Grosset/Putnam.

Diamond, G., & Siqueland, L. (1995). Family therapy for the treatment of depressed adolescents. *Psychotherapy: Theory, Research & Practice, 32,* 77–90.

Dunn, R., & Schwebel, A. (1995). Meta-analytic review of marital outcome research. *Journal of Family Psychology, 9,* 58–68.

Foa, E., Hearst-Ikeda, D., & Perry, K. (1995). Evaluation of a brief cognitive-behavioral program for the prevention of chronic PTSD in recent assault victims. *Journal of Consulting & Clinical Psychology, 63,* 948–955.

Gottman, J. (1994). *What predicts divorce?* Hillsdale, NJ: Erlbaum.

Gottman, J., Coan, J., Carrere, S., & Swanson, C. (1998). Predicting marital happiness and stability from newlywed interactions. *Journal of Marriage and the Family, 60,* 5–22.

Greenberg, L., Ford, C., Alden, L., & Johnson, S. (1993). Change processes in emotionally focused therapy. *Journal of Consulting & Clinical Psychology, 61,* 78–84.

Greenberg, L., & Johnson, S. M. (1988). *Emotionally focused therapy for couples.* New York: Guilford Press.

Greenberg, L., & Safran, J. (1987). *Emotion in psychotherapy: Affect and cognition in the process of change.* New York: Guilford Press.

Hoffman, L. (1998). Setting aside the models in family therapy. *Journal of Marital and Family Therapy, 24,* 145–156.

Holmes, J., Boon, S., & Adams, S. (1990). *The Relationship Trust Scale.* Unpublished manuscript, University of Waterloo, Waterloo, Canada.

Jacobson, N., & Addis, M. (1993). Research on couples and couple therapy: What do we know? Where are we going? *Journal of Consulting and Clinical Psychology, 61,* 85–93.

*Johnson, S. (1998). Emotionally focused couples therapy. In F. Dattilio (Ed.), *Case studies in couple and family therapy: Systemic & cognitive perspectives* (pp. 450–472). New York: Guilford Press.

Johnson, S. (1999). Emotionally focused couples therapy: Straight to the heart. In J. Donovan (Ed.), *Brief approaches to couples therapy* (pp. 13–42). New York: Guilford Press.

*Johnson, S. M. (1996). *The practice of emotionally focused marital therapy: Creating connection*. New York: Brunner/Mazel.

Johnson, S. M. (1986). Bonds or bargains: Relationship paradigms and their significance for marital therapy. *Journal of Marital & Family Therapy, 12,* 259–267.

Johnson, S., & Greenberg, L. (1985). The differential effectiveness of experiential and problem solving interventions in resolving marital conflict. *Journal of Consulting & Clinical Psychology, 53,* 175–184.

*Johnson, S., & Greenberg, L. (1988). Relating process to outcome in marital therapy. *Journal of Marital and Family Therapy, 14,* 175–183.

Johnson, S. M., & Greenberg, L. (Eds.) (1994). *The heart of the matter: Perspectives on emotion in marital therapy*. New York: Brunner/Mazel.

*Johnson, S., & Greenberg, L. (1995). The emotionally focused approach to problems in adult attachment. In N. Jacobson & A. Gurman (Eds.), *Clinical handbook of marital therapy* (2nd ed., pp. 121–141). New York: Guilford Press.

Johnson, S., & Greenberg, L. (1998). The use of emotion in couple and family therapy. *Journal of Systemic Therapies* (Special Edition), *17*. New York: Guilford Press.

Johnson, S. M., Hunsley, J., Greenberg, L., & Schindler, D. (1999). Emotionally focused couples therapy: Status and challenges. *Clinical Psychology, 6,* 67–79.

Johnson, S. M., & Talitman, E. (1997). Predictors of success in emotionally focused marital therapy. *Journal of Marital and Family Therapy, 23,* 135–152.

Johnson, S. M., & Whiffen, V. (1999). Made to measure: Adapting emotionally focused couples therapy to partner's attachment styles. *Clinical Psychology: Science and Practice, 6,* 366–381.

Johnson, S., & Williams-Keeler, L. (1998). Creating healing relationships for couples dealing with trauma: The use of emotionally focused couples therapy. *Journal of Marital and Family Therapy, 24,* 227–236.

Kierkegaard, S. (1948). The viewpoint for my authorship. *Synspunktet for min Forfattervirksomhet*. Finn Wangberg.

Kobak, R., & Cole, H. (1991). Attachment and meta-monitoring: Implications for adolescent autonomy and psychopathology. In D. Cicchetti & S. Toth (Eds.), *Disorders and dysfunctions of the self* (pp. 267–297). Rochester, NY: University of Rochester Press.

Kobak, R., & Hazan, C. (1991). Attachment in marriage: Effects of security and accurate working models. *Journal of Personality and Social Psychology, 60,* 861–869.

Kobak, R., Ruckdeschel, K., & Hazan, C. (1994). From symptom to signal: An attachment view of emotion in marital therapy. In S. Johnson & L. Greenberg (Eds.), *The heart of the matter: Perspectives on emotion in marital therapy* (pp. 46–71). New York: Brunner/Mazel.

---

*Suggested reading.

Kobak, R., & Sceery, A. (1988). Attachment in late adolescence. Working models, affect regulation and representations of self and other. *Child Development, 59,* 135–146.

LeDoux, J. (1994). Emotion, memory and the brain. *Scientific American, 27,* 32–39.

Lyons-Ruth, K. (1996). Attachment relationships among children with aggressive behavior problems: The role of disorganized early attachment patterns. *Journal of Consulting & Clinical Psychology, 64,* 64–73.

Marvin, R. S., & Stewart, R. B. (1990). A family systems framework for the study of attachment. In M. T. Greenberg, D. Cicchetti, & E. Cummings (Eds.), *Attachment in the pre-school years* (pp. 51–86). Chicago: University of Chicago Press.

Mikulincer, M. (1997). Adult attachment style and information processing: Individual differences in curiosity and cognitive closure. *Journal of Personality & Social Psychology, 72,* 1217–1230.

Mikulincer, M., Florian, V., & Tolmacz, R. (1990). Attachment styles and fear of death: A case of affect regulation. *Journal of Personality & Social Psychology, 58,* 273–280.

Mikulincer, M., Florian, V., & Weller, A. (1993). Attachment styles, coping strategies and post-traumatic psychological distress: The impact of the Gulf War. *Journal of Personality & Social Psychology, 64,* 817–826.

Miller, R., & Lefcourt, H. (1982). The assessment of intimacy. *Journal of Personality Assessment, 46,* 514–518.

Pinsof, W., & Catherall, D. (1986). The integrative psychotherapy alliance: Family, couple and individual therapy scales. *Journal of Marital and Family Therapy, 12,* 137–151.

Reimers, S., & Treacher, A. (1995). *Introducing user friendly family therapy.* New York: Routledge.

Rogers, C. (1951). *Client centered therapy.* Boston: Houghton-Mifflin.

Shadish, W. R., Montgomery, L., Wilson, P., Wilson, M., Bright, I., & Okwumabua, T. (1993). Effects of family and marital psychotherapies: A meta-analysis. *Journal of Consulting & Clinical Psychology, 61,* 992–1002.

Shaver, P., & Brenner, K. (1992). Attachment styles and the big 5 personality traits. *Personality & Social Psychology Bulletin, 5,* 536–545.

Shaver, P., & Hazan, C. (1993). Adult romantic attachment: Theory and evidence. In D. Perlman & W. Jones (Eds.), *Advances in personal relationships* (Vol. 4, pp. 29–70). London, PA: Jessica Kingsley.

Simpson, J. A. (1990). The influence of attachment styles on romantic relationships. *Journal of Personality & Social Psychology, 59,* 971–980.

Simpson, J. A., Rholes, W. S., & Nelligan, J. S. (1992). Support seeking and support giving within couples in an anxiety provoking situation: The role of attachment styles. *Journal of Personality & Social Psychology, 62,* 434–446.

Simpson, J. A., Rholes, W. S., & Phillips, D. (1996). Conflict in close relationships: An attachment perspective. *Journal of Personality & Social Psychology, 71,* 899–914.

Spanier, G. (1976). Measuring dyadic adjustment. *Journal of Marriage and Family, 13,* 113–126.

Walker, J., Manion, I., & Clouthier, P. (in press). A two year follow-up on an emotionally focused intervention for distressed couples with chronically ill children. *Journal of Consulting & Clinical Psychology.*

van der Kolk, B., Perry, C., & Herman, J. (1991). Childhood origins of self-destructive behavior. *American Journal of Psychiatry, 148,* 1665–1671.

Integrative Behavioral Couple Therapy

Janice Jones, Andrew Christensen, and Neil Jacobson

TREATMENT MODEL

Integrative Behavioral Couple Therapy, or simply Integrative Couple Therapy (ICT, Christensen, Jacobson, & Babcock, 1995; Jacobson & Christensen, 1996) builds on the behavior change strategies used in Traditional Behavioral Couples Therapy (TBCT, e.g., Jacobson & Margolin, 1979), but incorporates new strategies for promoting emotional acceptance. In TBCT the focus of treatment is on [decreasing negative behavior and increasing positive behavior.]In ICT, the emphasis shifts from attempts to merely change behavior to an emotional acceptance of each partner's behavior, even if the behavior remains at its current frequency and intensity.]However, [negative behaviors are reconceptualized and reexperienced in ways that soften each partner's responses to the other's negative behavior and make those behaviors more understandable and more acceptable] As a result of this process, the offending partner often spontaneously changes his or her negative behavior, so that emotional acceptance and behavior change are both achieved. If sufficient change does not spontaneously occur, the direct strategies of TBCT can be used to supplement the emotional acceptance strategies of ICT.

The ICT therapist's foremost task in the beginning of treatment is to conceptualize a formulation for the couple. The formulation is based on information-gathering in the first few sessions and is personalized to each couple. It reflects [the core differences with which they are struggling, the way each partner copes with these differences—often in a fruitless pursuit of change in the other—and finally, the subsequent emotional reactions each partner experiences, such as hopelessness or alienation. Developing an accurate formulation is critical to the success of ICT; an inaccurate description of a couple's problems and interactions renders the therapist's interventions less applicable or even ineffective, and will make the couple feel misunderstood.

The first component of the formulation is the couple's theme, which captures the essential differences with which they struggle. In presenting the differences between spouses, the therapist does not vilify or blame either spouse; rather, the therapist stresses that the couple's unique theme is reflective of common differences or incompatibilities between spouses. The therapist attempts to show that each spouse became the way he or she is for very good reasons, perhaps rooted in their personal history, culture, or current circumstances. The second component of the formulation is the polarization process, the emotional struggle that occurs as a result of disagreements about differences. Polarization is a natural consequence of the struggle by each partner to get the other to change. The more a couple argues about a particular difference between them, the more likely they are to become entrenched and extreme in their own positions. Eventually, polarization leads to the third component, the mutual trap. The spouses feel so distant that neither is willing to budge in their opinions. They feel trapped and helpless to do anything about the situation, and they feel alienated from each other.

The ICT therapist explains the couple's formulation to them in the feedback session, which follows the first few assessment and evaluation sessions. The therapist normalizes both the differences that the couple is experiencing and the way each partner is coping with these experiences. The therapist communicates empathy for each person's position in the struggle. A major goal of the feedback about the formulation is to move the couple toward a shared understanding of their difficulties and compassion for each partner's position in the struggle.

Intervention in ICT treatment uses the couple's formulation to advocate two key themes: promoting acceptance and promoting change. Acceptance, as conceptualized in ICT, is not resignation to the problems in the marriage; rather, at one extreme it is an active embrace of previously rejected aspects of the partner, and at the other extreme, a tolerance of negative aspects of the other. In essence, when partners become more emotionally accepting of each other, they view and experience their problems less personally and less negatively. One's partner may engage in the same or similar behaviors, but one won't be so pained by these actions. The therapist promotes acceptance in couples through three major strategies: empathic joining, unified detachment, and tolerance.

To promote empathic joining, the therapist draws on the formulation to emphasize the pain that each partner experiences as a result of the differences between them and the struggle over those differences. Spouses are encouraged to describe their own experiences, not in terms of what the other spouse does to aggravate them, but in terms of their own reactions of hurt and vulnerability. If a partner has difficulty describing his or her emotional injuries and instead focuses on the other's egregious acts and their anger and outrage at those acts, the therapist may suggest softer emotions, such as feelings of disappointment, neglect, or abandonment, which may exist beneath the harder feelings. As a result, instead of becoming defensive, the listening spouse can develop empathy for the other spouse's pain which can often be similar to their own. This shared experience of pain is particularly important in the evolution of acceptance: when each partner sees the other's distress without the distorting cloud of accusation, they no longer view the other as an enemy to be condemned, but as a fellow sufferer who deserves compassion. This newfound compassion may increase the intimacy between them.

In contrast to the close and tender stance therapists take when promoting empathic joining, they take a more distant, objective stance when they promote unified detachment. Here the goal is intellectual distance rather than emotional immediacy. ICT therapists engage the couple in an analysis of their problem—the triggers that precipitate their conflicts, the sequence of actions that occur between them, the escalation of their actions, and eventually the climax and recovery from conflict. ICT therapists may engage them in a comparison of different incidents or encourage them to give an appropriate name to their conflict. All of this is done to increase partners' awareness of their struggles, but in so doing to change the problem from a "you" to an "it." The problem is no longer "the bad things you do to me" but the "thing" they get into with each other. This transformation of the problem allows them to talk about the problem more objectively, without blaming the other spouse. It allows them perspective on the conflict, and may even allow them to laugh at their conflicts on occasion.

Tolerance becomes a goal when acceptance seems too difficult. Developing tolerance for behaviors that are merely reflective of differences between the spouses will mean that the behaviors will have less of an effect when they occur. (ICT would never advocate tolerance of harmful or dangerous behavior, which is why couples experiencing domestic violence or substance abuse are usually referred elsewhere for more appropriate treatment.) Several techniques can encourage tolerance-building. For example, the therapist can highlight the positive features of the spouse's currently intolerable behaviors to provide a more positive perspective, usually in relation to how the intent of the behavior may be to benefit the other spouse or the relationship. Another effective tolerance technique is to have the couple role-play negative behaviors during therapy sessions, so they can learn to prepare for future situations by practicing how to communicate and act, as well as become desensitized to the negative situations. The couple can take this desensitization a step further by faking incidents of negative behavior at home, allowing the spouse faking the behavior to observe the effects of their negative behavior on the other spouse.

The acceptance and tolerance that has now blossomed between the couple may have the seemingly paradoxical consequence of generating behavior change in both partners. Spouses will no longer be caught in the polarization process and mutual trap, intent on maintaining their behavioral patterns and expecting the other to change. Instead, their attitude of acceptance and tolerance will make them more likely to change their own negative behaviors that cause their partner pain.

The spontaneous behavior change that occurs in ICT is contingency-shaped rather than rule-governed (Skinner, 1966). This means the change comes not from a deliberate effort to change behavior to meet some agreed-upon rule; instead, the change develops from new experiences both spouses have of each other. Because each partner has developed a personally motivated desire to help the other, their new behaviors are intrinsically rewarding and likely to sustain themselves over time. Each spouse is able to see the relationship through the eyes of the other spouse, as well as through their own eyes. Thus, they are able to make adaptations to each other as circumstances change.

If acceptance and tolerance interventions are not so powerful as to create satisfaction within the couple, the ICT therapist may attempt some of the standard behavior change interventions of TBCT. These behavior change interventions are more directive than the acceptance interventions and require collaboration and compromise between partners. The acceptance interventions, even if they were insufficient to create satisfaction on their own, may generate the collaboration that makes direct behavior change interventions effective.

The standard behavior change interventions of TBCT include *behavior exchange*, in which partners collaborate to increase the positive actions that occur between them; *communication training*, in which partners learn a nonblaming way of discussion; and *problem-solving training*, in which partners learn a structured method for defining and solving problems. Because these interventions have been described in detail elsewhere (e.g., Jacobson & Margolin, 1979), they will not be described here.

In ICT, these behavior change interventions are implemented in a less structured way than in TBCT. Furthermore, if there is resistance to these interventions, the ICT therapist usually falls back on acceptance interventions. Thus, strategies of acceptance provide not only a backdrop for the directive work on change, but strategies of acceptance are a default option when directive strategies are ineffective.

THERAPIST SKILLS AND ATTRIBUTES

The qualities an ICT therapist should possess are very much those required for any successful clinician, and some of these characteristics are crucial when practicing ICT. Most generally, the therapist must be attentive to what the couple is communicating to him or her and to each other. Much of the important information will come from their descriptions; thus, good listening skills are vital to the success of an ICT therapist. The basis of the therapist's approach to the couple is a formulation of their difficulties, which is drawn from the couple's description of their conflicts and their associated feelings and thoughts. If the therapist is not attentive to these accounts, the formulation will be inadequate. But attentiveness also includes awareness of paralinguistic and nonverbal cues, including facial expression, body language and tone of voice, which can also provide a great deal of information regarding a spouse's emotions. Partners often reveal more about themselves in how they say something than in what they say. For example, a husband may state no negative feelings toward his wife, but his tone of voice reveals anger and irritation.

After the evaluation period, ICT is driven by the emotional state of the spouses rather than by an advance agenda by the therapist. Therefore, at each session, the ICT therapist must be sensitive to the issues that are emotionally salient for each spouse. The therapist should follow along with the couple and process the issues or incidents that are most significant to them at the moment. If a couple is distressed at an argument from the previous night, that argument serves as the starting content for the session. But the therapist's sensitivity must go beyond a mere reading of what is emotionally salient to the couple at the beginning of the session. As the therapist explores a particular incident or issue, he or she must be sensitive to the changing landscape of each spouse's feelings. Often, what is most emotionally salient to a couple is their interaction in the session. For example, as a couple discusses the argument from the previous night, they may react to the comments that each partner makes in the session. Then, the ICT therapist must read those emotional reactions and shift the focus from the emotional reactions last night to the current emotional reactions. Because partners often don't voice their emotions clearly or are only dimly aware of their emotions, the ICT therapist reads verbal and nonverbal cues and helps each partner articulate his or her experience.

Hand-in-hand with sensitivity to the couple's emotional reactions is the therapist's acceptance of each spouse's experience. A main conceptualization of a couple's experience is that underlying the strong negative feelings partners have for the other are their softer emotions, such as pain and loss. Therefore, progress in ICT treatment depends on each spouse developing sympathy and understanding for the other. To this end, the therapist must model such acceptance for the couple, regardless of how insensitively or thoughtlessly one or both spouses may have acted toward the other. Therapist acceptance also serves to validate each spouse's experience and reinforces their sense that the therapist has heard what each of them has said. Of course, any unsafe behavior, such as abuse or substance use, is not accepted and is addressed outside of the ICT.

Although ICT therapists are sympathetic and validating to each partner, they should remain objective and evenhanded with each of the partners throughout treatment. In order to maintain a therapeutic atmosphere, the therapist should not take sides or favor one spouse, particularly when the couple becomes involved in an argument during a session. Instead, the therapist must be impartial, seeing both sides and supporting both positions.

The ideal of following the client's emotional lead and of being validating and impartial may suggest a therapist who is passive and nondirective. Nothing could be further from the truth. In fact, ICT therapists are very active in reformulating each partner's position so their position is more understandable and sympathetic. Also, if a couple's anger and distress lead them to unconstructive actions in the session, such as yelling or interrupting, the therapist may actively direct the communication between the two.

Because of the central role of the formulation in Integrative Couple Therapy, a therapist's ability to develop such a formulation and adapt it to understand daily incidents in the couple's life is significant. First, an ICT therapist should be able to develop a logical, coherent, and accurate formulation of the couple's dilemma. If this formulation does not ring true for the couple, the treatment may not move forward, and the couple may make no progress in therapy. Second, the therapist must articulate this formulation clearly and persuasively for the couple. Ideally, the couple will adopt the formulation in thinking about their situation, which will help them to achieve unified detachment and empathic joining around their core issues. Finally, the therapist needs to use the formulation to make sense of the daily incidents and issues that couples bring up in therapy. The formulation will help them make sense of their diverse struggles and conceptualize them within the umbrella of their formulation.

More broadly, the effective ICT therapist communicates in a way that resonates with the couple. This is perhaps the most difficult skill to learn, as it involves shifting the language used during sessions to match what is most appropriate for each particular couple. This often involves using words the spouses use themselves; not only does this make the spouse feel understood by the therapist, but the therapist knows which words and terms are meaningful to the spouse. In addition, using humor and metaphors encourages the couple to become less emotionally vulnerable to their issues and take their problems less seriously, which can lead to unified detachment and empathic joining.

Lastly, the effective therapist should recognize when to end the therapy sessions. The goal of ICT therapy is not to solve all of a couple's problems; this is unlikely to happen, and if a couple thinks their problems are all solved, they will leave therapy unprepared for further problems that will inevitably arise. Instead, the main objective is to create an environment for the couple in which they can experience their relationship in a qualitatively different way. They understand the pain experienced by each and are sympathetic with that pain.

They see their relationship from a more obj~~ective distance~~, and can discuss their problems with some perspective. Their problems are no longer a "you" but an ~~"it."~~ When this qualitative change has taken place, the therapist may shift the couple to less frequent sessions. The couple will likely realize that they need the therapist less.

THE CASE OF MIKE AND JAN

Instruments and Assessment Tools

The first several sessions of ICT serve as an assessment and evaluation period. The therapist uses joint clinical interviews with the couple, individual clinical interviews with each spouse, and paper-and-pencil forms to gather essential information pertinent to treatment and to rule out possible exclusionary conditions.

First, the ICT therapist would use this initial evaluation period to determine if there is any reason to exclude Jan and Mike from ICT therapy. Couples exhibiting domestic violence that has led or would lead to injury and intimidation are not appropriate for ICT or any couple therapy, except perhaps couple therapy that is directed specifically at violence (e.g., Brannen & Rubin, 1996; O'Leary, Heyman, & Neidig, under review). Violence is not treated within the context of ICT because treatment may trigger violence and can support a relationship that threatens the safety of one of the members. The Conflict Tactics Scale (CTS-II; Straus, 1979; Straus, Hamby, Boney-McCoy, & Sugarman, 1996) can be used to gather information on the level of physical and emotional abuse between partners. The individual session with each spouse is also a point at which issues of domestic violence can be raised, and is one of the main reasons individual sessions are conducted. Couples will often not report violence during joint sessions, seeing it as a symptom of a larger, more pressing problem. Moreover, some spouses, usually the wife, will not admit the presence of abuse, fearing reprisals from her husband at home. Individual sessions and questionnaires completed separately from the husband or wife would allow a battered spouse to report violence confidentially. The therapist will also routinely assess for domestic violence throughout the course of therapy.

The ICT therapist also determines if there is some reason to believe that one or both of the spouses is suffering from a more debilitating psychological condition that may need to be addressed more urgently. These include severe depression or suicidality, psychosis, substance abuse or dependence, and antisocial, border-line, or schizotypal personality disorder, which will be assessed during the clinical interviews. These issues require more immediate attention which cannot be adequately addressed in couples therapy. These confounding factors will also limit the therapy itself, making success of treatment less likely.

The individual sessions also give the therapist an opportunity to evaluate each spouse's commitment to the relationship. Without the other present, Jan and Mike may be more forthcoming about their feelings about the relationship, involvement in other relationships, and willingness to work on their relationship. In some cases, a spouse may have already decided to separate or divorce and wants to use therapy to facilitate that process. Obviously, it is crucial for the therapist to learn this information as soon as possible. Separation or divorce therapy, rather than ICT, may be appropriate in this case. If either Mike or Jan is involved in an extramarital relationship, the therapist must assess his or her willingness to end that relationship or willingness to reveal the relationship to the other. ICT therapists are generally unwilling to continue marital therapy if one partner is involved in a current extramarital affair and is unwilling to end the affair or disclose it to the partner.

A second function of the evaluation period is to gather basic information from Mike and Jan regarding their levels of distress, their commitment to their relationship, their relationship history, and the problems they currently face. Much of the time spent in the first clinical interviews, both conjoint and individual, will focus on these issues. Jan and Mike will discuss the main problematic areas and how they are played out in their daily lives. The therapist will also ask them to describe the history of their relationship, including their initial attraction to each other, their courtship, and the development of their presenting issues. This information provides the therapist with an understanding of the reasons they became a couple, the characteristics they found attractive in each other, and what it is that still keeps them together. Other important information includes the progression and evolution of their problems and what has and has not helped in attempting to resolve them.

In addition to the clinical interviews, two questionnaires can be used to assess initial levels of distress. The Marital Satisfaction Inventory-Revised (MSI-R; Snyder, 1979; Snyder, 1997) generates a number of indices of relationship functioning, including a global measure relationship satisfaction (the Global Distress Scale). The Dyadic Adjustment Scale (DAS; Spanier, 1976) also measures several indices of relationship functioning, including a global measure of dyadic adjustment. These specific measurements identify the couple's strengths and weaknesses, as well as their sense of relationship well-being. Both instruments have extensive normative data on clinical and nonclinical groups. In addition to the individual sessions, the Marital Status Inventory (Weiss & Cerreto, 1980) is used to assess commitment. This questionnaire assesses what thoughts (e.g., thoughts of separation/divorce occur to me frequently) and actions (e.g., I have consulted an attorney) the respondent has taken toward separation and divorce.

The last component of the evaluation period is the feedback session, in which the therapist will give Mike and Jan a conceptualization of their relationship difficulties. The therapist will discuss the likely causes of their conflict and each of their contributions to this dynamic, as well as the strengths that are keeping them together and helping them cope with the problems they face.

Conceptualization of Mike and Jan

In ICT, the conceptualization of each spouse and their relationship is called the formulation, which consists of the theme (or themes), which are the couple's fundamental points of contention; polarization, the process through which a couple tries unsuccessfully to resolve their differences and often worsens the differences; and the mutual trap, in which the couple finds themselves at opposite ends as a result of the polarization process and experiences negative emotions such as hopelessness.

Two main themes emerge as the primary points of contention for Jan and Mike. The first centers around issues of trust, and is primarily a concern for Jan. She has had a long history of dealing with drug problems in people close to her and is therefore sensitized to the issue. First her younger brother, whom she helped to raise, used drugs extensively; then drug use and infidelity lead her to divorce her first husband; and now her second husband, Mike, has a drug problem. For his part, Mike has struggled with drugs for years, but with Jan's nagging, he often feels unsupported by her in his struggle to kick his habit.

The second theme is closeness, in which Mike and Jan differ about the level of emotional involvement versus personal independence that they each desire. Jan summed up their presenting problem as "difficulty achieving emotional intimacy due to continual conflicts and lack of effective solutions." Emotional closeness is important for Jan, who maintains close contact with parents and who sees her friends as her "real supports." Mike, on the other hand, was shy and tended to stay by himself as a child. Even during their courtship, Mike and Jan spent most of their time with Jan's acquaintances, and he now has few close friends. He prefers solitary activities, such as working on the computer or making furniture in his spare time. However, Jan wishes Mike wouldn't work so much on weekends and would spend more time with her.

As a result of their behavior around these core themes, Mike and Jan have become polarized, a natural consequence of the struggle to change each spouse. Jan is confrontational during their arguments and criticizes Mike, who tries to avoid conflict by withdrawing, dismissing what she says, and walking out of the room. His sensitivity to criticism probably developed from his relationship with his mother, who "tended to be very critical" of him and blamed any problems he had on something he had done. Jan perceives Mike's withdrawal as a lack of respect and a dismissal of her feelings. As a result, she may intensify her confrontation criticism of him and he may increase his withdrawal from her. As a result, the problems with trust and closeness are exacerbated rather than solved.

The result of their polarization is the mutual trap, a sense of hopelessness about the relationship, a sense that there is no way out. Mike and Jan both feel "confused" about their feelings and "ambivalent" and "frustrated" about the relationship. They are stuck in a pattern of their own making, but from which escape currently seems impossible. Faced with their own inability to extricate themselves from this trap, they considered divorce, but sought therapy.

Their most recent argument, the one that prompted them to finally come in for therapy, illustrates the themes that trouble Jan and Mike and provide glimpses into their polarization from each other and the mutual traps they experience. The argument concerned both trust and closeness. According to Jan and Mike, they had been "getting along fairly well" in the past several months. Mike had been calling Jan a lot to let her know "where he was and what time he was coming home." As a result, Jan had begun trusting Mike again. However, an incident around a party by a family friend, Jennifer, destroyed her trust.

Although both Jan and Mike were invited to Jennifer's party, Jan did not like Jennifer, did not want to go, and secretly wished that Mike would not go either. Mike knew that Jan did not like Jennifer and decided to go by himself, perhaps wanting some time away from Jan. Mike fell asleep at the party, awoke very late, and knowing Jan would be upset, drove home immediately. Jan was furious that he came home so late without calling. Jan described feeling "unappreciated" by Mike: "He could have at least called." She didn't want him to go alone to the party at all, yet thought she could trust him there. For her the trust was broken and she, in anger, threatened divorce. Mike, on the other hand, felt as if he were in a no-win situation: although he didn't want to upset Jan by going to the party, he also resented the restriction Jan put on his social life by disapproving of Jennifer. He wanted to be able to go to the party and have fun, regardless of whether Jan decided to come. He was angry that despite his weeks of faithful calling, this one incident sealed his fate: in Jan's eyes, he was no longer trustworthy.

Fortunately, Mike and Jan have several strengths that will help them through therapy. They were both willing to seek treatment, which demonstrates a commitment to improving their marriage. In fact, they both claim "that they remain together despite their differences because deep down inside they truly love each other. They want very much to be together . . . " Each has personal strengths as well; for example, Mike has been fairly successful in battling his substance abuse, and Jan was able to stop using drugs altogether. Their commitment to the relationship and their past experience in overcoming challenging personal problems will help them in trying to improve their marriage.

Treatment Goals

The predominant short-term therapeutic goals of ICT are to promote acceptance and change in Jan and Mike's relationship. Though these two notions may seem incompatible at first glance, they work in conjunction to increase satisfaction in the relationship. Acceptance as conceptualized in ICT is not resignation to the problems in the marriage; rather, it is at the very least a tolerance of the partner's "negative" characteristics and at the most an active embrace of those characteristics. Acceptance can also be seen as a form of change, but it involves an affective-cognitive shift, a change of perception and emotions, instead of in actions. Instead of the spouse changing in the direction one desires, there is a change in one's emotional reactions to the spouse. This change in emotional reactivity makes personal differences easier to accept, enhances intimacy, removes the pressure for change, and often, paradoxically, makes partners more willing to change. Without the pressure to change, partners often find it easier to accommodate to the other.

If partners become more accepting of each other but make only limited spontaneous changes in the behaviors that each desires, a focus on deliberate change is sometimes necessary. The strategies associated with Traditional Behavioral Couples Therapy, such as Behavior Exchange, Communication Training, and Problem Solving Training, are used to foster specific changes in each partner's behavior.

To measure Jan and Mike's progress in therapy, the therapist will observe and track their levels of acceptance and change over the course of treatment. Acceptance can be seen in how spouses respond to each other's negative behavior, both at the time of that negative behavior and later as they reconsider that behavior. Change occurs if spouses alter the frequency or intensity of their actions that are of concern to their partners. Jan would show acceptance if she, at least during therapy discussions, showed understanding of Mike's dilemma about Jennifer's party and, as a result, was less furious at what he had done. Mike would show change by calling her more consistently when his circumstances change.

In addition to interview assessments of acceptance and change, Christensen and Jacobson (1997) have created a questionnaire, the Frequency and Acceptability of Partner Behavior Inventory (FAPBI), to measure these dimensions. This questionnaire is currently in use in a longitudinal study of marital therapy conducted by Christensen and Jacobson. It asks each spouse to estimate the frequency of their various positive and negative behaviors of their partners. Then it asks them to rate the acceptability of those behaviors at their current frequencies. Respondents also indicate which behaviors of the other are most distressing.

The main long-term goal in treating Mike and Jan is greater satisfaction in their relationship. Thus, treatment success would be determined by a clinically significant increase in marital satisfaction, reported by the couple both in the therapy itself and on satisfaction questionnaires. Several of the measures used to assess levels of distress at the beginning of therapy may be used to assess long-term improvement, such as the Dyadic Adjustment Scale and the Marital Satisfaction Inventory. Levels of satisfaction both during and at the end of treatment can be compared with initial reported levels to determine the amount of improvement. Optimal success would be for Mike and Jan to achieve a level of satisfaction in their relationship comparable to that reported by nondistressed couples.

A second long-term goal is maintenance or enhancement of improved functioning as a result of treatment. Some couples improve in therapy, only to relapse later. Our goal for Mike and Jan, obviously, would be for them to improve their marital satisfaction and maintain that improvement. This goal can be assessed by giving couples the aforementioned satisfaction measures at follow-up periods after treatment. Christensen and Heavey (1999) recommend at least 2-year follow-ups after treatment.

For some couples, marital satisfaction is not a realistic possibility; separation and divorce is the more realistic goal. In that case, a constructive separation and divorce, rather than marital satisfaction, becomes the goal. However, "separation therapy" or "divorce therapy" is beyond the scope of this chapter.

Techniques and Interventions

The promotion of acceptance involves three major strategies: empathic joining, unified detachment, and tolerance building. In empathic joining around the problem, the therapist promotes a mutual sense of sympathy and regard for the partner's pain in relation to a problem they have together. The first step is for the therapist to provide the couple with a formulation of their problem. As described earlier, the new formulation the therapist gives the couple consists of three main components: the theme, the couple's main point of conflict; the polarization process, in which the couple exacerbates conflicts through unsuccessful attempts to resolve their differences; and the mutual trap, in which the couple is caught in an emotional bind in which neither will budge for the other. One of the major goals in describing the formulation to a couple is to foster a sense of compassion between them. Although each spouse knows his or her own sense of entrapment, hearing the therapist describe the other spouse's similar experiences may generate greater understanding and appreciation for the pain and sadness each of them is experiencing.

During the feedback session with Mike and Jan, an ICT therapist would normalize each of their negative responses to the other and show how these responses naturally arose from each one's respective situation in the relationship.

For example, the therapist might reformulate Jan's verbal requests, which Mike currently sees as "nagging," as her way of showing concern for Mike and an attempt to create emotional closeness. Mike's "withdrawal" might be reformulated as concern for the relationship by attempting to avoid conflict.

A second step in emphatic joining is to promote the expression of "soft" emotions versus "hard" ones. Hard emotions are ones like anger and resentment, which cast the self in a strong position vis-à-vis the other. In contrast, soft emotions are ones like disappointment and hurt, which cast the self in a vulnerable position vis-à-vis the other. Often, hard emotions such as anger are in reaction to soft emotions, such as hurt. Jan and Mike seem to generally use hard emotions during arguments: Jan criticizes Mike, while he dismisses her and stomps out of the house. In therapy, however, the therapist might encourage Jan to talk about what feelings underlie her criticism, and Mike to discuss how the criticism affects him. For example, an ICT therapist would encourage her to explore her fear that Mike may return to heavy drug use, or her loneliness at his distance from her. This strategy makes the listening spouse more likely to attend to the talking spouse without getting defensive, and to foster sympathy for how the spouse is feeling.

The second strategy, unified detachment, creates acceptance by promoting a more objective, less emotionally charged perspective on the problem. The problem is portrayed as an "it" that they both must struggle with, rather than a deficit in the other partner. The more descriptive and less emotional Jan and Mike are when talking about their reactions to each other, and ultimately about their theme and resulting pattern of behavior, the more likely it is that acceptance will occur. If they can describe their differences and their polarization around these differences without blame or withdrawal, they will move toward greater acceptance of each other and possibly some change in their positions.

To promote unified detachment, the therapist engages the couple in an intellectual analysis of their problems. The more objective a perspective they can get on the problem, the less emotionally involved they will be. For example, Jan and Mike might identify the triggers to their arguments, describe their process of escalation, discuss recovery after an argument, and compare and contrast various incidents. Adding the element of humor can also help Mike and Jan transform the way they view their problem. If they can take their problems less seriously, they are more likely to accept them. For example, if Jan and Mike can caricature themselves, with names such as Jan "The Nagger" and Mike "The Deserter," they may be more likely to see how extreme their own behaviors are, and even use these terms to diffuse a potentially volatile situation.

As material for both promoting unified detachment as well as empathic joining, the therapist uses emotionally salient material. In the early stages of treatment, therapist and clients will often discuss a recent negative event that led to distress in one or both. The incident around Jennifer's party would be an example of a negative incident that Jan and Mike might discuss. As treatment progresses, they may have more positive incidents in which they dealt with an issue related to their theme in a constructive way. These incidents also need to be debriefed. Finally, an upcoming situation that may provoke a reenactment of the couple's theme and polarization process is also useful for unified detachment and empathic joining.

Tolerance is the third major strategy for promoting acceptance. Developing tolerance for behaviors that are merely reflective of differences between the spouses will mean that the behaviors will have less of an emotional effect when they occur. (ICT would never advocate tolerance of harmful or dangerous behavior, which is why couples experiencing domestic violence or substance abuse are usually referred elsewhere for more appropriate treatment.)

Several techniques can encourage tolerance building. First, the therapist can highlight the positive features of the spouse's currently intolerable behaviors. For example, Mike's weekend work takes him away from Jan, but it also contributes income to their family. A second method for promoting tolerance is to have the couple reenact negative behaviors and scenarios during the therapy session. For example, let's assume that some of Mike and Jan's "checking in" scenarios go badly. Out of her fear and mistrust, Jan questions Mike about his behavior in ways that make him feel attacked and on the defensive. He responds by turning off to her and sometimes hanging up the phone abruptly. The therapist might have Mike and Jan replay such an interaction in therapy, making sure to present it as negatively as it actually was, or even more so. By changing the context in which this scenario occurs, the couple may experience it differently and desensitize themselves to it. Couples can often find some humor in their predicament when they reenact it in therapy, which leads to unified detachment from the problem. In addition, spouses sometimes feel embarrassed or even ashamed about their behaviors when they perform them in front of a third person. They may come to a realization of how their acts really influence the other spouse. If spouses get emotional during the replay, the therapist can stop the process and debrief their experiences in ways that lead to empathic joining.

A third strategy, similar to the second one, is to ask couples to fake negative behavior at home. For example, the therapist might ask Jan to fake her questioning of Mike's behavior some time when she is really not concerned about his behavior. Since she won't be emotionally aroused at the time, Jan can more accurately observe the effects of her behavior on Mike. If he responds negatively, then she can stop the interaction and reveal the "fake." This assignment is given in Mike's presence so he will know that some of Jan's behavior in the next week may be faked. With this knowledge, his automatic response to her may be interrupted. Thus, both may be able to achieve some distance from their negative interaction through this strategy.

Mike and Jan can also increase their tolerance of one another through greater self-care. Until specific needs are met in their relationship, Jan and Mike may seek to satisfy their needs through outside methods not detrimental to the relationship. For example, although Jan would ideally like greater closeness with Mike, she may find some fulfillment through closeness with a friend. This technique serves two fundamental purposes: first, it is sometimes a simpler way of meeting a basic need; second, it stresses to each spouse the importance of personal responsibility in satisfying one's own needs. However, the therapist must make certain that these methods are acceptable to each spouse and does not relieve them of the responsibility of working toward their joint goals of meeting each other's needs.

These strategies of acceptance often lead to a softening of partners' responses to each other. They become less accusatory and defensive, and are better able to explore their difficulties than to attack each other for them. Often, this greater acceptance leads to some spontaneous change in each spouse. As they listen more for the pain rather than the accusation in each other's experience, they may alter their behavior to lessen each other's pain.

However, in some couples, the promotion of acceptance does not bring sufficient change to foster marital satisfaction. Therefore, in the second stage of ICT, the therapist tries to bring about deliberate change. Whereas other types of therapy attempt to induce behavior change from the beginning of therapy, ICT recognizes the couple's initial reluctance and inherent difficulties involved in doing anything for the sake of the other spouse. This is why acceptance and tolerance techniques are implemented in ICT before attempting major work on deliberate behavior change. If changes in behavior are encouraged early on in therapy, most of these changes will be temporary unless the couple has a firmly established collaborative set; they must first share a sense of mutual responsibility for the problems in their relationship. Only then is the couple ready to make a commitment to permanent behavior change.

At this point, the therapist can teach two categories of behavior change techniques. First, behavior exchange (BE) emphasizes increasing the ratio of positive to negative behaviors between the couple. The goal of behavior exchange is not the unrealistic expectation of making all interactions between the couple positive. Instead, BE techniques encourage the couple to engage in behaviors that have a positive influence on their relationship on a day-to-day basis. Its main purpose is to prevent the inevitable reinforcement erosion that occurs when a couple makes little concerted effort to sustain interest in the relationship.

Second, communication and problem-solving training techniques teach more effective speaking and listening skills. Communication training involves both speaker and listener skills. When in the role of speaker, Jan and Mike would be taught to discuss their feelings in reaction to the other's specific behavior rather than to attack and accuse the other. When in the listening role, Jan and Mike would use active listening skills, such as paraphrasing and validation. Mike and Jan would also be taught how to define their problems clearly and how to generate, evaluate, and implement solutions to these problems. These strategies are described in greater detail elsewhere (e.g., Jacobson & Margolin, 1979). However, in ICT, these strategies are implemented with considerable flexibility and always include an option to fall back on acceptance strategies. If Mike and Jan were to get into a struggle during these sessions, the therapist would use empathic joining, unified detachment, and tolerance interventions to explore the struggle and soften each other's positions in it.

Pitfalls

The most hazardous, and perhaps most likely, pitfall for Mike and Jan would be the recurrence of Mike's drug and alcohol abuse. Given his long history of abuse, including arrest and loss of employment because of substance abuse, as well as the relatively short period of his current abstinence (7 months), Mike is at some risk for relapse. Continuing with his weekly attendance at Narcotics Anonymous meetings throughout the course of marital therapy would be highly advised for Mike.

In addition, a possible intervention early in therapy would be to ask Mike to make a written pledge to continue treatment and continue abstaining from drugs and alcohol. He may have already made a similar promise to his NA group, since abstinence is usually a goal of such self-help support groups. Given Mike's past behavior and his risk for recurrence, a promise from him to abstain from substance use may also be an effective tool for couples therapy. Such a contract would serve two primary purposes. First, it may reduce Jan's anxiety about a relapse. Second, the contract could be framed as a way of extricating Mike's substance abuse from the relationship. With a contract in place, Jan and Mike could work on the relationship issues most salient to them, without the shadow of his drug use. In particular, the contract might limit Jan's inclination to use the drug abuse as a scapegoat for their problems.

Should Mike start to develop symptoms of drug or alcohol abuse again, the therapist would need to reevaluate the appropriateness of ICT. The treatment of substance abuse and dependence is a more immediate and pressing issue than continuing couples therapy. ICT is not a model for the treatment of addictive behavior, and is not equipped to confront the myriad of issues that arise with drug and alcohol abuse.

Areas to Avoid

Because the ICT model stresses tolerance and acceptance as major goals of treatment, it does not generally avoid any area of discussion, particularly if it seems to cause conflict between a couple. The ideal in ICT is the couple's acceptance of each other on any issue that causes conflict. The couple's points of contention are actually used as tools for increasing intimacy, so they would be actively pursued in ICT.

In ICT, the determination of what topics to pursue is based on the topic's emotional saliency and its relevance to the couple's theme. If a topic has little or no emotional impact for the couple, then the ICT therapist would move toward one that did have impact. For example, if Jan and Mike discussed their weekend activities, but only with neutral sentiments, the therapist would move on to other, more fruitful topics. Traditionally, behavior therapists have eschewed a focus on the past. However, if the past were emotionally salient to Mike and Jan in the present or if it were relevant to their themes, the ICT therapist would not hesitate to focus on the past. For example, the therapist might bring up Mike's experience of his "critical mother" as a way of explaining his sensitivity to Jan's critical comments. Putting his sensitivity in this historical context might allow Jan to view it more sympathetically.

Inclusion of Other Family Members

Unlike some other forms of therapy, ICT does not generally seek the input from people outside of the couple seeking therapy. The main emphasis of ICT is helping the couple come to an understanding of the ways they become polarized from the interchanges they have with one another, and the involvement of other people in their formulation is usually not necessary.

Particularly because Jan and Mike are childless and have no other relatives living with them, nor do their disagreements revolve around or heavily involve another individual, the therapist will be unlikely to bring anyone else into the therapy session. If they did have children and one of the major areas of complaints centered around problems with their child, then an ICT therapist might have them bring the child to some sessions. Parent training would be taught as needed. If an adult relative, such as a mother-in-law, lived in the home with them and many of their problems focused on differences in dealing with her, then she might be brought into a therapy session as well. However, again the emphasis would be on how the spouses manage the issues about the child or mother-in-law, rather than a family therapy session. Other therapeutic techniques, such as individual or family therapy, may be suggested for other family problems. ICT, however, focuses solely on the marital partnership.

Homework

Homework assignments in ICT treatment serve to complement and further the material covered during therapy sessions. Although most of the work of ICT is done with the facilitative help of the therapist, Jan and Mike may also be given tasks to do between sessions. However, unlike structured treatments, ICT does not have fixed weekly homework assignments that must be completed between sessions. Instead, homework is assigned at the discretion of the therapist whenever therapeutically indicated over the course of treatment. In addition, the therapist must also be sensitive to the reaction of the couple to assignments and their compliance in doing the homework. If Jan and Mike resist doing the homework, the therapist does not pressure them to complete it. In ICT, noncompliance is thought to occur when the assignment was the wrong task for the couple to do at that point in their therapeutic progression. Rather than blaming the couple or pressuring them for compliance, the therapist takes the responsibility of modifying his or her conceptualization of the couple's progress in therapy as well as his or her method of explaining the assignments. In fact, homework assignments can be dropped completely if they don't seem to further the progress of therapy.

In addition to a manual for therapists (Christensen, Jacobson, & Babcock, 1995; Jacobson & Christensen, 1996), there is a book for couples in ICT (Christensen & Jacobson, 2000). Couples are assigned chapters in this book as they go through therapy. The amount of reading is adapted to the needs and abilities of the couple. Ideally, the couples read the first section of the book, which is an analysis of arguments, prior to the feedback session. Then, they read the second section of the book, on acceptance, early on in treatment. Later in treatment, they read the third section of the book, which is on change. Each chapter includes exercises relevant to the content of the chapter. Often, these are thought exercises, such as encouraging partners to describe a major incompatibility in their relationship or to describe a vulnerability that gets touched in themselves or their partners during conflict. There is a fourth section of the book on special problems such as infidelity and abuse. Material in this section is assigned only if relevant.

A major ongoing assignment for couples is to bring in incidents from outside of therapy to discuss in therapy. These incidents, positive or negative, are ones that illustrate the struggles between them. For example, Mike and Jan would bring in incidents related to their themes of trust and closeness (and any other themes that were developed in treatment). If, for example, they handled a potentially problematic issue around trust well, the therapist would want to debrief it in treatment, to examine how and why they dealt with it so effectively. If they had a hurtful exchange when Jan wanted to be close to Mike, the therapist would also want to debrief this negative incident to see what events triggered the pain in each. The therapist would help them process the escalation of emotions and the development of polarization during this incident. In addition to incidents that have already occurred between them, the couple should bring into therapy any upcoming incidents that may trigger problems between them. For example, if Mike were planning to attend another party by himself, the therapist would want to discuss that event in order to anticipate possible problems and prepare for those problems. This deconstruction of positive, negative, and upcoming events is designed to promote understanding and acceptance of each other's positions and emotional experiences. Out of this acceptance may come some spontaneous changes in the way each approaches future incidents.

Occasionally, ICT therapists assign homework that engages couples in novel tasks meant to change the actual experience of their interactions, so that they can become more empathic and objective observers of the conflicts. For example, faking a negative incident at home is a homework task based on the experiential emphasis of ICT. As was described above, the therapist will ask one partner to initiate a negative pattern when he or she is not feeling negative, to observe the consequent impact on the partner, and to end the pattern by revealing the fake before the pattern escalates. The therapist encourages the recipient to be on the lookout for faked negative behavior. Because the initiator will not be troubled by the usual negative feelings, he or she can be a better observer of their pattern. Because the recipient knows that the pattern may be faked, he or she may be able to respond differently to the initiator rather than repeat old, "knee-jerk" responses.

For example, the therapist may instruct Jan to feign irritation at Mike for not calling home to let her know where he is. She is to do this at a time when she is not feeling very bothered by it. Because she is not emotionally aroused as she usually is when discussing this topic with Mike, she can see more objectively his reactions to her complaints and nagging. She will experience their problem in a qualitatively different way and possibly see the effect her behavior has on escalating their interactions. Mike will also undergo a different experience that week as well. Although he won't know the precise moment Jan will decide to fake an incident, he knows it can happen at any time, and he may be less likely to engage in his automatic response to her. If the faked incident results in humor between them, they may achieve some emotional distance from their problem.

Homework assignments may also include tasks meant to promote deliberate change. For example, the therapist may have Jan and Mike rehearse communication strategies they have learned in therapy. Couples entering therapy often need some instruction in learning new ways of communicating with each other that are less accusatory than their current patterns. Couples often begin therapy in a blaming and defensive frame of mind, and teaching them to use more self-focused communication patterns can promote unified detachment and empathic joining around their problems. Mike and Jan may practice active listening and expressive skills, such as the use of "I" statements instead of the more accusing "you" statements. Practicing these techniques at home will enable Jan and Mike to effectively handle subsequent problematic issues.

The couple may also learn problem-solving techniques in therapy as a method of defining and resolving specific behavioral conflicts. In the beginning of treatment, the therapy session is often the only safe space for couples to talk about problems without spiraling out of control. The goal of the therapist is to facilitate Mike and Jan achieving such a space to discuss issues at home as well. Once Mike and Jan have become proficient in using these problem-solving strategies to resolve their conflicts during the sessions, they can create structured problem-solving sessions at home. To maximize the likelihood that they will resolve the issue effectively, the couple should designate a neutral setting in which to tackle a specific problem and try to keep the problem-solving session short and focused on one topic. At first, the couple will be encouraged to practice solving a minor problem using the methods learned in therapy and without reverting back to blaming and accusing each other. They can eventually work toward solving even major issues using the positive communication techniques at home as well as in the therapy session.

Behavioral exchange strategies are also techniques couples do at home. As mentioned earlier, behavior exchange techniques are useful in treating reinforcement erosion in a relationship by helping the couple find new positively reinforcing behaviors each partner can do for the other. The therapist may ask each partner to generate a list of behaviors that they could do to make the other happy. Each spouse may be encouraged to engage in these positive behaviors when they feel positive toward the other.

The experience of the couple outside of therapy is the criterion of success in any couple's therapy. Not matter what happens in therapy, if that in-therapy experience has no impact on their experience at home, therapy is a failure. Homework in ICT can facilitate this transfer between therapy to home.

Timeline for Therapy

Because the foundation of Integrative Couple Therapy is based on personalizing the course of therapy according to the needs of each couple, it is not a rigidly structured treatment. Instead, the therapeutic schedule is determined from one session to the next, depending on what issues the couple is currently facing and the extent of acceptance and change they are able to achieve. Specifically, the formulation of the couple's issues is the driving force behind the techniques used in therapy. For example, if Mike failed to call Jan one night before he left work, the therapist will ask each of them to discuss the event in terms of their theme of trust. If they are able to understand and discuss each other's experience with a measure of empathy or detachment, the therapist can opt to use techniques meant to foster direct behavioral change. If they cannot talk about the incident without becoming emotional and accusatory, the therapist will instead focus on achieving empathic joining, unified detachment, or tolerance instead. Thus, the various techniques and strategies involved in ICT are not laid out from week to week; rather, they are used when the therapist finds them appropriate throughout the course of treatment.

Therapy in ICT generally consists of approximately 25 weekly sessions of 50 minutes, leading to about 6 or 7 months of therapy. Sessions may spread out toward the end of treatment and occur every 2 or 3 weeks until termination. Again, the actual course of treatment will depend on the needs of the couple. As described earlier, the first several sessions are considered an evaluation phase, made up by the initial joint interview with both Mike and Jan, then individual sessions with each of them, and a joint feedback session.

The first session also aims to have a therapeutic effect with Mike and Jan, in addition to gathering information. The therapist's purpose is to give them a sense of hope for their relationship, rather than allowing them to become provoked by each other's complaints. The therapist will ask Jan and Mike to describe the history of their courtship, including their attractions to one another. By having the couple focus on the reasons they became attracted to each other, the therapist fosters in the couple a sense of hope about their relationship and orients the couple to the future and the goals they can think about working toward achieving. It also provides the therapist with valuable information about the basis of Jan and Mike's attraction to each other, their relationship before problems began, and their current relationship on days when they get along.

It is crucial that the therapist remain objective and evenhanded with each of the partners. Jan and Mike will each have an opportunity to describe their individual experiences in their relationship, both in the conjoint session and their individual sessions, and it is important that the therapist validates the experiences of both partners. Supporting the legitimacy of each of their experiences will help Mike and Jan feel that the therapist understands their perspectives. The individual sessions will give Jan and Mike each the opportunity to express their personal experiences with the conflict in their marriage without the influence of their partner in the room listening to them. This serves to bolster Mike and Jan's confidence that the therapist is truly attending to each of their personal perspectives.

In the feedback session, the therapist will present the formulation to Mike and Jan and describe the ways in which each of them plays a role in their problem and the way in which they polarize over their differences. Throughout this process, the therapist will again validate their positions, portraying their feelings and behaviors as understandable reactions to the issue with which they are struggling.

The couple's immediate issues and their progress with acceptance work structure the composition of later therapy sessions. The ICT therapist should not have an agenda for the couple; instead, the problems and issues that Jan and Mike bring to therapy each week will determine in which direction the therapy will go. Jan and Mike will see their therapist weekly in joint sessions for much of this time. As the couple masters the various acceptance and tolerance techniques and therapy seems to be coming to a close, sessions may switch to a biweekly schedule until a mutually agreed-upon termination date. Short individual sessions during therapy can also be used as a last-ditch effort when couples are fighting so intensely during therapy sessions that progress has been halted or reversed. Each spouse then has a chance to get the therapist's undivided attention regarding their views of the current argument, while the therapist continues with objectivity and acceptance.

Couples facing other very serious issues in their marriage or personal lives may be referred to other specialists for treatment of those issues. As discussed earlier, outside referrals are made for couples in which one or both spouse is suffering from untreated problematic symptoms of a major psychiatric disorder, such as psychosis, depression, bipolar disorder, or certain personality disorders. Again, professionals more experienced in handling these matters would be consulted in these situations, and psychopharmacological treatment can be pursued conjointly with ICT therapy.

Couples are also referred to outside therapists when pressing issues of the safety of one or both spouses arise. Although the central tenet in ICT therapy is a person's acceptance of his or her spouse, we certainly do not advocate acceptance of destructive behavior. Battering, emotional abuse, and drug or alcohol addiction are urgent issues that must be addressed immediately. ICT is inappropriate as a treatment for these issues. Thus, should Mike experience a significant relapse in his drug use, he would be referred for additional treatment. Depending upon the circumstances, marital therapy may even be discontinued until his drug problems are under control again.

Termination and Relapse Prevention

The decision of termination rests jointly with the therapist and couple. If Mike and Jan decide they no longer need therapy and the therapist believes they have improved, the couple can terminate easily. However, if Jan and Mike have difficulty deciding when to end therapy, the therapist can space their sessions further apart so that they become less and less frequent until they eventually stop. Increasing the time between sessions is an effective way of weaning couples off of therapy, giving them more opportunities to resolve conflicts on their own between therapy sessions.

Relapse prevention is built into ICT. The therapist often mentions that a couple's initial theme will reappear, and conflict over that theme is natural and inevitable. The therapist may comment that at her essence, Jan is more social than Mike and these differences in sociability are liable to lead to conflict on occasion. Using tolerance interventions, the therapist may have Jan and Mike rehearse "slip-ups" around their theme—occasions when they get back into their polarizing pattern as a result of one of their themes.

The final session, if a formal one is scheduled, will be a time for feedback from the therapist to the couple and vice versa. The therapist will review and summarize what has happened in the past few months the couple has spent in therapy, going over their formulation and the perspective they have gained in achieving a unified detachment and empathic joining around their problems. Jan and Mike will also have an opportunity to tell the therapist what they have gained from therapy, what was and was not helpful for them. The couple is also encouraged to recontact the therapist if they feel they need a booster session at some point in the future.

At the end of treatment, Jan and Mike will have learned the importance of acceptance and tolerance of their differences, which will allow them to have more empathy for each other. Although they will still have issues with each other, they will be more committed to staying together and working on improving the relationship. They will have come to perceive and understand the pain the other spouse has felt and see the spouse as a mutual partner in the dilemmas they share. Due to the unified detachment they have gained, Mike and Jan will also be able to describe their conflicts more objectively from a distance. As a result, their conflicts will be experienced as less intense as before therapy, and they will recover from them more quickly.

REFERENCES

Brannen, S., & Rubin, A. (1996). Comparing the effectiveness of gender-specific and couples groups in a court-mandated spouse abuse treatment program. *Research on Social Work Practice, 6,* 405–424.

Christensen, A., & Heavey, C. L. (1999). Interventions for couples. *Annual Review of Psychology, 50,* 165–190.

*Christensen, A., & Jacobson, N. S. (2000). *When lovers make war.* New York: Guilford Press.

Christensen, A., & Jacobson, N. S. (1997). *Frequency and acceptability of partner behavior inventory (FAPBI).* Unpublished questionnaire.

*Christensen, A., Jacobson, N. S., & Babcock, J. C. (1995). Integrative behavioral couple therapy. In N. S. Jacobson & A. S. Gurman (Eds.), *Clinical handbook of couples therapy* (pp. 31–64). New York: Guilford Press.

*Jacobson, N. S., & Christensen, A. (1996). *Integrative couple therapy: Promoting acceptance and change.* New York: Norton.

Jacobson, N. S., & Margolin, G. (1979). *Marital therapy: Strategies based on social learning and behavior exchange principles.* New York: Brunner/Mazel.

---

*Suggested reading.

O'Leary, K. D., Heyman, R. E., & Neidig, P. H. *Treatment of wife abuse: A comparison of gender-specific and conjoint approaches.* Under review.

Skinner, B. F. (1966). *The behavior of organisms: An experimental analysis.* Englewood Cliffs, NJ: Prentice-Hall.

Snyder, D. K. (1979). Multidimensional assessment of marital satisfaction. *Journal of Marriage and the Family, 41,* 813–823.

Snyder, D. K. (1997). *Marital Satisfaction Inventory, Revised (MSI-R): Manual.* Los Angeles: Western Psychological Services.

Spanier, G. B. (1976). Measuring dyadic adjustment: New scales for assessing the quality of marriage and similar dyads. *Journal of Marriage and the Family, 38,* 15–28.

Straus, M. A. (1979). Measuring intrafamily conflict and violence: The Conflict Tactics (CT) scales. *Journal of Marriage and the Family, 41,* 75–88.

Straus, M. A., Hamby, S. L., Boney-McCoy, S., & Sugarman, D. B. (1996). The revised Conflict Tactics Scale (CTS2): Development and preliminary psychometric data. *Journal of Family Issues, 17,* 283–316.

Weiss, R. L., & Cerreto, M. C. (1980). The Marital Status Inventory: Development of a measure of dissolution potential. *American Journal of Family Therapy, 8,* 80–85.

SUGGESTED READING

Christensen, A., & Jacobson, N. S. (1998). Acceptance and change in couples therapy. In K. S. Dobson & K. D. Craig (Eds.), *Empirically Supported Therapies: Best Practice in Professional Psychology* (pp. 133–156). Newbury Park, CA: Sage.

12

Integrative Marital Therapy

William C. Nichols

TREATMENT MODEL

Integrative marital therapy as an approach to understanding and working with married couples has been described in a variety of books and articles by William C. Nichols (Nichols, 1985, 1988, 1996, 1998, 2000; Nichols & Everett, 1986; Nichols & Pace-Nichols, 1993); and others Larry Feldman (1979, 1982, 1985, 1992; Feldman & Pinsof, 1982); William M. Pinsof (1983, 1995); Robert T. Seagraves (1982); Daniel Wile (1981).

Integrative Marital Therapy (IMT) combines family systems, psychodynamic, and social learning theories. From the family systems approach comes an emphasis on the contextual (interactive, systemic) dimensions in which clients live and function; a new epistemology; a broad systems outlook (emphasis on organization, subsystems, wholeness, boundaries, hierarchy, open systems, feedback, nonsummativity, equifinality, communication, stability and change, structure, and process), as well as change. Psychodynamic psychotherapy provides an emphasis on the individual, intrapsychic areas; on unconscious processes; on interpersonal processes borrowed from the work of Harry Stack Sullivan (1953a, 1953b, 1954); and an object relations emphasis (dyadic interactive and choice factors) stemming from the work of W. R. D. Fairbairn (1952, 1954, 1963) and Henry V. Dicks (1963, 1967). Particular attention is given to the processes of introjection, projection, collusion, and projective identification in marital couples. From behavioral approaches come an emphasis on individual, observable behavior; on learning/teaching processes (cognitive processes and techniques for achieving change); and on change.

How I attempt to synthesize these selected emphases from the three models was described in an earlier book (Nichols, 1996, pp. 52–56). The emphasis is on integration of theory rather than on blending various techniques of intervention. Integrative marital therapy does not consist of a set of techniques that can be specified for interventions in all cases. Rather, therapeutic interventions and the patterns of therapy are tailored to the clients and their personalities and needs, and depend also—as do the interventions of all therapists—on the personality and orientation of the therapist.

Integrative marital therapy is dedicated to a "both-and" rather than an "either-or" approach to working with marital couples. That is, it is focused on the person and the systems: on the person's dynamics, feelings, and thoughts as well as on the major systems and subsystems in which the person functions. It is not based on a purely systemic approach or solely on an individual orientation. Marital therapy is concerned with the lone voluntary relationship in the family, with a relationship that may or may not continue, and with two individual personalities and their strengths, problems, and vicissitudes, as well as their interaction and the patterns in which they are attached and engaged in the relationship. Put in another way, I am concerned with the significant contexts (systems and subsystems) into which the persons fit and the kinds of processes that characterize their lives and functioning. In therapy, the focus is on the communication and feedback processes that occur among the larger contexts, the interpersonal relations in the marital subsystem, and the individual behaviors and psychic processes of the persons in the marriage.

At a pragmatic level, I look for the "complementarity" that prevails, meaning how the two partners "fit together" in their current relationship and what attracted them originally (as far as I can ascertain). How has the complementarity changed? What kinds of needs do they fill for each other? As a heuristic guideline, I utilize a "five C's" framework for assessing the major areas of marital interaction. This simple framework, which has the value of being easily comprehensible to clients, was formed two decades ago in response to a request to provide guidelines or a type of checklist that would help them to understand how they were coping with the joint tasks in their relationship. The checklist and how it is used has been refined over the years.

The five "C's" refer to Commitment, Caring, Communication, Conflict and Compromise, and Contract (Nichols, 1988, 1996, 1998; Nichols & Everett, 1986). Commitment deals with the extent to which the spouses value the relationship and their intentions concerning maintaining it. They may be "preambivalent" (positively committed and have not considered ending the marriage), "ambivalent" (about whether or not to continue in the marriage), or "postambivalent" (have considered leaving but concluded that they will remain in the marriage— postambivalent positive, or decided that they will leave—postambivalent negative) (Nichols, 1988, 1996; Nichols & Everett, 1986). Up to a half-dozen ways of assessing the commitment of the partners to the spouse and marriage may be employed (Nichols, 1996). It is not clear from the case materials whether Jan and Mike have reached postambivalent states, or remain at an ambivalent stage, although the latter seems most likely.

Caring refers to the type of emotional attachment between the partners and involves being concerned with the well-being of the partner, rather than on what one gets from the other. In object relations terms, this refers to whether one is at the "object constancy" (object love) level, in which the partner is valued intrinsically (for herself or himself), or at the "need gratification" level, in which the partner is valued for the gratification provided. I would need to explore the object relations situation between Mike and Jan as an initial step in treatment. This would be accomplished by questioning them more in depth.

Communication refers to the manner in which meanings are conveyed, as well as to what is communicated. Communication segues readily over into Conflict and Compromise issues. How do the partners deal with their disagreements? How effectively do they compromise (i.e., give up some of what they want in order to effect a workable relationship)? Contracts are used here in the sense of facilitating a set of conscious and unconscious expectations held by each partner that the partner is expected to fulfill in the relationship (Sager, 1976).

At the same time the focus is on marital interaction, I am also concerned with the individual condition of the partners. Do they manifest psychopathology/ behavioral pathology individually? Are conventional diagnostic descriptions appropriate for them? If so, what relationship exists between the interactive and the individual problems and pathology? What is the prognosis for Mike's handling of his chemical addictive behavior?

Psychotherapy is both an influence process and an educational process. Clients are responsible for their own change, while the therapist is responsible for facilitating the process as one who creates to the extent possible conditions that lend themselves to commitment to change and learning. It is expected and hoped that clients will leave treatment with some improvement and an increased knowledge of how they function and how they can continue to change in desired directions.

THERAPIST'S SKILLS AND ATTRIBUTES

The ability to establish a relationship of trust—to be sufficiently trustworthy and trusting with the clients—and to form a therapeutic alliance with them is perhaps the single most significant factor in working with clients. While I regard knowledge as essential to the effectiveness of therapists, intellectual acumen does not necessarily rank above possession of kindness. In brief, if I had to make a choice between knowledge and technical skill and kindness and ethical sensitivity when referring a client to a therapist, kindness and trustworthiness on the part of the therapist probably would win the day, although, fortunately, such a choice is not forced upon one very often. The point is, as stated elsewhere, that what one does in therapy is significantly affected by what one is (Nichols, 1998).

This approach, recognizing as it does that therapy is an influence process and an educational process, requires also that the therapist respect each client's right to self-determination. At the same time, the therapist should strive to maintain a balance between the individual partners' needs and rights and the marital relationship needs and prerogatives. Maintaining such "multidirectionality partiality" (Boszormenyi-Nagy, 1966) in my approach does not mean that the therapist is morally neutral—he or she cannot be, in certain instances, such as the abuse of one partner by the other, in which ethical and often legal norms require a non-neutral stance—but that the therapist be equitable, committed to the clients and the treatment process.

The therapist needs to be able to review and process materials in an effective manner cognitively at the same time that he or she is existentially related to the clients, to be critically examining simultaneously with sensitively relating and empathically understanding.

The ability to stand equitably and effectively between two persons who are engaged in a troublesome marital relationship, and to help them to achieve meaningful contact and engage in successful problem resolution, requires that one also be able to weather the negative and/or seductive reactions that they sometimes launch in the therapist's direction. It is helpful in many instances to be able to recognize and acknowledge to oneself that the difficult-to-handle and hard-to-tolerate verbal and emotional currents issuing from the client are directed at you because you have offered to take on the role of therapist; that they go with the territory. We need to be able to "stand the heat or get out of the kitchen."

Recognizing and dealing effectively with gender considerations and ethnicity considerations poses an ongoing challenge for the therapist. Working to change gender inequities in marriage when possible has appropriately become a vital consideration in marital therapy. Similarly, the "shrinking" of the world makes it increasingly important to be respectful of cultural and ethnic factors as one works with representatives of humankind from varied backgrounds. Ongoing study of some of the excellent materials becoming available is certainly a requirement for doing marital therapy today (e.g., McGoldrick, Giordano, & Pearce, 1996).

In the midst of today's emphasis on narrative therapy and communication/conversation in therapy, I am reminded that "good" therapists have always listened and sought meaningful input and conversation from clients. While they "read" the nonverbal and verbal messages put forth by clients, they also are ready to respond sincerely: "I don't understand." "I'm not certain I understand." "Help me understand." "Teach me about yourself. About your background." "Help me to know what you feel and what your problems are, what troubles you." The therapist in this approach needs to be able to listen sensitively and to use her or his discriminatory abilities, as does a good therapist in any approach to marital therapy.

THE CASE OF MIKE AND JAN

Assessment

Typically, I use three approaches in assessment with the marital partners: interviews, observation, and, in some instances, formal assessment devices.

Clinical Interviews

Conjoint and individual interviews are the principal assessment tools used in my integrative approach to marital therapy. I want to hear what the clients say. General questions such as "What brings you in?" or "What are you looking for?" and focused queries such as "What attracted you to your mate, from what you are able to recall?" and "How has your relationship changed since your first meeting?" provide information relevant to treatment. These questions are accompanied by the use of background information forms that typically are completed individually by the partners immediately before the first interview and which provide pertinent dates, demographic data, and family background information. The information and the manner in which the partners complete or fail to complete portions of the form sometimes provide clues to individual and couple dynamics (e.g., a partner who fills in an obviously erroneous date of marriage alerts one to the presence of ambivalent feelings that may need to be pursued in a session).

At the initial assessment point, I generally see a couple conjointly. Sometimes, I split the initial appointment time, seeing each spouse separately, and then conclude with a conjoint session in which I offer feedback and we make decisions about how we will proceed from that point onward. In other cases, depending on what has been achieved and the time available in the first appointment, an individual history-taking and exploratory session is scheduled with each partner at later times. With some clients, a clinical judgment is made during the first sessions that all interviewing can be conducted conjointly, and no individual sessions are scheduled.

Observation

Most of my observation, like that of many clinicians, is essentially informal, and starts when I first observe them in the reception room, continuing when they seat themselves in my office. Not only do I wish to hear what clients say, but I also wish to observe how they relate their concerns, manifest their tensions, and provide behavioral signs of the nature of their relationship. As I explored some of the issues reflected in the case report, I would be observing: Do the partners appear to be apathetic, angry, hostile, caring for one another, competitive, cooperative, or what? Does there appear to be any hope or optimism, or is there a mood of hopelessness or pessimism? How do they communicate with each other? With the therapist? Who talks first? Does one of the partners seem to take the initiative most of the time, or to be in charge of their relationship? Do they listen and comprehend what is said? How do they respond to questions, to suggestions? Is there any humor manifested by either or both individual partner?

Formal Assessment Devices

As a matter of preference, I typically have used psychological testing primarily when working with a forensic case. However, in view of the fact that Mike had a recent hospitalization for drug and alcohol abuse, I would request a report of any psychological testing that was done at that time. Although there seem to be an abundance of psychodynamic basis for their low sexual activity, I would be interested in reports from physicians of both partners, primarily as a means of checking the possibility of contributory physical factors.

In the clinical interviews, I would explore as best as possible the history of the relationship. When and, as well as they remember and can relate, how did they experience change in their social activities and shared interpersonal activities, communication, and affectional and sexual relationship? We know that they enjoyed the "recreational, best foot forward" activities of their brief dating period, were involved in social activities with Jan's friends, and at one time enjoyed a good sexual relationship. I would also seek to establish an understanding of how each needs the other and of the nature of the significant psychodynamic processes of their relationship.

Conceptualization of Mike and Jan

It should be clear that the perceptions described in this section are held both firmly and loosely at the same time. They are held firmly as the best available guidelines for relating to the clients and planning treatment interventions and as hypotheses to be checked and appropriately discarded or altered as soon as new disconfirming information is discovered. Impressions of Jan and Mike, as gleaned from the case report, are as follows:

Jan and Mike do not have a marriage as much as they have "patterns of avoidance" in their relationship. They manifest a "distancer-pursuer" pattern, although one in which Jan seems to pursue for a limited time and then collude in maintaining the status quo by temporarily ceasing to pursue. (There appear to be some psychodynamic ties between this behavior and Jan's training as the "parent" for her younger brother. She seems to have received conflicting messages from her own parents to be responsible and to take care of him and then to "let it go" when she got concerned about his marijuana use.)

Mike and Jan spend very little time together. Both seem to require a significant amount of private time in which each is absorbed in his or her personal interests (e.g., reading, watching television, or using the computer). Their shared time essentially seems to consist of parallel activities or shared activity which is basically parallel, such as cleaning out the stables. Both seem to secure their major satisfactions from work and from "safe" activities, such as caring for their animals.

My impression is that the original complementarity, in which Jan seemed to be the dominant personality who had been attracted to a younger, socially shy, and uncomfortable male her brother's age, has slipped and does not work well now. How and why this has occurred is unclear, although speculation would be that with the passage of time the relationship failed to provide either of them with the satisfactions they sought. I can only speculate about their original expectations and "marital contract." Mike originally was exciting to Jan in part because he was safe and would not exert pressure for them to have children. Likewise, there is little information available that provides bases for good inferences about what they expect from one another today. Mike's behaviors and reports indicate that he does not wish to be criticized, and will leave the scene if Jan becomes critical. His historical pattern of being shy in regard to women, feeling somewhat inferior and fearful of trusting them, appears to continue, as does his childhood pattern of tending to stay by himself. Jan also does not seem to engage to any significant extent in social relationships, although she does talk with her parents almost weekly and has a long-term friendship with Nancy from college days. Neither partner appears to have a good history of dealing comfortably and effectively with heterosexual peers.

From the case material, it is possible to infer a few things about Jan and Mike's affective states. Jan reports feeling unfulfilled in the marriage; Mike, that he feels unappreciated. Understandably, Jan admits feeling confused and ambivalent about her feelings and Mike says he is frustrated. It seems that both are "walking around on eggshells," apprehensive that they cannot resolve their differences and could end up divorcing.

Mike has tended to "medicate" his anxiety with marijuana and alcohol. Even now, he follows a prescribed diet for his cholesterol and hypertensive problems inconsistently, and hopes or expects that his physician will prescribe medication for him.

On the strength side of the ledger, Jan and Mike have been married for 12 years, without any marital separations and without any hint of infidelity. Both claim that they stay together, despite their differences, because "deep down they truly love each other, want very much to be together and wish to avoid being divorced." There are indications that they can still enjoy some activities together (i.e., caring for the animals), and they seem to be able to spend a significant amount of "parallel" time, in the evening and on weekends. Their times of separation evidently occur only when their tension erupts in conflict.

Both work hard and also have stable work records, Jan throughout her occupational career and Mike specifically for the last decade and relatively so for his entire work career. Although Mike has a history of abandoning various activities, he has consistently stayed with his trade of welding, implying that he can and will stay with something that he chooses for himself and likes.

With the possible exception of Mike's chemically addictive behavior, there is an absence of serious emotional disturbance. He has manifested sufficient ego strength to decide that his drug use was out of control and to discontinue his use of marijuana, once for 3 years and currently for 7 months, remaining substance-free after completing a 28-day inpatient regimen of drug and alcohol treatment. He is attending Narcotics Anonymous regularly and using the appropriate support systems. Jan's substance abuse appears to be a thing of the past, and she appears quite supportive of Mike's recovery program.

Both have parents who have been supportive, within their rather severe limits. Mike recalls that his mother was critical of everyone in the family. Jan says that she has maintained a positive relationship with her parents. (How differentiated are the clients from their family of origin?)

Both Mike and Jan indicate that they are bothered by the tension that exists between them, and are interested in psychotherapy as a means of reducing this tension.

These facts can be reinforced with them as strengths and as a good base on which to build as they attempt to learn effective ways of communicating and coping with conflict and learning to compromise.

Treatment Goals

Goals are set by the couple in cooperation with the therapist. Mike and Jan have spoken directly about their goals regarding their marriage. Since therapy for me begins with an assumption of least pathology, I would start with a basic and straightforward approach. When straightforward approaches to the marital problems do not work, I move into larger systems interventions, dealing with extended family problems and attending to social and community factors that affect the situation for better or worse. If my continuing assessment supports the idea that Jan and Mike are currently handling their substance problems adequately, I would support the continuation of their present efforts in that area and move directly into concentrating on the relationship and marital problems. If not, then getting them to settle down in this area would be a preliminary step in working on the marriage.

My first treatment goal with Jan and Mike would be to engage in a feedback process in which we would discuss what they had revealed about their feelings and concerns and used the "Five C's" as a basis for elucidating what they felt ready to work on. They have already declared that they care about each other and wish to change their current relationship and remain married. There typically is a natural segue from the commitment and caring issues into exploring the kind of expectations and marital "contract" that is held. The basic trust issue would have to be dealt with immediately, and the clients helped to recognize that naive trust can never be possible again once it has been breached, but that a workable trust can be established. The exploration and interventions here would be basically psychodynamic in nature, questioning them about early childhood experiences and having them make connections between their marital issues and events that occurred during their upbringing.

A longer-term goal here, once the partners had been able to specify their expectations of their spouse and of themselves in their marital roles, would be to help them become aware of the sources of their expectations. Exploration of their parental and grandparental marriages would be pursued in order to elucidate not only their patterns of identification with the older generation, but also the "models of relationship" that they have internalized from exposure to how the significant adult persons in their lives as children had behaved in their marriages.

It is apparent that they do not have workable communication skills, either for maintaining satisfactory ongoing mutuality or for dealing with disagreements. A subgoal here would be to start teaching communication skills both by modeling and even didactically in the sessions (through largely behavioral and cognitive behavioral interventions). The psychodynamic aspects of attempting to improve communication would include recognition with Jan and Mike that anxiety and fear likely are inhibiting factors and that not communicating serves defensive purposes. This would open the way for exploring with them what would happen if they did learn to communicate and to get closer. In some ways they illustrate Schopenhauer's fable of the freezing porcupines, who are drawn together by their need for warmth but driven apart by the sting of their quills; except that they may be kept apart as much by fear of disappointment as by actual pain inflicted by their mate.

They are not comfortable with differences and conflict, but seem to have internalized their respective families of origin not only an understanding that conflict is inevitable, but, also, that there is nothing to be done about it (e.g., "Get over it," not to worry, and that "all marriages have their ups and downs"). An evolving goal would be that of respectfully disqualifying their parents (Haley, 1976) as authorities on marriage and beginning to help Jan and Mike to learn that it is possible to disagree openly and directly without getting into the familiar patterns of "nagging and withdrawal" or frustration, anger and avoidance of dealing with differences. This would involve a heavy cognitive component as well as exploration of the family backgrounds of their parents. This would shed light on the childhood experiences of their parents, which could help Jan and Mike to view their parents as children responding to their own parents' behaviors and establish a base for viewing their parents less as powerful figures and ogres. This may lessen the impact and influence of their parents on themselves. (See Nichols, 1996, pp. 6–8, for an example of a transformation of a young adult's perception of his father from ogre to that of a frightened son of an austere grandfather.)

Progress toward reaching the various treatment goals would be measured by the reports of Jan and Mike, as well as by observation of the spouses in their dealing with each other in the sessions. The "Five C's" provide a general guideline that can be used by the clients themselves and by the clients and therapist in determining progress toward reaching the treatment goals. How well are they doing? How well, individually and mutually, do they think they are doing in terms of satisfactorily expressing and implementing their commitment and caring, in their communication, in facing and dealing with their conflicts and in compromising, and in having comparatively clear expectations and a more workable marital "contract"?

Treatment goals—whether short-term or long-term—are not static. Two types of change that would be expected in working with Mike and Jan are emerging and reordered goals. As treatment proceeded, I would expect them to add new goals (emerging goals) to those they set at the beginning of therapy, as they recognized that things that were not originally included need to be addressed. Reordering goals pertains to prioritizing initial goals. Jan and Mike might, for example, decide that they needed to work on family-of-origin issues before they tackled some of the problems in their marital relationship and interaction. Alternatively, they might decide to work on financial issues before tackling other sets of marital problems.

Therapy would be considered successful to the extent that the clients reached their stated goals, the presenting complaint and revealed problems were diminished, and the clients were reasonably satisfied with the outcomes and with their new functioning. If their choice were to remain in the marriage, was a functional complementarity established?

Techniques and Interventions

Several specific kinds of interventions would be used, in addition to the typical conjoint sessions with the clients and the individual interviews frequently used during the initial assessment phase. (For an illustration of flexible treatment tailored to the individual and couple needs of a marital pair in which the following forms of intervention were used, see Nichols, 1985.)

Sexual Histories

Although I no longer secure a sexual history routinely with marital couples, doing so only when there are indications of problems in the sexual area, I would secure individual sexual histories with this couple, since they report sex to be a problem in the relationship. The sexual history would cover attitudes, cognitive factors, traumatic experiences, and the client's affectional/sexual experiences from earliest memory into the present, and typically involves reeducation for the client, both during the time in which the history is being secured and subsequently in other sessions. I would not automatically assume that Mike's experiences with his aunt were traumatic, but would be particularly interested in how he responded to the experiences, and in discovering any connections between Mike's being in an "inferior" position with regard to his aunt and his subsequent feelings of feeling "dumb" in relation to females.

Family Genograms

The background information forms mentioned above furnish a considerable amount of the family background data that is required to begin the construction of a family genogram for each of the partners. Unlike some family therapists, I do not routinely construct a family genogram (McGoldrick & Gerson, 1985) with all clients, but rather do it prescriptively. Two indications for constructing a genogram are: (1) The absence of some pertinent information in the initial session and the somewhat intuitive feeling that "something is missing" due to the client consciously or unconsciously withholding something that affects his or her behaviors and feelings. Constructing a genogram would likely bear out any missing pieces. (2) Any difficulty in making sense out of what has been offered verbally, and the perception that a structured approach of the kind used in constructing a genogram would be helpful in keeping the client on track. This would allow the client to "tell the story" of his or her troubles and help to elucidate significant patterns in his or her life ("the patterns which connect," Bateson, 1979, p. 8). Here, I would construct a family genogram with each partner in order to assess the marital and family patterns over at least three generations, with particular interest in the "models of relationship" (Nichols, 1996; Skynner, 1981) and parenting patterns that existed in grandparental marriages, as well as in the parental marriages.

I would construct the genogram of each in the presence of their spouse in order that the spouse could learn some things that he or she did not know previously. The spouse could also offer a close outsider's observations and insights regarding the other's family of origin. Over the years, I have witnessed a few dramatic reactions, including some that led to significant positive changes, when a husband or wife verbalized insights or asked pertinent questions during a history-taking or genogram session with his or her spouse.

Family-of-Origin Sessions

I would consider conducting one or two family-of-origin sessions with Jan and her family and, separately, with Mike and his family. Whether this would be done depends on whether we isolated one or more unresolved background issues that could best be handled in my judgment by meeting with the family of origin and the client (Nichols, 1996, pp. 7–8).

Potential Pitfalls

Impulsive behavior and lack of action directed toward change would be potential pitfalls with this couple. Although they both indicate that they are unhappy with things as they are and wish to secure change, they seem to have a limited ability to tolerate waiting, as evidenced more flamboyantly by Mike generally, but by both of them in their decision to get married and, to a lesser extent, in their recurrent quarreling. The absence of clear and trusting communication, fueled by their anxiety regarding the reactions of the other—as evidenced in the reactions to Mike's recent lateness after attending the party at Jennifer's—lead them to "brinksmanship" behaviors in some instances. In others, they both withdraw and seek to protect themselves by doing nothing. The challenge would be to help them keep going with therapy, risking a rapid escalation in their discomfort as they "break new ground" in their actions and in getting closer to each other, and at the same time trying to help them bind the anxiety and not impulsively dive into either "fight-or-flight" responses.

Limits or boundaries with this couple would be addressed in several ways. One, I would attempt to help them increase their cognitive knowledge concomitantly as I would work with them on improving their skills. For example, I would offer them the following explanation and constructs regarding non-work time: "We can divide our time into three compartments; private time, which is the time that we spend alone; parallel time, which involves a low level of interaction (i.e., watching television, the other reading), and interactive time, which is time in which we are dealing directly with one another (talking, making love, and so on). Most of us seem to need some of each of these types of time. The issue is to get the kind of balance that is satisfactory with us individually as well as with the couple." Exploration of these issues would be aimed at helping Mike and

Jan to work on improving the quality of their parallel and especially their inter-active time, while increasing their freedom to enjoy their private time minus the individual and marital tensions that currently prevail. Another way of addressing the boundary issues and attempting to head off the buildup of tension and the eruption of impulsive behavior would be through the construction of agreements about managing certain aspects of their interaction. An example would be the setting of ground rules for their conversation, particularly for the discussion of potentially disturbing matters. The ground rule that would be accepted by the clients would be an agreement that they would proceed in a "good faith" manner to talk, but that either of them could call "time out" if he or she began to get too uncomfortable. The other would agree to stop. As part of the "good faith" bargain, the person who called time out would be responsible for bringing the topic back up again at a later time, and would not use the time out as a "cop-out" but as a resting period.

Another way of dealing with such issues would be an agreement to bring anything that they did not feel ready to handle on their own back into the therapy session. This would include an agreement to try to refrain from "jumping to conclusions" or "rushing to judgment" in favor of trying to put something on hold until it could be handled in a conversation with the spouse or, if necessary, brought to a therapy session.

Areas to Avoid

It is impossible for me to determine whether or not I could comfortably and profitably address certain issues and areas with Jan and Mike without having had the experience of working with them face-to-face. I certainly would proceed slowly in any efforts directed toward bringing them closer together emotionally. There would need to be a considerable amount of work devoted to helping them lower their anxiety about closeness and intimacy, emotional or physical, before encouraging them to get closer. I would not wish to have the anxiety build up and result in destructive, impulsive behavior.

What kind of therapeutic alliance we could build cannot be determined in the abstract. How much and to what extent Jan and Mike would be able to form a temporary dependency relationship with me, and how and to what extent would I be able to "lend them my ego" so that they could move toward marital intimacy, could only be addressed in the context of live therapeutic experience with them.

In brief, I would surely wish to avoid expecting more of them than they would be able to tolerate in regard to marital intimacy and closeness.

Inclusion of Other Family Members

It is doubtful that I would include anyone else in the conjoint sessions with the spouses, except, as noted above, I possibly would conduct family-of-origin sessions in which Jan would be seen with members of her family and Mike would be seen separately with members of his family. Such sessions would be focused on specific issues previously identified by and with each client as troublesome and in need of exploration and/or remedy. Frequently, such sessions involve the client's needs to have questions answered, or to convey to the parents what they expect and need from them.

There are no other professionals involved in treating Jan or Mike. Jan's prescribed therapy following a hysterectomy occurred too long ago to offer much promise of currently relevant information, even if the therapist of 20 years past were available. As noted, I would attempt to secure reports on any psychological testing done with Mike during his recent inpatient substance hospitalization.

Homework

Jan and Mike would be encouraged to engage in or practice at home some of the communication patterns and exercises they were exposed to during the therapy sessions. This would be done in a manner in which whatever effort they made, and whatever success they achieved would be supported and rewarded in the subsequent sessions. They also would be encouraged to work out, as they were able, mutually satisfactory agreements regarding their use of private, parallel, and interactive time when they were at home. Again, some follow-up regarding their efforts would be done in the next following session, and attempts made to help them discuss their reactions to their endeavors and to "fine-tune" their patterns.

As their situation improved with a change in their evening and weekend behaviors, Jan and Mike would be encouraged to engage in more shared activities and to establish some social activities on a limited basis. The social activities would include going out to events that they enjoyed by themselves, such as movies or perhaps animal shows and, as emotionally and chemically "safe" relationships with other persons could be scheduled, engaging in some trial social interactions with others.

A part of these homework actions would include establishing "good faith contracts" in which the partners would do something that was known to be desired by the other. These contracts are different from "quid pro quo" agreements in which "I will do this for you if you will do that for me," and from contracts in which a partner earns rewards by engaging in specified behaviors. In the good faith contracts, nobody keeps score and there is room for volunteered behavior by each partner. With Jan and Mike, it would seem particularly important to respect their boundaries and to refrain from coercive pressures, leaving them a considerable amount of room to select their own strategies and activities.

Timeline for Therapy

The frequency of sessions is something that I am willing to negotiate with clients. "All right, we will try meeting every other week (or some other frequency) and see how it goes. If we find that it is not working, let's reconsider." I explicitly recognize with clients that there is nothing magical about seeing clients on a weekly basis. The question is, what kind of pattern would work best with this couple? What kind of pattern would provide sufficient support to keep their anxiety manageable? What kind of pattern would most readily break the "crust" that forms between sessions and keep the clients working at a productive level in therapy? How much work would they do between sessions? This is a case with chronic problems, not a crisis case that might require several sessions close together in a "major impact" approach to getting the crisis resolved.

With this couple, I would use an individual session or sessions to take sexual histories. Possibly I would use some additional time with Mike to deal with his sexual abuse experiences. Also, I would possibly use individual sessions to address his stated ambitions (real or otherwise) to work for himself.

Using combinations of individual and conjoint interviews in marital cases is something that I have done with many cases, particularly with cases involving rather complex individual and marital symptomatology (see Nichols, 1985, 1996).

As a rule, I do not consider it a wise move to refer a client who is in marital therapy to another therapist for individual psychotherapy concurrently with the marital therapy. Virtually every time I have agreed to see a couple for marital therapy when one or both were in individual therapy with another therapist or with other therapists, problems of priority of the therapies have arisen. The more professionals that become involved in a case, the more complex the situation becomes, and the greater the need for careful, conscientious collaboration between or among therapists. Rather than referring Jan or Mike for individual therapy, I would prefer to deal with them as described above while they were in marital therapy. If there were any concerns that were essentially individual in their impact, they could be referred for individual assistance later. Short-term consultation is sometimes helpful (e.g., with a child development specialist or child psychologist regarding parenting for couples with children, or with a vocational specialist regarding work matters), and might be considered for Mike if he has significant concerns regarding vocational changes.

Termination and Relapse Prevention

Termination can be either unplanned or planned. While an unplanned termination in which one or both partners decides not to continue—even though the therapeutic work is not completed and the goals not achieved—is undesirable, it sometimes happens. Occasionally the breakoff stems from factors with which the therapist is unacquainted and over which he or she has no control or influence. When a unilateral client decision is made to terminate therapy, it generally seems advisable to me from several perspectives to attempt to bring closure if possible, to have at least one conversation in which "loose ends" can be addressed as well as possible and the client's right to terminate is affirmed and his, her, or their judgment accepted, even if the therapist has a different judgment.

If the therapy with Jan and Mike were long-term and there had been an extended dependency on therapy and on the therapist, specific attention to preparing the couple to function without the therapist and the formal structure and process of therapy would be the responsible course to take. Appropriate opportunity to mourn the loss of something that had been an important part of their life would be a significant step toward the couple's well-being and preparation to function on their own and continued growth.

When the therapy has been long-term, there are several ways in which the treatment can be ended. In a "cold turkey" pattern the therapy ends with an appointment on the final scheduled date. No further contact is planned, and there is consensus that the treatment goals have been achieved and that the partners have "graduated" and seem to be able to handle things on their own at that juncture. In a "tapering off" process, the interval between sessions is increased (e.g., from weekly to every other week or monthly) until there is consensus that the termination point has been reached. There are some differences in the third pattern, "cold turkey with a scheduled checkup." The clients and therapists agree that the couple are ready to try functioning on their own, but with a scheduled appointment for the couple to come in after a reasonable interval such as after one to three months to evaluate how they are doing. The suggestion is typically made with couples who manifest any concern about their ability to function on their own that the supportive structures of therapy are there and that they likely will find themselves using them even though they are not coming in for appointments. At the checkup point, if the couple come in, a decision is made regarding whether to terminate then or to resume treatment. If treatment is resumed, it is likely to be for only a short period. Couples more frequently have canceled the scheduled checkup appointment, indicating that they did not think they needed it. The "will call if necessary" type of termination, the fourth pattern, may be used with other forms of termination (Nichols & Everett, 1986).

With couples in planned termination, I often use a review of the "Five C's" in which we go over where the partners think they are in terms of their commitment, their caring, their communication skills and functioning, their ability to deal with conflicts and to achieve adequate compromises, and in their understanding and agreement on the expectations in their marital "contract." I would also explore with the clients their ability to illustrate clearly the points they make regarding the "Five C's" in their current life and functioning.

With Mike and Jan, I would wish to conclude with them with a planned termination in which we enjoyed a consensus regarding what they had accomplished, how well the stated goals had been achieved, and some realistic statements regarding how they planned to handle their future relationship, both in terms of dealing with problems and in terms of proactive steps to engage in growth.

Specifically, I would like to see this couple achieve a greater degree of differentiation from their respective family-of-origin ties which have been restricting them and restraining their ability to trust others with a significant degree of intimacy. This would include lowered anxiety, greater flexibility in their functioning, and increased ability to select their own patterns of behaving and living and engage in realistic trusting. Specifically, getting the "ghosts of the past" out of major positions in their lives and eradicating the noxious effects of marriage and parenting that they internalized from their parents'—and possibly from their grandparents'—"models of relationships" would be something that I would wish to see for Jan and Mike. Additionally, I would hope to see the emergence of a good functional complementarity, in which the psychological and emotional needs of both partners were being met in a manner satisfactory to each of them and in a generally healthy fashion.

A good sign of ego strength, in technical terms, is the presence of an observing ego that permits one to be an observer and to exercise good judgment, rather than to be submerged inside one's impulses and feelings and lack the ability to make adequate discriminative observations and judgments. As indicated, I do not know what capabilities Mike and Jan have in this area—and could form an opinion only after working with them or perhaps after some psychological testing—but I would hope that if they could be helped to get free of some of the constraining family forces and to develop some increased ability to experience trust and growth with a spouse, they would begin to evidence a noticeable amount of improvement in ego strength.

REFERENCES

Bateson, G. (1979). *Mind and nature.* New York: Bantam Books.

Boszormenyi-Nagy, I. (1966). From family therapy to a psychology of relationships: Fictions of the individual and fictions of the family. *Comprehensive Psychiatry, 7,* 408–423.

Dicks, H. V. (1963). Object relations theory and marital studies. *British Journal of Medical Psychology, 36,* 125–129.

Dicks, H. V. (1967). *Marital tensions.* New York: Basic Books.

Fairbairn, W. R. D. (1952). *Psychoanalytic studies of the personality.* London: Routledge & Kegan Paul.

Fairbairn, W. R. D. (1954). *An object-relations theory of the personality.* New York: Basic Books.

Fairbairn, W. R. D. (1963). Synopsis of an object-relations theory of the personality. *International Journal of Psycho-Analysis, 44,* 224–225.

Feldman, L. B. (1979). Marital conflict and marital intimacy: An integrative psychodynamic-behavioral-systemic model. *Family Process, 18,* 69–79.

Feldman, L. B. (1982). Dysfunctional marital conflict: An integrative interpersonal-intrapsychic model. *Journal of Marital and Family Therapy, 8,* 417–428.

Feldman, L. B. (1985). Integrative multilevel therapy: A comprehensive interpersonal and intrapsychic approach. *Journal of Marital and Family Therapy, 11,* 357–372.

Feldman, L. B. (1992). *Integrating individual and family therapy.* New York: Brunner/ Mazel.

Feldman, L. B., & Pinsof, W. M. (1982). Problem maintenance in family systems: An integrative model. *Journal of Marital and Family Therapy, 8,* 295–308.

Haley, J. (1976). *Problem-solving therapy: New strategies for effective family therapy.* San Francisco: Jossey-Bass.

McGoldrick, M., & Gerson, R. (1985). *Genograms in family assessment.* New York: Norton.

McGoldrick, M., Giordano, J., & Pearce, J. K. (1996). *Ethnicity and family therapy* (2nd ed.). New York: Guilford Press.

*Nichols, W. C. (1985). A differentiating couple: Some transgenerational issues in marital therapy. In A. S. Gurman (Ed.), *Casebook of marital therapy* (pp. 199–229). New York: Guilford Press.

*Nichols, W. C. (1988). *Marital therapy: An integrative approach.* New York: Guilford Press.

*Nichols, W. C. (1996). *Treating people in families: An integrative framework.* New York: Guilford Press.

*Nichols, W. C. (1998). Integrative marital therapy. In F. M. Dattilio (Ed.), *Case studies in couple and family therapy* (pp. 233–256). New York: Guilford Press.

*Nichols, W. C. (2000). Integrative family therapy. In A. M. Horne & J. L. Passmore (Eds.), *Family counseling and therapy* (3rd ed., pp. 539–564). Itasca, IL: Peacock.

Nichols, W. C., & Everett, C. A. (1986). *Systemic family therapy: An integrative approach.* New York: Guilford Press.

Nichols, W. C., & Pace-Nichols, M. A. (1993). Developmental perspectives and family therapy: The marital life cycle. *Contemporary Family Therapy, 15,* 299–315.

Pinsof, W. M. (1983). Integrative problem centered therapy: Toward the synthesis of family and individual therapies. *Journal of Marital and Family Therapy, 9,* 19–35.

Pinsof, W. M. (1995). *Integrative problem-centered therapy: A synthesis of family, individual, and biological therapies.* New York: Basic Books.

Sager, C. J. (1976). *Marriage contracts and couples therapy.* New York: Brunner/Mazel.

Seagraves, R. T. (1982). *Marital therapy: A combined psychodynamic-behavioral approach.* New York: Plenum.

Skynner, A. C. R. (1981). An open-systems, group-analytic approach to family therapy. In A. S. Gurman & D. P. Kniskern (Eds.), *Handbook of family therapy* (pp. 39–84). New York: Brunner/Mazel.

_____

*Suggested reading.

Sullivan, H. S. (1953a). *Conceptions of modern psychiatry.* New York: Norton.
Sullivan, H. S. (1953b). *The interpersonal theory of psychiatry.* New York: Norton.
Sullivan, H. S. (1954). *The psychiatric interview.* New York: Norton.
Wile, D. B. (1981). *Couples therapy.* New York: John Wiley.

13

The Intersystem Model

April Westfall

TREATMENT MODEL

The development of the systems theories and therapies with their focus on interpersonal variables and the shared idea of the person-as-part-of-the-system represented a major paradigmatic shift in psychotherapy. The first 15 to 20 years of this new era resulted in a proliferation of different schools of thought (Gurman & Kniskern, 1981), all originally developed with an aim toward theoretical purity and exclusivity. The practice of marriage and family therapy, however, has always been far different than the theory, with clinicians borrowing freely from the different schools according to their usefulness. In subsequent years, the theorists have made efforts to catch up to the reality of the practitioners in a far-reaching movement toward psychotherapy integration.

In 1981, Berman, Lief, and Williams, all senior members of the Marriage Council (in 1994 changed to PENN Council for Relationships), first published a paper on marital interaction, illustrating how several theories could be combined into a coherent framework. Operating within a systems and developmental framework, they were able to successfully interweave contract theory, object-relations theory, multigenerational theory, and behavioral analysis into a unified whole. Their 1981 paper was followed by the popular text, *Integrating Sex and Marital Therapy: A Clinical Guide* (Weeks & Hof, 1987), creating a bridge between the then more individually oriented sex therapies and the systems-oriented marital therapies. This was followed by the publication of *Treating Couples: The Intersystem Model of the Marriage Council of Philadelphia* (Weeks, 1989), a more comprehensive presentation of this theoretical approach, outlining some basic principles and presenting research into the process elements of the model. Since then, Gerald Weeks and others at PENN Council have published three additional volumes elaborating on the Intersystem Model: the first dealing with techniques and basic approaches to effective practice (Weeks & Treat, 1992); the second consisting of an application of the theory to case study (Weeks & Hof, 1994); and the third continuing with an application to the more common problems of couple therapy (Weeks & Hof, 1995).

The Intersystem Model is a comprehensive, integrative, and contextual approach to treating couples. It requires the simultaneous consideration of three systems or subsystems: the individual, the interactional, and the intergenerational, all within a sociocultural and historical context. A couple is viewed as a system composed of two individuals. Consequently, individual issues, including defense mechanisms, life cycle stages, intrapsychic dynamics, and evidence of psychopathology are serious considerations in therapy. At the same time, a couple is more than the sum of its parts. From the beginning, the therapist observes the characteristic styles of communication and ways of resolving conflict between the pair, while attempting to understand the spoken and unspoken contractual agreements that have shaped their mutual expectations and disappointments through the marriage. Each partner enters the marriage with a unique family history. How that history has formed their expectations about marriage and their capacity to cope with its many challenges is critically important. To grasp the Intersystem Model, the therapist must come to understand the dialectical process that causes these three interlocking systems to impact on each other in continuous fashion. In so doing, the complexity and wholeness of individuals, couples, and families can be fully understood and appreciated.

THERAPIST SKILLS AND ATTRIBUTES

The Intersystem Model demands a breadth of conceptualization that views problems as multifaceted and therapeutic intervention as multidimensional. A specific problem can be approached in many ways, and must be viewed in the broad context of its many etiologies. A specific therapeutic intervention can have an impact on many different problems or different aspects of one problem. The therapist must maintain a constant awareness of the multifaceted problem and multidimensional intervention, while moving between facets, dimensions, and levels in a systematic way. He or she must decide how and when to intervene, choosing from an array of techniques and fluidly shifting among them as opportunities for change occur.

Even though the Intersystem Model calls for a multileveled formulation of the case, the actual work of therapy must be narrowed to a few key issues or recurrent themes at any one time. This narrowing of focus creates intensity to the therapeutic work, so that the couple is able to see below the surface rumblings of their many conflicts to their core issues (e.g., power or control, nurture, intimacy, trust, fidelity, and sense of order or lifestyle; see Goldberg, 1982).

While the Intersystem Model is construed in highly abstract terms, the therapist must make the model come alive in the sessions by rendering it in terms that make sense to the couple. As a staff psychologist at the Philadelphia Child Guidance Clinic in the late 1970s, I had the privilege of observing the family therapy sessions of Salvador Minuchin, a master in the use of language. Repeatedly, Minuchin was able to create metaphors that made the concepts of his Structural Family Therapy Model quite real to families. Perhaps it was the fact that English was a second language to this native Argentinian that allowed him to listen so attentively to the language patterns of his clients, using their own words and phrases, whenever possible, to bring home his point.

In a similar vein, the therapist operating within the Intersystem Model must make the three systems levels and their dynamic interrelationship seem real to the couple through a series of carefully framed questions. At the intergenerational level, a couple's continuing escalation of an argument to the point of name-calling will be interrupted with the question: "Where did you both learn to fight so poorly?" or "Were your parents able to stop their fights before they became so nasty?" At the individual level, this might be followed with a question to the husband: "If you were to choose not to fight back in kind, what would this say about you as a man?" At the interactional level, this might include an appeal to better behavior by both partners: "If you were to choose not to retaliate, what might you do instead?" These questions bring vivid definition to the Intersystem concepts, lost when conveyed in psychological jargon.

The Intersystem Model was developed with the goal of creating a model of therapy that permits the therapy to fit the client, rather than the client to the therapy. In practice, this means that the therapist will intervene in ways consistent with the way the client functions. Some clients may have undergone intensive analytic treatment prior to entering couple therapy. They are likely to respond well to an approach that helps them to appreciate their current marital difficulties with regard to early introjects, and to make spontaneous connections between their couple and individual therapies. Other clients would view this delving into their pasts as a waste of time. They will respond more enthusiastically to a therapy that aims directly to interrupt the destructive behavior patterns in their marriage and to teach them new skills. During the assessment phase, the therapist must remain acutely attuned to the couple's response to his or her probes, which should guide the treatment planning.

THE CASE OF MIKE AND JAN

Assessment

My initial work with couples tends to follow the Intersystem Model (see Westfall, 1994), in that I conduct a fairly lengthy evaluation of the couple before making a decision as to whether to see them in conjoint therapy, and if so, how to proceed with treatment. The assessment process routinely includes a series of structured interviews. When working with premarital couples with only a brief history together, I often make use of questionnaires and assessment instruments that help them project into the future and begin to envision a life together. I would not use them in my assessment of Mike and Jan, with their 12-year history, but instead, would rely on clinical interviews alone.

In the first interview, the couple and their relationship system are the primary focus. With both partners present, I am able to get a picture of their interactional style at the outset of treatment. I listen to how they each define the problems in their relationship and to their reasons for coming to therapy. I also want to understand how the couple system has evolved over time, so that their present difficulties can be placed within historical context.

In the more individually focused interviews, I get a detailed developmental and family history of each partner. In addition, these sessions help develop rapport with each partner, conveying the message that I understand and care about each of them as individual people. I prefer to conduct these interviews with both partners present because their mutual understanding of their individual histories is critical to my way of treatment.

Finally, I conduct a general feedback and review session leading to goal-setting and developing a preliminary treatment plan. This session tends to function as a dialogue between the couple and myself, rather than as a one-way presentation by me. What difference has our work together so far made to their understanding of their problems? How have their feelings about their relationship changed through our discussions? What has it been like for them to discuss such intimate matters with me? In this feedback session, I will also make a recommendation for a consultation with another professional, if necessary, for a more accurate and complete evaluation of their problems.

Given their presentation to treatment as a couple, I would want to begin with Mike and Jan in conjoint therapy. In addition, I would consider referring Mike for diagnostic psychological testing to determine a possible learning disability or attention disorder, which could have factored into his earlier mediocre school performance and general dislike of academics. Obviously, I would only make such a referral if Mike seemed genuinely responsive to the idea of knowing more about himself in this area. Given the excessive amount of time spent sleeping and the general social withdrawal from friends, I would also be concerned with depression in Jan. I would want to pay close attention to this issue in my early assessment, with a possible referral for psychiatric evaluation if indicated.

Conceptualization

Both Mike and Jan come from families where there was little emotional support and nurturance while growing up. Mike's academic struggles were overshadowed by his older brother's more severe learning difficulties and behavior problems. Jan's parents both had careers, and although they were generous with her in material ways, they had little time for her or her younger brother. Consequently, neither Mike nor Jan have come to expect much in the way of positive emotional support or shared intimacy from family. Instead, Jan has turned to her best friend for understanding and Mike to his drinking buddies, if to anyone at all, being more of a loner like his dad. More positively, Mike and Jan both report a great deal of job satisfaction in their chosen careers. Although Mike's job performance has been impaired by his substance abuse in the past, this appears to be less of a problem today, having remained with his present employer for the last 10 years.

Mike grew up in a family where he saw his father dominated by his mother. His father handled this situation by turning to other women through numerous affairs. Mike viewed these infidelities as justified by his mother's constant nagging and belittling remarks. Mike is unable to view their unhappiness in circular terms: considering his mother's critical remarks in relation to her helplessness in the face of his repeated betrayals, which, in turn, prompted his father to continue to look outside the marriage for emotional support. He also blamed his mother for their eventual divorce, and was furious with her at that time, rather than thinking of their breakup as mutually determined.

To some extent, this anger may have been brought on by his mother's increasingly critical attitude toward Mike after the divorce. While his older brother soon became involved with a woman and moved out within the next 2 years, Mike remained at home with his mother until his first marriage at age 29, thus remaining stuck in an uncomfortable situation where he was the brunt of his mother's negativity. This difficult living situation may have contributed to his worsening alcohol and drug problem during those years, which, in turn, would have only intensified his mother's criticisms. Mike coped with this difficult situation by adopting a reactive refusal to accept personal responsibility in the face of strong criticism, especially when coming from a woman, and has continued with this pattern in his marriage to Jan.

Two other factors are implicated in Mike's fear of women and his feelings of being in a one-down position to them. The early sexual molestation by his aunt surely contributed to his fear of being dominated by a woman and to a sense of shame. He also spoke of feeling "dumb" as a child, especially with his female classmates, possibly as a result of an undiagnosed learning disability. These feelings have persisted into adulthood, creating a need to compete favorably with women. When a female coworker was promoted over him in an earlier job, Mike was extremely upset and quit this job within weeks.

Jan was raised in a family with a much more positive role model of marriage in her parents. They have remained together without the history of acrimony or the repeated separations that occurred between Mike's parents. Her adjustment to school and her relationship to peers seems also to have been fairly positive.

Still, with two working parents, Jan was assigned adult responsibilities in the family (e.g., preparing meals, caretaking for her younger brother) at an early age. Although she appears to have handled these responsibilities well during her younger years, she reports feeling overwhelmed and overburdened later on, especially in attempting to deal with her younger brother's drug abuse. Moreover, she describes receiving little support from her parents in this regard, who assumed a highly permissive attitude toward the drug issue. Her parents continue to this day to minimize problems, as evidenced in their response to her marital conflicts with Mike: "All marriages have their ups and downs."

Jan experimented sporadically with alcohol and marijuana during her teens and early 20s, becoming a more frequent user during her first marriage. It was at that time that she first identified herself as having a problem and began attending Narcotics Anonymous (NA) meetings and discontinued using drugs altogether. She divorced her first husband a year later due to his continued drug dependence and sexual infidelity. Within months of the divorce she met and became involved with Mike, another man with a serious history of substance abuse. Four months later they rather impulsively married. In so doing, Jan seems to be caught in a repetitive pattern of overfunctioning in relation to an addictive partner, harkening back to her earlier relationship to her younger brother, 5 years her junior and the same age as Mike. In this marriage, Jan has wavered between denial, ignoring the signs of Mike's worsening condition, and anger, accusing him of irresponsibility.

Mike and Jan as a Couple

Mike and Jan report feeling a strong attraction to each other during their courtship, a fun and adventuresome time for them both. On the positive side, they share common goals, with both strongly committed to their respective careers and both in agreement in their decision not to have children, Jan by necessity and Mike by choice. Jan has been able to find a positive outlet for her nurturing, maternal feelings in her loving attention to her many animals, an endeavor which Mike appears to have devoted himself to with equal zeal. The decision to marry was mutual, although not carefully deliberated and with little attention to possible problems they might face in a life together. This fact is even more startling, coming in the aftermath of the failure of their first marriages, underscoring their inability to discuss problematic issues in a constructive fashion.

Although they spent considerable time together during their courtship and early years, they now participate in few activities together and there is very little common ground. They frequently even dine separately in the evenings, with Jan entertained by a book while Mike turns to television. Whereas in the beginning they spent time socializing with Jan's friends, they no longer do so, and when Jan visits her family, it is most often without Mike. Whereas at one time they both found sex mutually enjoyable, sexual intimacy seems now to have disappeared from their life altogether.

Mike's chronic drug and alcohol problem has taken its toll on the marital intimacy and trust between the couple. On the positive side, Mike's recent decision to enter a rehab and subsequent followthrough with NA meetings represent a real departure from his earlier failure to take responsibility for his substance abuse. He also has made a real effort to be more accountable to Jan for his whereabouts. Coincidentally, the couple report getting along much better in the last 4 months, which was about the same time that Mike entered rehab.

It is in the context of such evident improvement that the last serious incident happened, the one that finally led them to seek couples counseling. This incident can be viewed in a positive light, attesting to the fact that they will no longer tolerate a return to the former sorry state of affairs. The early period of sobriety can be quite stressful for couples with chronic addiction problems (Bepko & Krestan, 1985), and it is at this time that separation and divorce is more likely to occur. The disorienting effects of sobriety can include: sudden and confusing ambiguity about their roles, anxiety about a possible return to substance abuse, and bitterness associated with past problems caused by a spouse's addiction. Although Jan momentarily mentioned divorce, it soon became clear to her that this was not what she really wanted. Again, in a positive light, they spoke in therapy of their mutual wish to resolve their conflicts so that they might remain married, and, deep down, acknowledged a continuing love for one another through it all.

Treatment Goals

My first task would be to address the problem of emotional distancing in the marriage, with the goal of increasing the arenas of mutual involvement and fostering feelings of togetherness between the couple. I would frame this as a restorative endeavor, in that at one time Mike and Jan found numerous ways of enjoying time together. I would point to the fact that they have continued to care for their animals together as positive, in that they have managed to preserve some common ground in the face of chronic conflict. I would have them talk about their animals and describe what is involved in the care of them, as a way of highlighting their constructive cooperation in this arena.

I would begin with easier assignments, such as asking them to think creatively about how they could alter their eating habits so that they could keep each other company more often (e.g., preparing meals together, sitting at the table together to promote more conversation, trying out a new restaurant). I would caution them to avoid talking about conflictual issues during these times and would speak of the need to create a barrier between times designated for fun and enjoyment and times set aside to deal with problems.

I would also want to know more about what has happened to the friends they used to spend time with together. Who are the people they both enjoy, and how might they arrange to get together with them again? Some childless couples report becoming estranged from old friends whose lives can become largely determined by parental concerns, leaving them feeling that they no longer have much in common. Jan and Mike are now of an age where their friends are probably dealing with older and more independent children, and may welcome a friendship that is not so child-focused.

What has happened to Mike's relationship with Jan's family and to Jan's with Mike's? What can be done so that they begin to visit their families as a couple again? What about the relationship with each of their siblings, which was not mentioned in the information given to us? Have these relationships changed over the years to be more rewarding, and are there nieces or nephews who might offer a meaningful connection to the next generation?

At the same time that I would be working on creating a positive bond through renewed shared activity, I would use our sessions together to improve their poor conflict-resolution skills. My goal here would be to help the couple to appreciate the bind that has mutually entrapped them, especially around Mike's continued substance abuse. I would help them to see their dilemma in terms of circular causation, and also help them to appreciate the historical rootedness of this conflict, with each of their actions bringing about the worst fears of both. For Mike, Jan's frustrated anger and nagging behavior is horribly reminiscent of that of his mother. For Jan, her inability to get Mike to take his substance abuse seriously, either refusing to discuss the issue or fleeing the house, recalls her parents' failure to take her concerns about her younger brother seriously.

If successful, Mike and Jan would come to understand the reciprocal nature of their interactions, with each of their behaviors leading to an intensification of undesirable behavior by the other in a "more of the same" scenario, frustrating to both and polarizing them further. Mike would be able to enter into a more open discussion of problems with less defensiveness and withdrawal, and Jan would be able to present her concerns with less stridency and negative emotionality.

At some later point in therapy, I would address the couple's sexual estrangement, but only after they had shown some ability to problem-solve in more constructive ways and some desire to seek out each other's company on their own. Although sexual desire and a return to healthy sexual functioning may occur spontaneously for some couples as they successfully resolve their conflicts, this is by no means always the case. In their favor, Mike and Jan report feeling quite satisfied with their earlier sexual relationship. Still, I would want to know how the deterioration in their sexual functioning came about, whether gradually over time or more precipitously, and their explanation for what brought it on. Were there problems in their sexual relationship, even before the more obvious decline, and, if so, how were they handled? Given Jan's age at present, 49 years old, and her history of serious medical problems and early hysterectomy, I would need to consider the impact of these events and of any medical interventions on her sexual functioning and enjoyment of sex.

A further goal would be to address the pattern of overfunctioning/underfunctioning in their relationship, helping them to understand how Mike's continued drinking and drug use has contributed to this pattern. I would also underscore the familial roots of this pattern, with Jan's childhood role as the responsible older sister in the family being established very early in life. I would want to support Mike in his decision to enter rehab treatment and follow-up NA meetings, eliminating the need for Jan to overfunction as his caretaker. I would also look to ways where Mike could assume a dominant position in their relationship (e.g., having him teach Jan something about computers). There is also a need for more balance in their willingness to confront problems in the marriage. Over time, I would hope for Mike to raise concerns of his own in our sessions.

Eventually, I would want them to begin to make more long range plans for themselves as a couple by asking them to think into the future. Couples with children are in the habit of thinking about the future and the passage of life through stages in planning for their children's lives. This is typically less true for the childless. In addition, both Mike and Jan have had experiences that may have interfered with a more hopeful attitude toward the future. Jan suffered from a life-threatening illness in her late 20s and Mike witnessed the breakup of his parents' marriage rather late in their lives. Such a discussion would be too threatening in the beginning, given the deep rift between them at that time, and should be postponed to a later point in the therapy. If our earlier work together has been successful, a discussion that focuses on their future together should engender hope while alerting them to potential hazards.

Techniques and Interventions

The Intersystem Model allows for disparate techniques with different theoretical underpinnings to come into play in treatment. In order to accomplish my first goal of restoring a positive feeling of togetherness between Mike and Jan, I would likely make use of some version of behavior exchange procedures. Behavior exchange strategies (Jacobson & Christensen, 1996; Jacobson & Margolin, 1979) all aim to increase the ratio of positive to negative behaviors exchanged between partners. According to research by Gottman (1993), couples who report feeling greater marital satisfaction and stability are able to maintain an optimal balance of positive to negative exchanges, at least five to one. While the emphasis of these techniques is to increase the ratio of positive to negative exchanges as they occur at home rather than in session, the preliminary work must be done in the therapy session. Without active monitoring by the therapist, even an exercise designed to increase positive exchanges can quickly degenerate into an analysis of what is wrong in the marriage.

With Mike and Jan, I would most likely begin the process by asking each to think of ways the other has behaved, either in the past or present, that has made them feel loved or cared for. Such a framing builds on the fact that they once were able to give generously to each other, if not now, ensuring a more constructive outcome to the exercise. Still, couples who enter treatment in the highly conflicted state of Mike and Jan may have difficulty even thinking about the relationship in positive terms, instead converting the task into a discussion of problematic behaviors that need to be eliminated. It is here that the skill of the therapist is essential to redirect their thinking back to the task at hand, while supporting their urgent desire to resolve their divisive conflicts. I would also ask them to think of new ways they would like their partner to behave in the future that might convey a similar feeling of being loved or cared for. Such thinking may not come naturally for Mike and Jan, who were raised in families where they came to expect very little in the way of emotional nurturance.

Fairly early in the therapy, I would also want to begin communication and problem-solving skills training with the couple. There are numerous approaches to such training within the field of couple therapy. Personally, I find the approach of Markman, Stanley, and Blumberg (1994) and the other members of this Denver-based group most helpful to couples. They have coined the term PREP (Prevention and Relationship Enhancement Program) to refer to their particular combination of education and skills-based techniques. The PREP approach has the advantage of being straightforward and readily teachable to most couples. It has been well researched with demonstrable validity in preventing marital breakdown and divorce. In addition, their program can be introduced to couples through several well-produced formats (e.g., reading the popular book, *Fighting for Your Marriage*, viewing a series of training tapes, or attending one of a series of highly structured workshops for couples on the PREP approach), permitting the therapist to tailor the approach to the particular needs and personalities of their client couples.

With Mike and Jan, I would introduce the PREP training to them by having them sequentially view the series of videotapes, followed by some actual practice of the suggested exercises. Given the disparity in their educational attainment, with Jan graduating from college and Mike only completing high school, combined with Jan's stated pleasure in reading, I would want to avoid creating a situation that would create an obvious inequity between the couple from the outset. By having them view each tape prior to our sessions, I would be able to monitor their reactions to the material and provide immediate clarification if needed. Moreover, by having them practice the techniques in session, I would be able to coach them to use the techniques effectively and offer support and encouragement along the way.

Simultaneous to this more interactive work, I would help them to explore the familial roots of their conflicts. As outlined before, the importance of this work is made clear early on in the therapy by doing a comprehensive developmental and family history during the assessment phase. In this work, I ask many of the questions that are typically used by McGoldrick and Gerson (1985) in conducting a family genogram. I pay close attention to areas where there is little or no information and am careful to note the couple's affective responses to certain issues.

In marital therapy, I freely make use of several different intergenerational theories as appropriate to the particular couple. With Mike and Jan, the concepts of Murray Bowen (1978) and his suggested strategies for achieving a more differentiated position within one's family of origin would seem most helpful. For Mike, I can imagine at some point having him raise certain previously undiscussed issues with his father (e.g., some of the reasons behind his decision to never remarry). I would also consider ways that Jan could be supportive of Mike's desire to have a closer relationship with his father (e.g., inviting him to dinner, asking his assistance with a house project).

As we move into a discussion of their sexual relationship, I would also find the use of the sexual genogram (Hof & Berman, 1986) useful in examining the impact of sexual secrets, including the infidelity that occurred between Mike's parents and in Jan's first marriage. I would also hope to open up a discussion of Mike's early incestuous relationship with his aunt. Obviously, I would only make use of this instrument after there occurred some restoration of trust and return to more optimal functioning between the couple, and only after we had worked long enough together for them to gain confidence in me and the therapeutic process.

Pitfalls

I can envision a number of potential pitfalls that could undermine the effectiveness of my work with Mike and Jan. The most obvious concern is that there would be a return to substance abuse on Mike's part, given his long-term addiction and the failure of his efforts to stop in the past, even in the face of quite destructive consequences. Still, there are a number of things in Mike's favor at this juncture. This is the first time he has entered rehab, and he seems quite conscientious in his attendance of NA meetings. While not focusing directly on this problem, I would certainly inquire as to how his recovery is going, and would be supportive of Jan's accompanying him to NA meetings on occasion.

There is also the challenge of developing a positive therapeutic alliance with both Mike and Jan to begin with. Given the negative view of therapy that Mike was raised with—his father believing that only "crazy" people needed it—Mike would understandably enter treatment with some reluctance and skepticism, needing to be convinced of its practical value. In contrast, Jan was involved in individual therapy several years ago and found it to be quite helpful. In addition, Mike's longstanding fears of being dominated by women and his problem with women in authority would certainly pose a challenge to his developing a positive alliance with a female therapist. In order to work effectively with him, I would need to find a way of addressing problems without triggering his defenses and causing him to withdraw from treatment. In the face of his skepticism, I would want to intervene in some very practical ways at the outset, so that Mike could feel the immediate benefits of the work. I would also need to engage him in a collaborative way (i.e., checking out his reaction to my suggestions by asking "How does that sound to you?"), if he is to feel empowered in therapy.

I would also be concerned about the couple's premature termination of therapy after some slight improvement in their relationship and return of positive feeling. In the past, both Mike and Jan have ignored problems between them until reaching a critical state. Neither one is able to comfortably ask for help for themselves. They postponed entering couples therapy for years, despite worsening conflicts and strong encouragement from Jan's close friend, until they were on the brink of divorce. Consequently, I would need to underscore the need for practicing the skills-building exercises learned in our sessions until these skills were solidly in place before stopping therapy.

As stated before, I would also be concerned about Jan's mood state and the possibility of recurring depression, given her withdrawal from friends and excessive sleeping. I would want to carefully monitor her mood states in the course of treatment. If Jan is depressed, this could prove an impediment to her willingness to engage in activities together with Mike, or to her capacity to notice and respond positively to change.

Areas to Avoid

There is a definite possibility of sexual infidelity (see Westfall, 1995) on Mike's part, given the legacy of repeated affairs by his father and given the fact that, in the past, he would often socialize separately from Jan and would not return home until early morning. Furthermore, most of his socializing has occurred in the context of drugs or alcohol, often at the bar scene, where his judgment was impaired as well. The fact that the incident that brought them to treatment involved a party at a woman friend's home, with Mike attending alone and returning home at 2:30 AM after apparently falling asleep, leaves plenty of room for suspicion.

Still, I would not directly confront this possibility at the outset of treatment, and would want to respect the couple's mutual decision not to question the reason for Mike's falling asleep at her home—his explanation for the late return. The couple may not be able to tolerate the effects of sexual betrayal, if it indeed occurred, given the level of discontent and mistrust that already exists within the marriage, and might simply give up.

Instead, I would prefer to help them create a feeling of safety between them by supporting them in developing more of a social life together. I would also commend Mike in his most recent efforts to be more accountable for his time and whereabouts to Jan, so essential to restoring trust in the marriage. If, however, there is a return to the previous pattern of Mike fleeing the house for several hours with no explanation, I would certainly deal directly with the problem and would raise the possibility of both an affair and a drug relapse. I would want to do this in conjoint sessions with both parties present, rather than in an individual session, risking a secret alliance with either party.

Inclusion of Other Family Members

Although I would not include them in person in my sessions, I would want to confer with any consulting professionals working with Mike or Jan. As outlined earlier, I would consider referring Mike for psychological testing and Jan for psychiatric evaluation for depression if necessary.

The Intersystem model supports a therapeutic focus on intergenerational issues that contribute to a couple's overall identity of themselves as a couple and shape their image of what is normal and desirable in marriage. Such an analysis also allows them to appreciate the transmission of symptoms and the clustering of problematic issues across generations. It also permits them to begin to make changes in their current relationship to family members in line with their own needs and desires.

In the case of Mike and Jan, there are a number of important issues concerning their parental families that I would want to address in our sessions. I would want to know more about Mike's current relationship with his mother and her second husband. Has her greater satisfaction in this marriage, as understood by Mike, made a difference in her overall sense of well-being? Is she an easier person to get along with these days, and is she less critical of Mike than she once was? What is the nature of the relationship between Mike's father and Jan? Has he been supportive of their marriage in the past, despite his own inability to find fulfillment in marriage? How does Mike consider himself similar to and different from his father? Where Jan's family is concerned, I would want to know more about the nature of her parents' marriage and how the couple has functioned together since their children were grown. What are the reasons behind their inability to address problems head on? How have Mike's addictive problems affected his relationship with Jan's parents over the years? How might they be supportive of Mike and Jan today?

My preferred way to address these questions is to interweave these issues with the more interactional ones between Mike and Jan, deepening their appreciation of who they are, individually and as a couple. Such an exploration, when successful, can lead to greater intimacy and empathic understanding between the pair. I would not immediately consider bringing their parents into our conjoint sessions, rather coaching them to do the strategic work with their parents on their own. Should, however, either Mike or Jan request my assistance in creating a fruitful discussion of certain issues with their parents, I would not hesitate to meet with them, following the guidelines developed years ago by Framo (1992) for conducting these sessions.

Homework

Where homework assignments are concerned, I use them quite liberally, making suggestions from the outset of treatment as to how the couple might begin to change their more entrenched and unsatisfying patterns of behavior. If therapy is to be successful, it must yield some immediate, tangible results, restoring hope in the relationship as previously destructive behaviors are replaced by novel and more satisfying options. Still, I tend to be rather loose in the way I use homework, operating with more of a tone of suggestion than of an assignment. I like to put forth a number of possibilities and to do so only with the active participation of my clients, hoping to create a collaborative set. Although I often follow up in our next session with questions to see what they have done with my suggestions, I do not expect rigid compliance, but rather use this information to decide how next to intervene. Other clients respond well to more structured assignments and will want to report on their progress through the homework, sometimes with detailed notes.

With Mike and Jan, it is not enough to highlight the numerous problems in their relationship and to point out the progressive decline in shared intimacy over time without giving them some notion as to how to turn this around. As I listen to them describe their usual evening activities (e.g., Mike alone watching television or playing with his computer, Jan retreating to the bedroom to read before falling to sleep), I would want to ask them to begin to think of ways that they could spend more evening time together. If they seem to be at a loss to come up with anything, I might offer some suggestions of my own to get them started. In our next session, I would ask about the previous week with specific reference to the evening hours. Are they quickly able to make changes in their lives at home, automatically implementing my suggestions and creatively building on these with ideas of their own? Or does communication between them quickly break down in argument when I am not there to monitor these discussions? Is there an absence of direct conflict, but a failure to try out any new behaviors on their own? Their response to my suggestions will help me set the right pace for our sessions, so that I neither push them too hard for change nor lag too far behind what they are capable of doing.

With Mike and Jan, I would avoid having them do any exercises at home involving communications training or problem-solving in our beginning work. Given their long history of difficulty resolving conflicts, I would want them to practice these skills repeatedly in session, achieving some mastery, before having them attempt them on their own. I would want to avoid another failure experience, causing them to become unduly discouraged about ever resolving their differences.

Couples who have not shared sexual relations for a prolonged period, extending many months or even years, will likely have difficulty resuming regular sexual functioning together should they desire to do so. They have gotten out of "the habit" of being sexual with each other, and they have lost a responsiveness to the natural cues that once triggered sexual desire and excitement. An unnaturalness creeps into their responses that produces self-consciousness and sexual paralysis. These couples can benefit from specific suggestions and direction from the therapist in the form of homework assignments that help them get started again and circumvent some of the awkwardness they experience along the way.

Mike and Jan are likely to require such intervention when they feel ready to resume sexual relations. Asking them to set aside designated "date nights" where they approach the evening together in more romantic terms as something special can be helpful. Having them think of ways of countering their usual pattern of sexual avoidance (e.g., instead of sleeping back-to-back, cuddling together in bed; instead of the perfunctory peck, kissing with more feeling and passion) can break the existing stalemate, especially if they can bring some humor to their efforts. Of course, other problems may emerge as they resume sexual relations (e.g., residual anger and distrust, felt more keenly in the context of sexual intimacy; specific sexual dysfunctions that have emerged secondarily to other difficulties). These may require further therapeutic intervention.

Timeline for Therapy

After the completion of the initial evaluation with Mike and Jan, I would most likely contract with them, if both are agreeable, for intensive couple therapy for a 3- to 4-four month period. Given the longstanding nature of their conflicts, I believe this time would be necessary for any substantial progress to occur. I also believe it to be unfair and unrealistic to ask for a commitment to therapy beyond a 3- to 4-month period without proof of its effectiveness. If successful in achieving their goals, I can easily imagine their treatment extending beyond this initial period for an additional 3 to 4 months.

In terms of frequency of sessions, I prefer to meet with couples weekly during the first few months of therapy, reinforcing their commitment to and focus on the work and lending intensity to the process. From that point, I often move to see couples on a biweekly basis for the remainder of treatment. Biweekly sessions tend to promote more autonomous functioning in couples, so that they carry more responsibility for improving the relationship themselves. In today's health-care environment, with cost-effectiveness an important consideration, less frequent sessions permit the therapy to extend longer, so that the therapeutic gains can be more solidly in place before termination. Still, I would want to postpone a recommendation for less frequent sessions until the couple had reached a point where they would be unlikely to revert to former destructive patterns in the interim.

I will sometimes choose to meet with each member of the couple alone, usually later in the therapy, if I feel we have reached a stalemate where no further progress is being made. At other times, I may have formed an uncomfortable alliance with one partner, and need to re-establish rapport with the other partner to regain balance in the therapy. At some point, we may touch on an individual issue that results in a request by the client for an individual session to explore the matter further. I tend to honor such requests, if both parties are comfortable with the idea. Still, I use individual sessions sparingly in couples work, with the preponderance of therapy being conducted with both parties present. If, in the course of exploring an issue in an individual session, it becomes clear to me and the client that there is a need for further therapeutic work, I may recommend individual treatment with a different therapist.

Termination and Relapse Prevention

As stated above, I typically move from weekly to biweekly sessions after a few months of more intensive therapy. At this point, I will introduce the idea of couple meetings, having them set aside time each week where they talk about any problematic issues that have occurred during the week or any other relationship matter that requires some thoughtful discussion. These meetings serve the purpose of preparing them for a time when they will function completely on their own without therapeutic assistance.

At some point nearing termination, I will space our sessions even further apart, meeting once a month for a 2- to 4-month period, before stopping altogether. The effect of this spacing is to provide a forum for intermittent review and stock-taking of the relationship together with the therapist, while the spouses function largely on their own and with increasing confidence in their ability to do so.

Still, there is the safety of knowing there is therapeutic help to be called on as needed as they prepare for termination. I almost always invite couples to consider returning to treatment in the future, even for only one or two sessions, if they reach a point where they feel they are backtracking in serious ways, or if some new issue emerges where they might benefit from my therapeutic input. I have never had a client misuse this invitation to avoid disengaging from treatment. On the contrary, it has sometimes prevented a serious relapse, if only because the couple waited too long to return to therapy due to a sense of embarrassment at having failed in doing so.

I like to set the stage for termination during the first few sessions of therapy by asking the couple to consider the questions: "How will we know when our work together is finished?" and "What will be different about the way you relate to each other?" These questions establish how we will work together, empowering the couple to assume more control of the therapy and helping me to set goals that are more in line with their stated desires and resources.

At termination, I would hope for Mike and Jan to have reached many of the goals they set for themselves at the outset of treatment. Mike would have continued to make progress in his recovery program, so that the substance abuse issue is no longer the central focus of their lives. They would now be able to talk through problems of whatever sort with much greater ease and less defensiveness on both their parts. When they encounter conflict, they would be able to recover more quickly, no longer needing to leave the house or retreating to separate rooms for hours. Moreover, there would be more balance in their discussion of problems, with both Mike and Jan initiating these talks. There would be considerably more time spent in shared activities, including sex, with both looking forward to time together. The couple would be less socially isolated, spending time with friends they both enjoy and planning time with family in a way meaningful to each of them. They would be able to talk about the future with a deepening appreciation of their importance to each other. Of course, I would not expect them to be completely satisfied with their degree of progress on all issues before ending treatment. Still, they need to have come to a point where there can be real acceptance or, at least, greater toleration of the issues that remain unchanged, so that these problems are no longer so destructive to their marital happiness.

REFERENCES

Bepko, C., & Krestan, J. (1985). *The responsibility trap: A blueprint for treating the alcoholic family.* New York: Free Press.

Berman, E., Lief, H., & Williams, A. (1981). A model of marital interaction. In M. Scholevar (Ed.), *The handbook of marriage and marital therapy* (pp. 3–34). New York: S. P. Medical and Scientific Books.

Bowen, M. (1978). *Family therapy in clinical practice.* New York: Jason Aronson.

Framo, J. L. (1992). *Family-of-origin therapy: An intergenerational approach.* New York: Brunner/Mazel.

Goldberg, M. (1982). The dynamics of marital interaction and marital conflict. In M. Goldberg (Ed.), *Psychiatric Clinics of North America: Marital Therapy* (pp. 449–467). Philadelphia: Saunders.

Gottman, J. M. (1993). A theory of marital dissolution and stability. *Journal of Family Psychology, 7,* 57–75.

Gurman, A., & Kniskern, D. (Eds.). (1981). *Handbook of family therapy.* New York: Brunner/Mazel.

Hof, L., & Berman, E. (1986). The sexual genogram. *Journal of Marital and Family Therapy, 12*(1), 39–47.

Jacobson, N. S., & Christensen, A. (1996). *Integrative couple therapy: Promoting acceptance and change.* New York: Norton.

Jacobson, N. S., & Margolin, G. (1979). *Marital therapy: Strategies based on social learning and behavior exchange principles.* New York: Brunner/Mazel.

Markman, H., Stanley, S., & Blumberg, S. L. (1994). *Fighting for your marriage: Positive steps for preventing divorce and preserving a lasting love.* San Francisco: Jossey-Bass.

McGoldrick, M., & Gerson, R. (1985). *Genograms in family assessment.* New York: Norton.

*Weeks, G. R. (1989). *Treating couples: The intersystem model of the Marriage Council of Philadelphia.* New York: Brunner/Mazel.

*Weeks, G. R., & Hof, L. (Eds.). (1987). *Integrating sex and marital therapy: A clinical guide.* New York: Brunner/Mazel.

*Weeks, G. R., & Hof, L. (Eds.). (1994). *The marital-relationship therapy casebook: Theory and application of the Intersystem model.* New York: Brunner/Mazel.

*Weeks, G. R., & Hof, L. (Eds.). (1995). *Integrative solutions: Treating common problems in couples therapy.* New York: Brunner/Mazel.

*Weeks, G. R., & Treat, S. (1992). *Couples in treatment: Techniques and approaches for effective practice.* New York: Brunner/Mazel.

Westfall, A. (1994). Too old to go steady: The case of Marcia and Barry. In G. R. Weeks & L. Hof (Eds.), *The marital-relationship therapy casebook: Theory and application of the intersystem model* (pp. 63–82). New York: Brunner/Mazel.

Westfall, A. (1995). Working through the extramarital trauma: An exploration of common themes. In G. R. Weeks & L. Hof (Eds.), *Integrative solutions: Treating common problems in couples therapy* (pp. 148–194). New York: Brunner/Mazel.

---

*Suggested reading.

14

Conflict Resolution Therapy

Susan Heitler

TREATMENT MODEL

Conflict resolution theory offers a comprehensive framework for understanding emotional health, explaining psychopathology, and guiding efficient, comprehensive, and effective treatment. The theory is based on a simple premise: conflict produces tensions; conflict resolution yields relief of tensions and resumption of well-being. Conceptualizing treatment as conflict resolution dovetails closely with what patients generally describe as what they want from therapy. In her initial telephone call requesting therapy, for instance, Jan "stated that she and her husband were experiencing difficulty achieving emotional intimacy due to continued conflicts and lack of effective resolutions" (Heitler, 1993, p. 12).

What Is Conflict and What Is Effective Conflict Resolution?

In this theoretical system the term conflict is defined as "a situation in which seemingly incompatible elements exert force in opposing or divergent directions" (Heitler, 1993, p. 5). Conflict thus implies tensions but not necessarily fighting.

Conflicts routinely occur in everyone's lives in at least three realms (Heitler, 1993). Conflicts within an individual's intrapsychic realm involve an individual's competing preferences, values, beliefs, fears, and desires. Mike, for instance, experiences inner conflict between, on the one hand, wanting to sustain a relationship with his wife and, on the other hand, wanting to avoid her for fear of unpleasant arguments. Conflicts occur between people, such as in Jan and Mike's argument after Jennifer's party. Thirdly, conflicts occur between people and circumstances—illness, infertility, financial difficulties, work disappointments, etc.

When conflicts are handled effectively, feelings of emotional distress give way to relief and closure. "Effective" resolution implies that:

- The process is based on information sharing, not on verbal or physical domination.
- The attitude of participants is collaborative and mutually respectful, not deprecatory, judgmental, avoidant, antagonistic, or coercive.
- The process includes exploration of both parties' concerns.
- The outcome leaves all parties feeling satisfied that the solution is responsive to their concerns.

Three main steps of collaborative problem solving constitute what I refer to as "the win-win waltz" (Heitler, 1997, p. 192):

- Identification of the conflict by expression of both parties' initial positions;
- Exploration of both sides' underlying concerns; and
- Creation of solutions responsive to both parties' underlying concerns.

For instance, if Jan wants to talk in the evening with Mike, while Mike prefers to work on his computer, Jan and Mike have a conflict. Jan's immediate concern might be to refresh her sense of connection with Mike; a deeper underlying concern may be to feel reassured that Mike values her and their partnership. Mike's underlying concern may be to avoid interaction for fear of fights; his deeper concern may be to feel that Jan respects him. If Jan and Mike then decide to go together to a movie, this solution could give them shared time, refreshing their sense of connection, and yet giving them enough structure that arguments will be unlikely and mutual respect will prevail. Note that this collaborative solution would not be a compromise. A compromise is a solution in which both sides each give up on some of what they want. Rather, Jan and Mike would have created a solution set that is fully responsive to all of their concerns.

The Conflict Resolution Theory of Emotional Health and Healthy Marriage

Emotionally healthy individuals, couples, families, and groups sustain well-being by collaboratively resolving the various dilemmas life inevitably presents. When differences arise in a well-functioning couple, they have the skills and attitudes set forth in Table 14.1, enabling them to discuss the challenge cooperatively.

TABLE 14.1 Dysfunctional Versus Emotionally Skillful Individuals and Couples

Dysfunctional	Emotionally skillful
Express concerns as blame and criticism.	Express concerns with tact and insight.
Disparage or ignore concerns.	Listen respectfully to concerns.
Smother and/or escalate emotions.	Heed emotions as indicators of concerns.
Escalate anger, and use it to coerce or to hurt.	Hear anger as a sign of a problem to address.
Make decisions based on one side's concerns.	Make decisions based on both sides' concerns.
After upsets, allot blame and seek to punish.	After upsets, apologize and prevent repeats.
Endure or fight over frustrating situations.	Find solutions to frustrating situations.

The Conflict Theory of Emotional Distress

People feel tension when they experience conflict. If the problem or conflict is not handled effectively, the problem continues to generate stress. At the same time, poor conflict management strategies in themselves produce additional negative effects. For instance, when Mike responds to conflicts with Jan by trying to avoid discussing them, important disagreements remain unresolved—and his wife erupts in fury at his attempt to exit.

Conflict resolution theory posits that there are four ineffective conflict patterns, as listed in Table 14.2. Each of these patterns results in a specific type of clinical pathology (Heitler, 1993). Conflict resolution theory further notes that a given

TABLE 14.2 Conflict Resolution Patterns and Their Consequences

Conflict pattern	Behaviors	Clinical symptom
I. Submission	Give up, give in. Excessive altruism.	Depression
II. Fight	Attempt to prevail via domination.	Anger
III. Freeze	Take no action: remain immobilized.	Anxiety
IV. Flight	Change the subject, leave the situation, distraction.	Addiction, obsessive-compulsive habits
V. Discuss	Collaborative problem-solving.	Well-being

individual will tend to utilize the same patterns in both intra- and interpersonal conflict handling.

The Conflict Resolution Theory of Treatment

Conflict resolution theory facilitates comprehensive treatment by interweaving three goals—

a. removal of symptoms,
b. prevention of subsequent tensions by improving conflict resolution skills and
c. resolution of current conflicts.

In what order should these therapeutic tasks be addressed? In general:

- If symptoms such as anger, depression, addictions, or anxiety are interfering with ability to function, focus on symptom reduction first, then guide and coach.
- When a couple bickers regularly, or is upset by frequent disturbing fights, start with brief coaching of the basics of talking, listening, and anger management. To accelerate teaching of the fundamentals, assign homework reading and audiotapes.
- Barring these conditions, use what I term the "laundry list strategy" (Heitler, 1993).

With the laundry list strategy each session begins with the couple selecting a specific conflict to resolve. The conflict may be one from their laundry list of on-going differences or from a recent argument. The therapist guides resolution of this conflict, and along the way also coaches at least one communication skill. This coaching may include a brief exercise for skill consolidation. As the couple explores the emotions and concerns raised by each conflict, they gain insight into themselves. Softening occurs in their attitudes toward each other (Rice & Greenberg, 1984). Optimism increases as they resolve one-by-one the issues that had been creating tension, and also as they see that they can learn skills for discussing sensitive issues productively.

Relationship of Conflict Resolution Theory to Other Treatment Philosophies

When therapists use the terms "problems," "dilemmas," and "issues," these words imply conflicts. Conflict resolution therapy guides the next steps: specifying exactly what is in conflict with what (a psychodynamic component), and moving toward resolution with practical plans of action (behavioral and solution-focused components).

A conflict resolution theoretical model thus offers a broadly integrative treatment map. The therapy extends the basic Freudian idea "where id (feelings) were, let ego be (thinking about feelings)." Thinking about underlying concerns, including at times the childhood origins of these concerns, leads to practical solutions to life dilemmas. The treatment includes behavioral learning, especially of communication and conflict resolution skills, to sustain marital well-being. The treatment rests on a systemic basis, with simultaneous treatment of intra-, inter-, and extrapersonal factors.

Conflict resolution therapy also resonates with attachment theory. Conflict resolution theory posits that each unit of interaction, and especially of verbal interaction, is a microcosm of the overall relationship, that is, of the attachment bond. Collaborative dialogue thus re-enacts, and reinforces, a secure attachment of mutual respect, empowerment, and affection. By contrast, avoidant or antagonistic communications perpetuate unsatisfactory attachments.

Templates for conflict resolution and their associated attachment patterns begin to be formed in childhood (Ainsworth, Blehar, Waters, & Wall, 1978; Bowlby, 1980). Positive attachment grows out of parents' utilization of effective conflict resolution. For instance, when a child wants to make noise and the parent wants quiet, a skilled parent capable of offering a secure attachment handles the conflict in a way that is respectful of both participants. The parent invites the child to come sit quietly in his/her lap for a story, or perhaps distracts the child with a puzzle more compelling than noisemaking. That is, secure attachment emerges out of cooperative conflict resolution, which in turn both reflects and causes mutual affection. By contrast, negative conflict resolution patterns— evidenced in unskilled, neglectful, or domineering parenting—yield avoidant, ambivalent, or hostile attachments.

THERAPIST SKILLS AND ATTRIBUTES

Therapist attributes essential to this kind of therapy begin with those relevant to most treatments—ability to listen accurately; warmth that conveys caring; intelligence, life experience, and wisdom. Personal attractiveness helps, motivating couples to want to do their best because they like you, want to be like you, and want you to like them. In addition, conflict-focused therapists need conviction that conflicts can be resolved. This confidence typically rests on therapists' success with cooperative conflict resolution in their own personal and business affairs.

With regard to technical skills, to conduct a conflict resolution treatment a therapist needs to be able to wear at least four hats:

- *Healer.* Healing psychological symptoms can be accomplished with a broad array of techniques, including conflict-focused interventions (Heitler, 1993), for reducing depression, anxiety, excessive anger, and obsessive-compulsive syndromes.
- *Guide.* Guiding conflicts to resolution necessitates mediator skills plus Gestalt-type techniques for exploring subconscious underlying family-of-origin concerns.
- *Coach.* Effective coaching rests on a repertoire of skill-building exercises, plus detailed understanding of the skills that enable couples to negotiate differences, recover from upsets, and make shared decisions.
- *Traffic police.* The therapist is responsible for keeping sessions safe, and therefore needs skills both for prompting positive communication habits and for halting negative interactions.

THE CASE OF MIKE AND JAN

Mike and Jan are two reasonably well-functioning individuals whose marriage has involved a history of disappointment and frustration, but who would like their marriage to improve and endure.

Assessment

Conflict resolution assessment organizes diagnostic data into the three areas defined above as treatment goals: symptoms; content of conflicts; and process of handling conflicts.

Symptoms

To gather rapid initial information about symptoms, I ask new couples to fill out a symptom checklist (Heitler, 1995) included in their packet of registration materials handed out in the waiting room prior to their first session.

Content of Conflicts

To assess the content of a couple's conflicts, I request that the couple, talking with each other, compile together a laundry list of the issues that they find controversial or tension-producing. I suggest that they include the issues that they fight about and also those that they avoid. As I listen, I serve as the couple's secretary, writing down the issues they enumerate. The list, I explain, will serve as an informal outline for their treatment. I usually suggest that they take turns adding to the list, and encourage them to give just titles that identify each controversial issue rather than longer explanations.

Process of Conflict Resolution

To assess a couple's skills in communication and conflict handling, I would observe what occurs when the spouses talk with each other. Assignment of any topic for them to discuss together can serve this purpose. I might ask them, for instance, to discuss when their tensions began and what events were transpiring in their lives at that time. In this case, as they are talking I would be gathering information simultaneously on their dialogue skills, and on the history of their attachment.

Alternatively, to simplify data gathering, I might assign my "Going Out to Dinner" diagnostic exercise (Heitler, 1993). In this exercise, I ask the couple to pretend they have decided to go out together and need to pick a restaurant. This nonthreatening shared problem-solving situation quickly illuminates the couple's strengths and deficits in communication. I note, for instance, if the individuals:

- verbalize their preferences or either refrain from saying their preferences or use crossovers (my term for speaking for or about each other);
- have symmetry in their dialogue;
- demonstrate bilateral listening (my term for ability to hear their own and also their partner's concerns), or either insist on their own way or err on the side of excessive altruism;
- access insight or slip into blame and criticism;
- integrate both partners' perspectives or engage in power struggles over whose ideas will prevail.

Eventually, I would obtain a history of each individual's key life events and of their relationship as a couple. Similarly, family background, including relationships with parents, parents' personalities, and the parents' marital history, are important data. I typically gradually amass this historical perspective, however, in the context of issue explorations, rather than necessarily in the first session.

I would want to answer two remaining key questions in the first session. First, I would want us to build together a non-blaming explanation of what has gone wrong in the relationship. A typical explanation might run as follows: The couple married with ample love but insufficient skills for handling differences. As they encountered stresses from various life events, their insufficient partnership problem-solving skills became frustrations with each other. In addition, transference and modeling from their families-of-origin may have further contaminated their affection for each other.

Second and lastly, I would want to find out what strengths and attractions drew, and continue to draw, the partners to each other. Concluding with a focus on this last question ends assessment sessions on a high note.

Case Conceptualization

The Couple

As described above, conflict resolution theory conceptualizes individual and couple difficulties by focusing on their conflicts: look at the symptoms their conflicts are producing, the content of their conflicts, and the processes by which they handle their conflicts.

Symptoms

Distance, tension, depressive discouragement, and episodic arguments are the main troubling elements in Jan and Mike's marriage. When Mike and Jan end each day together in bed, instead of lying open to sexual intimacy, they sleep back to back. In their daytime hours, instead of shared activities and verbal intercourse, they live similarly "back to back." While Mike and Jan do say that they love each other and want to stay together, they are poignantly limited in being able to connect in loving, trusting, playful, supportive, or other positive ways.

Content of Conflicts

Jan and Mike have identified multiple areas of controversy:

- The fight that followed Mike's late return from Jennifer's party. Converting upsets into positive growth experiences is an important subcategory of conflict resolution.
- Wanting more trust. (Jan)
- Emotional intimacy. (Jan)
- Feeling unfulfilled and unappreciated in the marriage. (Jan)
- "Mike not being dependable." (Jan)
- Mike's concerns about what he refers to as Jan's "nagging," and Mike's behaviors about which Jan "nags."
- Mike's working on the weekends, and related issues of what Jan and Mike could do for shared leisure activities, socializing, and fun.

- The fact that Jan makes more money than Mike; other ways in which their relationship feels competitive or unequal; and how to establish a sense of symmetrical power and value in the relationship.

Process

Discussing issues of serious concern generally turns on a flow of tensions, resentments, and criticism, so Jan and Mike mostly avoid talking. Conflicts hover instead, and periodically erupt. When Jan and Mike do try to discuss sensitive issues, the dialogue quickly deteriorates. Criticisms and complaints from Jan lead to withdrawal from Mike. This withdrawal further agitates Jan, who escalates to shouting and crying. If Jan and Mike do reach solutions, these evolve from Jan dominating and Mike acquiescing. Mike then does not keep the agreement he had accepted under pressure (e.g., about calling her) and the tensions are renewed.

Further examples of the couple's actual dialogue would be necessary to identify the full range of specific communication glitches that interfere with Jan and Mike's ability to talk together about serious matters. A few, however, are immediately evident. For instance, Jan tends not to share her positive thoughts or feelings, such as her appreciation of Mike's alcohol recovery, with her husband. When she feels hurt, Jan is quick to interpret judgmentally, rather than to ask for more information about what happened ("He could have at least called. How much thought does that take?"). Similarly, instead of listening to understand Jan's concerns, Mike "simply dismisses what Jan says as being trivial."

Detailed observation of a couple's dialogue is critical for a conflict-focused therapist. Dysfunctional communication habits, such as "buts" or asymmetrical "air time," often prove to be the subtle but powerful elements that are most corrosive in a marriage—perhaps because these habits are the visible elements of so-called personality traits, such as self-absorption, competitiveness, etc. Detailed sensitivity to these patterns enables the conflict focused therapist to zero in very quickly and repair detrimental relationship dynamics.

Mike

Symptoms

While Mike seems to function fine outside of the household, at home Mike's problematic symptoms include depressive resignation and avoidance-inspired behaviors. Jan says that she married Mike because she found him fascinating, but the Mike that is portrayed in this case sounds more inhibited than intriguing, more limited than likable, and more resentful than resilient or robust. On the other hand, Mike does seem to enjoy himself when he is on his own, with his computer for instance. After he and Jan have had good talks, Mike seems to

become more participatory in the relationship, and to enjoy it more. It is noteworthy also that Mike has for the most part been quite steadfast in wanting to
stay married.

Content

The main issue Mike expresses distress about is his wife's "nagging." Like many
people who avoid troubling situations by using denial to stay clear of unpleasant
thoughts and feelings, Mike may have additional concerns in the marriage that
he has not articulated.

Process

Submissive giving up and avoidance are Mike's two main modes of response to
conflict situations. Giving up, the conflict style associated with depression, is a
problem-solving tendency Mike first showed in childhood toward schoolwork,
in sports, and in his social life. Giving-up strategies are often the coping/conflict
strategies of choice for children with a tendency to shyness, a temperament which
Mike showed. Mike's possible attention-focusing weaknesses (there are signs of
ADD), may have made success difficult for him at many of the activities kids
do, from baseball to academic work. In addition, his father modeled depressive
giving-up patterns.

Mike similarly learned self-protective avoidance early in his youth. For many
years he implemented avoidance with drinking and drug use. While he does not
appear to have been drinking or using drugs during the 7 months prior to treatment,
avoidance continues to predominate as Mike's strategy for handling marriage.
Avoidance seems to motivate his dismissive listening style. Avoidance of talking
with Jan when she might have been critical after his late stay at Jennifer's party
provoked their most recent upset.

Mike developed avoidance, rather than a secure positive attachment, with both
of his parents. Distance characterized much of his relationship with his father.
Throughout much of his youth, Mike experienced few friends and a "disinterest"
in school, music, and baseball, an attitude similar to the basic stance his father
seemed to take toward him, with the exception of attending Mike's football
games, which Mike appreciated. Even when Mike was an adult, his father modeled
avoidance of feelings by disengaging and avoiding emotional situations. If Mike
felt troubled, his father would tell Mike to "Get over it."

Mike's attachment to his mother was more active, but often demoralizing.
Her chronic disapproval, guilt induction, and blame must have invited avoidance
of her, and also contributed to Mike's negative feelings about himself: "No matter
what problems he was experiencing, his mother always pointed out that it was
somehow related to something he himself did to cause it." His mother probably

was depressed during much of Mike's youth, which could account to some extent for her chronic negativity. She also felt angry much of the time at her husband, Mike's father, which could have conveyed generalized anger at males, including Mike. The sum impact on Mike was vast experience in remaining in a relationship with a dominant and critical woman and yet avoiding interactions with her. It is striking that Mike continued to live with his mother until his late 20s.

Mike's depressive/avoidant conflict resolution behavior was further imprinted by his parents' behavior toward each other. During the years that children learn words and a grammar of spoken language, children also learn a grammar of interaction of loving, enjoying, and fighting—from their parents' spousal relationship. The model of marriage that Mike grew up with consisted of a wife who criticized and a husband who avoided. Mike viewed his mother as powerful with her controlling and critical behavior, and viewed his father as ineffective. Given this power differential, the father probably was chronically depressed. Though her family viewed her as powerful, Mike's mother's angry negativity probably was an outcome of depression as well. The father self-medicated for his depression with periodic escapes into affairs, blaming these affairs on his wife's angry "nagging" and "put-downs." Mutual depression, plus circular patterns of escapes into inappropriate marriage behavior (affairs, etc.) on the part of the husband and angry negativity (complaints, criticism) on the part of the wife, characterize Mike's parents' marriage and also his own.

Sibling patterns in the family of origin can serve similarly as templates for adult marriage partnership patterns. Mike resented his older brother, whom he experienced as getting "more" than he, at least with regard to parental attention. Mike experiences Jan likewise as "bigger," that is, as dominant and as getting more. She makes more money, has more friends, and does not share the self-shaming history he has of drug abuse.

Jan

Symptoms

Jan's clinical symptoms of negativity and social withdrawal suggest depression and anger. Jan sounds more critical than kind, which must be difficult for a relatively shy and not very self-confident fellow like Mike. Like her husband, Jan seems robust enough when she is on her own. Jan in college seemed to have reached her optimum level of social functioning with many friends and multiple active interests. Now she enjoys personal pursuits like reading and does seem still to have a network of friendships and a positive relationship with her parents. During her years of marriage, however, Jan's interests have shifted more toward reading than experiencing life, and her enthusiastic participation in social activities seems to have shrunken considerably. For instance, she did not want to attend their friend Jennifer's party with Mike. Rather than her old enthusiasm, Jan's predominant emotions at home seem to be negative.

Content

Jan's expressions of disgruntlement at Mike focus primarily on what she experiences as his "lack of dependability" and lack of clear expressions of caring for her. She wants more interaction, more intimacy, more affection, and more sense of receiving positives from their relationship. Exactly what kind of positives she wants from her marriage would need to be clarified in the couple's discussions.

Process

Jan's primary conflict resolution mode is attack. If she does not feel heard, or if Mike attempts to withdraw from a sensitive discussion, Jan escalates with shouting and crying. She sometimes also shows depressive resignation, particularly in response to the scarcity of interaction in her marriage. With regard to Jan's overall attachment pattern with Mike, the other notable feature is how little positive communications she (or he) seems to give forth.

Jan's rather sparse relationship with her parents growing up has been repeated with Mike in her marriage. In response to the relative lack of parental involvement in her youth, Jan turned resiliently to her younger brother, serving as caretaker for him throughout their growing-up years. For some time, this relationship seems to have been mutually satisfying. Later, when her brother was in his teens, and especially around issues of drugs, Jan transitioned from nurturing to criticizing him. In her marriage, Jan has "parented" Mike as she did her younger brother. Initially quite enamored of him, she eventually has become critical, first around his drug and alcohol abuse, and gradually more broadly.

Back to the Couple

Adults can modify and improve the patterns they learned from child-parent, parent-parent, and sibling interactions, but Jan and Mike have retained them. In the co-choreography of husband and wife, perhaps because Jan and Mike's conflict styles from each of their families-of-origin dovetailed so well, they have continued the interaction patterns they had experienced as children.

Furthermore, as Paul Wachtel (1977) has described, when one spouse acts in ways he or she learned as a child, this behavior is likely to pull complementary responses from the other. Behavior like Mike's not calling from his late party does not consider the partner's preferences, and consequently engenders irritation in the other, regardless of who the other may be. Similarly, Jan's criticisms would be likely to trigger avoidance of open discussion in anyone, particularly with regard to potentially sensitive topics.

Moreover, attachment patterns are based on skill and habit acquisition. Neither Jan nor Mike had parents who modeled positive conflict resolution. Their parents did not consistently listen to their children's needs, express their parental concerns in ways that were positive rather than critical, or routinely find mutually respectful solutions to differences. They modeled nonresponsive, dominant-submissive, and avoidant patterns, rather than open emotional sharing and problem-solving, leaving both Jan and Mike poorly equipped for marriage partnership.

Lastly, attachment patterns are impacted by the quantity of affection expressed in a relationship. Couples who share vast amounts of joyful or loving interaction seem better able to tolerate difficulties from poor conflict-handling skills. Neither Jan nor Mike received very much overt positive affection from their families of origin. As a couple, they have gradually slipped into similarly non-nutritive co-living. They often spend dinner eating separately. Evenings consist of Mike "in front of the television" and Jan "at the kitchen table while she pages through a magazine." Though their relationship began with a sense of fun in a courtship filled with activity (movies, restaurants, parties, skiing, and caring for Mike's animals), in marriage their life has been whittled down to inconsistent meals together, occasional animal care together, and back-to-back sleeping. Mike and Jan "rarely venture out socially." Fun leisure activities, friends, shared evenings and weekends, and sexual intimacy—most of life's pleasures—seem to have slipped away. Their marriage at this point is a relatively empty shell.

Strengths

Mike and Jan do nonetheless share several strengths: continuity of jobs, interests in caring for animals, and love for each other, however limited its expression. They do each have at least one individual interest—Jan's mystery reading and Mike's computers and TV watching, which are compatible as parallel play.

Jan for many years in her youth enjoyed a very loving relationship with her brother, and as an adult has a reasonably positive relationship with both parents. She also enjoys excellent relationships with friends. These successes show strong potential for positive connections.

Fortunately also, Mike has long enjoyed using his hands to make things, an arena of positive functioning, which has become the basis for a positive and relatively stable career path. He and his dad shared Mike's success as a football player, and at present share an interest in making things. Mike and his mother did get along well enough that he lived with her until he was 29, and he reports a positive relationship with his stepfather.

In summary, Jan and Mike's poor conflict resolution skills are linchpins for understanding Jan and Mike's unsatisfying marriage. Any discussion of differences risks turning on a flow of tensions, resentments, and criticism. At best, their marriage has evolved into a relatively comfortable if distant cohabitation. At its low points, the marriage becomes a partnership of mutually irritable, disappointed, and defensive adversaries.

Jan and Mike's inadequate conflict resolution skills help us to understand why the circular pattern of Mike's "undependable behavior" and Jan's "nagging" do not change. The skill deficits, especially Mike's avoidance of dialogue and Jan's criticisms, lock them into mutual frustration and erosion of goodwill. The good news, however, is that these deficits also point the way toward intervention strategies that can help Mike and Jan build the kind of marriage partnership they would like to enjoy together.

Treatment Goals

The most immediate short-term goal for this couple would probably be to talk constructively about the incident after Jennifer's party, a therapeutic task I refer to as "clean up after toxic spills" (Heitler, 1997). This dialogue would help Mike and Jan identify the concerns they each had that night—Mike's dread of criticism, perhaps, and Jan's sense of feeling unappreciated. It would be important for this dialogue to include depth explorations of childhood experiences of similar feelings, and to identify the behaviors each spouse contributes that re-trigger their partner's long-standing concerns. Apologies would help if Jan could focus on her quickness to blame and condemn, and Mike could acknowledge his reluctance to communicate in the possible face of criticism. Clarifying how Jan could begin to feel more trusting and fulfilled in the marriage, and helping Mike to articulate what would help him to feel more comfortable as well, would further convert the upset into an opportunity for mutual growth. Each spouse summarizing what s/he has learned would complete the cleanup on a high and harmonious note.

Jan has articulated three longer-term goals for treatment: better communication, better conflict resolution, and to feel that her husband is dependable. Jan defines dependable as when her husband communicates with her. To invite this openness, Jan needs to become safer, less judgmental, to talk with.

Mike also has articulated three treatment goals: to be trusted, to prevent arguments, and to insure that the relationship will stay permanent, and not end in divorce. These goals similarly boil down to communication issues. To attain his goals, instead of avoiding sensitive topics for fear of fights, Mike needs to learn to verbalize his concerns, to be willing to hear his wife's concerns, and to do his part in creating mutually satisfactory solutions.

In summary, to heal their relationship Jan and Mike need to learn to talk in a cooperative manner that can give them deeper understandings of themselves and each other, enabling them to resolve difficulties instead of polarizing when differences emerge. With skills of cooperative dialogue, they would be able to talk openly and frequently enough to feel more connected and more intimate. Better communication could prevent the upsets that have threatened the permanence of their relationship. When mishaps do occur, Jan and Mike would be able to discuss them, converting their upsets to shared learning experiences. With these gains, both partners would have received from therapy the changes they are seeking.

Jan and Mike need to practice their developing dialogue skills on their many conflicts, and particularly on the topic of re-choreography of their marital life. What changes could each of them make to bring their relationship out of hibernation? As they both feel more alive in terms of increased social life, sex life, fun, and shared leisure, both will hopefully experience more positive self-image, well-being, and mutual love. If they then also both learn to be more expressive of their positive feelings toward each other, the changes will be complete.

In general, how does a conflict resolution therapist know when treatment is complete? There are three indicators, corresponding to the three aspects of treatment.

- *Symptoms:* Anger, depression, and tension will be replaced by affection, laughter, emotional well-being, and comfortable connecting.
- *The issues which had been in dispute* will all be resolved.
- *The couple will be able to dialogue* without the therapist's help. When the therapist can roll his/her chair back, leaving Jan and Mike to discuss even sensitive matters constructively on their own, the couple will be ready to terminate treatment.

Techniques and Interventions

Conflict resolution interventions braid together the same three strands: symptom removal, resolution of specific conflicts, and coaching of skills.

The laundry list strategy explained earlier in this article gives the therapist an overall game plan. The therapist still, however, needs a means of selecting specific goals for each session. To set this agenda at the beginning of each session, I would ask Jan and Mike each to identify what they would like to focus on in that session. They will know best where their energies lie, which issues are of prime import at any given time, and what has been and will be going on in their lives. Reluctance to specify goals is usually diagnostic of a skill deficit of some sort and merits early therapeutic attention.

Alleviating Symptoms

Jan and Mike need help with all four categories of symptoms: anger, depression, anxiety, and avoidance.

Treating Anger

Anger offers a helpful alert to where problems lie. Anger is not effective however as a mode of problem solving. To reduce Jan and Mike's anger I would suggest that they treat anger as a stop sign. Each time either of them feels angry, I would suggest that they stop, look, and listen, just as they would at a traffic stop sign. They need to *stop* to identify what the problem is that their anger is indicating, *look* inward to find the sensitive concerns the situation has triggered, and *listen* to understand also their spouse's concerns in the dilemma. By quietly and cooperatively discussing the problem that had triggered the anger, the problem can be resolved, and the anger will dissipate.

Anger often emerges from breaches in cooperative communication. For instance, Jan wanted Mike to skip going to Jennifer's party and instead stay home with her, but she did not express this preference directly to Mike. Jan's deficit in verbalizing her concerns gave rise to anger when Mike went to the party against her unspoken wishes. Similarly, when Jan says she wants to talk about their conflicts and Mike brushes aside her request, Mike's listening-skill deficit evokes anger in Jan. Likewise, when Jan criticizes Mike—"You shouldn't have . . . "—instead of expressing her concerns and preferences—"I would love to . . . "—Mike reacts to the deprecation with anger.

Anger indicates unilateral instead of bilateral decision-making. Anger indicates attempts to resolve conflicts by overpowering rather than by understanding. Jan, for instance, has a tendency to use anger to try to force Mike to make the changes she wants in his behaviors; that is, she engages in what I refer to as "force-it talk" as opposed to "fix-it dialogue" (Heitler, 1997). Force-it approaches to conflict resolution invite anger and/or depression in response.

Anger often functions as a Geiger counter; its activation may indicate important underlying concerns. In these cases, a depth-dive intervention can be appropriate. Later in this chapter, this technique for accessing subconscious concerns will be detailed.

Lastly, the therapist needs to teach Jan and Mike about the costs of trying to resolve conflicts with anger. For instance, when we feel angry, we tend to believe that our own concerns are sacred, and that the other's are irrelevant. Anger in this regard makes us selfish. When we feel angry, we tend to regard the other in a far more negative light than the way we see them once we have calmed down. Anger in this regard distorts our vision. Lastly, anger is repulsive, not attractive; anger pushes others away, often at the times when we most want to connect. These understandings would hopefully increase Jan and Mike's motivation to treat anger as a stop sign, rather than as a green light for attacking.

Treating Depression

Depression pervades Jan and Mike's relationship. Both spouses show the negativity, irritability, and social withdrawal characteristic of depressive functioning.

Their mutual hopelessness about the future is so serious that it leads them to consider divorce, the equivalent in a marriage to suicide in an individual.

From a conflict-focused perspective, depression is a disorder of power. Therefore, mutual empowerment by walking Jan and Mike through successful conflict resolution will be key.

Depression emerges with submissive responses to conflicts. Mike feels hopeless about Jan ceasing her "nagging." Jan feels that she cannot convince Mike to listen constructively to her concerns. As long as they feel powerless with regard to these deeply felt desires, Mike and Jan will continue to experience depression. By contrast, as they mutually empower themselves and the other with cooperative dialogue, gain empathic understandings of each other, and settle each arena of argument, their individual feelings of depression will lift. Positive moods, including capacity for mutual affection, will reemerge.

Treating Anxiety

Anxiety, while not a prominent symptom for Jan or Mike as individuals, permeates this tension-ridden marriage. Anxiety indicates conflicts that hover without resolution. As Jan and Mike focus on and successfully talk through each area of differences, the tensions around that conflict will dissolve. To stay relaxed with each other, they need the skills to be able to discuss subsequent potentially upsetting issues in a manner that leads similarly to mutually satisfying solutions.

Treating Avoidance

Avoidance has been a major coping strategy for Mike, as manifest in his history of substance abuse and his tendency to stay away from any discussions that could result in conflict. By learning ways to talk about sensitive subjects constructively, Mike will no longer need to rely on avoidance to stay emotionally safe. For instance, Mike's attempts to avoid conflicts by minimizing his wife's concerns or leaving the discussions have in the past triggered Jan's emotional escalations—her episodes of yelling and crying. As Mike and Jan learn to talk openly and safely with each other, Mike will be able to make himself far safer than by avoiding discussions.

As with many individuals in recovery from substance abuse patterns, ceasing to drink or smoke is only the first step. Learning to dialogue constructively rather than avoid conflicts is also vital for full "recovery" from addictions into emotional health.

Guiding Resolution of the Specific Conflicts That Have Evoked Tensions in the Marriage

Jan and Mike need help resolving their outstanding disputes. The therapist guides the way through the three steps of this process, serving also as traffic policeperson who keeps information flowing smoothly and safely, particularly with regard to what I refer to as the four s's:

- *Symmetry:* Are both spouses' concerns being explored? Is Mike monosyllabic and Jan a lengthy talker? They need more or less equivalent air time.
- *Specifics:* Exactly what behaviors do words like "trust" and "dependency" mean for each spouse?
- *Short chunks:* Long monologues lose data. Dialogue is more productive when each spouse makes only one point per air time, in no more than several sentences.
- *Summary:* Circling back to review the concerns made by both spouses assures both spouses that what they say matters.

Another of the therapist's tasks will be to highlight concerns that are either deeply felt or recurrent, concerns which I term core concerns. These are called "core relationship themes" by some theorists (Luborsky, Crits-Christoph, & Mellon, 1986), and transference issues in psychodynamic lingo. In response to core concerns—which are indicated by frequency, a surprisingly intense feeling, or an idiosyncratic interpretation of what the spouse has said or done—a *depth dive intervention* (Heitler, 1995) can explore the unconscious roots.

For instance, Jan describes her reaction to Mike's coming home late from Jennifer's party as "feeling unappreciated." To conduct a depth dive visualization the therapist suggests that Jan close her eyes and focus on that unappreciated feeling, and then asks:

- As you experience that unappreciated feeling, allow your image of Mike to begin to dissolve. In its place allow another image to come up, another moment in your life when you felt similarly unappreciated. *(Jan may see her younger brother going off with his friends.)*
- As you re-experience that moment, notice who is involved, and what that person has done that feels unappreciative to you. *(As her brother leaves, he ignores her.)*
- What about the two incidents feels the same? *(She loved both. And neither paid attention to her once they went off with drugs and/or friends.)*
- Here comes the hard question. As you focus again on Mike, what can you see about Mike and this more recent experience that is different from the experience with your brother? Different in a way that is encouraging, that opens up new possibilities. *(Her brother needed to begin to find his own friendships separate from her. And he was addicted to drugs. Mike and I want to stay together, and he has broken his drug and alcohol habits.)*
- Given these encouraging different aspects of the situation with Mike, what can you visualize that you could do differently in this situation? What would

give the current situation a different, much nicer, kind of ending? *(She could talk plans over ahead of time with Mike, express her preferences, listen to his, and choose activities they will be able to enjoy together.)*

- Now as you open your eyes again, let's discuss what you experienced, what you have discovered about similarities and differences between the past and the present.

The same depth dive visualization could prove useful for helping Mike explore his core concerns such as, for instance, his tendency to feel chronically one-down vis-à-vis women, or the fear that he is about to be berated by his wife. These concerns probably stem from early patterning vis-à-vis his mother. Note that the depth dive is based on the early Freud adage, "where id was let ego be." That is, the depth dive brings origins of emotional reactions up to the light of consciousness, where present and past can be clearly distinguished and new response patterns developed.

As Mike and Jan progress toward understanding the concerns involved with each controversial issue, they will reach a point where they can begin to find solutions. The therapist needs to encourage Mike and Jan to think in terms not of a simple solution, but of a *solution set,* that is, a plan that includes elements responsive to each of the various concerns either of them have expressed. For instance, in order for Mike and Jan to feel full mutual trust, they might choose to institute regular evening times to talk together, make shared decisions and plan upcoming events. They might decide to ask each other, at the end of each discussion, "Are there any pieces of this that still feel unfinished for you?" This question would counter their mutual tendency to leave key concerns unspoken. They might agree also that when plans suddenly change, as happened with Jennifer's party, they both will assume good intentions on the part of the other, so that phoning to touch base feels comfortable, not frightening.

Coaching Collaborative Communication and Conflict Resolution

Dialogue patterns offer a microcosm of the whole relationship. The predominant styles of attachment that Mike and Jan experienced growing up were critical interactions (from Mike's mother) and remoteness (from Mike's father and Jan's parents). These two patterns currently characterize Jan and Mike's marriage. Changing these patterns would change the whole nature of their attachment.

Jan currently expresses her desires as criticisms. For example, after the Jennifer's party debacle, Jan focused on Mike and spoke, "You erred in your judgment. You could at least have called. How much thought does that take?" Jan's critical style of expressing her concerns exacerbates Mike's tendencies to experience his wife as dominating and himself as lacking—tendencies exacerbated by Jan being 5 years older, a better student, and a higher wage-earner.

Jan needs to learn to focus instead on herself and to express insight—her feelings and desires—rather than criticism. "I felt worried about you when you came home so late from the party. I began to wish we communicated more and was hoping desperately for a phone call." Expressing the underlying feeling of worry will engender more empathy, less defensiveness, than her subsequent feeling at anger.

At the same time, Mike needs to learn skills of listening to replace his habit of fending off words from Jan. As long as he minimizes the importance of what his wife says and does not take her concerns seriously (as per the modeling of avoidant listening in his family), he will continue to generate anger in Jan. The more she feels angry, the more she will be tempted to try to get through to him by angry shouting instead of cooperative talking. Changing their circular interaction of anger/avoidance to a cooperative pattern of expression of insights and mutually respectful listening requires that both Jan and Mike learn new skills.

The majority of Jan and Mike's arguments involve Mike "not being dependable" and Jan "nagging." Interestingly, these two factors both refer to communication skill deficits. What Jan calls "not dependable" are instances in which Mike has avoided talking instead of following the first two rules of collaborative dialogue, "Say it" and "Verbalize feelings" (Heitler, 1997). Had he been able to follow these guidelines, after Jennifer's party, Mike would have phoned his wife, told her how embarrassed and regretful he felt, and come home to an appreciative wife.

Similarly, what Mike calls "nagging" is Jan's difficulties with the third and fourth basic guidelines for constructive dialogue: "No trespassing," and "No polluting" (Heitler, 1997). When she tells him not to drink or that he has to be more dependable, Jan is issuing what I call "crossovers" (Heitler, 1997). That is, instead of following the No Trespassing rule by either talking about herself or asking about Mike, Jan is talking about Mike, crossing into his territory and compromising his autonomy by telling him what she thinks he should be doing. And her deprecatory "You're not OK" tone pollutes Mike's self-space with negative implications about him as a person.

Instead of "nagging," i.e., repeatedly telling the other person in a deprecatory tone what you want them to do, Jan needs to learn to give feedback about her concerns. The "When-you" format can be especially helpful for structuring this kind of feedback, keeping the subject of the sentence "I" and the focus of her reference to Mike on behaviors, not personality traits. For example, Jan might tell Mike "I lose trust in you *when you* go to bars," or "*When you* stay away from drinking like you have been the past 7 months, I find my trust growing that maybe you do care more about me than about drinking." At the same time, Mike needs to allow himself to heed Jan's concerns. Otherwise, he is actively inviting repetitions.

How does a therapist coach new skills? Coaching requires that the therapist devise exercises that highlight and repeat each new skill (Heitler, 1992). Repetitions make new skills into habits.

Jan and Mike need to choreograph a disengagement-reengagement routine (Heitler, 1995, 1997) to ensure that they will no longer engage in fighting. A good exit routine includes a method for re-engaging and launching quieter dialogue after both partners have self-soothed. Jan and Mike also need to agree upon anger ceilings, that is, on the level of escalation at which they will discontinue dialogue once one or both of them begin to feel irritated. To keep their dialogues productive and eliminate yelling and crying altogether, they would be well advised to set their anger ceilings at the first rumblings of irritability, and to use their mutually agreed-upon exit-reentry routines for bailing out temporarily of any discussion beyond that point. Note that exits, if initiated early enough, often take only a few minutes of pause time—just long enough for both parties to self-soothe to calmer states.

To consolidate their exit choreography, it is important that the couple practice, several times, how they would implement their exit-reentry routines. Role plays identify potential glitches in a couple's attempts to use new skills and also consolidate learning. As Mike gives a sign that he wants a time out, for instance, Jan might find that she experiences anger at what seems to her to be another avoidance of talking. Playing the sequence out to the end, however, would enable Jan to experience Mike's return and reengagement in discussion, which would build her confidence that this routine will increase rather than end dialogue.

In sum, Jan and Mike need to switch from angry/avoidant interaction cycles to mutually respectful talking and listening. This change in their dialogue patterns would improve both the power and the love aspects of their partnership. Collaborative dialogue creates shared empowerment and allows a secure and loving attachment to flourish.

Pitfalls

Mike's history of quitting activities he tries suggests significant risk for dropping out of treatment, especially given his wariness of whether treatment can make a difference. Giving Mike and Jan frequent feedback on the specific progress they are making in treatment would be vital. Emphasizing Mike's strengths and adding to his skill repertoire rather than focusing on his deficits, will be essential.

Lastly, making an explicit contract with Mike with regard to what he and the therapist each need to do if Mike has an impulse to leave treatment could avert a premature termination. Like a No Suicide contract, a prearranged plan for Mike to contact the therapist and discuss any impulses he might feel to drop out could prevent this pitfall.

With regard to pitfalls on Jan's side of the treatment, Jan's stance has generally been quite blaming. Sometimes a therapist's attempt to refocus a spouse from blame and emphasis on fixing the partner to a self-focus backfires. Instead of yielding insight, the maneuver can rigidify the blaming stance. Fortunately, however, Jan shows capacity for focusing on herself and what she can do differently.

Jan's tendency to bring up the trump card of divorce and the ambivalence she has expressed about her marriage suggest that she would benefit from exploring the concerns that prompt her to want to leave. Instead of blaming Mike, she needs to clarify the unfulfilled personal desires that tempt her to exit. For instance, Jan seems considerably more sociable and interactive than her husband. Once she has identified her concerns, Jan could brainstorm with Mike on solutions.

Finally, both Jan and Mike need to stop engaging in high-risk marriage behavior. Long and loud arguments must be stopped. Threats of divorce must be ended. Threats of divorce, like threats of suicide, may be intended as calls for help, but they erode secure marital attachment. I would want to see Mike and Jan declare arguments and divorce threats, like drug/alcohol abuse and violations of monogamy, out of bounds.

Areas Mike and Jan May Want to Avoid

Did Mike have an affair at the party? Why would he have fallen asleep there? The couple seems not to be delving into this question, and may prefer here to let sleeping dogs lie. It would probably be preferable to explore this question. Openness about affairs is generally preferable to secrecy. On the other hand, I would respect a couple's mutual preference not to discuss an error that would be humiliating for Mike to admit and wounding for Jan to hear. Individual sessions could be helpful for exploring these preferences and also Mike's father's history of infidelities.

Mike may avoid discussing his sexual molestation at ages 7 and 9; avoidance would be consistent with his general style of coping with troubling events and concerns. On the other hand, this molestation may have had profound impact on Mike's attitude toward sexual activity, his tendency to feel dominated or controlled by women, and on his ability to feel self-respect rather than shame and guilt. One of the depth dive explorations of Mike's underlying concerns should access this potent life event. Like affairs, molestation might best be explored initially in an individual therapy session.

Inclusion of Other Family Members

I would include Jan and Mike together in most sessions, and from time to time would meet individually with each of them. Families of origin can be included in treatment from time to time, adding depth and breadth to the treatment. I find, however, that few couples want to add this additional complexity to their treatment.

If Mike and Jan had children, I would discuss ways in which their marriage difficulties may have modeled problematic behavior and I might encourage them to bring their children for at least a session or two to assess their emotional health. They do not, however, have offspring.

Homework

Jan and Mike need to learn basic skills of marital dialogue. Doling out this information piece by piece in therapy sessions takes time. Homework accelerates the learning process. I would therefore assign:

1. *Reading from The Power of Two: Secrets to a Strong & Loving Marriage* (Heitler, 1997). To combat enmeshment as well as to increase the learning, I would encourage Jan and Mike each to have their own book to underline important passages. I suggest that they read to learn about themselves, not with a focus on what they would like the other to do. The specific chapter assigned each week would be correlated with the skills addressed that session.

2. *Listening to the audiotape Conflict Resolution for Couples* (Heitler, 1994). Mike may not be a reader, as Jan seems to be. Audiotapes can bypass reading inhibitions, sparing Mike a one-up situation in which Jan does her reading homework and Mike "fails" by avoiding a project that he does not feel he will do as well as his wife.

3. *Listening to the audiotapes we record of each session.* I tape sessions routinely, and give the tape to the couple at the end of each session. Therapy sessions are like dreams, vivid immediately upon completion, but quick to fade. They also tend to be dense, with more information than people can absorb in one experience. Listening a second time to sessions consolidates learning.

4. *Viewing of the video The Angry Couple* (loaned by the therapist). My clinical experience suggests that when couples watch the couple on the video transition from fighting to cooperation, their own progress accelerates.

Timeline, Referrals, and Policies for Individual Therapy Sessions

I would expect this case to be a relatively straightforward treatment, completed within 3 to 6 months, that is, in 12 to 25 sessions. One key factor in treatment length would be how much energy each partner puts into homework study. Also, however, people seem to have an internal rate of change that would have to be respected.

With regard to referrals, if the negative thinking of either partner continued, I might request that we add a medication component to treatment to ease depressive physiology. I would expect Mike to continue in some kind of post-alcohol supportive treatment such as AA. If I suspect that ADD may be complicating Mike's functioning, I might refer him to an ADD specialist for further assessment and medication.

As to individual therapy, I would insist that these sessions be handled by me. Involving a second therapist for individual treatment components is a recipe for unsuccessful treatment. An individual therapist, seeing only one member of the couple, operates with too little understanding of the couple's interactions. By working with the two individuals plus the couple aspects of treatment, a single therapist can keep these three treatment arenas coordinated with positive synergies.

Many therapists fear the confidentiality issues that can arise if they sometimes work individually with the spouses. What if, for instance, one partner is having an affair? This concern for holding secrets is appropriate. The solution I prefer however is to make clear at the outset what rules will govern confidentiality. I would clarify to both Mike and Jan, at a marital session prior to working with them individually, that any information shared with me when I am talking with one of them alone will be held confidential by me. They can choose to share what we have discussed with their partner or to keep it private; I will not be at liberty, however, to disclose to the partner anything that is told to me in individual sessions.

A marriage therapist must be able to work individually with each member of the couple, with clear confidentiality, as well as conjointly. If Mike or Jan, for instance, is in fact involved in activity counter to a healthy marriage, such as having an affair, considering suicide, or running into financial difficulties, their therapist needs to know about it. Otherwise the therapist cannot help them with the elephant in the room; without addressing the elephants in a relationship, treatment is doomed.

In offering couples individual sessions, symmetry is essential. Sometimes one partner seems more troubled or more frozen in terms of treatment progress. Nonetheless, keeping the number of individual sessions symmetrical allows the other partner also to grow, and avoids the appearance either of favoritism or of pathologizing one party. In rare instances, when there is a highly significant difference in levels of symptomatology, this principle needs to be modified, but Mike and Jan do not show this kind of extreme difference.

Early in treatment I would want at least some time alone with each partner to be sure that all the relevant information is on the table. Most of the work of individual treatment with a disengaged couple like Mike and Jan, however, is best accomplished with both partners in the room. When one partner explores the impact of his or her past on present feelings and habits, if both spouses are in the room the listener gains empathic understanding while the other is gaining insight. Empathic understanding is as vital to the growth of a more loving relationship as self-knowledge.

Termination and Relapse Prevention

Some couples can terminate treatment with a summary session or two. Others do better tapering off gradually, with a concluding phase of sessions every other week, a 6-week check up, or a followup after 3 months. Whatever their termination arrangement, Jan and Mike would be encouraged to return if problems re-emerge. We would specify the signs that could indicate slippage into old patterns. Scheduling a booster session in 6 months or a year also can be helpful.

Termination would include a treatment review, perhaps utilizing the following visualizations:

- Close your eyes and picture your first therapy session here. Recall how you were feeling, how you felt toward your partner, what you were doing and wanting, and what your partner seemed to be doing. Then bring your focus to the present. How would you answer these same questions as you sit together in this session today? What has changed?
- Thinking back on the course of your treatment, what moment(s) stands out for you as particularly vivid or as a turning point in your process of growth?
- Thinking ahead to the future, what challenges do you anticipate may prove difficult for you in the coming months? What strengths and skills have you discovered that will aid you? What can you remind yourself that will help sustain your positive feelings toward yourself and toward each other?

REFERENCES

Ainsworth, M. D. S., Blehar, M. C., Waters, E., & Wall, S. (1978). *Patterns of attachment.* Hillsdale, NJ: Erlbaum.
Bowlby, J. (1980). *Attachment and loss: Vol. 3. Loss: Sadness and depression.* New York: Basic Books.
Fisher, R., & Ury, W., (1991). *Getting to yes.* New York: Penguin.
*Heitler, S. (1992). *Working with couples in conflict* (Audiotape with listener's outline). New York: Norton.

---

*Suggested reading.

*Heitler, S. (1993). *From conflict to resolution.* New York: Norton.

Heitler, S. (1994). *Conflict resolution for couples.* (Audiotape). Denver, CO: Listen to Learn. (Available: 1-800-919-8899).

*Heitler, S. (1995). *The angry couple: Conflict-focused treatment* (Video and viewer's manual). Denver, CO: Listen to Learn (Available: 1-800-919-8899).

*Heitler, S. (1997). *The power of two.* Oakland, CA: New Harbinger.

Luborsky, L., Crits-Christoph, P., & Mellon, J. (1986). Advent of objective measures of the transference concept. *Journal of Consulting and Clinical Psychology, 54,* 39–47.

Rice, L., & Greenberg, L. (1984). *Patterns of change.* New York: Guilford Press.

Wachtel, P. (1977). *Psychoanalysis and behavior therapy.* New York: Basic Books.

SUGGESTED READING

Simpson, J. A., & Rholes, W. S. (1998). *Attachment theory and close relationships.* New York: Guilford Press.

15

Relationship Enhancement Couples Therapy

Barry G. Ginsberg

TREATMENT MODEL

Relationship Enhancement Therapy (RE), developed by Bernard G. Guerney in the 1960s, combines psychodynamic, behavioral communication, and experiential and relationship (family) systems perspectives into an integrative whole. This approach was one of the earliest to recognize the benefits of an educational skill-training model over the traditional diagnosis and treatment that has been popular for decades. Central to the development of RE is the belief that one's personality is "shaped by his or her relationships, which in turn shape relationships over the life span. The individual is seen as developing interpersonal reflexes (Leary, 1957; Shannon & Guerney, 1973) which trigger the same kind of response in others" (Ginsberg, 1997, p. 5). These reflexes, or habits are seen as automatic and non-conscious and operate reciprocally. Shannon and Guerney (1973) found that these interpersonal reflexes elicit like responses. For example, positives elicit positive responses and negatives elicit negatives. From this perspective, Guerney conceived of the idea of training people in constructive relationship skills, which became the foundation of RE therapy.

From an RE framework, the key issue in a couple's relationship is their ability to maintain a context of intimacy and engagement that allows them to experience a sense of trust and security in which they can be "safely vulnerable." Couples can do this if they feel attached, which in turn depends on the ability to emotionally engage with one another, a quality that enables people to develop in healthy ways and to trust themselves.

Interpersonal reflexes, or the ways in which a person habitually relates to others, almost certainly influences two people coming together. Once the relationship becomes significant, these reflexes become the signposts around which emotional engagement can deepen. In the process, each partner's reflexes are modified to accommodate the other. New reflexes then evolve that help secure the relationship. Stress and conflict arise from this process and provide opportunities for change. It is important for the relationship to be flexible enough to cope with these forces; at the same time, the couple has to maintain sufficient emotional engagement to maintain the trust and security of the relationship.

Stress and conflict, then, are the vehicles that both challenge the maintenance of emotional engagement between two people, and often provide the opportunity to deepen this engagement. The key in couples therapy is not to directly help couples solve problems, but to have them skillfully maintain emotional engagement under stress. In fact, it is likely that a couple's difficulty in resolving conflict has more to do with emotional disengagement than with an inability to solve problems. Most often, couples seek therapy when the degree of emotional disengagement threatens the stability of their relationship. RE attempts to help couples return to closer, more intimate levels of emotional engagement and to help them learn the skills necessary to maintain the security of their relationship.

It's instructive to consider the benefits of RE therapy in the context of John Gottman's esteemed research on marriage. Gottman (1995) proposes that the most consistent determinant of marital unhappiness is the expression of negative emotions in response to one's spouse's expression of negative emotions. He found that when spouses react with particular negative behaviors—criticism, contempt, defensiveness, and stonewalling, which he termed the "Four Horsemen of the Apocalypse"—divorce could be predicted 85% of the time. The constructive relationship skills that are taught to couples in RE directly mitigate against these behaviors. In particular, couples are asked not to make judgements or accusations, and not to ask questions while listening to one another. Instead, they are asked to acknowledge the underlying feelings that motivate their spouse's expressions and actions. They are asked to avoid judgement and acknowledge (own) their feelings when speaking. This helps to keep the relationship on a more equivalent basis.

By agreeing to follow these rules, couples create a relationship context that reduces the frequency of criticism and prevents stonewalling. Specifically, when couples stop judging each other, they become less defensive—defensiveness is a hallmark of all troubled relationships—and embark together on a process of "softening," which refers to a change in the hardness of the quality of confrontation (Greenberg & Johnson, 1988).

Gottman not only stresses the importance of "softening" (Gottman, Coan, Carrere, & Swanson, 1998), but he also includes acceptance as an important variable in this softening process. According to the precepts of RE, non-judgement and acceptance are taught together, because these two skills are integrally related. Rogers (1957, 1959) describes acceptance as a letting go (of judgement), and as an interpersonal process of trying to understand another's motivations without confounding this understanding by one's own motivations. Thus, when a member of a couple acknowledges the "feelings" of the other person while inhibiting his own feelings and judgments, that person is practicing nonjudgement and acceptance.

According to Greenberg (1994), acceptance has two components. The first he describes as the "valuing of the partner's internal experience in a non-judgmental fashion, free of expectation of how they should be or feel about themselves, or what attitudes they should hold" (p. 65). The second facet of acceptance is the ability to renounce attempts to control or change the other's behavior. In RE, couples learn to access their internal experience by exploring the emotions that motivate behavior. When people perceive that an interpersonal context is safe enough, they are freer to reveal these motivating feelings to themselves as well as their partners. Rogers (1951) extends this notion of acceptance to oneself: "When the individual perceives and accepts into one consistent and integrated system all his sensory and visceral experiences, then he is necessarily more understanding of others and is more accepting of others as separate individuals" (p. 520).

RE rests on three core skills which, taken together, allow couples to become emotionally engaged. The first is *Expressive (owning)* skill. By practicing ownership, each member of a couple learns to recognize his or her own feelings, take responsibility for them without projecting them onto others, and assert them. *Empathic Responding (receptive)*, the second skill, enables each partner to wait longer before expressing his or her own feelings and perspective, to understand the underlying motivations (feelings) of the other, and to incorporate this understanding into one's own expression.

In RE, each member of a couple practices expressing his or her feelings and owning these feelings; this then enables each person to accept the other. By reciprocally practicing the skill of acknowledging the internal experience of the other—through receptive listening—a context of acceptance is created (see Peterson, 1994). Ultimately, through supervised and then unsupervised practice, couples learn to create an ongoing relationship context of acceptance that operates in their day-to-day lives. Establishing this context is a critical outcome of RE therapy.

The third core skill of RE—the "relationship" or *Conversive (discussion-negotiation/engagement)* skill—solidifies emotional engagement (Ginsberg, 1997). This critical skill depends on the ability of each person, after understanding the other person's feelings, to give meaning to the importance of the relationship, that is, to make a connection to their shared internal experience. To practice the conversive skill, one partner is designated as the "expressor" or "speaker," and is instructed to say "Switch" when he wishes to stop talking and begin listening (empathic responder). In other words, couples are asked to maintain distinct positions of either "listener" or "speaker," and agree that the "speaker" is responsible for switching these positions. This acknowledges the fact that the speaker is in the more vulnerable position. At the switch, the new speaker (the former listener) must then indicate how she feels to know her partner's feelings about what was just expressed (e.g., "I feel bad that you were hurt by . . . ").

The conversive skill encompasses two component skills: the ability to interact and to engage. The interactive component helps couples learn to differentiate from one another; the engagement component fosters emotional engagement. In those cases in which the conversation takes place in a climate of openness and acceptance, couples are able to both interact independently and to emotionally engage with each other.

Two additional RE skills are *Generalization* and *Maintenance*. These two skills are included with owning expression, receptive listening and conversive (discussion-negotiation/engagement) skills as the Core RE skills.

The success of the therapy lies in clients' abilities to extend these skills to their real everyday lives. The development of client's generalization and maintenance skills begin with the very first session of RE therapy. (See Ginsberg, 1997, for guidelines for generalization and maintenance skills.)

As couples learn and apply these skills, they create an ongoing context of acceptance and engagement. Once couples begin to grasp the Core skills and perhaps begin to practice them at home, other skills can be incorporated in the learning process. Secondary (related) skills (Ginsberg, 1997) include problem/conflict resolution; facilitative, self-change, and helping others. It is the author's belief that these related skills are mostly learned by couples as an outgrowth of practicing the Core skills and are specifically taught when pertinent to a particular couple's needs. (For further elaboration of the secondary skills, see Ginsberg 1997, pp. 41–49.)

THERAPIST SKILLS AND ATTRIBUTES

Probably the most difficult aspect of couples therapy is engaging couples under the conditions of conflict and high arousal levels that motivate them to come to therapy. In fact, it is likely that these factors and how the therapist responds to them are critical to the success of the therapy. According to Gottman (1995), engaging successfully around these variables determines whether couples remain together. The RE therapist uses RE skills—empathic responding, owning of one's own motivation (expressive skill), and conversive skill to connect with the emotional dissonance that makes couples therapy so difficult—engaging the couple in a constructive way to elicit the positive feelings and resources underlying the relationship.

Helping couples learn and apply the Core RE skills in their everyday lives is the key to sustaining emotional engagement and improving their coping skills. It is essential that the RE therapist act as a model for clients, as this enhances learning and fosters trust. In particular, the therapist employs good interpersonal skills such as genuineness, empathy, and acceptance. Furthermore, the RE therapist uses his or her skills to emotionally engage clients without being triangulated into the dynamics of their relationships.

Effective RE therapists draw upon the principles and skills of RE. Two essential attitudes which impact on therapist effectiveness are having "humility" regarding one's ability to understand and directly influence the clients' problems, and having "trust" in the clients' ability to resolve their own difficulties. The very idea of helping them learn skills is based on these attitudes. RE therapists have developed good teaching skills that help clients see that learning RE skills could have a positive impact on the quality of their relationship and their problems. They also believe that clients can learn the skills and change, and can be motivated to practice and maintain the skills over time.

Therapists must create a climate that is safe and take responsibility to maintain this safety during the process of therapy. The principles and structure of RE, including the rules of conversation, provide a framework to accomplish this. Therapists also need to maintain fairness and impartiality, while being free to form coalitions to balance power. The therapist draws from ten specific therapist/ leadership skills.

1. **Administering** (directive), managing the therapy in a directive way
2. **Instructing/structuring** (didactic), structuring the therapy and guiding home assignments
3. **Demonstrating** (didactic), providing examples, expressing guidelines, and indicating how skills can be used
4. **Reinforcing**, applying principles of operant conditioning
5. **Modeling**, expressing skills and feelings in a way that is consonant with RE principles
6. **Prompting/encouraging**, encouraging clients to express thoughts and feelings, and encouraging client participation
7. **Supervising home assignments**, structuring and reviewing homework
8. **Troubleshooting for clients**, helping clients resolve their difficulty or anxiety using RE skills
9. **Becoming/doubling**, helping clients who feel too overwhelmed or upset to respond
10. **Troubleshooting for self**, using RE skills when difficulties arise in the therapist-client relationship.

The RE therapist draws upon these skills and attitudes, and applies them in a structured, systematic, and time-designated way to facilitate optimal outcomes in couples therapy.

THE CASE OF MIKE AND JAN

The Conceptualization of Mike and Jan

Because RE is non-diagnostic, it makes no distinction between prevention and amelioration. However, when couples present themselves for therapy rather than education, it is helpful to the therapist to formulate some hypotheses regarding the functioning of each individual member and the couple relationship. This enhances the therapist's skill in working effectively with the couple and helps to identify other concerns that may require referral to other professionals.

Mike

Mike's background reveals a developmental history of dependency and insecurity. He tends to be a loner who is insecure with men and women. He appears to have developed a dependent relationship with a critical mother in a context in which his father was distant. There is a question of whether he received sufficient nurturance during the early developmental years to achieve a satisfying level of intimacy. His 20-year dependency on alcohol may reflect his effort to relieve his underlying anxiety and unhappiness. After so many years of substance abuse and dependency, the question of an endogenous depression cannot be ruled out.

There are many benchmarks in Mike's family history to be considered. Certainly, trauma has affected his life. He was the youngest brother (the good one?) of two, his older brother getting more attention due to his "behavioral" problems. Mike himself may have had "attentional problems" exacerbating his feelings of inadequacy and insecurity. Fortunately, he found working with his hands very rewarding. Between the ages of 7 and 9, he had an overinvolved, perhaps sexually abusive relationship with an aunt. It is possible that this close, sexual relationship created ambivalence in him between his need for intimacy and the threat of the violation of boundaries. Significantly, he is reluctant to reveal this relationship to anybody but his wife and therapist. He is still in conflict over it.

Even when Mike tried to please his dad, he felt abandoned by his father. This sense of abandonment is accentuated by his father's leaving at the time of his parent's divorce, causing Mike to become more dependent on his critical and controlling mother. Though after he continued to live with her until age 29, she abandoned him as well by remarrying. He married a year later (rebounding from the abandonment of his mother?), but it appeared to be a disengaged relationship exacerbated by pregnancy and miscarriage. Drugs and alcohol became more of consolation during this period. He also had an auto accident (a DUI offense), lost his job, and became divorced. Shortly thereafter, he met and married Jan. More than 10 years later he had a blackout episode which led him to drug and alcohol rehabilitation. Seven months later he and his wife entered couples therapy.

This isn't surprising. The rehabilitation process puts tremendous stress on the primary and significant relationships of the person in recovery. The old relationship habits based on dependency are no longer viable, which creates stress and provides the opportunity for change. This may very well have been the stimulus for Jan and Mike to enter marital therapy.

Jan

Jan's history does not seem to be as revealing as Mike's. However, her claim that she didn't want children because she did her share of raising her brother is significant. She expressed this feeling after having had a traumatic hysterectomy at age 29. It is not clear whether her first marriage occurred before or after this event. Eight years after it, she married Mike. She is relieved that he doesn't want to have children. She states that her parents were quite lenient, even when she seemed to need stronger limits. She seems to have functioned as a co-parent, taking care of her brother, and at times of her mother as well. Often, a child in this position develops a mistrust of depending on others, and ends up depending only on herself. It is easier for her to take care of others than to depend on them. This often leads to problems with intimacy and rigid ways of coping. Jan's statement "I did my share of parenting when I was raising my younger brother John" reveals an underlying anger and ambivalence towards her family. It addresses Jan's issue of the role of trust in relationships and her need to care for others to feel secure and maintain distance in the relationship. This complements Mike's need for dependency and his own difficulty in trusting others.

Jan's reaction to Mike's behavior at Jennifer's party (asking for a divorce) seems stronger than this episode warrants. It underscores the rigidity with which she copes with her issues of trust and intimacy. Her reaction may be representative of the changes in their relationship fostered by Mike's sobriety.

The Couple Relationship

Jan stated the presenting problem as "difficulty achieving emotional intimacy due to continual conflicts and lack of effective resolutions." These concerns are a good generalization of the couple's dynamics. Their relationship can be seen as a dependent one that protects their insecurity, vulnerability, and emotional distance. Mike has emerged from a dependent relationship with a critical mother against whom he defends himself through avoidance and disengagement. Jan is accustomed to taking care of others, but harbors dissatisfaction because her needs for emotional intimacy remain unmet. These characteristics complement each other to elicit a cyclical dynamic, which repeats the habits they learned while growing up, and with which they are comfortable. It seems likely that escalation of their difficulties (leading to seek marital therapy) may have been precipitated by Mike's 28-day treatment program and his subsequent 7-month sobriety. The fact that Jan didn't want Mike to attend Jennifer's party, yet couldn't assert herself effectively, suggests difficulties in communication. Furthermore, her reaction (not wanting to continue the relationship and asking for a divorce) exemplifies rigid coping mechanisms.

Mike's response is rigid as well. That he expects her to react less angrily because "in the last 6 weeks he has done everything he said he would" reinforces their rigid habits and inefficient communication skills. They avoid discussing conflicts with each other, which leads to more conflict, and when they do argue, Jan criticizes and Mike stonewalls and disengages. These are the very characteristics that Gottman (1995) has demonstrated lead to separation and divorce. Recently, Gottman et al. (1998) have identified the importance of marital therapy's role to help the husband increasingly accept his wife's influence. Stung by Jan's criticism, Mike resists this.

It is also important to consider that both Jan and Mike are in mid-life, and that after 12 years of marriage, their needs have changed. The crisis created by such changes provides the opportunity to build on the resources they have developed in their relationship to form an improved, more emotionally engaged and stable relationship.

Instruments and Assessment Tools

RE is nondiagnostic because of its emphasis on skill learning. In a traditional diagnosis and treatment approach, the "patient" depends on the assessment and diagnosis of the "expert," and treatment depends on this diagnosis. Under these conditions, patients concede some or most of their own perspective to the superior knowledge and experience of the provider.

One of the important principles of RE therapy is the notion of equivalence. This is as important in the client-therapist relationship as it is in the client-client relationship. In RE, a collaborative relationship is formed where clients and therapist agree on the problems and formulate together how to obtain the best outcomes. It is the therapist's responsibility to inform the clients of the value of the skill training approach and its relevance to the problems. Ultimately, clients and therapist agree on the course of treatment, which typically includes skill learning as its central focus.

The therapist's power, guidance, and leadership depend on the collaboration between clients and therapist. Once this collaboration is established, the therapist has the clients' permission to proceed under the conditions agreed to by the clients. Only when clients understand the relevance of the principles and methods of RE to their presenting problem can this collaboration and permission emerge.

The clinical interview forms the basis for this collaborative process. It establishes the trust necessary to gain mutual understanding and develop this collaborative relationship. The therapist and clients together review those factors that led to the decision to seek therapy. It is helpful for the therapist to acknowledge the feelings (receptive skill) that have driven this process. Not only is this good modeling, but it also helps reframe the problems by attaching feelings to them. All of these efforts help clients and therapist develop a mutual understanding of the problem and how RE therapy will help them achieve a meaningful outcome. Commonly, couples are eager to relate the history of their problems and relationship. This naturally leads to discussion of family-of-origin issues, and can add to the understanding of clients and therapist. Taking time to do this can enhance the trust between clients and therapist and lead to additional strategies to ameliorate the problems.

Inventories and assessment materials can be useful as part of a structured, time-limited, educational-based therapy. Asking couples to complete standardized questionnaires can be a valuable tool to help clients learn about themselves and their relationship. Some examples of these measures are Prepare/Enrich (Olson & Hawley, 1992) and the Interpersonal Check List (Leary, 1957), which emphasize the reflexive nature of human functioning. Also, Guerney has developed manuals that include measures for couples to assess their relationship (Guerney, 1989; Nordling, Skuca, & Guerney, 1998; Preston & Guerney, 1982).

Strengths

One of the most important values and methods of RE therapy is to assist couples to elicit and acknowledge the underlying positives in their relationship. There are many strengths in Jan and Mike's relationship that point to an optimistic therapy outcome. They have a 12-year marriage, which itself speaks of the strength of their relationship and the degree to which it has met their needs. Both have held jobs for a long time, indicating stability. After their conflict, both recovered from their impasse of the night before and demonstrated an ability to "soften" towards each other. In RE, softening is seen as the emergence of an openness to the partner and increased acceptance of the other person's perspective. This will be discussed more in the section on goals. Jan recovered from her initial threat of divorce, and both were able to verbalize their unhappiness.

This fits Greenberg and Johnson's (1988) definition of "softening" as a time "when a blaming spouse accesses vulnerability and asks for closeness or comfort from a previously distant partner. This event . . . constitutes a redefinition of relationship structure" (p. 176). Their agreement to seek therapy represents an acknowledgment of their problem-solving skills, which can be called upon in therapy. Because they love each other, they possess the underlying positive motivation that can propel them to learn the skills they need to improve and maintain emotional engagement over time.

Treatment Goals

It is important to review some of the basic assumptions of RE when considering goals. Implicit in the formulation of RE is the concept of interpersonal reflexes. The RE therapist believes that the difficulties couples experience arise from habits each person has acquired over the course of his or her life, and are also derived from within their relationship with each other. These habits are expressed as ineffective or inadequate communication/relationship behaviors. Helping couples learn the constructive communication/relationship skills fostered by RE shifts these defensive habits to interactions that are more openly accepting and emotionally engaging.

In RE therapy, clients and therapists negotiate mutually agreeable goals for the therapy. Typically, this is determined in the first session and evaluated at agreed-upon time-designated periods throughout the therapy. Judging from Jan's comments when she made the appointment for marital therapy, Jan and Mike wanted to improve their emotional intimacy, reduce conflicts, and be better able to resolve their differences. These are realistic goals, and ones with which clients and therapist could agree. It is important, however, to help couples be realistic in their expectations and evaluate these objectives as they continue therapy.

Techniques and Interventions

The RE therapist needs to draw upon the specific therapist/leadership skills. Demonstrating and modeling are particularly important interventions throughout the therapy. The RE therapist also needs to make the therapeutic context safe enough for couples to learn and practice the skills. He or she must also be concerned about any disruptions in the couple's relationship that occur between sessions. Specifically, the therapist/leadership skills of troubleshooting for the client, becoming/doubling, and troubleshooting for self (therapist) are important interventions under those conditions (see Ginsberg, 1997). These interventions would be used throughout the therapy whenever disengagement is evident. The therapist's objectives would be to help the couple reengage and continuing practicing the skills. Ultimately, therapeutic change lies in the practice of these skills.

One of the difficulties that couples have when they are initially engaged in RE skill training is that they feel frustrated with the stilted and artificial way the conversation is structured. It is essential that the therapist openly address this difficulty to ease client resistance. In some ways, this is the nub of RE therapy, because once the couple is engaged in the structured, slowed-down conversation, the old habits of their interaction begin to break down and be replaced by new, constructive ones. Holding couples within this speaker-listener conversive skill framework opens up the relationship, helps to develop softening, elicits the underlying positives in the relationship, and subtly shifts the interaction to one that is more emotionally engaged.

A short example of an imagined beginning session with Jan and Mike will help to illustrate this process.

This portion of the session begins with the therapist instructing the husband (Mike) about being in the listener's role. The therapist has already instructed the wife (Jan) in the speaker's position. She is the first speaker.

Ginsberg: (to Mike) I would prefer you start out doing it slowly and rotelike. After a while, it will become much more easy to do and much more comfortable, much more fluid, natural, but right now I would much rather you do it more straightforward, just to get into this way of working with each other. I'll help you with that. I'll model it for you and you tell it to her. It's a very good way for you to learn. If what you're saying tends to be judgmental, or if you give your opinion, I'll come in and help you try to say it back to her in a way so she feels you are really understanding it.

(*to Jan*) Now, we're going to have to give you some time to stay in the speaker's position so you'll (to Mike) be in the listener position for a period of time.

(*To Jan*) And, then after a while, because you're the vulnerable one, when you feel fairly understood—and I'll try and help you with that—you'll say, "Switch." That will mean that you are willing to be a listener now, and it's his turn to be a speaker. At that time I'll introduce a new role.

Jan: I know what he's going to say—I don't want to hear it. He's going to tell me it's a certain thing and it's not what I did. *(She is anxious and defensive)*

Ginsberg: I know you're worried about that, and that would make it hard if you're already anticipating what he's going to say. I'm hopeful that what he is going to say at that point will be different because of the rules that come into play. (*The therapist uses Receptive, Expressive and Conversive skills*). My purpose is to help you, not to make it harder for you. We're going to do this slowly and carefully, and I'll be very much involved in your conversation at the beginning because I want to help you learn this. So, you're going to talk to him, no judgements, no accusations, no questions. (Structuring.)

Jan: I thought you said I was going to be talking to you.

Ginsberg: Oh no, the best way for me to help you is for you to talk to him, so you can learn something together and take it home with you and make your relationship better.

Jan: I guess I misunderstood.

Ginsberg: I hope it's still okay for us to do this.

Jan: No, I'm fine.

Ginsberg: It's really important for me that you understand what we are doing and that we get a chance to help you see the value of what we are doing. So, you're going to talk to him, and I would encourage you to express only one or two sentences to start with. Don't give him the whole thing at once, because it would be too hard for him to respond. Remember, we are just practicing. *(Notice how much structure the therapist provides to help keep the context safe.)*

Jan: I'm very upset about the way you spoke to me in front of my parents when we took them out to dinner last month. I want you to know that.

Mike: Well, you want me to know that you are really upset. . . . *(Mike sounds judgmental)*

Jan: *(Interrupted him)* I'm sorry, he already . . . *(She's defensive)*

Ginsberg: I see it, I hear it. *(to Mike)* It would be helpful if you would try to convey judgement in the way you're talking, *(To Jan)* but I wasn't going to be too strong with him because it's the first time he's doing it. *(To Mike)* But, she's right, the way you are saying it is judging her. Try again without the judgement. *(Notice how the therapist intervenes to acknowledge and engage both of them in this process.)*

Mike: You're upset with me because of the way I spoke to you when we were out with your parents, and you want me to know that.

Ginsberg: Good. *(Reinforcement)*

Jan: When I tried to talk to you about it, you said that you were angry at me because I deliberately turned the radio up so loud that you couldn't hear my parents, and then I tried to explain to you that I didn't realize the speaker on your side of the car was working and mine wasn't and I didn't know how loud it was, and I'm just appalled that you would think that I would do something deliberately to cut you out of the conversation. That upsets me.

Mike:	You're appalled to think that I would think that you deliberately cut me out of the conversation with your parents when you turned up the radio and that really upset you.
Jan:	I felt humiliated in front of my father and that made me feel pissed at you.
Mike:	You're pissed because you felt I humiliated you in front of your father and that you were really embarrassed and that you were pissed at me about that.
Jan:	I never talked to you that way in front of your parents, because I expect you to treat me the same way in front of my parents as I do in front of your parents. I am courteous to you even when I'm pissed that your mother is treating me like shit. (*She's judgmental—talking in a one-up position*)
Ginsberg:	This is hard! It's really important to you that he respect your feelings because you try hard to respect his, particularly when you're with each others' parents. I'd like you to say that to him.

(The therapist intervenes immediately to help shape the expression before the husband can respond. This helps to reduce defensiveness and limits the wife's judgment.)

Jan:	(*to Ginsberg*) Please repeat what you just said.
Ginsberg:	(*Modeling*) It's very important to me to be respectful of you when you're with your parents, and that's why it hurt me so much when I thought you weren't being that way when we were with mine.
Jan:	I try to be always respectful to you and to your parents, no matter what's going on, and it hurt me very much that you wouldn't return the same courtesies to me.
Mike:	You're upset because you feel I didn't extend you the same courtesy that you extend me around my parents. (*His response picks up her judgment anyway. He is defensive.*)
Ginsberg:	(*to Mike*) That's not bad, but it's not exactly what she meant. It's important to her that you respect her feelings when she's with her parents, because she tries to do that with you. She was hurt because she didn't think you were doing that. I would like you to say: "You feel hurt because you don't think I was being respectful of your feelings when we were with your parents." (*Again, the therapist uses modeling to shape the response and limit defensiveness.*)
Mike:	You feel hurt because I wasn't respectful of your feelings when we were with your parents because you respect me when we are around my parents. And you're hurt by that.
Ginsberg:	Excellent! This would be a good time for a switch. What do you

think?

(It's important in the beginning for the therapist to guide the switch to help pace the conversation and reduce emotional arousal. This keeps the couple engaged.)

Jan: Yeah, I'm out of steam.
Ginsberg: Okay, it's your vulnerability that's on the line here, so you're the one that has to say, "Switch," to acknowledge that you're ready to be a listener. So say "Switch."
Jan: Switch. Are we going to be discussing the same issue?
Ginsberg: You'll see how this goes.
Jan: Okay, I'm ready to switch.
Ginsberg: Now hold on, you have to know what the rule is—we haven't talked about this rule yet. It's a very important rule, it's a rule everybody forgets, because most of us would be inclined now to give my side of the story; where I'm coming from about this. But what you would be doing is you would be ignoring the meaning of your relationship with her. So the part that you have to do first before you get into your side of things is do what I call the relationship rule, and that is you have to tell her how it makes you feel to know that she was hurt thinking that you weren't respectful of her feelings when you were with her parents. How does that make you feel to know she was hurt by that? One word—I'd like to hear one word from you—a feeling word.
Mike: I guess I'm flabbergasted, surprised, because I didn't think I really did anything.
Ginsberg: Good. Will you say that to her?
Mike: I'm surprised at how upset you were because I just didn't feel like I did anything much.
Jan: You're surprised that I'm upset because you didn't think you did anything much.
Ginsberg: Good, good. But how does it make you feel to know that nevertheless she was hurt? How does that make you feel? (*This is an effort to try to elicit more emotional engagement.*)
Mike: Again, I'm surprised that you were hurt, and I guess I'm sorry that you were upset and hurt by that—it wasn't something—I didn't mean to hurt you, and I do feel bad about that and I want you to know that. (*He is softening.*)
Ginsberg: Good.
Jan: You feel bad . . . I don't believe him . . .
Ginsberg: I understand, it would be hard for you to do that . . .
Mike: I feel like I'm getting all the blame.

Ginsberg: Yeah, this is hard, this is hard. Understand his perspective; maybe it will help. He didn't realize that what he was doing was being disrespectful of your feelings. Now, you may have a lot of feelings about that, but just understand that he is surprised to learn that his actions when you were with your parents caused you to feel so hurt. (*Notice how much receptivity the therapist expresses as he helps shape her response.*)

Jan: Yeah, but it goes deeper than that. He thought I did it deliberately. That says a lot about the kind of person that I am that I would deliberately do something to make him mad, to hurt him, to make him uncomfortable.

Ginsberg: That is important, but we haven't had a chance to get to that. Remember, you agreed to be the listener, and he's entitled to a perspective and this is only really part of the situation. It's very hard for you to wait, but it's very important that he also gets heard. And, he said to you that he was surprised that what he did hurt you, and knowing that you're hurt he feels bad. (*The therapist is heavily structuring the conversation.*)

Jan: You're surprised that you hurt me and you feel badly. (*She is softening a little.*)

Ginsberg: Good. (*to Mike*) She's really eager to talk more, so this would be a good time to switch again. Would you like to, or would you like to say more? It's your decision.

Mike: Well, again I feel like I'm kind of made out to be the bad guy.

Ginsberg: And, that makes you feel bad.

Mike: Yeah, that makes me feel bad.

Ginsberg: Tell her that.

Mike: I feel like I'm having to take all the blame for the situation we had when we were out with your folks, and that makes me feel bad and hurt by that.

Jan: You're hurt that I'm putting all the blame for this situation on you.

Ginsberg: Good, now say it in a way that he understands. He's very hurt by that, right?

Jan: You're very hurt.

Ginsberg: Good. It's very hard for her to be a listener because I think she needs to speak. Now, remember that the rule is when you switch, you have to say how you feel to know how he feels.

Jan: I don't care how he feels right now. (*Jan is defensive and highly emotionally aroused.*)

Ginsberg: Okay, that's how angry you are, but I'm concerned that it's going to be very hard for him to hear what you have to say next. I'm very concerned about that. It's really important that you respect how he's feeling. And if you're not going to listen to how he feels and express how you feel about that, then it's very hard to help you have a conversation with him.

Jan: That's how I feel. I feel that I don't care about what he feels about what I feel.

Ginsberg: You believe that you don't care about his feelings any more.

Jan: No, I didn't say that—about this situation.

Ginsberg: Well, I'm not sure I understand.

Jan: I don't either.

Ginsberg: Just try to follow me. I'm trying to guide you. Since you're so frustrated, this is hard for you. He says to you—and I believe that it sounded genuine—that he was surprised because he didn't recognize that his actions hurt you, and knowing they hurt you makes him feel hurt. Furthermore, he's hurt because he feels like he's the bad guy all the time. Now, I'd like to know how that makes you feel to know that he's hurt by that.

Jan: He should feel hurt, he is the bad guy. He did it.

Ginsberg: So, you feel good that he's hurt.

Jan: No, I don't feel good.

Ginsberg: That's kind of what you're saying. Well, I understand that you feel he's responsible, but I want to know how it makes you feel to know that he's hurt because he thinks he's always the bad guy with you. *(Reframing)*

Jan: I'm surprised you're hurt. *(Softening)*

Ginsberg: Good. *(To Mike)* Tell her that, she's surprised.

Mike: You're surprised I'm hurt.

Ginsberg: Good, and how does it make you feel that he is hurt?

Jan: I don't know.

Ginsberg: Well, maybe it would be important to think about that. Let's take some time. Maybe we can't do it right away, but I think that's what we have to get to.

Jan: To know how I feel about the fact that he's hurt.

Ginsberg: Yeah, for you recover those feelings which you've lost in your relationship. That's what is making you so upset.

Jan: Well, I don't like it that he is hurt.

Ginsberg: *(To Mike)* Could you say that back to her.

Mike: You don't like it that I'm hurt.

Ginsberg: Good. *(To Mike)* How does it make you feel to know that? *(Switching)*

Mike: Makes me feel a little better.

Ginsberg: *(To Jan)* Could you say that back to him?

Jan: That makes you feel a little better.
Ginsberg: Good. So let's stop here.
Ginsberg: This was hard and I appreciate your hard work. I think it's true that you have to get to the underlying feelings that brought you together in the first place. That's why practicing this is so important.

In this intervention, the therapist is very engaged with Jan and Mike's conversation. He uses all the therapist/leadership skills to keep them engaged, reduce emotional arousal, shape responses, and help them learn to pace their interaction to keep them more engaged.

Pitfalls and Limits

Because of the dynamics that are involved in any dyadic relationship, pitfalls are inevitable in couples therapy. Bowen (1978) explains that the inherent instability of the two-person relationship results in triangulation with other parties in order to stabilize the relationship. Therefore, therapists may expect to encounter myriad triangulations throughout the therapeutic process.

It would not be surprising, for example, to have a family-of-origin issue or an issue pertinent to a child emerge as the focus of the couple's attention. In structural and strategic approaches to family therapy, Minuchin (1974) and Haley (1980, 1987) describe how commonly children become the identified patient in order to restabilize the marital relationship. The marital conflict then proceeds around the triangle, which includes the child. It is important for the therapist to be receptive to the stress that this dynamic creates in the couple, but at the same time not to allow it to divert the therapy away from the structured systematic process and practice of RE therapy. It would be important to assess, with the couple, the relevance of this newly emergent issue and to determine whether to reformulate the therapeutic agreement to include and/or address these issues. Because of the structured systematic and time-designated nature of RE, these issues can be postponed until the couple is in home practice and meeting less regularly with the therapist. Sessions could be scheduled to attend to these issues more directly and/or bring the relevant parties into the process. (For a more extensive discussion, see Ginsberg, 1997.)

In Relationship Enhancement Therapy, most of these issues would be addressed and/or encountered as part of the management of the therapy. The key issue would be to triangulate with Jan and Mike so that there can be enough security and stability in the therapeutic relationship to continue to practice the skills and thereby shift the rigid habit systems. Their relationship would be freed to become more flexible and triangulations more functional. The level of their emotional engagement would improve and lead to the gradual disengagement by the therapist.

These difficulties can be minimized by the way in which the therapist paces the process of therapy, as described in the earlier vignette. The relationship enhancement process engages people very quickly so that they move into more intimate, and potentially, significantly more vulnerable positions in relation to each other. This could easily cause an escalation of defensiveness and conflict, even disengagement, in the relationship between Jan and Mike.

A common pitfall encountered regularly in RE couple therapy is the egocentrism of one or both individuals. This egocentrism could very well have been derived from the personal experience of each person and/or it may be exacerbated by the defensiveness the couple has developed over the years. Origins notwithstanding, defensiveness makes each person unreceptive to his or her partner. Egocentric people are unable to recognize their own motivations and actions, and believe that their partner's behavior is responsible for their difficulties. In other words, they may tend to project the responsibility for their difficulties on their partner without considering their own contribution to that process. Elements of this exist in Jan and Mike's relationship. The therapist's skill in maintaining the rules of engagement that are part of the RE therapy process is the key to preventing this from undermining their therapy.

However, no matter how fervently the therapist may believe that he or she understands the dynamics of the couple, every couple exchanges significant, subtle cues that elicit conflict. These cues are beyond the consciousness of the therapist, and he or she cannot prepare for them when they surface. However, RE therapists draw upon their leadership/therapist skills to help couples keep to the boundaries and structure of the RE process. This eases the difficulties deriving from these conflicts. One skill in particular, troubleshooting, can be the most instrumental skill in not letting these eruptions undermine the process of therapy. It is important to note that the therapist stays within the context of the principles, structure, and rules of RE when dealing with these problems (see the preceding vignette).

When couples in RE therapy begin to have regular weekly home practice sessions and meet with the therapist less frequently, regression can occur. The couple may not be ready to be on their own without the security of the therapist's involvement. The RE therapist helps the couple prepare for this time from the beginning of the therapy (generalization). When the time seems right for home practice to begin, the therapist asks couples to establish a weekly home practice time and try it out before beginning a structured conversation. When that is in place, couples are asked to have a home practice session and audiotape it. Together, therapist and couple review the tape at the next weekly session. This continues until both clients and therapist agree that the couple knows how to conduct these sessions and keep them safe. Office sessions, then, are scheduled less often. Couples are encouraged to contact the therapist in between office sessions, if they encounter any difficulties. Clients who call the therapist between sessions are usually able to wait until the next scheduled session. As couples become more confident in engaging on their issues and conflicts on their own, office sessions are scheduled less and less frequently.

All of the pitfalls mentioned above could surface in Jan and Mike's therapy. Both Jan and Mike have issues of loss, which may affect their capacity for trust and intimacy. Mike is in a process of recovering from drug and alcohol dependence, and this could present many difficulties. Regression is common during this period, as is relapse. It is important that Jan and Mike are involved in 12-step programs and that Mike has a sponsor. Because of his long-term history of dependency, the possibility of physiological effects is quite likely, and these would need to be evaluated and perhaps treated medically along with therapy. Jan's unresolved anger at having been so responsible for her brother may be another pitfall that would need to be considered in their couple therapy.

Finally, limits and boundaries are naturally maintained in RE therapy because of its structure and the manner in which the skills help to maintain differentiation in the context of emotional engagement. Furthermore, the emphasis in RE therapy is on the interaction between the couple themselves, rather than that between the therapist and the couple. The objective is for the presence of the therapist to gradually diminish as the couple learns RE skills, and generalize them to their everyday lives and maintain these skills over time.

Areas to Avoid

It is incumbent on the RE therapist to stay within the boundaries of the principles and structure of RE therapy. It's particularly important for the therapist to trust that the couple can be responsible for their own therapy. The therapist's trust in the value of learning and practicing the RE skills, and in the subsequent changes that emerge in the couple relationship, is also critical.

The RE therapist would be open to Jan and Mike discussing any areas that they want to bring to the therapy. Any proscription on what issues could be addressed in the therapy would inhibit them and limit the effect of the therapy. Furthermore, RE strongly emphasizes that the speaker, whether Jan or Mike, be responsible for the topics initiated in the therapy. Any judgements on the part of the therapist or other partner would compromise the speaker and make that person more defensive.

In RE, Jan and Mike would be encouraged to begin practice by discussing positive and more benign subjects before tackling the difficult ones. The more difficult the subject under discussion, the harder it is for clients to inhibit themselves and keep themselves from blurting out emotionally arousing material. It is important that the therapist help structure the interaction to allow Jan and Mike to face difficult subjects. Should the conversation get out of control, the therapist would employ troubleshooting to help keep both Jan and Mike feeling safe.

RE therapy is directed to the process of their interactions—how two people relate to each other, communicate, and develop an emotionally engaged relationship, and one in which they can resolve their differences and the stresses of their lives much better. Couples are encouraged to raise issues that are important to them. These issues become the vehicles for skill practice. As couples engage around these issues, they soften, and the issues change. Experiencing this change motivates couples to practice the RE skills. Some issues, however, may be outside the expertise of the RE therapist. It is important that the RE therapist consider talking with the couple about an appropriate referral. It would be the responsibility of the RE therapist to guide a couple to the appropriate resource for problems that arise that may be outside the therapists' expertise. Couple therapy can continue concurrently with other therapies.

An obvious example of this would be when one member of the couple has a major mental illness which has not been stabilized. It would seem unlikely that couple therapy could be greatly successful under such a condition. Treatment for this disorder may be required before couple therapy can continue. However, once the condition is stabilized, the couple therapy can again emerge as the primary therapy for the couple.

Inclusion of Other Family Members

RE therapy is a whole family therapy, so that including other family members is very much a part of the way RE therapy is conducted. However, the problems to be addressed might very well change when others are included in the therapy. For example, if children are included, the focus of the therapy may very well shift to the concerns regarding the children's development. Though this might be considered part of the continuity of the couple relationship and their responsibility, it would be a diversion from a focus on the couple relationship itself.

In RE therapy we would encourage the couple not to include other parties until they have begun to practice at home regularly on a consistent basis. Child-centered family therapy (Filial Therapy) Ginsberg (1997), is a relationship enhancement therapy when the child is identified as the patient and the motivation for therapy focuses on child outcomes. Couples engaged in home practice of their relationship are better prepared for the inclusion of filial therapy, which draws from the same principles and methods.

This is not to say that teaching couples to conduct home play therapy sessions with their children does not also impact vividly on the dynamics in the marital relationship. It is just that the contract is different. It's very important that the contract between therapist and client is clear, and that when the focus is shifted to other relationships besides the couple relationships, a new agreement or understanding is negotiated to accommodate inclusion of these other parties in the therapy. The RE therapist does this to maintain the structured systematic and time-designated nature of RE therapy.

RE therapy can include members of the families of origin of the couple. These family-of-origin sessions are typically one-time and intensive (6–18 hours). Typical RE family-of-origin therapy is scheduled to include all members. The spouse or partner is not usually included in these sessions. This has been discussed more extensively in Ginsberg (1997).

Jan and Mike's history does not indicate the need to include anyone else in their therapy. They have no children, and family-of-origin issues do not appear to be relevant when they began therapy. If these issues arise as therapy proceeds, members of the family can be included. In Mike's case, he continues to be conflicted over the early incestuous relationship with his aunt. Assuming that Mike's aunt is alive, RE Family-of-Origin therapy (see Ginsberg, 1997, pp. 181–229) for Mike and his aunt could be helpful. Typically, with all couples, family-of-origin issues are discussed in RE couple therapy. This background helps couples better understand the etiology of their difficulties and improves their acceptance of themselves and each other. In the course of that discussion, family-of-origin therapy is introduced as something that could be helpful once the couple is engaged in weekly RE home practice sessions.

In Mike and Jan's early sessions, Mike's continued ambivalence regarding his relationship with his aunt would be explored. An understanding of his present relationship with her, and how it impacts him and his relationship with Jan, would be insightful and useful in their couple therapy. At that time, the benefits of RE family-of-origin therapy would be raised. It is typical for such a session to be held once the couple is having regular RE home practice sessions, because they are then adequately prepared: they understand the RE process, have developed increased skills in relating to each other, and are more emotionally engaged.

The RE therapist would emphasize that the decision to schedule a family-of-origin session, and the responsibility to invite the relevant parties, would rest with Mike. Session time would be devoted to helping him decide his course of action. Mike might consider inviting both his aunt and her sibling (his mother or father). On the other hand, he might choose to have a session with only his aunt. Generally, clients are discouraged from inviting their spouse, since the family-of-origin issues that will be discussed occurred before the couple met. Even if Mike ultimately decides not to schedule a family-of-origin session, he would probably find the discussion of this possibility helpful; it may even ease some of his conflicts.

RE family-of-origin therapy has two basic objectives: Mike would review his family history, and become engaged with his family member(s) in RE conversations. It is assumed that this process puts a boundary around past events, brings them into the present, and juxtaposes them with present-tense reality. Profound changes occur gradually following such a session.

Homework

Homework is an essential and integral component of RE therapy. The objective is for couples to carry on the practice, generalize, and maintain the skills over time. The skills of generalization and maintenance are incorporated into the Core RE skill because of the importance that the clients bring the skills and subsequent changes into their real lives. Homework becomes the means by which the therapist is able to transfer the implementation of the skills from office to home.

In the first session, couples agree to participate in tasks developed in collaboration with the therapist. A significant advantage of this methodology is that it provides continuity between sessions. RE therapists begin each session by reviewing the homework reinforcing the couple's efforts to fulfill the assignment and modifying it to fit the couple's needs. Not only is the continuity of the therapy maintained, but the task orientation of this approach is conveyed. Furthermore, the consistent emphasis on homework assists in conveying and transferring the responsibility of the success of the therapy to the clients' own efforts.

At the end of the first session, clients are asked to observe how they interact and communicate with others. Additionally, they are given a handout, *Client Guidelines for the Goal Hierarchy List* (see Ginsberg, 1997, p. 48). This helps clients focus on specific issues and helps to make these issues more behaviorally specific. Clients are encouraged to modify the list as therapy proceeds and bring it to each session.

When asked, couples frequently report that they have few opportunities to be together to nurture their relationship and that they don't have much fun together. A simple task is to encourage them to schedule a special time to be together, usually outside the home, and have fun together.

Another assignment, typically given at the fourth or fifth session, asks the couple to set aside a special time once a week (usually for an hour) during which they ignore all interruptions, whether from children or the telephone. This prepares them for the audiotaped home practice. Once couples are engaged in weekly home practice sessions, the office sessions focus mostly on the supervision of the home practice tapes. Couples continue to practice the RE conversations after they no longer attend regular office sessions. Subsequent booster sessions, usually at the couple's invitation, include review of the home audiotapes. The couple's home practice supervision of audiotapes is such a powerful method to enhance couple learning and responsibility that it becomes the primary focus of this subsequent session.

Timeline for Therapy

The basic 10-session model of RE typically extends over a 3–6-month period. This 10-session model becomes the guideline for evaluating the progress of therapy.

RE is structured, systematic, and time-designated. Typically, it is formulated as a 10-session model, but RE is very flexible, and other formats have been described (Ginsberg, 1997). The first session, which can be extended, is an intake during which Jan and Mike are introduced to the RE approach, agree to engage in learning the communication/relationship skills (speaking, listening, conversive), and learn to generalize and maintain these skills over time. They are asked to agree to supervised practice of the skills in the therapist's office for the next four sessions. The objective is to become skillful enough to conduct structured home practice sessions on their own. Of course, they would need to experience sufficient softening and improvement in their relationship to motivate them to continue.

At the end of the fifth session, Jan and Mike and the therapist evaluate the benefit of learning and practicing these skills, as well as the couple's readiness to continue practicing on their own. They are asked to consider whether they see the following changes in their relationship: an increase in the number of episodes during which they experienced emotional engagement; an increasing ability to resolve their differences; a quicker recovery time after conflict; and fewer episodes of conflict. Along with these objectives, Jan and Mike and the therapist assess the degree of softening.

Assuming that they are willing, Jan and Mike are asked to set aside a specific time each week for home practice, and to audiotape these sessions (see Ginsberg, 1997, pp. 172–176). The audiotapes are brought to the sessions with the therapist for supervision by them and the therapist together. As Jan and Mike become more skillful in conducting these practice sessions, meetings with the therapist become less frequent. During this transition period, sessions with the therapist emphasize the secondary skills. At the tenth session, Jan and Mike and the therapist review the progress of therapy and determine the therapist's future role. The objective is for the therapist to become more of a consultant and see them at their request. Jan and Mike would be encouraged to continue weekly home practices for 6 months to a year before changing the process. After this period of time, a booster session is scheduled to assess whether they are more emotionally engaged, have fewer conflicts, and are better able to resolve their differences.

In effect, by learning and practicing Core RE skills, Jan and Mike regain improved levels of emotional engagement and become skillful in generalizing these skills to their real lives over time. Thus, they are more readily able to recover from conflict and draw upon their relationship to cope with the stresses that they face.

Sometimes, however, more time is required to engage the couple. B. G. Guerney (1977) developed the concept of "extended intake or early stage of therapy," which encourages the therapist to take more time to engage the family and establish the collaborative relationship necessary to conduct the intensive practice sessions that are to follow. Three important considerations are identified in the extended intake concept:

> That couples 1) air their feelings and be open to structured retraining; 2) feel that they have been able to fully present their perspectives, including the depth and scope of their problems; and 3) be able to listen to each other without emotional breakdown or interruptions. (Ginsberg, 1997, p. 124)

The extended intake sessions would potentially extend the number of sessions beyond the ten sessions.

Another RE concept is the notion of "booster sessions" to encourage clients to continue to practice the skills and principles of RE. Booster sessions can be scheduled at varying intervals to reinforce RE practice and the improved emotionally engagement and stability in the relationship. These sessions could be scheduled at 2- or 3-month intervals over a period of 6 months to a year. They are an important part of securing the improved relationship functioning derived from the RE practice.

The decision to intersperse individual sessions with the couple sessions depends on the needs of Jan and Mike. It's important that they initiate this decision. One of the underlying principles of RE is the importance of primary and significant relationships and the conversations between the partners in such a relationship which give meaning to the relationship and enhance one's own personal worth. In RE, the relationship is the client. Therefore, the decision to include individual sessions would be based on its benefit to Jan and Mike's relationship. If individual sessions are included, the RE therapist would inform them that absolute confidence could not be maintained, as it would compromise the therapist's ability to maintain the trust of both parties. They would also be encouraged to discuss these individual sessions together. These individual sessions occur infrequently in RE couple therapy, but when they do, they usually are important to help one member of the couple to clarify his or her own thoughts before expressing these issues in the couple session.

If the individual issues for Jan and Mike are an overriding consideration, referral to another therapist is preferable. For the couple therapist to attempt to include individual therapy in the agreement skews the therapy away from the emphasis on their relationship and may undermine relationship therapy. Sometimes, couples initiate couple therapy when one or both already are engaged in individual therapy. Under such a circumstance, RE couple therapy can be conducted along with individual therapy.

Termination and Relapse Prevention

In RE therapy, termination is a gradual process, which begins the first session. Jan and Mike would be informed of the timeline of the therapy, and be prepared for termination in each session. Many aspects of RE—the intensive training component, home practice with supervision of audiotapes, and the scheduling of regular booster sessions to follow the formal termination of therapy—all address termination. Jan and Mike would be encouraged to contact the therapist when they want to initiate a booster session, once the regular booster sessions have ended. Under the structured and systematic procedures of RE, termination becomes a constructive reinforcement of their progress. At the same time, relapse is prevented by preparing Jan and Mike to request a booster session when they begin to experience regression.

This enhances the constructive outcomes that result from the structured, systematic, and time-designated nature of RE therapy.

REFERENCES

Bowen, M. (1978). *Family therapy in clinical practice.* Northvale, NJ: Jason Aronson.

*Ginsberg, B. G. (1997). *Relationship Enhancement Family Therapy.* New York: Wiley.

Gottman, J. M. (1995). The dissolution of the American family. In W. J. O'Neill, Jr. (Ed.), *Family: The first imperative* (pp. 103–116). Cleveland, OH: The William and Dorothy K. O'Neill Foundation.

Gottman, J. M., Coan, J., Carrere, S., & Swanson, C. (1998). Predicting marital happiness and stability from newlywed interactions. *Journal of Marriage and the Family, 60,* 5–22.

Greenberg, L. S. (1994). The investigation of change: Its measurement and explanation. In R. L. Russell (Ed.), *Reassessing psychotherapy research* (pp. 114–143). New York: Guilford Press.

Greenberg, L. S., & Johnson, S. M. (1988). *Emotionally focused therapy for couples.* New York: Guilford Press.

*Guerney, B. G., Jr. (1977). *Relationship enhancement.* San Francisco: Jossey-Bass.

Haley, J. (1980). *Leaving home: The therapy of disturbed young people.* New York: McGraw-Hill.

Haley, J. (1987). *Problem-solving therapy* (2nd ed.). San Francisco: Jossey-Bass.

Leary, T. (1957). *Interpersonal diagnosis of personality.* New York: Ronald.

Minuchin, S. (1974). *Families and family therapy.* Cambridge, MA: Harvard University Press.

*Nordling, W., Scuka, R. F., & Guerney, B. G., Jr. (1998). *Couples Relationship Enhancement program.* Bethesda, MD: IDEALS.

Olson, D. H., & Hawley, D. R. (1992). *Prepare/enrich.* Minneapolis, MN: Life Innovations, Inc.

*Suggested reading.

Peterson, R. F. (1994). Acceptance, experience and choice. In S. C. Hayes, N. S. Jacobson, V. M. Follette, & M. J. Dougher, *Acceptance and change: Content and context in psychotherapy* (pp. 68–72). Reno, NY: Context Press.

Preston, J. C., & Guerney, B. G., Jr. (1982). *Relationship Enhancement skill training.* State College, PA: IDEALS.

Rogers, C. R. (1951). *Client-centered therapy.* Boston: Houghton Mifflin.

Rogers, C. R. (1957). The necessary and sufficient conditions of therapeutic change. *Journal of Consulting Psychology, 21,* 95–103.

Rogers, C. R. (1959). A theory of therapy, personality, and interpersonal relations as developed in the client-centered framework. In S. Koch (Ed.), *Psychology: A study of a science* (Vol. 3; pp. 185–256). New York: McGraw-Hill.

Shannon, J., & Guerney, B. G., Jr. (1973). Interpersonal effects of interpersonal behavior. *Journal of Personality and Social Psychology, 26,* 142–150.

SUGGESTED READINGS

Guerney, B. G., Jr. (1982). Relationship enhancement. In E. K. Marshall & P. D. Kurtz (Eds.), *Interpersonal helping skills* (pp. 482–518). San Francisco: Jossey-Bass.

Guerney, B. G., Jr. (1983). Marital and family relationship enhancement therapy. In P. A. Keller & L. G. Ritt (Eds.), *Innovations in clinical practice: A source book* (pp. 40–53). Sarasota, FL: Professional Resource Press.

PART V

POSTMODERN THEORIES

16

Recasting the Therapeutic Drama: A Client-Directed, Outcome-Informed Approach

Barry L. Duncan, Jacqueline A. Sparks, and Scott D. Miller

> Until lions have their own historians, tales of hunting will always glorify the hunter.
>
> African Proverb

The request to describe the therapy with Mike and Jan based on "background information" provided by the editors presented an interesting dilemma for the authors. A client-directed, outcome-informed approach is not charted a priori based on information from non-client sources, such as theory, case notes, personal viewpoints, or referring clinicians. Such "facts" occur apart from the "heart" of the therapy, and can jeopardize factors critical to success. Further, others' descriptions of clients can interfere with the therapist's utilization of the client's own theory of change, i.e., the clients' uniquely personal ideas about their concerns and how they may be changed. The authors reject devising goals or interventions for any case disembodied from the words of clients and the flow of an actual therapy encounter.

In an effort to address the challenging questions posed by the editors in a way that we could live with, this chapter brings to life Jan and Mike's voices in an imagined therapy. In constructed dialogue, the reader may get a feel for the in-the-moment reliance on the clients' resources, experiences, goals, and

301

perspectives that predominates our approach. Hopefully, then, Jan and Mike become more real than "Case #401" or "The Substance Abuse Couple"—and, instead, become persons with whom the reader can interact, form a relationship, and commiserate through the struggles and triumphs of therapy.

A CLIENT-DIRECTED, OUTCOME-INFORMED APPROACH

The ride home after their first session was a welcome respite from arguing. Both Mike and Jan felt closer than in recent memory. "What do you think?" queried Mike. Jan considered his question. "Well, it's a start. We got some stuff out and I think she has a picture of what we're dealing with." "Yeah," agreed Mike. "Maybe it's not a lost cause." He reached across the front seat and took hold of her hand. Jan smiled, "We're supposed to start the homework tomorrow, not tonight." "Why waste time?" Mike responded, giving her hand an affectionate squeeze.

Mike and Jan could be returning from their first session after meeting with a Bowenian, psychodynamic, or cognitive behavioral couple therapist. All of the available data indicate that the different therapy models work about equally well (Miller, Duncan, & Hubble, 1997). If we can't talk about differences that make one model better or faster, how can we account for what works, and what opened the door for Mike and Jan's new feelings of warmth and optimism for the future? Research indicates that, as mundane as it sounds, positive outcomes are more associated with characteristics shared by most clinical models (Asay & Lambert, 1999).

Lambert (1992) analyzed 40 years of outcome research and identified four factors common to effective therapies. Extra-therapeutic or client factors are part of the client or the client's life circumstances that aid in recovery despite the client's participation in therapy. In short, they are what clients bring to the therapy room and influence their lives outside it. Examples of these factors include persistence, faith, a supportive grandmother, membership in a religious community, sense of personal responsibility, a new job, a good day at the tracks, or a crisis successfully managed (Duncan, Hubble, & Miller, 1997). Client factors account for 40% of change in therapy. This hefty percentage represents a departure from convention, considering that most of what is written about therapy celebrates the contribution of the therapist, the therapist's model, or the technique(s) employed.

The next common factor is a positive therapeutic relationship. This class of factors contributes to 30% of outcome variance (Lambert, 1992) and represents a wide range of relationship variables. Caring, empathy, warmth, acceptance, mutual affirmation, and encouragement of risk-taking are but a few. Recent conceptualizations, termed the "alliance," include these relationship qualities as well as agreement between the client and the therapist regarding the goals and tasks of therapy. Client ratings of the alliance are the best predictor of success (Bachelor & Horvath, 1999). Except what the client brings to therapy, these variables are probably responsible for most of the gains resulting from psychotherapy interventions (Assay & Lambert, 1999).

Placebo, hope, and expectancy, the next class of factors, account for 15% of psychotherapy outcome. They contribute to change by virtue of clients' knowledge of being treated. Expectancy parallels the Franks' (Frank & Frank, 1991) idea that in successful therapies both client and therapist believe in the restorative power of the treatment's procedures or rituals. Models and techniques are the last of the four factors. Like expectancy, Lambert suggests that they account for 15% of improvement in therapy. In a narrow sense, model/technique factors may be regarded as beliefs and procedures unique to specific treatments. The miracle question in solution-focused brief therapy, cognitive restructuring in cognitive-behavioral therapy, and the respective theoretical premises attending these practices are exemplary.

Therapy models evolve specialized languages and interventions that delineate them from competitors. All such articulations take place outside the awareness of those most affected. Until recently, it seemed perfectly reasonable to conduct case reviews, analyze tapes, endlessly conjecture about client motivation, and construct therapy goals without consulting the source—the client. To the degree that models grow and thrive apart from the heart—the client's world view and experience—they spin their shop talk and tales of therapy adventure into disembodied therapeutic "realities"—starring, who else, the therapist.

The recurrent finding that theories and their associated technical operations do not significantly contribute to outcome is very important news. It deserves more notice. Accordingly, as unpopular as it may be among the separate therapy schools, the stand taken in this work is that the common factors require utmost attention. An approach based on common factors casts clients in their rightful role as stars on the therapy stage. Clients bring the resources upon which success is built and are the ultimate arbiters of whether therapy, and the therapeutic relationship, is "on track." A client-directed therapy identifies and expands what many therapists already do, while avoiding those practices that counter client participation. Clearly, Jan and Mike's therapist, whatever model he/she espoused, knew well, and practiced, what works.

Already, Mike and Jan believe that their therapist has heard their story (alliance) and maintain hope that, with the therapist's assistance, they can solve their difficulties (client factors and expectancy). Jan and Mike decided to take their therapist's homework assignment into their own hands (client factors and technique). Whatever else happened, the therapist tapped the gold mine of common factors; Jan and Mike are off to a good start.

Therapist Skills and Attributes

Heroic clients get center stage in this account of therapy. So what about therapists? Are they merely helpful stage hands—holding up prompt cards, making sure the scenery and props are in place, collecting ticket money at the door?

A client-directed approach requires that therapists know how and when to complement, provide counterpoint to, and showcase client talent. Therapists who take advantage of common factors are skilled at maximizing client resources, forming alliances with those that others find difficult, and structuring therapy around client goals and expectations. Above all, these therapists share a fundamental belief that clients know what's best for their own lives and have the motivation and the wherewithal to reach their goals.

Client-directed therapists are simply "people persons," possessing a natural way of connecting, showing appreciation, listening, and expressing understanding. Like good hosts and hostesses, they are friendly, respectful, and courteous— actively courting their client's positive favor and regard. Such qualities are not feigned, but genuine expressions of their liking and respect for human beings.

Secondly, client-directed therapists are flexible and able to readily adapt to the values and beliefs of clients and match their expectations. Client-directed therapists focus on the client's own theory of change with relative ease and psychological comfort. They have a "sixth sense" about where the client is and what is wanted, along with the patience and skill to seek information that clarifies and confirms these hunches. Following Milton Erickson's seminal contribution of utilization methods, client-directed therapists have an uninhibited determination (to some, a reckless abandon) to conduct therapy within the client's world view and follow a client's idea to its logical conclusion.

Finally, therapists committed to privileging the client's voice as the source of wisdom and solution tend to be dyed-in-the-wool optimists. While they empathically resonate with client despair, they refuse to succumb. Their unwavering belief in human potential and the inevitability of change tempers the realism that goes with the territory of working with people struggling in dire and oppressive circumstances. The realistic optimism of client-directed therapists gives life to the belief that personal control over adversity is possible, spreading hope to the most discouraged.

In a practice based on common factors, the therapist, like a magnifying glass, brings together, focuses, and concentrates the forces of change, narrows them to a point in place and time, and causes them to ignite into action (Miller et al., 1997).

Assessment

"What would you each like to see different in your relationship?"
"I would just like Jan to feel she can trust me."

"How can I trust you when every time it starts to come back, you pull something else and we're right back where we started?"

"What would be the first thing each of you would notice that would tell you this time is different—the first step in real trust coming back?"

The therapist continues with Mike and Jan, clarifying their goals for therapy and possible routes to those goals. At the close of the session, she asks, "Do you feel we're on track with figuring out where you all are and where you want to go? Have we been talking about the things you feel are most important to focus on?"

Mike responds, "I like it that we are talking about where we want to go—in the future. A lot of things have happened, but if we get stuck there, we may never get on with things."

"I think so, too," Jan adds. "But the things that have happened in the past keep us from going on into the future. I think we're talking about what's important, but we haven't dealt with—Mike hasn't dealt with—how he's let me down."

The therapist has gathered significant data in just these small interchanges. She has learned that re-establishing trust is an important goal for both Mike and Jan. She has learned that, for Jan, some discussion of, and reparation for, past wrongs, as well as safeguards for the future are important ingredients in achieving trust. In addition, she has learned that Mike and Jan have slightly different views about the best route to change—Jan desires some exploration of the past, while Mike wants to "put the past in the past" and focus on the future. With a few targeted lines of inquiry, a specific direction for therapy is emerging.

Assessment in client-directed, outcome informed therapy is a dynamic process of determining how common factors are at play throughout therapy. Therapists informed by common factors assess client resources, client goals, their beliefs about the best route to get what they want, the strength of the alliance, and the client's perception of progress. This assessment dictates every step the therapist takes and is open to constant revision; the therapist's next step is directed toward strengthening client participation and input in the process.

"Checking-out questions" sprinkled throughout the interview involve clients in an evolving assessment process. Specific instruments can also monitor progress and the alliance. For example, the *Session Rating Scale* (SRS) (Johnson & Shaha, 1996) is a 10-item satisfaction survey specifically designed to be sensitive to clients' perceptions of the therapeutic relationship.

Regarding outcome, therapists can choose from a host of well-established, taken in minutes, instruments. For example, the *Outcome Questionnaire 45* (OQ-45.2; Lambert et al., 1996), assesses three different dimensions:

1. symptoms (e.g., measuring depression, alcohol and drug use, etc.);
2. interpersonal relationship (measuring how well the client thinks she or he gets along in important relationships); and

3. social role (how well the client rates his or her functioning at work or school).

As such, the measure taps into the three variables that researchers and practicing therapists consider relevant and strong predictors of client progress (Orlinsky, Grawe, & Parks, 1994).

Information learned from these instruments is "fed back" throughout the therapy process itself (Duncan & Miller, 2000). Typically, clients are given the OQ prior to each session and the SRS toward the end. Results are quickly scored and discussed with clients. This radical departure from traditional use of assessment instruments gives clients a new way to look at and comment on their own progress and their ongoing therapy.

The process is simple—clients who are informed, and who inform, whether with "checking out" questions or more formal instruments, feel connected to their therapist and the therapy process; their participation, the most significant contributor to positive outcome, is courted and secured. Assessment no longer precedes and dictates intervention, but weaves in and out of the therapeutic process as a pivotal component of change itself.

For example, knowing Jan's wish to examine how past events impact her current ability to forgive and "move on," and Mike's hope to "get over it" and "move on," might prompt the therapist to conclude the first session with the following:

"Jan, I realize how important it is for you to look back at how things that happened in the past are roadblocks to your wish to have a stronger relationship with Mike. And, Mike, I understand that you don't want to get stuck in the past and are concerned that spending a lot of time on that might just make things worse. What I both hear you say is that, in spite of what has happened, a bond of love has held you together and you both want to move forward in a way that the past no longer haunts you. What we can do in our next meeting is to find a way for the past to help you build trust in the present and move on. Is that okay?"

The therapist makes sure that both Mike and Jan know that she has heard their preferred way of working and their goals, thereby strengthening the therapy relationship, and suggests coming up with a way to connect both their hopes. She then checks it out for "fit." The response to "checking it out" always directs whether therapy is on track or whether a new or slightly altered frame or direction needs cofashioning with clients.

Therapist's View

Jan lamented, "We've been having these problems on and off now for at least 5 years. Nothing we do seems to make a difference."

Mike agreed. "Maybe it's time to think of something else. After that last fight, I just figured, what's the use. She wants a divorce, so why not?"

The therapist listens, waits, and encourages their story to unfold, then adds, "How is it that you decided to come here? How did you think this might be helpful for you both?"

Jan responds, "After the fight, the next day, we were both kind of quiet. When we were in the barn, cleaning up, we started to talk. We felt it was worth a shot. We . . . I . . . never wanted this to happen."

The therapist explores, "Tell me about that—about the talk in the barn."

Mike explains. "We never fight in the barn. We're always working together to get the job done. We just start talking and don't even know we're talking." Mike and Jan both chuckle as they consider this phenomenon.

In a client-directed, outcome-informed approach, a therapist's view of clients take shape from the interaction present in the room—in face-to-face conversation. At the same time, client-directed therapists are aware that their *lens* (theoretical perspective or world view) has much to do with how these views form. Depending on the lens, the above interaction may lead a therapist to:

a. search for underlying causes (perhaps located in individual histories or current problematic patterns, such as conflict avoidance or distance regulation);
b. request for more information about the past 5 years and their history of fighting; or
c. suggest a trial separation for the couple.

Another lens may suggest that the therapist:

a. explore Jan and Mike's barn conversations;
b. discover how these conversations differed from other times; and
c. wonder if this was the first time they both noticed that they talked together, if there are other times they talk together and don't realize it, and if they can somehow take more notice of these wonderful instances and make them happen more often.

A client-directed, outcome-informed approach views change as constant and inevitable, and clients as capable of solving their problems. As Soto Zen Masters believe, those seeking help have answers within their grasp; what matters is waking up to—becoming aware of—this reality (Uchiyama, 1993). In this scenario, clients are the prime movers—the sources of solutions—and therapists are there simply to "wake up" what already exists. This view not only allows therapists (and clients) to escape from the hopelessness and helplessness that often contaminates therapy, but also more closely conforms with research indicating that clients' preexisting abilities in combination with outside events are the largest contributors to positive outcome.

Jan and Mike's therapist understands any past therapist's "progress notes," assessments, or reports about Mike and Jan that may arrive on her desk as products of that therapist's lens rather than objective truth (e.g., "Their sex life has deteriorated to the point where they now sleep back-to-back."). Such proclamations exude an air of authority that disguises their origin as explanations and language of the therapist/author, reflecting his or her unique lens. She is also aware that themes that exist in case files may never arise within any given therapy hour, and may be irrelevant and perhaps detrimental to the evolving therapy conversation. Most importantly, she is aware that these same events might be rewritten, or retold: "Despite stating that their sex life is not what they would prefer, they continue to sleep together." In this rewriting of the text, both the voices of the clients take prominence, while the therapist consciously chooses to reject language that might crystallize problems.

Preferring a change- and resource-oriented lens as more likely to promote desired changes, Jan and Mike's therapist looks at their situation as brimming with hopeful possibility. Attune to any and every indication of change and strengths during the interview, she notes they mention their mutual interests, their triumphs over past health and emotional challenges, their job satisfaction and stability, their personal outside interests, and their common bond of love and desire to stay together. Taken together, these comprise significant prognosticators of positive outcome.

Treatment Goals

The therapy hour was winding down. Jan and Mike's therapist had listened attentively to the stories each had told. Still, she remained unclear about what they wanted from therapy.

She asked, "Jan, what would you like to see different? When we come to the end of our work together, what would have to be in place for you to say that our work together had been successful?"

"I want to know that I can trust him—that he won't keep letting me down. And I want him to listen to me and talk with me when I have a problem. He just leaves, and that's the end of it. It's so frustrating."

"Okay, so you'd like to trust Mike more—and to have him listen and talk to you instead of leaving?'

"Yes."

"Mike, what about you? What would you like to see come out of this process that would tell you we were successful in our work together?"

"I don't want to feel I'm always under a microscope. I need her to know that I love her and that I'm not going to do anything intentionally to hurt her. It seems like whatever I do, I can't win, so I just leave and hope it will blow over. She needs to not worry so much."

"Sounds like you would like Jan to trust you more as well?"

"Yeah. I'm not perfect. Nobody is. But if she'd just know that I'm doing the best I can and relax a little, maybe I could talk more."

"So, if that trust came back more, then you'd feel more likely to want to stay and talk with Jan about whatever you both are concerned about?"

"Yeah."

Recall that it is the *client's* view of the client-therapist relationship that is the best predictor of a positive outcome. Blatt, Zuroff, Quinlan, and Pilkonis (1996) analyzed client perceptions of the relationship in the largest, most sophisticated outcome study ever done: the NIMH depression project. This study compared cognitive, interpersonal, and pharmacological treatment of depression. Like hundreds of other studies, improvement was minimally related to the type of treatment received (even drug treatment), but substantially determined by the client-rated quality of the relationship.

While intuitively valued by most therapists, relationship factors often appear too vague or ephemeral to be of use. However, research on the significance of the "therapeutic alliance" to positive outcome offers specific, doable guidelines for accessing this powerful variable (Bachelor & Horvath, 1999). Alliance research points to the importance of the therapist's accommodation of the *client's goals* for therapy.

In fact, even when tempted to pursue theory-driven goals (e.g., address substance abuse, release repressed emotion, clarify diffuse boundaries, etc.), therapists who listen for and "go with" what *clients* say they want, more fully tap client motivation and strengthen the therapeutic alliance. Treatment is more effective and more efficient not only when client goals are accepted at face value *without* reformulation along doctrinal lines—psychiatric diagnosis, theory-specific problem etiology, or therapist-generated treatment plans—but when those goals, in turn, determine the focus and structure of the intervention process. The more conscious, deliberate, and focused the attempt to draw the client into goal and intervention construction, the less significant explanatory models and techniques become.

Research also indicates that treatment goals that have been specified in small, concrete, specific, and behavioral terms, and that clients perceive as both desirable and attainable, are more likely to influence their behavior (e.g., Bandura & Schunk, 1981). Therefore, outcome questions that generate broad expressions of change may need to be "worked backward" to develop more specific steps. Mining for goals in this way intertwines with intervention—the more the therapist (and clients) struggle to articulate precisely what *clients* want and what constitutes (for *clients*) measurable change, the more the steps needed for accomplishing change become evident. And the more discussion about change and its precise nature, the more the preferred reality takes shape and is likely to influence behavior in its direction outside of therapy. Goal "talk" is not merely something that happens prior to intervention and prior to change—it both shapes and is change itself.

Finally, clearly articulated goals provide evident and measurable means for assessing progress. Therapists can not only monitor their own thoughts, hopes, and interventions for fit with clients' stated goals, but can, with clients, gauge whether progress toward goals recommends reworking steps for change, continuing on a particular path, or planning for termination. Lack of progress may suggest revisiting "goal talk"—perhaps the therapist has inadequately understood what clients want, or clients may yet be unclear about the exact nature of what, for them, constitutes change. Therapists can simply ask about progress during the therapy hour or incorporate outcome instruments (e.g., OQ45) into therapy conversation. On-going therapist and client goal clarification, construction of steps for goal achievement, and progress measurement provide the blueprint for therapy and ensure the best possible outcome.

For example, Jan and Mike's therapist ascertained that Jan would like to trust Mike more and Mike would like Jan to trust him more. The therapist can then inquire further:

"Jan, what would need to happen for you to take the first step toward trusting Mike more?"

"Well, sometimes he does well for a while, and I think everything is okay. Then he lets me down again—stays out and doesn't call. I guess he would have to show me over time."

"How long a time would be required, or how many times of Mike not letting you down, before you could say 'this is different—something's different?' "

The therapist could then more narrowly define the kinds of behaviors that would need to occur to indicate, *to the client*, significant change. Similarly, the therapist might inquire further about Jan and Mike's talking together: what do they mean by "talking together;" how often would each expect it to occur; what does Mike mean by wanting Jan to "relax"; what behaviors would he want to see from Jan that would help him feel less "under a microscope;" and so forth. In so doing, Jan, Mike and their therapist gain specific knowledge of the steps required to reach broader goals.

Making the Most of What Works

"Between now and next week, notice those times when you are talking and it's working—Mike, you're not feeling under a microscope and Jan, you feel Mike is really listening to you, whether he agrees or not. Just notice those times and come back here and we'll discuss that. Since you've both had some ups and downs over the past years, it's important that you take this slow—don't expect trust to come back overnight. At the same time, it's not too soon to be thinking about how you want your relationship to be as you move into the next half of your lives together. Does this seem reasonable?"

"Sure." Jan agrees. Mike follows, "Yeah, that makes sense—See when things are going okay now and think about the future."

Technique and model accounts for 15% of the variance in therapeutic outcome (Lambert, 1992). Models and techniques provide focus and structure, essential elements of any effective psychotherapy (Mohl, 1995). However, given that the various therapeutic approaches achieve roughly equivalent outcomes and the large number of techniques available, the challenging question is which intervention the therapist should adopt when working with a particular client (Dattilio, 1998).

A client-directed, outcome-informed approach is less concerned with the intervention itself than with whether it enhances the utilization of common factors. Does the intervention:

a. fit with, support, or complement the client's world view;
b. fit with or complement the client's expectations and goals for treatment;
c. capitalize on client strengths, resources, and abilities;
d. take into account and use the client's environment and existing support network;
e. identify or build on the spontaneous changes that clients experience while in therapy;
f. be considered by the client as empathic, respectful, and genuine;
g. increase the client's sense of hope, expectancy, or personal control; and
h. contribute to the client's sense of self-esteem, self-efficacy, and self-mastery?

A common, but challenging situation for the therapist was matching the intervention to both Jan and Mike's ideas about the problem and its potential solutions. The therapist took note that Jan felt particularly wounded by breaches in trust from Mike's past behavior. Mike, too, expressed hurt that Jan trusted him so little that she could not forgive "slip ups." Fortunately, trust surfaced as pivotal for both. Drawing on the couple's report of numerous times (even since the incident precipitating therapy) of talking together in the barn, the therapist amplified these positive occurrences already at play in their lives, and attempted to expand them into other settings and other times. At the same time, she attempted to match Jan's concerns about the past with Mike's desire to move forward by inserting a "go slow" caution coupled with a future focus. All together, the intervention spoke to each individual while taking advantage of their joint wish to turn 50 as a married couple.

This intervention is not THE correct client-directed intervention—any number of interventions might fit, as long as they are constructed using the client's language, world view, hopes, and abilities that surface during the therapy hour. Interventions are simply "jumping-off spots" for change. Clients invariably take what they hear the therapist recommend and make it their own. It would not be surprising for Mike and Jan to return for a session having gone out for a candlelight meal instead of having a talk at the kitchen table as assigned. Rather than argue with success, the therapist expands all positive movement toward stated goals, regardless of its origin or degree of compliance with the prescribed intervention. In an approach that glorifies client contribution, therapists often takes a lackluster second to the creative and spontaneous "interventions" devised by motivated clients.

Like goals, interventions are cofashioned by clients and therapists. And, like goals, to the degree that interventions fit client's unique world views and expectations, they garner trust in the therapist, enhance the alliance, engender hope, and invite and expand client participation in the process. Intervention's 15% piece of the outcome pie, when connected to and supporting other common factors, gains new meaning and prominence in promoting change.

The Royal Road to Ruin: Not Minding Common Factors

"How did the week go?" Jan and Mike's therapists begins her second session with the couple.

"I guess pretty good." Mike looks over at Jan. "What do you think, honey?"

"Yeah. We went out Friday night—something we haven't done in, oh, a long time."

Their therapist interjects. "It seems like we didn't talk a lot last week, Mike, about your recovery. Could we spend a little time now filling me in on how that's gone for you, your history with that problem—because I feel we'll never get to the bottom of yours and Jan's relationship problem unless this is really dealt with."

Jan frowns. "It's really not a problem now, I don't think. I believe he's on top of it. It was hell before. His dad had a problem."

"What do you mean "Dad had a problem"? He only drank occasionally. We've been through this." Mike folds his arms and turns in his chair away from the therapist and his wife.

The session is off and running—to where? Instead of a couple coming in, eager to talk about the first fun time they've spent together in perhaps the past year, the therapist redirects conversation toward a problem—not Jan or Mike's problem, but a therapist-identified problem. The rather instantaneous result of this redirection is the deflation of positive feelings, a "closing down" of Mike towards the therapist and towards his wife, and the stage set to rehash an area of discussion that has had a notoriously poor track record of resolution for the couple. Should the therapist insist on continuing this line of inquiry, it is doubtful that the session will end well. In fact, it is likely that Mike might leave the room, or that either he or Jan will not return to therapy for another demoralizing encounter with the past.

The above illustrates three pitfalls to avoid. One rapid freeway to failure arises from what we call *attribution creep* (Duncan et al., 1997). Whether the experience is borne in simple trait ascriptions or by establishing a formal diagnosis, once set in motion, the expectancy of hard going can be surprisingly resilient. If left unchecked, the expectation becomes the person, and clinicians will unwittingly select or distort information to conform to their expectations. Attribution creep erodes therapists' ability to confirm and affirm clients' strengths. Case in point: the above therapist's attribution of "alcoholism." Similarly, theory and tradition provide another avenue for the onslaught of attribution creep. Clients eventually take on the characteristics defined by the therapist's theoretical premises. Perhaps Mike would soon look like he was in denial, and Jan, like an enabler.

Failure also arises by persisting in approaches that are not working. One of the contributions of the Mental Research Institute (MRI) is their assertion that the unyielding nature of a problem arises in the very efforts to solve it (Watzlawick, Weakland, & Fisch, 1974). The attempted solution has become the problem. Intractability develops in clinical situations when therapists repeatedly apply the same or similar strategies. Facilitating a discussion of Mike's recovery may provide a slippery slope of repeated negative exchanges between the couple.

The final road to failure is paved by the *neglect of the client's motivations and perceptions*. There is no such individual as an unmotivated client. Clients may not share our motivations, but they certainly hold strong ones of their own. In short, when their theories of change are ignored, dismissed, or trampled by the therapist's theory, "resistance" is a predictable outcome.

Granting clients the right to define the problem does not dismiss the complexity of addiction, depression, or any host of distress found in people's lives. While acknowledging complexity, therapy that privileges client formulations also underscores the belief that people fashion solutions far more effective than those derived from therapeutic texts and theories. Being change sensitive and respectful of the variety of ways people undertake to solve dilemmas means trusting that *any* positive change promotes overall change, including resolution of the presenting problem.

The fact that Jan and Mike had a dinner out would not be viewed as incidental, but rather fundamental to their goal to have greater trust. It is not uncommon for a client-directed therapist to construct an entire session around such an "aside" mention of a positive event—*as long as clients are engaged in and appreciating this discussion.* Instead of directing attention away from their description of the evening out, a client-directed therapist relentlessly pursues and amplifies this event: Whose idea was it to go out? What did the other think about this, were they surprised? What does that tell that person about the other? Might they see this event as a turning point for their new life together, and so forth. Talking about an evening out is not seen as a distraction away from more serious, "deep-seated" issues like boundaries, substance use, etc. Instead, it may well be a catalyst for transformation—the realignment of distance, the modification of communication patterns, and the restructuring of trust—when the natural tendency to health and change are recognized and promoted in the therapy encounter.

The Royal Road to Change: Utilizing the Client's Theory of Change

Because all approaches are equivalent with respect to outcome, and technique pales in comparison to client and relationship factors, the client is cast as not only the star of the therapeutic stage, but also the director of the change process. We now consider our clients' world view, their map of the territory, as the determining "theory" for therapy (Duncan et al., 1997), directing both the destination desired and the routes of restoration.

Rather than reformulating the client's theory into the language of the therapist's orientation, client-directed therapists elevate the client's perceptions and experiences above theoretical conceptualizations, thereby allowing the client to direct therapeutic choices. Force-feeding change and competency on clients who have not yet felt that their problem and pain have been heard, understood, or acknowledged is equally as deleterious to the alliance as forcing theory-driven problems. Similarly, clients who expect or want a theory-driven therapy may do better when their problem is explained "scientifically" by an expert. Client-directed therapists, taking their cue from clients, may have to let go their theory to not have a theory, in order to build rapport, hope, and client motivation.

Within the client is a uniquely personal theory of change waiting for discovery, a framework for intervention to be unfolded and utilized for a successful outcome. To learn the client's theory, therapists may be best served by viewing themselves as "aliens" seeking a pristine understanding of a close encounter with the client's interpretations and cultural experiences. Clinicians must adopt clients' views in their terms with a very strong bias in their favor. What the client wants from treatment and how those goals can be accomplished may be the most important pieces of information that can be obtained. Client responses provide a snapshot of the client's theory and a route to a successful conclusion.

It is also helpful to simply listen for or inquire about the client's usual method of or experience with change. The credibility of a procedure is enhanced when it is based on, paired with, or elicits a previously successful experience of the client. How does change usually happen in the client's life?

Utilizing the client's theory occurs when a given therapeutic procedure fits or complements clients' preexisting beliefs about their problems and the change process. We, therefore, simply listen and then amplify the stories, experiences, and interpretations that clients offer about their problems as well as their thoughts, feelings, and ideas about how those problems might be best addressed. The degree and intensity of our input varies and is driven by the client's expectations of our role. *The client's theory of change is an "emergent reality" that unfolds from a conversation structured by the therapist's curiosity about the client's ideas, attitudes, and speculations about change.* As the client's theory evolves, we implement the client's identified solutions or seek an approach that both fits the client's theory and provides possibilities for change.

Whereas Mike may want to overlook the pain of the past and the danger, or fears, of relapse, Jan may see these, and dealing with these, as the heart of their difficulty and the only road to improvement. The therapist may find herself dealing with two conflicting theories of change that may mirror the conflict experienced in the couple system. The challenge, then, for a client-directed therapist working with Jan and Mike, is to artfully balance each individual's views about the best route to change while remaining connected to and respectful of each. Again, the therapist takes not one true road, siding with and validating one client's view over the other, but adopts a "both-and" perspective in which each is "right."

In Mike and Jan's situation, should Jan want to confront Mike's unreliability as connected with a substance use pattern, the therapist can help Jan articulate this and her theory of how change should occur. At the same time, the therapist invites Mike to articulate his theory of the problem and possible routes to change. The rendering of these "theories of change" may not ultimately require agreement or "common ground." Solutions can occur in spite of divergent client theories— e.g., Jan and Mike may agree to talk together in the barn while doing chores— which do not negate either individual's preferred picture of the situation. What is important is that the therapist uses the theory of each to talk about and "frame" the therapy conversation.

Minding the Client's Life Outside of Therapy

Whether the therapist is making interpretations, pointing out dysfunctional communication, or realigning boundaries, stories of successful psychotherapy most often emphasize the therapist's contribution. These stories perpetuate a belief in the "guru" therapist's contribution to change that is simply not supported by the facts. Worse, focusing attention on the therapist's prowess inadvertently leads helping professionals to discount or even ignore the larger contribution to change made by the client.

Therapists can begin to cast their clients in their deserved role as the primary agents of change by recognizing that clients invariably make use of whatever is available in their own lives as resources for problem resolution. This may include friends, relatives, a religious leader, a self-help book, or fortuitous events, such as meeting a new neighbor or joining a health club. As researchers Lambert and Bergin (1994) have noted, "Distressed human beings do not sit still like rats in cages waiting for the experiment to end. They act to relieve their stress . . . " (p. 175). From this perspective, the therapist is *not* the only show in town—clients have, and use, a vast range of personal resources to overcome difficulties.

With this in mind, therapists can simply listen for and then be curious about what happens in the client's life outside of therapy. However, because clients are part of a culture that elevates the power of the therapist, they, themselves, may often minimize the importance of these personal resources or fail to bring them up in therapy. Therefore, therapists can ask pointed questions about helpful aspects of the client's existing social support networks and about the circumstances outside of therapy in which the client feels most capable, successful, and at ease. The therapist may then actively incorporate these elements into the treatment process. In some cases, for example, the therapist may wish to invite someone from the client's existing social support network (e.g., parent, employer, friend) to participate in the therapy, or to refer the client to resources in the community (e.g., self-help groups, support lines, social clubs).

Couples present both opportunities and challenges for therapists interested in accessing clients' outside resources. Both members of a couple may share a resource, or may support a particular resource used by the other. Or, in some cases, one member's resource may be the other's enemy—for example, the wife who objects to her husband's association with "buddies" at the expense of their time together, or the husband who decries his wife's liberal discussions with a girlfriend after their fights. The following illustrates how Mike and Jan's therapist might choose to make use of resources mentioned by each.

"Jan, a few minutes ago you talked about going to Nancy last week after you and Mike argued. Can you tell me about that—how that helps you."

"Yeah. She's definitely my best friend. She just knows how to listen. I just feel better after we've talked."

"Mike, how is this for you, when Jan goes over to Nancy's?"

"Fine with me. It gives us a time out, and she's always calmer when she gets back. Then I don't have to hear the yelling. Nancy's okay. Sometimes she's over and we talk too."

In this case, Nancy serves as a natural de-escalator, or buffer, for Mike and Jan. The therapist might consider inviting Nancy in to discuss her unique role with her friends, and how she can further support the changes Jan and Mike are trying to accomplish in therapy. Nancy, becomes, a "therapist helper," as well as Mike and Jan's helper—and the help she offers is likely to be part of their lives long after therapy has ended.

Consider, however, the following.

Jan complains, "I just don't understand it. He makes such a big deal going to see Jennifer. He seems to get more excited about going to see her than going out with me on the weekend. And she's part of that group. They're no good for Mike, the way things are now. He's trying to stay clean, and that's all they do—smoke and drink."

Mike retorts, "I just like to go for a little while. You could go, too. We never go out. They're just having a good time. What's wrong with that?"

Mike appears to be making use of a friend network to have the "let-down" time he craves. He also expresses a desire for Jan to be part of that—perhaps in ways similar to their dating experiences at the beginning of their relationship. The therapist may choose to balance Mike's needs and Jan's concerns for Mike's sobriety by inquiring about other ways they can "unwind" together that are "safer."

After some debate, Jan recalls, "We did go to this line dancing class last month. We had a blast! We haven't had that much fun since when we first got married. The best thing is there was this couple that we both knew from a few years ago but had no idea they had moved up here. And no one, really, was drinking."

"Yeah. How come we didn't go back?"

"You said you wanted to go to Jennifer's."

The therapist can encourage Mike and Jan to experiment further with how the dance group might work for them to have fun without worrying about alcohol. Who knows—rather than cathartic breakthrough, an arduous negotiation, or communication training, line dancing may, in fact, be the "turning point" of Mike and Jan's therapy. The therapist's sensitivity to and incorporation of the bountiful instances of informal helping networks in people's lives can be *the* pivotal interventions that help clients reach their goals.

Home Is Where the Heart Is: Homework That Capitalizes on Common Factors

Jan and Mike were animated as they talked about their whirlwind courtship and impromptu marriage. Each detailed what attracted them to the other—Jan felt easy around Mike and able to talk with him; she appreciated his sense of humor. Mike felt that Jan was the "woman of his dreams," and couldn't spend enough time with her. They smiled, recalling the fun of going out to parties, seeing friends, caring for the animals, and just being together. Their therapist noticed the hour was up and moved to end the session:

"Thanks for sharing those times with me. It's clear that what you two shared was very special. Our next step is to figure out what went wrong. What I'd like each of you to do for next week is write down when and how things started going away from that special relationship you had. Bring those in and we can spend some time looking at those changes and how they progressed over the years. That will bring us up to the present. Then we can go from there. Okay? See you next week."

In a matter of seconds, Jan and Mike's mood was transformed from happily reminiscent to grim. They left the office with the menacing specter of the homework looming over like a storm cloud. As Jan went out the door, she gave Mike an irritated look. "Why don't you hold the door for me like you used to?" Mike quickly retorted, "Don't start that again."

To assign or not assign, what type and how often—these are some of the choices therapists make daily with clients. Recall that the outcome literature suggests that as much as 15% of the variance in outcome is attributable to model-specific interventions; models provide a specific structure for therapy and give therapists a repertoire of novel interventions for "stuck" situations. Homework provides both a linking between sessions, an opportunity for the therapy to be "alive" in a person's natural environment, and a sense of "we're doing something—we're working hard" that can engender hope for meeting therapeutic objectives. It may also be a vehicle for shifting away from nonproductive therapeutic directions.

In the above example, the homework may fit Jan's or Mike's view of their situation, and their view of possible routes to change, differently. Mike may be most uncomfortable with unearthing past transgressions, whereas Jan may believe this to be a reasonable, or even best, way to move forward. Simply assigning a task communicates to Jan and Mike that their therapist believes that each is motivated and capable of accomplishing work outside the therapist's purview.

However, the homework ignores Mike and Jan's reports of relationship strengths that emerged during their discussion of happier times of courtship, including their mutual commitment to caring for their animals and enjoyment of social events and friends. The therapist's assignment to explore the difficulties of the past fails to capitalize on the positive, spontaneous momentum of goodwill provided by Jan and Mike's tale of courtship. Despite acknowledging the special bond between them, the somewhat abrupt shift in focus from positive to negative tends to discount their tale; it is difficult to see how Jan and Mike might experience their therapist as understanding when their romantic account is so quickly side-stepped.

Mike and Jan appear to leave dreading their upcoming encounter with the past. The stress of dealing with the homework, then "facing the music" at the next session, could lead to increased arguing during the week, an increased sense of hopelessness, and a possible next session "no-show" or premature termination of therapy by one or both. Let's revisit the close of the session and a different, more client-directed, outcome-informed choice:

"I am really moved by the story you've told today—the way the two of you were so instantly attracted to each other, had so much in common. You each seemed to recognize and relate to what was special about each of you—Mike, your sense of humor and enjoyment of life, your commitment to Jan; and Jan, your caring for others, your ability to show love and affection. I would like to suggest that these are some characteristics that each of you still have. I think it would be interesting, over the next week, to watch for those times when you notice the other doing or being that person you fell in love with—and those times when the two of you come together in any way that reminds you of how it felt then. Sometimes it's helpful to write these down, so we will be sure to cover it next time. How does that sound?"

The therapist, in this case, capitalizes on the positive mood generated in the session—bridging it into their home and everyday lives. She utilizes the warmth and caring demonstrated not only in their account, but in the expressions toward one another during the telling of that account. She orients the homework toward their mutual goal of moving into the next half of their lives married to one another in a satisfying relationship. And she offers a relatively painless (even fun!) way to move forward to the next session, giving a sense that change is indeed possible and within reach.

Finally, the therapist checks on the assignment's fit. It may be possible that Jan will protest that "just looking at positives" is not enough, or Mike may lament the loss of their past rapport in the present. Ask and you shall receive; the therapist can now fine-tune her assignment or offer a comment that shows she hears and will address those concerns, staying "on track" with the therapy alliance.

Therapists who are comfortable with a range of techniques can "do something different" when clients indicate dissatisfaction. In this way, we use models to change our minds about directions to take, not make our minds up about clients. Whatever the choice, it is not the technique or homework assignment that causes change. Rather, models and techniques either promote or work against those factors most responsible for change—the client's personal resources, the strength of the therapeutic relationship, and the climate of hope and positive expectation for change.

Unfolding the Story: Clients Lead and Therapists Follow

Therapy is frequently planned and implemented based on diagnosis and standard treatment protocols. For example, addictions compel hospitalization, personality disorders require long-term psychotherapy, couples dealing with violence are assigned to separate therapies, and medication plus cognitive-behavioral psychotherapy reign with anxiety and depression. Once the diagnosis has been determined, advocates of so-called empirically supported treatments (EST) would have us believe that it is then only a matter of consulting the cookbook and following the recipe. Even before engaging clients, therapists may have a preset idea about what, where, and how their intervention will proceed, including length of treatment, model or technique most appropriate, whether medication is indicated, and/or who should attend sessions.

However, what is genuinely alarming about this common practice is its serious lack of scientific support. Data from over 40 years of increasingly sophisticated outcome research provides little empirical support for:

- the differential effectiveness of competing therapeutic approaches;
- the superiority of psychopharmacological over psychological intervention; or
- the utility of psychiatric classifications in either determining the appropriate course or predicting the outcome of treatment.

Therapy selection, therefore, must go beyond the mere prescriptive matching of client problems with ESTs toward a more individualized tailoring of treatment. In this light, models are merely potentially helpful "lenses" to be shared as they fit the client's "frame" and "prescription." Therapy becomes a dynamic dance of collaborative problem and solution definition that unfolds—at times, unevenly and discontinuously—throughout therapy. Therapists constantly assess how well treatment is matching client's concerns, utilizing client resources, strengthening the therapeutic alliance, and achieving progress. Monitoring fit, the alliance, and progress allows therapists to systematically alter failing strategies. Therapists can routinely inquire about these factors or incorporate results from a plethora of rating scales.

While clients and their unique points of view shape each therapy, studies tracking the occurrence of change indicate that, regardless of the treatment approach, *the general trajectory of change in successful treatment is consistent and highly predictable.* Nearly all meta-analytic studies, for example, have found that between 60–65% of clients experience significant symptomatic relief within one to seven visits—figures which increase to 70–75% after six months and 85% at one year (Howard, Kopte, Krause, & Orlinksy, 1986; Steenbarger, 1994). These same data also show, "a course of diminishing returns with more and more effort required to achieve just noticeable differences in patient [sic] improvement" as time in treatment lengthens (Howard et al., 1986, p. 361). Clearly, the bulk of change occurs earlier rather than later in the treatment process. In fact, studies indicate that, in psychotherapy, less may be more; if clients report no improvement by the third session, they are not likely to show improvement over the entire course of treatment (Brown, Dreis, & Nace, 1999).

These results should not be construed as an indictment of therapies that extend beyond a handful of sessions. On the contrary, they indicate that in cases where progress is being made, more treatment is actually better than less. At the same time, however, the data strongly suggest that therapies in which little or no change occurs *early* in the treatment process are at significant risk for a null or even negative outcome. Indeed, early improvement—specifically, the client's experience of meaningful change in the first few visits—is emerging as one of the best predictors of eventual treatment outcome (Brown et al., 1999).

Information that confirms the general trajectory of successful therapy gives therapists guideposts for measuring their own therapy practice. In the second session, Jan and Mike's therapist learned of the positive events that followed their first session. Tracking these and other reported changes throughout therapy indicated what was working and what was wise to continue. Early indications of progress and a positive therapeutic alliance boded well for a brief therapy and successful outcome. With clients, not theories, in the lead, therapy inexorably unfolded toward Jan and Mike's preferred future.

If conjoint efforts seemed unhelpful and did not result in the client's experience of progress, other avenues of intervention would be explored. Individual sessions would offer one such option. Individual sessions would also be appropriate if either person requested them. It is important to honor client requests because such requests often indicate how the client sees change happening. Further, if the alliance was assessed to be unfavorable to success, individual sessions may allow the therapist to understand where the alliance was suffering and correct any therapist misunderstandings of the client's view of the relationship, goals, or theory of change.

The client has been woefully left out of the loop regarding outcome and service accountability. Using measures that privilege the client's experience of progress and satisfaction radically focuses therapy on clients *really* directing therapy. The client's voice, formally utilized in all aspects of therapy, establishes an entirely different discourse—not pathology or treatment approach, but rather the discourse of the client.

Knowing When to Say When in Client-Directed Therapy

"So how has the week gone?" Jan and Mike's therapist opens their fifth session.

"Great." Jan begins. "We went out again. He's talking to me now. At least I feel like he's listening and taking into account how I feel. I know we're not completely out of the woods, but I think we're definitely seeing the light."

"Mike, what about you?"

"Yeah, I agree. We had an argument, but she didn't get all worked up. We took a break and then did like you suggested, talked about things when we were doing the chores. I feel like we're getting somewhere."

The conversation continues as Jan and Mike recount other instances of progress.

"So who danced the longest Saturday night?"

"She did."

"He did."

Laughing, Jan and Mike talked much of the rest of the session about a new dance step they had learned and how their dance club had elected them to represent the group at an upcoming competition.

Over the previous several weeks, Jan and Mike redirected their attention and effort toward productive communication patterns already present in their lives. They achieved success separating when arguments occurred and talking through issues later after each "cooled down." Jan had spontaneously decided to reconnect with her brother, and Mike was considering teaching a metalworking course at the local vocational school. Their new social life included weekly dance outings and the rekindling of friendship with a couple they had known years before.

Clients' assessments of progress are trusted as indications of their resourcefulness in action and the inevitability of change. When clients report change, the therapist chooses a minimalist approach, stepping back quickly and allowing those natural forces to have full sway. Well-timed termination that addresses client concerns about leaving and the sustainability of progress reinforces forward momentum and clients' felt sense of personal control.

Research show that change is more likely to be long-lasting in clients who attribute their changes to their own efforts (Lambert & Bergin, 1994). Therapists, therefore, can remind their clients that *they*, not the therapist, achieved results, magnifying clients' sense of personal agency and solidifying change for the future. Most importantly, therapists assist clients to terminate by helping them decide the degree to which they feel they have reached their therapy goals. Ultimately, clients make the decision to end or to return.

Termination without any trace of a problem or the possibility of any recurrence is an ideal seldom realized. In all probability, Mike and Jan will experience future arguments. Mike continues to struggle with his newly won sobriety, and both are only recently adapting to changed communication patterns. Therapists can assist clients to expect and prepare for setbacks by reviewing newly acquired skills and devising "retention plans" that specifically detail what to do when problems re-emerge.

In a good good-bye, the door is left open for future visits, and the rituals of goodbye acknowledge and celebrate the mutual experience of learning and giving.

"I feel a little funny leaving. I know I said I don't worry so much about his drinking. It's just that he's let me down so many times in other ways and I really don't know if that will happen again. I guess I just don't completely trust yet."

Mike turns toward her. "Look, I guess I'm a little unsure myself. It's sort of like they say at meetings—one day at a time. I've had a few slip-ups there, and then I get back. I want this to work just as much, more, than that."

Their therapist interjects. "You know you can always schedule another appointment. But you've both had some rough spots in the past few weeks and you've handled them. You both have a lot of skills—it may just take some practice. And remember, you can be sure you'll need to pull out those skills again."

After reviewing a "retention plan" for slip-ups and after discussing the pros and cons of ending therapy, the decision is reached. Mike and Jan agree to try it on their own. Before standing to end the session, their therapist thanks them both.

"You have both taught me a lot—about how couples can get over some major hurdles—and how to keep at it. Would it be okay with you if I share with other couples experiencing similar problems (anonymously, of course) some of the solutions you have used? I believe they could be of use to others."

From helped to helper, the therapy circle is complete. Mike and Jan leave feeling "one up" with their therapist, in their relationship with each other, and their relationship with the future. Good therapy endings and good therapy goodbyes are tinged with the sadness of parting and the reasonable fears of the future, along with the satisfaction of having achieved together mutual learning and change.

REFERENCES

Asay, T., & Lambert, M. (1999). The empirical case for the common factors in therapy. In M. Hubble, B. Duncan, & S. Miller (Eds.), *The heart and soul of change* (pp. 33–56). Washington, DC: APA Books.

Bachelor, A., & Horvath, A. (1999). The therapeutic relationship. In M. Hubble, B. Duncan, & S. Miller (Eds.), *The heart and soul of change* (pp. 133–178). Washington, DC: APA Books.

Bandura, A., & Schunk, D. H. (1981). Cultivating competence, self-efficacy, and intrinsic interest through proximal self-motivation. *Journal of Personality and Social Psychology, 41,* 586–598.

Blatt, S., Zaroff, D., Quinlan, D., & Pilkonis, P. (1996). Interpersonal factors in brief treatment of depression. *Journal of Consulting and Clinical Psychology, 64,* 162–171.

Brown, J., Dreis, S., & Nace, D. (1999). What really makes a difference in psychotherapy outcome? In M. Hubble, B. Duncan, & S. Miller (Eds.), *The heart and soul of change* (pp. 389–406). Washington, DC: APA Press.

Dattilio, F. M. (1998). Epilogue. In F. M. Dattilio (Ed.), *Case studies in couple and family therapy: Systemic and cognitive perspectives* (pp. 473–479). New York: Guilford Press.

Duncan, B., Hubble, M., & Miller, S. (1997). *Psychotherapy with "impossible" cases.* New York: Norton.

Duncan, B., & Miller, S. (2000). *The heroic client. Doing client-directed, outcome-informed therapy.* San Francisco: Jossey Bass.

Frank, J. D., & Frank, J. B. (1991). *Persuasion and healing: A comparative study of psychotherapy* (3rd ed.). Baltimore: John Hopkins University Press.

Howard, K. I., Kopte, S. M., Krause, M. S., & Orlinsky, D. E. (1986). The dose-effect relationship in psychotherapy. *American Psychologist, 41,* 159–164.

Johnson, L. D., & Shaha, S. H. (1996). Continuous Quality Improvement in psychotherapy. *Psychotherapy, 33,* 225–236.

Lambert, M., Burlingame, G., Umphress, V., Hansen, N., Vermeersch, D., Clouse, G., & Yanchar, S. (1996). The reliability and validity of the outcome questionnaire. *Clinical Psychology and Psychotherapy, 3*(4), 249–258.

Lambert, M. E., & Bergin, A. E. (1994). The effectiveness of psychotherapy. In A. E. Bergin & S. L. Garfield (Eds.), *Handbook of psychotherapy and behavior change* (pp. 143–189). New York: Wiley.

Lambert, M. J. (1992). Implications of outcome research for psychotherapy integration. In J. C. Norcross & M. R. Goldfried (Eds.), *Handbook of psychotherapy integration* (pp. 94–129). New York: Basic.

Miller, S. D., Duncan, M. A., & Hubble, M. A. (1997). *Escape from Babel: Toward a unifying language for psychotherapy practice.* New York: Norton.

Mohl, D. C. (1995). Negative outcome in psychotherapy: A critical review. *Clinical Psychology: Science and Practice, 2,* 1–27.

Orlinsky, D. E., Grawe, K., & Parks, B. K. (1994). Process and outcome in psychotherapy— noch einmal. In A. E. Bergin & S. L. Garfield (Eds.), *Handbook of psychotherapy and behavior change* (4th ed.) (pp. 270–378). New York: Wiley.

Steenbarger, B. N. (1994). Duration and outcome in psychotherapy: An integrative review. *Professional Psychology, 25,* 111–119.

Uchiyama, K. (1993). *Opening the hand of thought: Approach to Zen.* New York: Penguin.

Watzlawick, P., Weakland, J., & Fisch, R. (1974). *Change: Principles of problem formation and problem resolution.* New York: Norton.

SUGGESTED READINGS

Berg, I. K., & Miller, S. D. (1992). *Working with the problem drinker: A solution-focused approach.* New York: Norton.

Bergin, A. E., & Garfield, S. L. (Eds.). (1994). *Handbook of psychotherapy and behavior change* (4th ed.). New York: Wiley.

Hubble, M., Duncan, B., & Miller, S. (1999). *The heart and soul of change.* Washington, DC: APA Books.

Smith, M. L., Glass, G. V., & Miller, T. I. (1980). *The benefits of psychotherapy.* Baltimore: Johns Hopkins University Press.

Tallman, K., & Bohart, A. (1999). The client as a common factor. In M. Hubble, B. Duncan, & S. Miller (Eds.), *The heart and soul of change* (pp. 91–132). Washington, DC: APA Books.

17

Feminist Couples Therapy

Cheryl Rampage

TREATMENT MODEL

To say that one practices feminist couples therapy is to say that one believes that the distribution of power, privilege, and responsibilities between men and women in intimate relationships must be thoroughly addressed in both assessment and treatment of couples. Aside from the belief that males have historically held rather more than their fair share of power and privilege, and that this imbalance has had deleterious effects on women, as well as on men, there are few universally held beliefs among therapists who attempt to bring feminism into the therapy room. Feminist therapists may practice within a psychodynamic model, or Bowenian, or behavioral, or a score of others. Therefore, it is misleading to define this chapter as *the* feminist approach to couples therapy. Instead, let me suggest that I will describe *an* approach to working with couples that is informed by feminist sensibilities as well as by a methodology that draws from many other sources.

My approach to therapy is consistent with a model that has been developed by my colleagues at the Family Institute over the past 15 years (Breunlin, Schwartz, & Mac Kune-Karrer, 1992; Goodrich, Rampage, Ellman, & Halstead, 1988; Pinsof, 1995). The Family Institute (FI) model is based on several premises, which I shall note briefly. First, human problems occur within a matrix of relationships, and solving those problems will be most efficiently accomplished by working with as many people as possible who influence and are influenced by the problem. Second, clients are presumed to be healthy until and unless there is clear evidence to the contrary. A corollary of this second premise is that intervention to ameliorate the presenting problem ought to be parsimonious, and address the problem in the most direct and simple way possible. The therapist does not pursue issues or character traits because they seem odd or even pathological to the therapist, but only if those issues or traits are clearly related to the presenting problem.

These premises lead to a general model of therapy which specifies that the change process should start with the present, here-and-now issues, and address those issues at the most overt and behavioral level. Only if working at this level does not provide relief should the therapist move toward the more intrapsychic and historical. All therapists try to help clients create change in one or more of three domains of experience: behavior, belief, and feeling. Since behavior is usually the simplest domain within which to effect change, therapy in the FI model starts by seeking to produce changes in action. Sometimes changing actions leads to changes in belief as well as feeling, allowing the problem to be solved by behavior change alone, even if it was originally defined by the client(s) as a problem of belief or feeling. If a change in behavior or action does not lead to resolution of the problem, the therapist must move the therapeutic inquiry into the domain of belief or meaning, exploring how what the clients think about the problem and its solution might actually be getting in the way of resolution. If that still doesn't lead to a shift in the problem, the therapist will need to focus more directly on the feelings of the clients, and examine how those feelings hold the problem in place. Obviously, in the course of a single session, the therapist may address all three domains of experience, attempting to understand how each is influencing the other.

Just as the therapist starts with the behavioral and moves inward (psychologically) only if necessary, likewise the therapist should begin with the present, and only move to the historical if it proves to be necessary in order to solve the presenting problem. For example, if the presenting problem is sexual dissatisfaction, modification of the behavior of each partner might be sufficient to achieve resolution. On the other hand, if the problem is held in place by beliefs and feelings resulting from one partner's past sexual abuse, then successful resolution of the problem may very well require a detailed exploration of the historical bases of that partner's beliefs and feelings about sex.

Whatever model of change the therapist has operating in her head, the *sine qua non* of successful therapy lies in a strong alliance between client and therapist. Decades of psychotherapy research have repeatedly shown that clients report more improvement when they regard their therapist as genuine, caring, and empathic, no matter what the therapist's theoretical orientation. Alliance issues are notoriously tricky when working with couples, as each partner may feel concern that the therapist is more interested in what the other partner has to say, or believes the other partner is more "right." Working with couples requires that the therapist pay exquisite attention to balancing attention, care, and validation between the partners. Practicing as a feminist makes this task even more challenging, as the very premise of feminism—that men as a group have been privileged over women—may draw the therapist into challenging the male partner or working directly to change the power balance in the couple to favor the woman more and the man less. Such interventions, although they may be necessary to solve the problem, put an undeniable burden on the alliance that must be attended to by the therapist. Most feminist therapists who work with heterosexual couples address this dilemma by attending overtly to the costs that privilege have exacted from the man, and by eliciting from him the ways in which he has been injured or hindered by patriarchy. The translation of a political reality like gender inequality into a clinical conversation about a marital dilemma requires care and subtlety. The fact that *some* men exploit women is not a sufficient explanatory concept to understand the experience of any particular male client. Neither is the notion that women are disempowered by the institution of marriage sufficient to understand how a particular female client perceives and uses power within her marriage. Feminist couples therapy will attend to the details and daily practices that determine how privilege and responsibility are allocated and enacted within the relationship.

Within the FI model, there are several lenses through which the therapist examines the problem, to see what is constraining the client(s) from solving it. We call these lenses "metaframeworks." Not every metaframework will be relevant for any given problem brought to therapy, but each is considered by the therapist. There are six metaframeworks in the model: internal process, sequences, organization, development, culture, and gender (Breunlin et al., 1992). Internal process includes the beliefs, feelings, and attitudes of a person, patterns of thinking and responding to the world that are the consequence of a lifetime of accumulated experience. Sequences are patterns of interactions over time. Some sequences may be very brief, and may be completely enacted within a few seconds. Others may be transgenerational, involving patterns that extend over many years, such as alcoholism which traces back from son to father to grandfather. Organization refers to how the system operates in terms of roles, rules, and boundaries. The development metaframework considers the problem in the light of the system's life course stage, and the accomplishments required to successfully complete that stage. The multicultural metaframework considers how the problem is influenced by the cultural beliefs and experience of the family system. Finally, the gender metaframework examines how gender beliefs and roles may be constraining the system and preventing the problem from being solved.

Within the FI model, therapy consists of identifying and removing constraints which are preventing clients from living their lives in the way they would like to be doing. Some problems that clients bring to therapy will have few constraints, and therefore be easily resolved. An example of such a problem might be a couple who are in conflict over managing their young child's refusal to go to sleep without a parent's presence. If this is a relatively isolated conflict within a marriage where the partners are generally able to come to agreement over parenting issues, and there is no physiological reason for the child's difficulty, a single session of therapy might be sufficient to develop a successful intervention strategy. On the other end of the spectrum, problems may exist within a complicated web of constraints that includes intrapsychic and family-of-origin issues, biological or developmental conditions, cultural differences, and gender conflict. In general, the more constraints, the more difficult it will be to relieve the problem.

THERAPIST SKILLS AND ATTRIBUTES

This is a complex model to work with. To use it properly, the therapist must be familiar and comfortable with a variety of methodologies, from behavioral to narrative to psychodynamic. Because it is a collaborative model, the therapist must be comfortable working within an egalitarian relationship structure. While there are moments when the therapist might need to speak or act authoritatively (for example, to de-escalate a conflict), for the most part, the therapist minimizes power and expertise differences between herself and the client(s). Because therapy involves moving between the domains of behavior, belief, and feeling, the therapist must be willing to take an active, sometimes even a directive role in conducting the therapy.

Because the model assumes that gender is a significant category of clinical analysis, the therapist must be interested in and attuned to his/her personal beliefs about the meaning of gender, and be able to bring gender into the therapeutic conversation in a way that is not shaming, aggressive, naive, or polemical. A sense of humor helps, as does the ability to separate the evils of patriarchy from the behavior of the particular male client in the room. I find it useful to bear in mind (and sometimes to share with the clients) that male/female relationships have changed more in the past three decades than they had in the previous 300,000 years. All of us are in the midst of this great cultural transformation, and the fact that we experience stress, confusion, and conflict about what constitutes gender and how it should be enacted is a normal, albeit uncomfortable consequence of that transformation.

THE CASE OF MIKE AND JAN

Assessment Tools

The primary assessment tool I would use is the protocol my colleagues and I have developed here at the Family Institute. Using this protocol, I would conduct a series of sessions in which I would engage Jan and Mike in an inquiry of how the problem gets in the way of their relationship, and what constrains them from solving it. We would explore the problem from the standpoint of each metaframework, to understand as much as possible about what has kept it from being solved. Given the complexity of this problem and its long history, I suspect that I will need to consider more than one metaframework to have an adequate understanding of it. I will be particularly interested in the internal process, sequence, organization, and gender metaframeworks.

Internal process will be of interest because the case information describes a long history of unsatisfying relationships for Mike, going back to his original family. What he believes about his own potential, as well as how his relational expectations of Jan have been shaped by earlier experiences with other significant women, may critically affect the problem. For her part, Jan's marriage to Mike is so reminiscent of her relationship to her younger brother that it draws attention to the question of how she perceives herself and her proper role vis-à-vis a significant male in her life.

The sequence metaframework is obviously important to examine in this case because it will focus attention on the troubling, repetitive patterns of the marriage. For example, the sequence around their conflicts (Mikes underfunctions; Jan becomes angry and confronts him; he feels shame and withdraws; she loses hope and retreats also) needs to be sufficiently understood so that it can be modified into a more useful pattern.

An examination of the organization metaframework will focus on the structure of the relationship, its boundaries, rules, and roles. One thing that may be revealed is that Jan and Mike's relationship lacks balance, that Jan functions as the relationship "leader" to such an extent that she feels burdened, while Mike feels superfluous, and that his needs and wishes are not regarded as important.

Finally, the gender metaframework will be applied to analyze how power is distributed within the relationship, and to determine how Jan and Mike have constructed their marital roles along gender lines. Analyzing gender issues in marriage must take place on several levels. First, there are the overt and explicit beliefs each partner is willing to state about what it means to be a man or a woman, and how that affects their marital role. Then there are the most implicit, sometimes even unconscious beliefs about gender, which may be enacted in the relationship, but cannot be admitted to by the participants. People may believe one thing about gender, but act otherwise, so a therapist interested in understanding gender must observe as well as listen. Ultimately, the purpose of using gender as a category of analysis in marital therapy is to reveal any ways in which their very notions of maleness and femaleness are constricting couples from finding more satisfying modes of participation in the relationship.

Early in the assessment process, probably by the third session, I would conduct at least one session in which I would interview Jan and Mike separately. We have recently added this component to the assessment process in order to screen for partner violence, a relatively common and under-reported problem of couples. Family therapists have unwittingly contributed to the underassessment of violence in relationships by the very fact that we see couples and families as whole groups. Victims of domestic violence are often unwilling to speak about the problem in the presence of the abusive person for fear of later recrimination. If the individual interview reveals violence as an issue in the relationship, the organization and direction of subsequent sessions would be modified accordingly.

In any assessment, it is not enough to understand what's wrong. Successful therapy will depend on identifying and capitalizing on the client(s) strengths. Therefore, the assessment process will also address what Jan and Mike regard as their relational assets, gathering data on which aspects of their relationships and what kinds of interactional transactions tend to be the most successful between them.

Conceptualization of Mike and Jan

Jan is the oldest daughter of two busy and preoccupied parents. She seems to have given more care in her life than she has received, first stepping in as a substitute parent for her younger brother, then marrying two men who both had significant substance abuse problems. In addition, she spends a great deal of attention nurturing her animals. She is probably severely undernurtured herself, but seems to have limited awareness of her own emotional needs, and little idea of how to get those needs met.

Jan is disciplined and goal-directed. She successfully completed college and has maintained a stable job history in a responsible career. Her methods of soothing herself, including reading and taking care of her animals, are adaptive, although probably limited in their usefulness. While she once had a community of friends who seemed to support and nurture her, she now appears to be very isolated socially, which limits her opportunities to receive care from others. Although she has maintained contact with her parents and clearly feels some attachment to them, they do not seem any more open to hearing about her concerns now than they were when she was younger, leaving the impression that the relationships are fairly superficial.

Jan may be suffering from chronic mild depression, which could have its origin back in her own undernurtured childhood. The feeling that she is most aware of is anger, which she does not know how to direct in a useful way, so that her experience must be that even when she does share how she feels, nobody seems to care. Additional contributing factors to her depression could be the physiological and psychological consequences of her early hysterectomy. Jan reports having been understandably devastated by her diagnosis of ovarian cancer at the age of 29. Given that she was not in an intimate relationship at the time, and that her parents are generally under-responsive, it is easy to imagine how isolated and frightened she might have felt. Furthermore, since it was a reproductive cancer, she would not have been eligible for hormone replacement therapy for several years. I am interested in knowing whether she now receives such therapy, because of its potential impact on depression, as well as its impact on sexual drive and function. This is an area where the gender metaframework might be of critical importance in addressing one possible constraint around marital satisfaction. Feminists have long asserted that traditional gynecology has understated both the psychological and physiological consequences of hysterectomy on women. Jan may have received little, or no, attention from her physicians around how to minimize the psychological and sexual effects of the hysterectomy.

Mike is the younger of two brothers, and seems to have been the "forgotten child" in his original family. In addition to feeling that his parents were preoccupied with his older brother, Mike had the unfortunate, probably traumatic experience of being sexually molested by a family member for 2 years. For these reasons, and possibly because he is biologically vulnerable to it, he turned to substance abuse at a fairly young age. He seems to have used alcohol and marijuana to numb himself for most of his life. Consequently, he has little experience managing his affect, including anxiety, in a sober state. His social life also seems to have revolved largely around being with others who were using substances. At this point in his life, he is extremely isolated socially. This is problematic in two ways: first, it keeps him too dependent on Jan, a dangerous position since so much of their interaction is negatively charged right now, and second, it limits his opportunities to get some of his needs for validation satisfied by others. A significant factor in Mike's intrapsychic world is that he had a dependent relationship with a mother he regarded as hostile and critical, and a longing for greater contact with a father who seemed mostly unavailable. His relationship with his mother probably taught him to expect criticism from women, and that such criticism cannot be responded to in a useful or safe way, so it's best to simply block it by refusing to becoming engaged. This may explain his pattern of stonewalling in response to Jan's attempts to discuss problems with him.

Like Jan, Mike brings some real strengths to the psychotherapy enterprise. First, he has made a major intervention on his own life by becoming sober. After decades of using chemicals to manage his painful affect, Mike has courageously and with great determination given up the most powerful method he knows for avoiding pain. Second, he has a stable work history in a job that he likes and does well. Third, he finds real enjoyment in doing things with his hands. Finally, he knows that he loves his wife and really wants to make their marriage work.

As a couple, Mike and Jan bring several assets to the project of changing their relationship. First, their relationship had an unambiguously positive beginning. They were attracted to each other, fell in love, went through a courtship that affirmed for each of them how wonderful the other one was, and can still say they love each other in spite of the stress in their marriage. Even now they can work collaboratively around shared goals, although that currently seems limited to caring for their animals. They also seem to have a clear understanding that their method of conflict resolution is inadequate, so they will probably be open to suggestions for how to do it differently.

Conflict management seems to be the primary behavioral issue of concern to the couple, probably because of the volatility their conflicts have created. There is a highly gendered quality to their methods of dealing with conflict: she criticizes (like his mother) and he withdraws, a typical male strategy (Gottman, 1995). Although there is no apparent history of violence between them, this pattern of fighting is very damaging to the marriage. Each of their fighting styles creates a gendered wound. His withdrawal from her makes her feel unimportant and unheard, a position that replicates both her family-of-origin experience and the way in which women frequently feel received by the external world. At the same time, her criticism of him inverts what is still commonly felt as the "natural" order of things, in which men are supposed to be in the expert position relative to women. Mike may know that Jan is the "expert" and "leader" in their marriage, but he may nonetheless resent her for it, and feel it as emasculating.

At another level, Mike and Jan fit together hand in glove. She is an older sister used to taking care of younger, underfunctioning males. It may not be entirely coincidental that Mike is the exact age of her brother. For his part, Mike is used to being dependent on women who cannot be pleased, and blame him for everything that goes wrong. On his side also, the age difference between him and Jan may not be coincidental.

Many factors about Jan and Mike's marriage seem to suggest that if there is a power difference between the two, it is in her favor. She is older, has a better job, is better educated. It might be tempting to conclude that there are no relevant gender issues in the case. But if power is defined as the ability to have one's way, Jan does not look so powerful. She is lonely, unhappy, and has lived for years with a man who showed more loyalty to his bottle than to his wife. To understand Jan's power, a therapist must think about why she didn't use it. Why didn't she leave Mike during those long lonely years when he was drinking? As it happens, husbands of alcoholic wives are far more likely to leave their spouses than are wives of alcoholic husbands. Power in such cases seems mitigated by something else. Perhaps it is Jan's sense of responsibility for Mike that has kept her in the marriage, and prevented her from directly exercising her power by leaving.

As for Mike, he certainly has not appeared to be a powerful person in his marriage, except for the power to resist his wife's efforts to get him to change. Like many alcoholics, his power has often taken a passive-aggressive form. He has not been a leader in the marriage, but he has effectively blocked Jan's efforts to change him or their relationship.

Thus, however well Jan and Mike have chosen partners who replicate some important aspect of a significant early relationship, there are obvious ways in which these choices have failed. Each partner feels uncared for (which, of course, is also a replication of those early relationships) and resentful of the other. At this point, each has so withdrawn from the other that little meaningful interaction takes place at all.

In summary, my initial understanding of this couple suggests that their marriage is constrained from being satisfying by several factors:

1. They have a well-established sequence of conflict, which is unproductive and even destabilizing to the marriage, and in which they both enact highly gender-stereotyped roles. At the same time, they lack effective sequences that would demonstrate caregiving and attachment, and might provide a stabilizing influence.
2. The fundamental organization of the relationship is hierarchical instead of egalitarian. Jan functions as the responsible, critical parent, while Mike acts as the underfunctioning, sometimes rebellious child.
3. A sense of their options within the relationship is constrained by their own internal process, which predisposes each of them to participate in the relationship in ways that are reminiscent of roles they held in their original families.

Treatment Goals

To my mind, the most important single fact in this case is that Mike has a long history of substance abuse, and has been sober for only 7 months. This fact would significantly influence my approach to working with the couple, since I believe that staying sober must be Mike's number one goal, and that doing so will demand a great deal of effort on his part. Having spent his entire adult life numbing himself to avoid feeling things, he has little experience managing anxiety in a sober state. Therefore, I would proceed cautiously, wanting to avoid creating intense conflict. I would support Mike's sobriety in every way I could think of, and encourage Jan to attend AlAnon meetings, or at least read literature on the effects of alcohol and drug abuse on the family.

In a perfect world, I might want to delay any intensive couple therapy until Mike's sobriety has been more firmly established, but it is not a perfect world, and I understand that Mike and Jan are coming to therapy now because they have become discouraged about whether their marriage can survive. Probably they were both initially optimistic that when Mike stopped drinking things would get better between them. What they have learned in the past 7 months is that Mike's sobriety is a necessary, but not sufficient, change to repair the marriage.

A second goal I would have is to immediately increase the number of caregiving and attachment behaviors that Mike and Jan demonstrate toward each other. During much of the marriage they have operated effectively as ships passing in the night, having little interaction with each other. They have thus lacked for opportunities to nurture and care for each other in the many small, but meaningful ways that satisfied couples do. Not only do they not have a sexual life (a problem I would not directly address for a while), but they do not even eat meals together. An early therapeutic goal would be to help them each find ways to behave like a more loving, thoughtful spouse toward their partner.

A third short-term goal would be to put in place some sort of method of addressing conflict besides Jan's complaining and Mike's stonewalling. In the short run, I would encourage them to leave their fights for my office as much as possible, until I can help them find a more effective way of resolving differences. I might suggest some sort of structure and rules for them to adopt, to change the repetitive and damaging sequence that they enact when they fight

In the longer run, I would hope to participate in conversations with Mike and Jan about what kind of marriage each of them wants. I would use Mike's sobriety as a great opportunity to rethink and reconstruct the roles each of them plays in marriage. This may be the first time in their married lives that it is possible for them to participate as equals in a discussion about what they want from their marriage, how they wish to be treated by each other, what they are willing to do to improve the relationship. While the initial focus of such conversations might be very specific, behavioral changes, I would hope that eventually therapy could be a forum in which Jan and Mike could discuss the values they want to be enacted in their marriage. When such discussions occur in marital therapy there is a great deal of redundancy in what spouses say they want, almost always including respect, caring, and attention. Whether or not the therapist chooses to make it explicit, these are values that are most congruent with an egalitarian, non-sexist relationship.

At some point in therapy, Jan and/or Mike may explicitly state that greater intimacy is one of their therapeutic goals. This would not be realistic early in the therapy, because sustained intimacy is dependent on self-awareness as well as an understanding and acceptance of the other—both qualities that this couple currently lacks. Intimacy is a relatively higher-order relational skill, one which many couples never achieve, and is based on a foundation of caregiving and attachment behaviors (Wynne & Wynne, 1986). At this point in their marriage, Mike and Jan lack the foundation for intimacy, even if that were their goal.

My only outcome measures are the self-report of my clients and my own observations about the changes that I observe in them. If Mike and Jan continued therapy with me until they were able to say that their marriage felt "good enough" to them, and they demonstrated an ability to solve problems together and to enjoy each other, I would regard the therapy as successful. At the same time, I do not regard staying together as a necessary criterion for success. If Mike were to relapse into drinking and refuse to work on recovery, the definition of success might change to helping Jan extricate herself from a chronically stressed marriage in which she can have little hope of satisfaction. Even if Mike does maintain his sobriety, he or he and Jan together might decide that they simply cannot overcome the long history of marital troubles, and decide to separate. Then my definition of success would shift to helping them accomplish that goal in a way that does no further damage to either of them.

Techniques and Interventions

Early in couples therapy, I often prescribe a variant of Stuart's (1980) "Caring Days" exercise. This exercise is designed to increase the frequency and awareness of small, positive exchanges between partners. It is especially helpful in situations like Mike and Jan's, where the accumulated experience of disappointment in the relationship has created such discouragement that neither partner reaches out to the other in a caring, loving way anymore.

To summarize the exercise, each partner is asked to generate a list of 15 small things that the other person could do to indicate caring. The lists are then exchanged, and any ambiguities clarified. Items on the list are to be concrete, positive, and easily accomplished. For example, "Kiss me hello when you come in at night" would be an appropriate item for the list, while "Stop being so mean to me" would not. The former item is specific, positive, and could be accomplished in a few seconds, while the latter is both vague and negative. Partners take home each other's list and are instructed to do at least three things each day that appear on the other person's list, noting the response received. At the next session, the couple discuss the impact of these small, behavioral adjustments on their sense of well-being. Success with the exercise serves to encourage partners about their ability to make a positive difference in the relationship. Lack of success is often diagnostic, indicating that there is significant inertia that will have to be addressed before any positive change will be possible. In other words, there are constraints that must be identified and removed before even such a simple and behavioral intervention can be accomplished.

Another specific intervention I would make with Jan and Mike would be to teach them a method of conflict management. They have clearly indicated that they do not know how to resolve differences between them, and so have developed a strategy based on avoidance. When that fails, it is usually Jan who disrupts the avoidance by a complaint of some sort, which triggers Mike's defensiveness, and eventually his stonewalling.

There are a number of conflict resolution techniques that have been developed over the years. The one I recommend most frequently was developed by Notarius and Markman (1994). This method involves teaching couples to listen to each other and reflect back what they are hearing instead of reacting, then to work on finding common threads in their description of both the problem and potential solutions, and finally to negotiate a solution that both can accept. I would probably ask Mike and Jan to read Notarius and Markman's book, and then practice the method in my office, so I could help them identify and work through difficulties in applying the technique.

Pitfalls

There are three pitfalls that I would need to stay conscious of in this case. Of course, as the therapy proceeded, more pitfalls would probably emerge. These are just the ones I can already see. Most of them are related to Mike's addiction.

First, I could easily make an error by minimizing Mike's addiction, and therefore his vulnerability to relapse. By not continuing to make the issue visible, I could reinforce the denial and minimization that are hallmarks of the problem, and also contribute to its persistence. And yet (and herein lies the second pitfall) by focusing on the addiction, I risk making Mike the problem, which will discourage him, and is certainly not an adequate description of the dilemma facing the couple in any case. The third related pitfall is that without the substances he has historically used to manage his painful feelings, Mike is probably going to have a low tolerance for strong affect until he can develop alternate methods of managing it without being overwhelmed. Since therapy (and especially couples therapy) often creates a highly charged emotional atmosphere, I may be exposing Mike to exactly the circumstance most likely to threaten his sobriety. Finally, because Jan is so apparently "in charge," I could make the error of assuming that power is not an issue in the relationship, thus missing an important element of what holds the relationship in place.

Areas to Avoid

The question for me is not what areas to avoid, but rather how to approach certain areas and when to do so. In 25 years of doing therapy I cannot remember a client ever refusing to discuss a topic with me, but I can think of many therapeutic conversations that did not go well, either because I framed the conversation poorly, or pursued it at a time when the client was not ready to discuss it with me (often because our alliance was not yet strong enough). Because it is fundamental to the general understanding of psychotherapy in this culture that it requires candor about even the most secret, private aspects of our lives, clients are predisposed to be receptive to whatever topic the therapist feels is essential to solve the problem. This presumes, of course, that the client has chosen to enter therapy, rather than having been coerced into it.

So, rather than thinking of what areas I'd avoid with Mike and Jan, I would think about what areas are going to be more difficult, and will therefore require particularly careful attention to issues of framing, timing, and the quality of the therapeutic alliance I have formed with them. Putting the question that way, I can identify several areas of concern. First, Mike will be reluctant to be open with me about his history of substance abuse unless I make it clear that I do not regard it as the whole problem, but merely as one of the constraints that has kept his life from being how he would like it to be. Second, I would avoid pushing for intimacy, even if Jan and Mike present it as a desire, until there is a better foundation of caregiving and attachment behaviors between them. This would probably include any lengthy conversation about what is wrong with their sexual relationship.

Consistent with the FI model, I would not pursue detailed conversations about the impact of their particular families of origin on Jan and Mike's marital difficulties until I had determined that the beliefs and feelings each of them developed in their original families are constraining the relationship now. Given the case description, I suspect that this is indeed the case, but I would defer the conversation in favor of first pursuing more immediate obstacles to change.

Inclusion of Other Family Members

I think it is unlikely that I would want to include anyone other than Jan and Mike in the sessions. If at some point either Jan or Mike were to pursue individual therapy concurrent to the marital therapy, I would think it very important that I establish contact with the individual therapist(s), but a telephone consultation would usually be sufficient for my purposes. Maintaining some dialogue with clients' individual therapists can serve to attenuate the therapist's distortions of the unseen partner, and thereby decrease the pathologizing of that person in the partner's therapy.

Another possibility is that if the marital therapy does eventually become focused around family-of-origin issues, then Jan or Mike might wish to invite one or more members of their families into a session. But that is a decision that would be made at a later point in the therapy.

Homework

The negative associations that most people have to the word "homework" are so bad that it is almost never a useful word to employ in psychotherapy. It has connotations of hierarchy and punishment (not to mention boredom and futility) that far outweigh any positive value. So I never give clients "homework." I do, however, suggest ways that they could extend the work we do together into the other 167 hours of the week. Sometimes these suggestions take the form of "experiments" or "data collection." Sometimes they are more oblique suggestions about things that "may be worth noticing."

Timeline for Therapy

As part of the assessment of the couple, I routinely do an individual session with each partner early in the therapy, usually by the third session. The primary purpose of this format is to screen for possible abuse. In addition to screening for abuse, an individual session is a useful vehicle for ascertaining other information that each person would be reluctant to reveal in front of their partner, such as how committed they are to the process of therapy. Of course, the hazard of individual sessions, particularly early in the process, is that the client may reveal a secret that then compromises the therapist by creating a collusion between her and the secret-holder. I try to get around this dilemma by stipulating before the individual sessions that while I will not be reporting to each spouse on the session with their partner, I will not keep secrets which I believe are harmful. Each partner is then free to make their own decision about what to share with me. Although this stance probably prevents me from knowing some kinds of information, long experience has shown me that this is a lesser price to pay than being caught in a triangle.

I am always flummoxed when clients ask me in the first session how long therapy will take. There are so many variables that influence the length of therapy, including how constrained the clients are from changing, how high their aspirations are, how much they like the process, how flexible their time is, and what their financial resources are. I do tell them that if we can't create some sense of hopefulness and encouragement within the first couple of months, it is unlikely to happen at all. I am deeply interested in the therapy being useful to my clients, and if it isn't, then I am the first one who would want to make a change, either by bringing in a consultant, by changing the direction of the therapy, or by altering the configuration of who gets seen and how often.

All that being said, I would probably encourage Jan and Mike to commit to a series of weekly sessions. Once the themes of the therapy are established, and the alliance is reasonably strong, it is often feasible to move to a biweekly schedule, but initially I like to have at least weekly contact to establish some intensity and rhythm in the work.

As far as individual therapy is concerned, I only recommend it when there is evidence that the couple's progress toward their goals is being constrained by the intrapsychic issues of one or both partners, and these constraints cannot be addressed conjointly. The recommendation usually emanates directly from the client's own recognition that some internal struggle (which could be an unresolved family-of-origin issue, post-traumatic stress disorder, or a host of others) is preventing movement in the couple treatment. At that point I might recommend individual therapy, and would suggest a specific therapist whose thinking is sufficiently similar to my own that I feel confident there will be no conflict between the individual and conjoint work. More problematic is when individual therapy for one or both partners predates the conjoint therapy. In that case, the individual therapist has often formed a very solid and also distorted impression of the partner who is not their client, and is actively engaged in encouraging the individual client to see the spouse as the problem.

Termination and Relapse Prevention

My initial training as a psychotherapist taught me that therapy was a closed-ended process, and that working toward termination in long-term therapy was a multi-session task and might even go on for several months. The corollary to this was that therapy was a once-in-a-lifetime event, and that when clients were "cured," they stayed cured. The past decade of work at the Family Institute, which is set in a large and fairly stable community, has led me to completely rework my model for termination.

It is still true that many clients come to therapy for a while, get what they want, and go on to lead their lives with no further involvement from the mental health community. But for roughly a third of my clients, I have become their family therapist for life, and have the same sort of standing with them as their family doctor. They come to me episodically, when some new life crisis or transition befuddles them or causes them pain. I might start out as the marital therapist and eventually become involved with an issue regarding the family of origin, or a child who will not cooperate. Or the same couple who came to see me 10 years ago because of a marital crisis might bring back their adolescent daughter who is having difficulty making the adjustment to college.

So termination has a more conditional connotation than used to be the case. Still, when people have let you into their lives to the extent of discussing issues and feelings they wouldn't dream of telling their best friends; have let you witness their fights, their fears and pains, their tears and sorrows; then bringing the relationship to a close, even if only temporarily, requires some sort of closure ritual.

I like to have couples wind down slowly from therapy, stretching out the time between sessions until they feel confident that not seeing me for a month at a time will not create any significant perturbation in their system. If I have been working with them for more than 6 months (and often I do work with couples for a year or more) the termination phase will consist of continued refinement of the solutions they are implementing to their problems, as well as some review about what they have learned about themselves and each other, and about how to maintain the relationship they have developed during therapy. In the last session, I often take time to express to the couple my sense of gratitude for what they have shared with me during therapy, and I try to articulate a personal and specific acknowledgment about the work that they have done and the changes they have made. I invite them to give me any feedback they would care to share that might help me understand how to better help other couples. Sometimes I ask them to tell me how they want to be remembered by me.

I think that to have the kind of relationship that Jan and Mike seem to want, they would need to do a lot of work, over a fairly long time. There are two reasons for this; first, Mike has a very brief history of sobriety, and needs to work hard at firmly establishing that pattern in his life. For at least several months, I would be more focused on stabilizing his relationship with Jan than on challenging it, or on stimulating intense affect. Second, this couple has a very long history of enacting some very corrosive marital patterns. They need to establish new habits of thought and action about what it means to be part of a married couple. This will involve things as concrete as eating together at a table together several times a week, as well as more complex processes, like learning how to recognize their own needs and ask their partner for what they want. They need to learn to collaborate, to manage conflict effectively, to read each other's nonverbal signals. They might very well be the kind of couple who will stay in therapy for a while, reach some plateau, and then take a break, returning when they are ready to go further, or when some new challenge presents itself.

Conclusion

Jan and Mike have not had an easy time of it as a married couple. Like most couples who seek therapy, they are in a highly distressed state, each feeling deeply disappointed by the relationship and their partner, and each fearing that there is no real hope that they can be happy together. The therapeutic challenge is to create some real cause for hope and encouragement, to discover and enhance the strengths and resources of the couple while creating a safe environment in which they can safely confront those factors in themselves and the relationship that have undermined the health and satisfaction of the marriage. This is an enterprise that requires strength, flexibility, tenacity, optimism, and creativity on the part of the therapist, as well as an approach that is robust enough to be adapted to the particular style and needs of the clients' relationship.

REFERENCES

Breunlin, D., Schwartz, R., & MacKune-Karrer, B. (1992). *Metaframeworks: Transcending the models of family therapy*. San Francisco: Jossey-Bass.

Goodrich, T. J., Rampage, C., Ellman, B., & Halstead, K. (1988). *Feminist family therapy: A casebook*. New York: Norton.

Gottman, J. (1995). *Why marriages succeed or fail, and how you can make yours last*. New York: Fireside.

Notarius, C., & Markman, H. (Eds.) (1994). *We can work it out: How to solve conflicts, save your marriage, and strengthen your love for each other*. New York: Perigee.

Pinsof, W. (1995). *Integrative problem-centered therapy*. New York: Basic Books.

Stuart, R. B. (1980). *Helping couples change*. New York: Guilford Press.

Wynne, L. C., & Wynne, A. R. (1986). The quest for intimacy. *Journal of Marital and Family Therapy, 12*, 383–394.

SUGGESTED READINGS

Rampage, C. (1994). Power, gender and marital intimacy. *Journal of Family Therapy, 16*, 125–137.

Rampage, C. (1995). Gendered aspects of marital therapy. In N. Jacobson & A. Gurman (Eds.), *Clinical handbook of couple therapy* (pp. 261–273). New York: Guilford Press.

18

Narrative Therapy with Couples

Jill Freedman and Gene Combs

TREATMENT MODEL

Narrative therapy, as we use the term, refers to an interrelated set of values, attitudes, stories, and practices that flow from the work of Michel White and David Epston (Freedman & Combs, 1996b; Monk, Winslade, Crocket, & Epston, 1997; White & Epston, 1990, 1992; Zimmerman & Dickerson, 1996). White and Epston have drawn on the ideas of post-structuralist scholars such as Michel Foucault (1980), Jerome Bruner (1990), and Barbara Meyerhoff (1986) to articulate and embody a creative and inspiring approach to therapy. An important idea in narrative therapy is that stories shape our experience. The stories that we enact with each other are not about our lives; they *are* our lives.

Narrative therapists collaborate with people to change their lives by changing their stories. This would be easy work if we could simply construct any story we wanted, tell it, and have it taken up and lived out by the people who consult with us. But it's not that simple. Some stories have more staying power than others. In any culture at any given time, certain stories are much more a part of the fabric of day-to-day reality than are others. We are born into stories, and those stories shape our perceptions of what is possible. However, we don't usually think of the stories we are born into as stories. We think of them as "reality." Stories have the power to shape our experience of reality.

The way we see it, the dominant stories in any society are kept in power by richly interconnected networks of language, beliefs, institutions, customs, laws, etc. We call these networks "discourses" (Hare-Mustin, 1994; Madigan, 1996), and we think an important part of therapy is making limiting discourses visible so that people have the opportunity to revise their relationships with them. The dominant discourses in any social network determine (and are determined by) what counts as "knowledge" or "truth" in that network. The dominant discourses determine who does and does not have access to power. For example, when our founding fathers wrote the phrase "all men are created equal," the discourses of their day led people to take for granted that "men" (when applied to the right to vote) meant "land-owning White males." It took, among other things, a civil war to change the discourses so that the taken-for-granted meaning of "men" in relation to the right to vote was "males of any color, as long as they are U.S. citizens and not in jail." It took lots more sweat and strife to change the discourses so that "men" applied to women as well.[1]

A distinguishing feature of narrative work is that we seek to make visible the discourses that support problematic life narratives. We believe that when the partners in a couple decide to consult with a therapist, they are caught up in limiting and unsatisfying stories of themselves, each other, and the world. We believe that those stories are supported by discourses, and that the discourses tend to be invisible (taken for granted). Highlighting the discourses that support a couple's problems makes it possible for the partners to see each other in the light of different discourses. In that light, they can imagine, experience, and live out more satisfying stories of their relationship.

In the day-to-day work of narrative therapy, we start by getting to know people. In an initial interview, we want to hear at least a few things about people's lives outside of the problem—their interests, their living situation, etc. People often begin to tell us about their problems without being asked. If they don't, after a while we might ask a general question like, "What brought you here?" We listen to their responses as stories. This is a very different mindset from listening for symptoms that will help establish a diagnosis, for surface clues to deep meaning, for self-defeating cognitions, or for "facts." We try to understand what is problematic in people's stories, and we search for descriptions of the problem(s) that are "experience near" (fitting with their vocabulary and worldview, not ours).

We listen with an attitude of not-knowing (Anderson & Goolishian, 1992), that is, we cultivate a genuine curiosity about what people will say. We are not trying to lead people toward some predetermined outcome. At the same time—and this can be a tricky balancing act—we don't want to let the dominant discourses in people's worlds predetermine the outcome. With couples, this often means that we must stay aware of gender discourses (Freedman & Combs, 1996a; Goldner, 1985; Hare-Mustin, 1994; Laird, 1989) and how they shape each part-

---

[1]We heard this example in a snippet of a radio interview with a Derrida scholar, whose name we did not hear.

ner's experience and expectations. As we listen, we ask questions that invite people to consider the effects of the problem(s) on their lives and relationships. This combined focus on discourses and the effects of problems tends to bring forth stories of people's struggles with the limiting effects of dominant cultural narratives on their lives. With couples, this can shift each partner's experience from one of struggling with the other person to one of struggling together to overcome problems coming from outside their relationship. Whether this happens or not, this kind of inquiry tends to deconstruct (White, 1991) the problematic story, opening space for the perception of "unique outcomes" (events that would not have been predicted by the problematic story). As unique outcomes are brought forth, we ask questions that invite people to expand or "thicken" (Geertz, 1978) them into memorable, experientially vivid stories.

Stories need listeners as well as tellers. It is through the interpersonal, societal practice of telling and retelling of stories that people's lives can change. For this reason, narrative therapists have developed many ways of working that involve witnessing. We provide space and time for people to reflect on their own narratives as they emerge. Whenever possible, we use reflecting teams (Andersen, 1989) or "outsider-witness groups" (White, 1997) to increase the audience for tellings and retellings. As we will illustrate more fully later in this chapter, when working with couples, we often work so that one partner is in a telling mode while the other is in a witnessing mode. There is a rhythmic alternation between telling and listening, between acting and reflecting, that runs through narrative therapy.

When we say, "telling and retelling," we are speaking of *embodied* expressions. White often quotes Edward Bruner (1986) to emphasize this point:

> A ritual must be enacted, a myth recited, a narrative told, a novel read, a drama performed, for these enactments, recitals, tellings, readings, and performances are what make the text transformative. . . . Expressions are constitutive and shaping, not as abstract texts but in the activity that actualizes the text. (p. 7)

Because we believe that the new stories that emerge in therapy only become transformative as they are enacted outside of the therapy room, we are interested in documenting and circulating the new stories. To facilitate documentation, we sometimes write letters between therapy meetings. In these letters we might reflect on unique outcomes and ask questions that we didn't ask in the session, hoping that this will thicken and extend the knowledge that had begun to emerge there. We might generate formal documents that list important elements of new narratives and, to encourage the circulation of this knowledge, invite people to share these documents with other people in their lives. Another way we might facilitate circulation of alternative stories as they develop is to invite members of people's social networks (friends, co-workers, bosses, teachers, ministers, etc.) to therapy sessions.

THERAPIST SKILLS AND ATTRIBUTES

Many people in the narrative therapy community have noted that the ideas that have come to be known as narrative therapy constitute a worldview, a way of life. We would not think about skills and attributes a therapist should have, but instead whether she situates herself in a way of living that supports collaboration, social justice, and local, situated, context-specific knowledge rather than normative thinking, diagnostic labeling, and generalized (non-contextualized) "expert" knowledge. This worldview leads to improvisation and creativity and a commitment to confront the discourses that oppress or limit people as they pursue their preferred directions in life. We think that situating ourselves in this worldview is an ongoing process. An important part of that process for us is asking ourselves certain questions.[2]

Here is a representative list of the kinds of questions we ask ourselves:

- Whose language is being privileged here? Am I bringing forth the stories that these people want to tell in their own words, or am I pushing for the stories that I want to hear, told in my jargon?
- Are there dominant stories that are oppressing or limiting these people's lives? Am I inviting awareness of those stories without becoming oppressive myself?
- Am I evaluating these people, or am I inviting them to evaluate things (how therapy is going, the effects of various practices, preferred directions in life, etc.)?
- Who am I viewing as the "expert" here, myself or the people I am working with?
- Am I working so as to require these people to enter my expert knowledge, or so as to require myself to enter their worlds?
- Is what I am doing dividing and isolating these people, or bringing forth a sense of community and collaboration?
- Am I situating my opinions in my personal experience? Am I being transparent about my context, my values, and my intentions so that these people can evaluate the effects of my biases?
- Do the questions I am asking conserve dominant social practices or propose alternative practices?
- How am I embodying "professionalism"? Am I more concerned with how I am looking to my professional colleagues or how I am being experienced by the people who are seeking my help?

---

[2]The original questions on this list came to us in a personal communication from David Epston, who said that he and Michael White had developed them for themselves. Over the years, we have revised the list so much that we can no longer remember which questions originated with Michael and David, which came from us, and which came from other people.

THE CASE OF MIKE AND JAN

Assessment

Two ideas that inform narrative work seem particularly relevant in responding to this question. The first is "the interpretive turn" (J. Bruner, 1986), which supports the idea that people are in a better position to interpret their own experience than outsiders are. In keeping with this idea, as stated in the previous sections, we encourage those with whom we work to be in an evaluative position about the work and about their experience. Insofar as possible, we avoid the position of making professional, "knowing," assessments. Because we are interested in detailed, context-specific narratives, we shy away from standardized instruments and psychological testing.

The second idea is that we think about information as being *generated*, rather than "gathered" in therapeutic conversations. In a rather literal way, we believe that we are making ourselves and each other up as we go along. This is a poststructuralist idea. We do not assume that a couple has a particular interactional or relational structure that we can assess. We do not think of people or relationships as having stable, quantifiable identities or "typical" characteristics, so we do not try to uncover or gather information about such characteristics. Instead, we think of people's lives as being multistoried, and we believe that each new telling generates new possibilities for interpretation and action.

We would be interested in asking questions that would invite Jan and Mike to tell more satisfying and useful stories of their relationship. As these stories took shape, we would invite them to assess their usefulness. We would want to know whether the new stories spoke to them of a more satisfying identity as a couple. In telling these stories and reflecting on them, Jan and Mike would be collaborating with us in an ongoing assessment of the new expressions of themselves and their relationship.

Here are some questions we might ask in eliciting Jan's and Mike's assessments:

- What name would you give the problem?
- What is it like to have the experience of the problem?
- What effect does the problem have on your life?
- What effect does the problem have on your relationship with each other?
- What effect does the problem have on other relationships?
- How does the problem affect your relationship with yourself?
- Is this what you want for your relationship? Why or why not?
- Is this what you want for yourself? Why or why not?
- Are we talking about what you want to be talking about?

- Is this conversation useful?
- How is it useful?

While we favor leaving assessment in the hands of the people who consult with us, it would be misleading to imply that we make no assessments of any kind. Rachel Hare-Mustin (1994) makes the argument that if we simply reflect what our clients say in therapy, nothing new will happen. We see it as our responsibility to bring in new discourses. One kind of assessment, then, that we make has to do with which parts of Jan and Mike's story might be located in discourses that are invisible to them. We would be interested in asking questions to locate their problems in such discourses and to give Jan and Mike an opportunity to decide (in this way leaving "assessment" as much as possible still in their hands) where they stand and where they would like their relationship to be in the face of such discourses. Because each question leads to the next in ways that none of us can know until they are spoken, it is quite difficult to describe exactly how this might go. However, we might initiate such a conversation with some of the following questions:

- In the pattern you describe of avoiding conflict, part of the description included a reference to Jan "nagging." Do you think that description of nagging is more often applied to men or women?
- *(If the answer is "women")* Do you think there is a comparable way of relating that men would be described as using? What would that be called?
- What do you think supports women and men trying to influence each other in such different ways?

Case Conceptualization

The worldview that we subscribe to influences how we read the material in the case presentation. Within our worldview, we do not think of the material as descriptions of or clues to personality. Within that worldview, we are not looking for healthy or unhealthy behavior, normal or abnormal affective states, rational or irrational cognitions. We are not making global assessments of Jan's and Mike's functioning. Instead, we read the material as stories which are expressions of Jan's and Mike's experience. In working with them we would remain steadfast in our belief that other experiences could be storied, and that these other stories would speak differently of their lives and identities. We would consider it part of our task not to let the problem-filled stories dominate our view of Jan and Mike or of their relationship.

As we described in our answer to the question about assessment, we would hope to find ways for Jan and Mike to be doing any evaluating that was done.

In keeping with that stand, we would want to know how Mike and Jan might describe their desired directions in life in relation to the problems that beset them, both individually and as a couple. We would be looking for sparkling moments—events in their stories that would not have been predicted by the problem-filled stories that have brought them to therapy.

For example, if they had named the pattern of avoiding conflict as a problem which has brought distrust, emotional distance, avoidance, criticism, and tension into their lives, we would be listening for moments that seem to stand outside of the stories of conflict avoidance and its effects. As we heard about events that sounded like such moments, we would ask questions about them. Here are some of the questions we might ask:

- You have described your courtship as a fun time you will always remember. When you think about it what stands out for you?
- What do you notice in your partner that the distrust and tension may have kept you from seeing lately? What do you see about your relationship?
- We are interested to hear that although you have talked about therapy before from time to time, you did not follow through because things got better. Can you tell us about this getting better? What did each of you contribute to it? How did it happen? Was there preparation involved or did you simply find yourselves doing things differently? How would you explain that?
- As you hear your partner describe his or her part in things getting better, what does it tell you about his or her motivation and intentions in the relationship? Is that something that you already knew about? If so, how did you know it?
- You've told us that for the past 7 months you have been getting along fairly well. Could you describe a typical evening or Saturday during that time of getting along well? When you look at that, what do you learn about your relationship and about each other?
- Can you see moments during that evening or Saturday when you could have been derailed by the pattern of avoiding conflict, but you weren't?
- What went into keeping your relationship the way you wanted it instead of the way the pattern of conflict-avoidance might have wanted it? What can you see that your partner contributed to that happening? How would you name that quality in your partner?

We might also ask similar kinds of questions about Jan's and Mike's individual stories.

Through questions of this kind, we might develop a list of events that would not have been predicted by the stories of conflict avoidance, distrust, emotional distance, criticism, and tension. Each of these events, pending Jan and Mike's confirmation, would be a candidate for "unique outcome" status. To build on these unique outcomes in the treatment process, we would ask questions that invited the telling and retelling of stories having to do with them. As such stories were told, we would hear descriptions of qualities or characteristics in the relationship and in each partner that were not part of the pattern of avoiding conflict.

Hypothetically, let's suppose that the couple named "commitment" and "closeness" as qualities of their relationship that emerged in these stories, and that they named "warmth" and "understanding" as qualities that Jan showed and "strength" and "fun-loving" as qualities that Mike showed.

To thicken the stories of these qualities, we might ask questions such as the following:

- Have there been other times that you have seen the commitment and closeness in your relationship?
- Can you tell us about these times?
- What do these experiences mean to you?
- If you held these memories close to you in your heart and mind at some of the times that the conflict avoidance pattern (or distrust, etc.) tends to take over, how would that make a difference?

To Jan:

- Do you like being described as understanding and warm?
- Why do you like that?
- Who from your past do you think would have noticed these qualities in you at a very early age?
- What would they have observed?

To Mike:

- What is it like hearing Jan's memory of that?
- Does it put the story you told about the "nagging" in a different light? How?
- Which of those ways of looking at it do you prefer? Why?
- Do you often think of yourself as fun and strong?
- In which contexts do you think those aspects of yourself are most at play?
- What do you think it would be like if Jan had more experience of you the way you are in those contexts?

To Jan:

- What do you think it would be like if you were more in on the way Mike is in those contexts?

To Mike:

- If you were going to create that context more at home, what would be your first step?

Treatment Goals

A general goal for our work is to help the members of couples experience themselves as living out preferred stories of themselves and their relationships. Because we strive to conduct our conversations in the realm of the not-yet-spoken, we do not set goals at the outset with the couples we see. We listen for sparkling moments or hidden presences that would not have been predicted by the problematic story. When we hear what sounds to us like such moments, we ask questions about them to see if they might be openings to new stories. None of us know where these stories will take us.

We speak of "projects" or "directions in life" more often than we speak of goals. We believe that this language leaves more room for revision and redecision along the way. It fits better with the "making it up as we go along" atmosphere that we value. Projects are usually identified and named in relation to problems. If Jan and Mike had named the problem "the conflict-avoiding pattern," or "distrust," or "tension," they might name the project "closeness," "strength," or "warmth." The names emerge through the telling of counterstories to the problem.

In the course of therapy, we would often ask Jan and Mike to make evaluations of how things are going in terms of the problem and the project. They may come in and tell about something that happened since they last met and we might say, "Is that way of being more on the side of avoiding conflict or more on the side of closeness?" In this way they continually evaluate their experience in terms of the problem and the project.

While we would not set goals for Jan and Mike based on our ideas of how a couple should be, or on any established norms, or ideas of "health," we would not say that we think all stories are equal. We take strong stands against (for example) oppression, violence, and exploitation, and we strive to be transparent about our own values and biases. Even in taking a strong stand against something, we would seek Jan and Mike's collaboration.

Techniques and Interventions

Because we place such a high premium on collaboration and avoidance of "expert" knowledge, we prefer not to use words like "techniques" or "interventions." We speak instead of "practices." While certain practices are widely used and perhaps even characteristic of narrative therapy, we would not want anyone to use these practices in a rote or standardized way. That said, it is very likely that we would use questions, transparency, externalizing conversations, developing a history of the present, some reflective practices, and taking-it-back practices in working with Jan and Mike. We might also use an outsider witness group or reflecting team, letter writing, documents, and internalized other questioning.

Questions

We would strive to do most of the interview through questions. We find that questions help construct a collaborative atmosphere. There are not particular questions that we would use or decide upon beforehand outside of the conversation. We would propose a domain through a question and Jan or Mike's response would further the story within that domain. We will sketch an idealized map here, emphasizing that there is not a particular sequence to how we would do this work. It would evolve in conversation with Mike and Jan.

We would begin the interview by asking questions of both Mike and Jan, to get to know them as people—not in terms of the problems that brought them. They might fill us in on their work or some of the interests mentioned in the case material or anything else of interest to them. This initial conversation would be important in communicating our understanding that their identities include much more than the problems that brought them.

Transparency

We would then invite them to ask us any questions. Our interest in putting forward this invitation would be to minimize the power differential inherent in client-therapist relationships. For many people, this invitation signals that the context of working in this way may be "different" than other therapies. It would offer us the opportunity to begin the practice of transparency—making our biases and ideas visible and traceable to particular experience, rather than representing the voice of family therapy or professional discourse. We think that practices of transparency, which would continue throughout the work, would help the couple know how to take our ideas. At this same point, especially with a heterosexual couple, we might introduce a conversation about gender, especially if only one of us were working with Jan and Mike. In that case, we would want to mention that our own gender would make it more likely that we understand one of their experiences more fully than the other's.

Externalizing Conversations

After we had gotten to know each other a bit, we would be interested in having a conversation about the problem. We would hope to engage in a deconstructive, externalizing conversation in which we asked Mike and Jan to name problems (these could be different problems for each of them or a shared problem). We would have at least three ideas in mind: first, to separate Jan and Mike from the problem by speaking about it in an externalized way; second, to unmask what contributes to and supports the problem; and third, to note the effects of the problem on their lives, relationships, and identities (both as a couple and individually).

In the second purpose we mentioned—to unmask with them what contributes to and supports the problem—we would be wondering about power. With both heterosexual and same-sex couples, we wonder if gender and cultural specifications play a role in power inequities. With Jan and Mike, we wonder, for example, if gender specifications may be intertwined with some social class differences. Specifically, the material indicates that Jan graduated from college and Mike began working straight out of high school. Jan works as a sales associate for a pharmaceutical company and Mike works as a welder/fitter. We might ask about whether Jan earns more money and if she does, what the effects of that have been for this couple. In our culture, the traditional expectations are that men should be more responsible as wage-earners and that as "the head of the family" men should have greater qualifications, such as more education. If there is a discrepancy in earning, we would wonder if the cultural expectations have created problems for this couple around the meaning of their different salaries. We would also wonder about the different status and symbols of status involved in each of their jobs and levels of education and how those interact with gender specifications. We would explore this area through many questions, following their experience. Our intention would be to expose the role that cultural specifications play, so that this couple could consider whether the problems are lodged in those specifications, rather than in each other.

As problems are named and externalized and their effects are mapped out, we would be listening for hidden presences—sparkling moments whose existence would not be predicted by the problematic stories. We would view these sparkling moments or unique outcomes as possible entryways to alternative stories. Through questions, we would invite Jan and Mike to thicken the stories of experiences that stand outside of the problems. As these stories developed, we would ask them to evaluate whether these stories fit with their preferences in life. For example, the material indicates that Jan is 49 and that Mike is 44. In our culture, the normative story is that in heterosexual relationships the man is older. Somehow this couple made up their own mind instead of letting cultural specifications come between them in regard to age. We would be interested in the story of this, and particularly in what good things it says about them as a couple.

We would think about this process as the deconstruction of problematic stories and development of preferred stories. As preferred stories are told and retold, we would expect that they would speak to Jan and Mike of preferred directions and possibilities for their relationship and their identities within it.

Developing a History of the Present

As new stories develop we would be interested in developing their roots. This has also been referred to as mapping a "history of the present." For example, it might emerge that one of the ways that Mike has turned his back on drugs for the last 7 months has been through telling himself how important this is to Jan. Jan, in reflecting on this new aspect of the story, might name the quality this shows in Mike as "loyalty." To develop a history of the present, we might begin to ask Mike if he could tell other stories in which his loyalty really showed.

In response to our questions, Mike might tell of his devotion to a high school friend who was badly injured in an accident—how he had helped him with his homework, driven him to school, and visited him during extended stays in the hospital. He might then talk about how, later on in their lives, he risked his own job to help the friend find work. Jan would hear these stories from a witnessing, reflective position and they might remind her of other times in which Mike's loyalty has been evident. We could ask her questions to bring forth thick descriptions of those stories.

This whole conversation would invite both partners to step into a world where Mike is a loyal person and has been a loyal person for a long time. In that world, their relationship might feel more full of good possibilities. This is just a tiny example of how alternative stories could be developed that the couple could then decide if they preferred.

Reflecting Practices

We would expect Jan and Mike to have different stories about the same events in their relationship, just as we would expect each of them to name different events in their relationship as especially significant. These differences often lead to conflict. Many couples approach therapy as a venue where only one version of the truth can prevail. Some people interrupt their partner to argue or correct. Others keep track of the errors they hear so that they can set the therapist straight. Others are intent on explaining how they see the situation their partner is describing differently. These common practices get in the way of each person really witnessing or even hearing his or her partner's story.

We would structure much of the work by speaking directly with either Jan or Mike and asking the other to be in a listening position. At intervals, we would switch and ask the listener to reflect on what he or she heard. Much of our work with couples involves this practice of speaking with one member at a time and then turning to the other to ask for reflections. In this atmosphere, with our questions facilitating, the person in the "witnessing" position often understands his or her partner in ways that are relatively free of defensiveness, argumentation, and competition.

Taking-It-Back Practices

We find that invariably in our work with couples we gain something. We hope that we always include taking-it-back practices in our work. These consist of finding respectful ways to let the people we work with know that the conversations they have included us in have given something to us. We would "take it back" by acknowledging to Jan and Mike what the work with them means to us. We might do this by telling how some step they had taken together had given us the courage to take a risky step in our own lives. Or we might share how something we had learned in working with them had been useful in our work with another couple.

Other Practices

There are other practices that we might use in working with Jan and Mike. An *outsider witness group* or *reflecting team* who could witness the couple's new, preferred, stories and participate in the definitional ceremony (Meyerhoff, 1986) of telling and retelling them would be additive. Also, we might collaborate with Jan and Mike to create *letters* and *documents* (White & Epston, 1990) to thicken and document their preferred stories and stands on life. Additionally, some of the conversations might make use of internalized other interviewing (Epston, 1993; MacCormack & Tomm, 1998) in which we would ask questions of the internalized Jan in Mike and the internalized Mike in Jan.

Pitfalls

We would not anticipate pitfalls, just as we would not be able to anticipate what will be the preferred stories that Jan and Mike author over the course of the therapy. In general, when things were not going in a direction that Jan and Mike clearly preferred, we would think again about deconstructing problematic stories. Perhaps the problem as Jan and Mike first named it was "distrust" and the project was "closeness." If, after a time of moving in the direction of more closeness, they come in complaining of being distant from each other, we would wonder what is getting in the way of closeness now. Perhaps distrust has taken over again. Perhaps we haven't facilitated the telling and retelling of closeness stories enough, or thickened and circulated the stories enough, for them to have become a dependable part of Jan and Mike's reality. Maybe what is getting in the way is no longer distrust. Perhaps the drug culture has gotten a grip on Mike again.[3] If the drug culture was what was getting in the way of closeness now, we would inquire about its effects on Mike and Jan and on their relationship. In the course of this inquiry, we would be on the lookout for unique outcomes and preferred directions in life. As they emerged, we would seek thick, memorable, widely circulated stories of them.

It is difficult for us to say how we might address boundaries or limits with Mike and Jan. As we have already stated, we are clearly and outspokenly against violence, oppression, and exploitation. We think more in these terms than we do in terms of "boundaries" or "limits." To us, the discourse of separation and individuation has been overly valued, and these terms derive from that discourse. We would be interested in finding ways for Mike and Jan to consider their relationship in the light of discourses that support collaboration, connection, and interdependence.

Areas to Avoid

There are no areas that we would want to avoid addressing with Mike and Jan.

Inclusion of Other Family Members

Since ours is a social constructionist therapy, we value community. We are always on the lookout for other people to participate in the tellings and retellings of people's preferred stories. Cultivating an audience for new stories can thicken them and create a support system for them. At the very least we would include other people through inquiring about them and their viewpoints in our conversations with Jan and Mike. We would ask them questions that include other people, such as the following:

- Who would have predicted this step you are taking?
- What do they know about your relationship that would have led them to predict this?
- If I were to interview them, what memory might they tell me about that fits with this step?
- What words would they use to describe this quality in your relationship?
- Would it be helpful to hold this person's view of your relationship closer?

---

[3]We do not mean to imply here that we would not have talked with them about the drug culture until this point in therapy. We may well have asked about it, but perhaps they thought at the time that that particular problem was behind them.

We would also be interested in having other people actually join our sessions. This could be in the form of an outsider witness group or reflecting team, if Jan and Mike were agreeable and if that fit with the therapy context.

With the couple's permission, we might ask others who might be part of a supporting community, whether or not they are family members, to join us. It would emerge in conversation who might be relevant to invite. For example, if the problem is named as "distrust," the drug culture might have played a big role in luring Mike away from closeness and in alienating Jan. This distance and alienation might have been identified as contributing to the distrust. If the couple has a friend who has successfully walked away from drugs and has supported this couple in staying away from drugs, it might be appropriate to invite that friend as a witness who could reflect on the stories that came forth in therapy. Mike's AA sponsor might be a possibility.

Another way we might include other people would be to initiate a letter-writing campaign. We might ask friends, relatives, and associates, often people from different periods and places in Mike's and Jan's lives, to send letters about their experience of that person.

We would certainly, with Mike and Jan's permission, be interested in including other involved professionals. In the work of deconstructing problematic stories and authoring preferred ones, we are very interested in facilitating community inclusion and support for preferred stories. As we talked with other professionals, we would be interested in circulating alternative strands of story that we hoped would become part of their way of relating to Jan and Mike. Their involvement in the therapy process would be negotiated, first with Jan and Mike and then with each particular professional person.

Homework

Our associations to "homework" and "assignments" are hierarchical. When we use these words, we imagine one person telling the others what to do (and usually when and how to do it). Since we are interested in contributing to a collaborative context that minimizes hierarchy, we would not choose to use these metaphors. However, an implication in the idea of homework is that things happen outside of the therapy room that contribute to the process. That idea is very much a part of our work.

Lynn Hoffman (1990) writes that in moving into a social constructionist way of working it is not that she doesn't do what she did before, she just does it more tentatively. If, in the developing of a preferred story in therapy, either Jan or Mike had the idea of doing something in keeping with that story—or if we had a thought of something they might do—we might (tentatively) wonder what it would be like to actually do it. For example, if we were developing stories of trust, and Jan and Mike told us about long, sharing conversations that contributed to trust they used to have while eating out together during their courtship, we might wonder if that would be something they would be interested in doing again. If they decide to follow through on this, it would probably have something in common with doing a homework assignment.

Our hope is that in the telling and retelling of preferred stories, Jan and Mike would begin to live out the preferred stories, rather than the ones that they find problematic. We would hope that between meetings they would be doing things and thinking in ways that would be in keeping with their preferred stories. One thing that we might do to aid in this process is write letters summarizing preferred stories as they are developing and asking questions that might contribute to the further development of those stories. Or we might send a document summarizing the stand they decided to take in relationship to the problem. Most couples who receive such letters or documents in the mail tell us that they read and reread them, sometimes posting them, and sometimes carrying them around to consult with when problems seem to be on the verge of making a comeback.

Here is a letter that we might send, based simply on the information supplied. Since we would ask different questions if we had interviewed the couple ourselves, our letter would be somewhat different and would probably include a brief summary of our understanding of the couple's stories.

Dear Jan and Mike,

We enjoyed getting to know you a bit at our first meeting. We are sending this letter simply to raise a few questions that occurred to us after you left. If you would like, we can talk about them next time.

One part of the interview that stayed with us was your comment that for the last 7 months, with the exception of the event that led to your coming here, you have been getting along fairly well. We would be interested in what getting along fairly well means to each of you. What kinds of things are different? What would you each say that your partner contributes to the difference? What are you each aware of contributing? If you could tell us about a particular time that was characteristic of getting along, what would you tell us about? What do you think it says about your potential as a couple that you could get along fairly well for 7 months? Did each of you do things in the months prior to the 7 months that laid the groundwork for this time?

If we understood you correctly, one important characteristic of your relationship during this time was trust. The trust seemed to be in danger when Mike came home at 2:30 AM without calling. Within a day, you as a couple came together and decided to begin couples therapy. Do you think that that says something about your motivation to keep trust in your relationship?

We also noted that Mike has been substance-free for 7 months. Is there a connection between your getting along and the elimination of drugs? The correlation leads us to wonder if the drugs came between you or got in the way of your being able to see what might be possible. Does that fit for you? If it does, now that drugs aren't blurring your vision, what do you see in your relationship that drugs had obscured?

Another thing we noticed, Jan, probably because we both enjoy reading mysteries, is that you are a mystery reader too. You know how a good mystery has clues leading up to its resolution? We were just wondering if there are clues in your life together that point in the direction of how you would like things to be.

If any of our thoughts or questions are of interest to you, we would be happy to talk about them together.

'Til next time,
Jill and Gene

Even if no ideas were suggested and no letters were sent, we would expect that things would happen between meetings that could contribute to alternative stories. We might begin a therapy conversation with Mike and Jan by reading our notes from the previous conversation. The notes would summarize the developing stories, and we could then ask the couple what has happened since our last conversation that would extend these stories. They can then reflect on the time between meetings in relation to the stand they have taken and the preferences for their lives and relationship that they have named in previous therapy conversations.

Timeline for Therapy

At the end of each meeting, we would ask Jan and Mike if the interview was helpful and if so, how it was helpful. Then we would ask if they wanted to come back and if so, when they wanted to come back. For most people, this is an unexpected way of negotiating timing. We do it this way because we want to privilege the experience and wisdom of the people we work with, rather than our own.

Some couples find our asking them about the timing confusing. They may ask how often we *usually* see people. We generally say something like the following: "You have decided that you want to do something about a problem and we see ourselves as consultants in that project. How often you want to consult us really is your choice. Some people have told us it works best for them if it is often enough to keep them organized and reminded of the work they are engaged in, and not so often that they haven't had time to reflect on the last interview and to try out any ideas they have had. Different couples have different schedules and different amounts of time available to them, so we don't know what would be most fitting for you."

Other couples are delighted to hear that they don't have to come every week. Some may want to come more frequently at times of intense difficulty and less frequently as they become more securely situated in preferred stories.

How long the therapy extends over time would again be up to Jan and Mike. Some couples name a problem, begin to develop preferred stories, and experience themselves as being "over a hump" in just a few meetings. They may end therapy for good or they may come back at times they feel stuck. Other couples value having a format where they can reflect on their ongoing experience. Over the course of therapy, they may name a number of different problems and develop many rich strands of story. They value having witnesses and a time they can set aside for this process.

We would be flexible about whether and when to see either Mike or Jan individually. If Jan came to an appointment greeting us by saying, "Mike called me on his way here. He couldn't leave his job so we decided I'd come alone," we would see her alone. We might well write a letter to Mike filling him in on the conversation and asking some questions about what he would have contributed if he had been there. We would see either Mike or Jan individually by plan if they requested it. In such instances, the other would also have the opportunity to be seen alone.

If either Mike or Jan was asking to be seen alone because they thought a particular problem was "theirs," we would wonder if it might be useful to have the other as a witness. Although we would try to be flexible, one thing we would think about and perhaps talk with Mike and Jan about is the possibility that we might become more involved in the stories we heard from the couple member we were seeing alone rather than being equally immersed in both of their stories. That would be a reason to confer with them about a possible referral to someone else for individual therapy. Another reason would be if one of them was interested in talking about something they both agreed was separate from their relationship and not important to work with together, for example, something having to do with work.

Termination and Relapse Prevention

Since we would be thinking of ourselves as consultants to Jan and Mike, they would have more say in when and how the consultation ended than we would. People make only one appointment at a time with us. They don't have a regular appointment time unless their schedules demand it. At the end of each time, we ask if they would like to come back and if so, when. There would come a time when Mike and Jan would decide not to come back. Most likely they would realize that they were nearing the end of the process and tell us that a few sessions before they actually stopped.

We feel most satisfied if therapy ends with people living out stories that they prefer. We are more certain that this is the case when those stories have been told and retold in the consulting room and contrasted with the way things were before. If a couple suddenly and unexpectedly feels "done," we might suggest another meeting to look at how far they've come, and what it means about them as a couple that they have been able to do this work together.

We do know that Jan and Mike would have the final say in when therapy ended, but we don't know where this work would lead them and what stories would unfold as they began taking the problems apart.

Although therapy with Mike and Jan would end, our relationship with them would not necessarily end. We might ask them if they would be willing to serve as consultants to us about a particular problem that they had conquered. They could do this by being interviewed to make a consultation tape that we might show to other couples facing similar problems, or we might ask if they would be willing to come back and serve as outsider witnesses on a reflecting team for people struggling with problems similar to the ones they had overcome.

REFERENCES

Andersen, T. (1989). The reflecting team: Dialogue and meta-dialogue in clinical work. *Family Process, 26,* 415–428.

Anderson, H., & Goolishian, H. (1992). The client is the expert: A not-knowing approach to therapy. In S. McNamee & K. J. Gergen (Eds.), *Therapy as social construction* (pp. 25–39). Newbury Park, CA: Sage.

Bruner, E. (1986). Experience and its expressions. In E. Bruner & V. Turner (Eds.), *The anthropology of experience* (pp. 3–20). Chicago: University of Illinois Press.

Bruner, J. (1990). *Acts of meaning.* Cambridge: Harvard University Press.

*Epston, D. (1993). Internalized other questioning with couples: The New Zealand version. In S. Gilligan & R. Price (Eds.), *Therapeutic conversations* (pp. 183–189). New York: Norton.

Foucault, M. (C. Gordon, Ed.) (1980). *Power/knowledge: Selected interviews and other writings, 1972–1977.* New York: Pantheon.

*Freedman, J., & Combs, G. (1996b). *Narrative Therapy: The social construction of preferred realities.* New York: Norton.

*Freedman, J., & Combs, G. (1996b). Gender stories. *Journal of Systemic Therapies, 15*(1), 31–46.

Geertz, C. (1978). *The interpretation of cultures.* New York: Basic Books.

Goldner, V. (1985). Feminism and family therapy. *Family Process, 24,* 31–47.

Hare-Mustin, R. (1994). Discourses in the mirrored room: A postmodern analysis of therapy. *Family Process, 33*(1), 19–35.

---

*Suggested reading.

Hoffman, L. (1990). Constructing realities: An art of lenses. *Family Process, 29,* 1–12.

Laird, J. (1989). Women and stories: Restorying women's self-constructions. In M. McGoldrick, C. Anderson, & F. Walsh (Eds.), *Women in families: A framework for family therapy* (pp. 427–450). New York: Norton.

MacCormack, T., & Tomm, K. (1998). Social constructionist/narrative couple therapy. In F. M. Dattilio (Ed.), *Case studies in couple and family therapy: Systemic and cognitive perspectives* (pp. 303–330). New York: Guilford Press.

Madigan, S. (1996). Undermining the problem in the privatization of problems in persons: Considering the socio-political and cultural context in the externalizing of internalized problem conversations. *Journal of Systemic Therapies, 15,* 47–62.

Meyerhoff, B. (1986). "Life not death in Venice": Its second life. In V. W. Turner & E. M. Bruner (Eds.), *The anthropology of experience* (pp. 261–286). Chicago: University of Illinois Press.

Monk, G., Winslade, J., Crocket, K., & Epston, D. (Eds.) (1997). *Narrative therapy in practice: The archaeology of hope.* New York: Jossey-Bass.

White, M. (1991). Deconstruction and therapy. *Dulwich Centre Newsletter,* (3), 21–40.

White, M. (1997). *Narratives of therapists' lives.* Adelaide, South Australia: Dulwich Centre Publications.

White, M., & Epston, D. (1990). *Narrative means to therapeutic ends.* New York: Norton.

White, M., & Epston, D. (1992). *Experience, contradiction, narrative, and imagination.* Adelaide, South Australia: Dulwich Centre Publications.

Zimmerman, J., & Dickerson, V. (1996). *If problems talked: Narrative therapy in action.* New York: Guilford Press.

Epilogue

Frank M. Dattilio and Louis J. Bevilacqua

The famous artist Leonardo da Vinci once said that there are many different ways to view just about anything in life—an adage that has rung true countless times throughout our lifespan. So, who's to say that any given psychotherapeutic modality is right or wrong, or that any one is any better than any other in treating the case of Mike and Jan. This compendium of 18 different modalities demonstrates that just about any type of approach might be effective with this or any other case at any given time.

What's important is that the reader has an opportunity to see what approach might feel best to them, and then have the opportunity to compare and contrast the potential strengths and weaknesses as it applies to a particular case. The fact of the matter is that no one approach can be all things to all people. Any stated approach to couples therapy is only as good as the therapist applying it and the chemistry that ensues between the clients and the therapist.

We can only imagine what type of chemistry could develop between Mike and Jan and each therapist and their respected approach. This book of comparative treatments demonstrates the rich variety of interventions available, as well as some common threads present in each model of therapy.

ASSESSMENT

The majority of approaches described in this text indicate that the clinical inter-view—which incorporates listening skills, being able to identify patterns of interaction verbally and behaviorally, as well as eliciting a thorough individual and family history (i.e., family diagrams or genograms and critical life events)—would be the primary assessment tool utilized. Most contributors also described how they would incorporate various self-report inventories in the work with Mike and Jan. Only the strategic therapist, James Keim, suggested that Mike be referred for a full medical evaluation, including a physical and neurological work-up. The Narrative approach supports the idea of the couple assessing themselves and their experience in therapy. The Narrative therapist, in general, does not use psychological tests and self-report inventories.

CASE CONCEPTUALIZATION

From the standpoint of case conceptualization, most contributors perceived Mike and Jan as experiencing chronic tension and lacking an emotional connection. Their typical pattern of interaction viewed Jan being the pursuer, which Mike interpreted as aggressive and nagging/critical; Mike was perceived as avoidant, which escalated Jan's anger and frustration. The result frequently ended without any resolution. Most approaches also indicated family-of-origin factors as contributing to the current relationship dysfunction. Only the Narrative approach declined a description of case conceptualization. Rather, they explain that the information presented are stories or expressions of Jan and Mike's experience.

GOALS, TECHNIQUES, AND INTERVENTIONS

The most common goal cited involved having Mike and Jan increase the number of shared activities. The most common way of achieving this involved behavioral exchange exercises. Communication skills training was another common goal as well as an intervention technique. Some of the other shared objectives included developing greater trust and intimacy, conflict resolution skills training, and learning acceptance. The Narrative approach reframed the concept of goals with the idea of projects such as pursuing closeness, strength, and warmth. A reliance on self-report inventories and verbal feedback from Mike and Jan was the main form of measurement for the various treatment goals and objectives of those approaches that look to measure progress.

POSSIBLE PITFALLS

The number one pitfall cited by the majority of models was related to Mike's substance abuse history and the possibility of relapse. A second common pitfall was the idea of Mike not following through with treatment, or that Mike and Jan only deal with "problems" when there is a crisis, and therefore would discontinue treatment prematurely. It is interesting to note that many models indicated specific areas as possible pitfalls which were not mentioned by the other approaches. Some of these include concerns of Jan's criticalness (Adlerian), lack of trust (Intersystems), and minimizing or overfocusing on Mike's addiction (Feminist).

AREAS TO AVOID

The overwhelming response from the various models regarding areas to avoid was "none," or that the issues to be addressed would be up to Jan and Mike. Some approaches did mention specific areas that they would avoid, such as Jan's hysterectomy and history of cancer (Imago); the concern of infidelity (Adlerian, Imago, Intersystems, and Conflict Resolution); and Mike's sexual abuse history (CBT). Most approaches explained that any sensitive topics would need to be dealt with slowly.

WHOM ELSE TO INCLUDE

Almost every model touched on issues relating to family of origin. Almost half indicated that they would include other family members if Jan and Mike were interested in addressing such issues. Keim, Freedman and Combs, and Duncan, Sparks, and Miller suggested that anyone who would be of assistance, such as co-workers, might also be included in the treatment. Freedman and Combs also described how others could be included by asking them to write letters regarding their view of Jan and Mike. Only the Object Relations, Adlerian, Imago, and Emotionally Focused Therapy models indicated that they would only include Jan and Mike and no others.

HOMEWORK

The main homework tasks/objectives revolved around having Mike and Jan learn ways to resolve their conflicts and tension by practicing negotiation exercises (Strategic), problem solving skills (CBT, IBCT), and specific ways to communicate (i.e., IRT dialogue, or the conversive skill in RE). Another form of homework suggested by many involved changes in behavior. This could be based on a want list that each partner created, as described by Luquet in the Imago model, or behavioral experiments and behavior exchange exercises, as described by the CBT, IBCT, Integrative, RE, Adlerian, and Feminist approaches. The Narrative approach described the therapists writing letters to Jan and Mike, summarizing

Jan and Mike's preferred stories and asking questions that could enhance further development of those stories. These letters would also include questions that Jan and Mike could think about and possibly discuss in the next session.

TIMELINE AND INDIVIDUAL VERSUS COUPLE

Some models were not able to indicate a specific time frame, but rather stated that duration and frequency would be determined by Jan and Mike (SFT, Object Relations, Narrative, Bowen, and Strategic). Others believed that treatment could be completed within 10 sessions (RE model, Imago, and Adlerian). Conflict Resolution-Conflict Focused and EFT suggested 12 and 15 sessions, respectively. Still other models recommended that treatment involve approximately 25 sessions or more than 6 months (CBT and IBCT). Intersystems suggested an intensive (at least twice a week) approach for the first 3 to 4 months and then weekly and biweekly for another 3 to 4 months. Most models suggested booster sessions, while others simply stated that treatment could resume at any future time.

As far as individual treatment, the great majority said that they would provide the individual if it was needed. Object Relations, Relationship Enhancement, Narrative, and Intersystems therapists agree that a referral would be made if individual treatment were necessary. Only the Imago therapist stated that no individual treatment would be needed.

TERMINATION AND RELAPSE PREVENTION

The majority of models viewed Mike and Jan being ready for termination when they would be able to resolve conflicts in an emotionally safe way (Strategic). This would be evident when problems could be discussed with more ease and less defensiveness (Intersystems, Feminist, Emotionally Focused Therapy), when they could be more objective in discussing conflicts (IBCT) and when dealing with their fears and insecurities, less negative affect would be present during interactions (EFT and Imago).

This would lead them to experiencing more intimacy, comfort, trust, and commitment in the relationship (EFT) and a higher balance in their emotional bank account (Imago). Other contributors described that Mike and Jan would be ready for termination when each could understand the other's struggles (SFT), where they were living out their preferred stories, or were feeling that their emotional and psychological needs were being met (Integrative, Feminist, and Object Relations). Relapse Prevention would be seen as involving a review of new strategies learned (CBT and RE), which would be heightened (EFT), and discussed in an attempt to plan ways to handle future external stressors (Adlerian).

Similarly IBCT and Conflict Resolution described common themes that lead to conflicts would be reviewed. The majority stated that they would be available for future sessions (Bowen, Strategic, Narrative, RE, Intersystems, IBCT, Conflict Resolution, and Object Relations). Some models explicitly described scheduling booster sessions (CBT, Adlerian, and Imago).

As can be seen in the following matrix of therapy models, there are numerous similarities and differences with each model. The following pages were designed to provide the reader with a quick overview of each model's summary, therapist's skills and attributes, modes of assessment, conceptualization, techniques, interventions, and goals of therapy.

TABLE E1 Treatment Model and Attributes

Treatment Model

	Bowen Family Systems	Strategic—Washington School	Structural Family Therapy
Summary of Model	Relationship difficulties develop from a mixture of poor differentiation of self; as a result, anxiety develops creating the forces of "togetherness" and "differentiation." Each partner's physiological and behavioral reactions within the relationship stem from family of origin.	Problem formulation is informed by a constructivist view and focuses on a therapist's optimism and client strengths. The family life-cycle stage is considered. "The problem" is viewed as "love gone wrong" (Protection) and described within an interactional context (Unit). These interactions need to be resequenced (Sequences). Marital hierarchy is also addressed.	SFT considers an ecosystemic perspective of the individual, the couple, and their social context and relates this to the issues at hand. SFT goes beyond the here-and-now and incorporates family-of-origin work. Today, SFT is much more integrative, and places greater emphasis on the therapists involvement and his/her use of self.
Therapist Skills and Attributes	Acts as a consultant or coach from an emotionally neutral stance. Engages the couple in specifying the nature of the disturbance, perception of how it should be addressed, and to supervise the couple's efforts to modify functioning. Must be able to modify his/her own emotional reactivity.	Competent in developing/maintaining the therapeutic relationship, being a catalyst to change, a skillful listener, elicit the client's worldview, understand the family life cycle, comfortable with adjusting the emotional tempo, and give directives, while being aware of the degree of the clients' motivation.	Central to SFT is focused thinking. Critical thinking is used to employ precise interventions with specific purposes in mind. The therapist must constantly evaluate the effectiveness of each intervention in order to plan his/her next move. Another key skill is the active use of self.

(continued)

TABLE E1 *(continued)*

Treatment Model

	Bowen Family Systems	Strategic—Washington School	Structural Family Therapy
Assessment Instruments	Multigenerational family diagram to broaden the perspective and connect it to family of origin. Timeline of critical events or when symptoms appeared. Elicit subjective information (i.e., what attracted you to each other?, What is your perception of the marriage?)	After the first session, both would complete an 8-page questionnaire eliciting individual and family history. Mike would be referred for a physical, neuropsychological evaluation, electroencephalogram, and endocrine work-up.	Observation of family interactions and transactions between therapist and the couple to generate structural and functional hypotheses. Use of genogram and structural diagram to assess spiritual and moral values and use them as strengths.
Conceptualization	Avoid interpretations but infers on the basis of data. Chronic tension between Mike and Jan and emotional reactivity, which leads to greater sensitivity to one another. Cognitive frameworks develop to explain or justify tension and sensitivity that is present.	Utilize the PUSH construct. There is a decrease in emotional intimacy. Both engage in a conflict-avoidant pattern. Mike often sees Jan's request as controlling. Mike presents as a loner and Jan is a caretaker. Mike's negative view of Jan resembles that of his mother.	SFT looks to identify the issue that activated the couple to seek treatment. SFT views Jan and Mike as having developmental deficits that preclude intimacy from getting started.

Goals	The short-term goals would involve defining precisely what is the nature of the problem and what Jan and Mike want to do about it. In general, the short-term goal is to decrease the intensity of anxiety. This can be measured by self-report or charting. The long-term goals would focus on enhancing differentiation of self. Success is determined by Jan and Mike.	Long-term goals would include a return to intimacy and trust, to solve conflicts in an emotionally safe way, and for both to feel safe, positive, and committed to each other. Short-term goals would be to participate in treatment, and to seek a balance between acceptance and change.	Put off discussion of divorce. Confront conflict and mutually negotiate solutions. Develop trust and intimacy. Claim personal power and responsibility for their part of the relationship.
Techniques and Interventions	The Bowenian therapist acts as a coach to help Jan and Mike think objectively in order to implement plans. S/he also works to clarify and define the relationship between partners. Emotional neutrality is a key to staying detriangled from the emotional system. S/he works to describe the family system functioning, ways to self-regulate and talk about feelings without sparking an affective charge to initiate a chain reaction and anxiety. S/he must also relate actively to each partner with an attitude of inquiry.	Each to record a list of items to be negotiated or a "want" list. Coach them into a negotiation utilizing a fun activity. Triangulate with the couple to balance each other's influence. Provide written rules for negotiating.	Focus on the free moral choices people make in their family and social interactions. Therapist and couple must view the origin and present nature of the problem in the same way. Treat couple as sharing responsibility for the problem. Personal empowerment through personal ownership of the problem.

(continued)

369

TABLE E1 (*continued*)

Treatment Model

	Bowen Family Systems	Strategic—Washington School	Structural Family Therapy
Possible Pitfalls	No pitfalls were addressed in the chapter on Bowen Family Systems.	Failure to pace the treatment process according to the needs and situation of the client. Other pitfalls would be Mike relapsing, the influence of a third party on the relationship, or failure to establish a strong therapeutic relationship.	Protecting their vulnerabilities. Confronting conflict of Jan's nagging and Mike's panicky-flight response. Need the strength of the therapist's personal connection with each to protect these vulnerabilities.
Areas to Avoid	There would be no areas avoided by the Bowenian therapist. Any issues addressed or not would be up to Jan and Mike.	If Jan and Mike explicitly asked that an issue not be addressed or if the therapist could not bring up an issue in a professional or empathic manner.	None. To feel safe, Jan and Mike must believe that they can speak about and expect understanding and caring from each other.
Whom Else to Include	This would be based on the clinician's knowledge and understanding of theory, knowledge of current situation or problem, and experience and willingness to include anyone else.	Adding people would be pursued if treatment were not meeting with success. If Mike relapsed, co-workers may be included to support sobriety.	SFT would not include anyone else with Jan and Mike in the session. They would encourage the development of a social ecosystem that would support their marriage.

Homework	Homework would be determined by Jan and Mike. A focus on increasing self-regulation skills. Possible drills and exercises in effective listening and behavior modification would also be addressed.	Homework must meet the motivation of Jan and Mike. They would be given the negotiation exercise, which involves agreeing to the rules of negotiation, exchanging a "want" list, and practicing negotiations after receiving coaching by the therapist.	Any homework given is directly related to the work done in the session. Jan and Mike may benefit by practicing volunteering their insecurities. This would be strengthened by improved listening skills: Listening to understand without analyzing or trying suggesting remedies.
Timeline for Treatment? Individual vs. couple?	This would be determined by Jan and Mike. Treatment would start weekly, then cut back to every 2 to 4 weeks. Individual sessions would be pursued if the level of emotional reactivity were too high.	The first 3 or 4 sessions would be weekly. The next 3 or 4 would be every other week. Then, sessions would be monthly or on an emergency basis. The average session would involve seeing the couple for the first half and then each individual for a quarter of the session.	No timeline would be designated. Treatment may involve some individual sessions to address each one's own insecurities and reframe them as personal wounds. A focus on helping each to communicate what they are struggling with in ways that elicit more empathy.
Termination and Relapse Prevention	When Jan and Mike are able to readjust without the help of the clinician, when the level of anxiety has decreased, and each is in better contact with the other, treatment would no longer be necessary. The clinician is always available for future consultations.	When Mike feels that Jan trusts him and does not feel overwhelmed when talking with Jan. Jan would feel that Mike is dependable and stable with regard to his sobriety. Conflicts would be solved in an emotionally safe way. Both would feel a return to intimacy and committed to the marriage. Future check-up sessions can always be scheduled.	When Mike and Jan have taken charge of solving their own problems because they have accepted responsibility for their own difficulties and can understand their partner's struggles.

(continued)

TABLE E1 *(continued)*

Treatment Model

The Intersystem Model	Cognitive-Behavioral Approach	Integrative Behavioral Couple Therapy	Integrative Marital Therapy
Views couples according to three systems: the individual, the interactional, and the intergenerational. All three are seen within a sociocultural and historical context.	Short-term structured approach, which addresses the interrelationship of partner's behaviors, cognitions, and affect. CBT with couples emanates from the behavioral treatment, which focuses on increasing positive interactions. Special attention is given to themes and patterns of responses between partners, especially automatic thoughts stemming from one's schema and common cognitive distortions. Primary treatment focus is on beliefs about the relationship, unrealistic expectations, and causal attributions and misattributions.	Builds on traditional behavioral therapy with an emphasis on promoting acceptance of the partners behavior. Primary task is conceptualizing a formulation of the couple. This includes identifying the differences each are struggling with, the polarization process that ensues and the mutual trap that results. Interventions target acceptance through emotional joining and change through objective problem analysis.	Combines a broad family systems perspective, psychodynamic therapy with an emphasis on object relations, and social learning theories. Focus is on the communication/feedback processes among the larger contexts, the couple, and the individual behaviors and psychic processes of each individual. Marital interaction is assessed based on the Five "C's": Commitment, Communication, Caring, Conflict and Compromise, and Contract. Treatment is an influence process and an educational process.

Must view problems as multifaceted and treatment as multidimensional. From this multileveled conceptualization s/he must focus on a few key issues or themes. Framed questions are used to explain the interrelationship of the three systems. Awareness of the couple's response to her/his probes will direct the process of treatment.

A directive approach using deductive reasoning skills to coach the couple in identifying the impact of their beliefs and perceptions. Provide warmth and empathy through a structured and collaborative process.

Develop a logical and accurate formulation of the couple's dilemma. Mirror the language of the couple. Attentive and active listening skills. Sensitive to emotionally salient issues, accepting of each partner. Encourage an objective perspective to problems ("it" vs. "you").

Ability to establish a trusting relationship based on kindness and sensitivity. Must be equitably committed to each client and the treatment process. Recognize and effectively address gender, cultural, and ethnic issues. Sensitively listen and elicit meaningful input from clients.

Clinical interview would be the main assessment tool. This would entail one to two sessions addressing problems and dynamics, two to explore individual histories, and a feedback/review session to develop goals. Possible testing of Mike for Attention Deficit Disorder or learning difficulties and possible psychiatric evaluation for Jan to assess depression.

Numerous self-report inventories can be used to assess attitudes, beliefs, and behaviors (i.e., ISRS, MAS, DAS, MHS, and MSI), as well as the clinical interview, would be used.

Joint and individual interviews to gather history, relationship commitment, and current problems. Two questionnaires such as the DAS and MSI-R would also be used. A feedback session concludes the evaluation process.

Conjoint and individual interviews are the principal assessment tools, which are used to explore the relationship history. Observe how each relate their concerns and manage tension.

(continued)

TABLE E1 (continued)

Treatment Model

The Intersystem Model	Cognitive-Behavioral Approach	Integrative Behavioral Couple Therapy	Integrative Marital Therapy
Jan and Mike had little emotional support/nurturance growing up. Jan has assumed a caretaker role and overfunctions in relationships. Mike avoids responsibility when faced with criticism and sees himself in a one-down position to women.	Mike presents as more needy, and his dependency seems to exacerbate within intimate relationships. Mike also appears to have been depressed for most of his life and has tried to self-medicate his pain. Mike's schema's center around self-protection and danger, as well as shortcomings in relating in intimate relationships. Jan is likely to compensate for feelings of low self-worth by being a caretaker for others, which may also be how she maintains power in relationships.	Two themes characterize the main points of contention: trust and closeness. This has resulted in polarization in which Jan is confrontational and critical and Mike is avoidant. Both feel mutually trapped, hopeless and confused, which has led to seeking treatment.	They engage in a "distancer-pursuer" pattern of interaction. Both require a significant amount of private time. Mike feels inferior to women and fearful of trusting them. He feels unappreciated by Jan. Jan feels unfulfilled.

Increase mutual involvement and feelings of togetherness. Increase social contacts (peers as well as family). Improve conflict resolution skills by understanding the circular causation of their problem and the historical context to it. Help them understand the reciprocal nature of their interactions and the role of their own behaviors. Address the pattern of over- and underfunctioning within the relationship.

Long-term goals include remaining content; learning communication and problem solving skills; understanding that a relationship takes work; and maintain sobriety. Short-term goals would include redefining the problems as objectives and identifying which are realistic in being able to change; encouraging acceptance; identify schema's about the relationship; address expectations, attributions, distortions; and target problem areas in problem-solving and communication. Progress would be based primarily on Mike and Jan's feedback, as well as self-report inventories. Success would be seen when Jan and Mike are able to identify automatic thoughts and distortions and change maladaptive behaviors.

Long-term goals: increase marital satisfaction and maintenance of improved functioning, which is measured by self-report and questionnaires (FAPBI). The short-term goals are to promote change and acceptance or tolerance, which involves an affective-cognitive shift.

Goals are set by Jan and Mike. The "Five C's" are used to determine the areas needed to be addressed. Initial goals may be "reordered" and "emerging" goals may be added. Addressing the basic trust issue would be an initial and ongoing goal. A long-term goal would involve family-of-origin issues (i.e., respectfully disqualifying their parents as authorities on marriage). Teaching communication skills and identifying that anxiety and fear are inhibiting factors to their communication problems. Progress is measured by their reports and observing them in sessions. Success would be when the treatment goals were reached, the presenting complaints were diminished, and Jan and Mike were satisfied with their new functioning.

(continued)

TABLE E1 (continued)

Treatment Model

The Intersystem Model	Cognitive-Behavioral Approach	Integrative Behavioral Couple Therapy	Integrative Marital Therapy
Behavioral exchange strategies and a focus on the positive past and present behaviors. Communication and problem solving skills (PREP approach). Explore family-of-origin issues and work toward self-differentiation. Sexual genogram to examine the impact of sexual secrets, once there was a return of trust and optimal functioning between Mike and Jan and a level of confidence in the therapeutic process was achieved.	Communication and problem solving training, behavioral change agreements, cognitive restructuring, identify automatic thoughts (i.e., use of the Dysfunctional Thought Record).	Empathic joining involves normalizing each partner's negative reaction to the other as well as promoting the expression of soft emotions. Unified detachment is used to create objectivity when problem solving. A third strategy used is tolerance building to lower the emotional reactivity. Lastly, behavior exchange, communication, and problem solving techniques would be utilized.	Sexual histories and family genograms would be obtained. Family-of-origin sessions would be pursued if unresolved background issues were isolated and thought to be best handled this way.

Mike relapsing, the negative view of treatment in Mike's family, Mike's fear of female domination (i.e., female therapist), premature termination due to a decrease in conflict and pattern of waiting until critical state within the relationship, and lastly, Jan becoming depressed.	Substance relapse and being able to identify any of Jan's enabling behaviors. Changes in behaviors when Mike is sober. Ways they avoid intimacy and problems with limits and boundaries (i.e., Mike attending Jennifer's party).	The most likely pitfall would involve Mike relapsing.	Impulsive behavior and lack of action directed toward change. Lack of trusting communication fueled by anxiety regarding the reactions of the other. Being able to refrain from jumping to conclusions or rushing to judgment.
Reasons why each chose the other for marriage, and the concern of infidelity, would be two areas the Intersystem Model would avoid with Mike and Jan.	Mike's sexual abuse would most likely be best dealt with on an individual basis. In order to avoid separating Jan and Mike, this issue would most likely be avoided.	Topics pursued would be based on the emotional saliency and relevance to the couple's theme. Therefore, only those topics that have little or no emotional impact would not be addressed.	Issues of intimacy and closeness would be addressed slowly, based on the relationship that develops between the therapist and Jan and Mike.
If Mike and Jan were interested, family-of-origin work would include sessions with their parents under the guidelines developed by Framo (1992).	Unless Jan and Mike were interested in dealing with family-of-origin issues, Jan and Mike would be the only ones included in treatment.	If Jan and Mike had children or an in-law living with them, perhaps those individuals would be included at times. Otherwise, ICT would focus solely on the marital relationship.	Others would be included if family-of-origin issues were to be addressed.

(continued)

TABLE E1 (continued)

Treatment Model

The Intersystem Model	Cognitive-Behavioral Approach	Integrative Behavioral Couple Therapy	Integrative Marital Therapy
Homework is used liberally and presented in a suggestive tone, such as psychoeducational readings and ways for them to spend more time together. Communication and conflict resolution skills practiced within the session until some mastery is achieved. Steps to becoming sexual again (i.e., cuddling instead of sleeping back-to-back).	Observational tasks involving self-monitoring and other monitoring. Experimental tasks such as trying out new behaviors, communication styles, or problem-solving strategies. An example would be to have Jan and Mike practice active listening without interrupting each other.	Chapters from the ICT book for couples would be assigned as needed. Fake negative incidents to observe the pattern of interaction that results. Communication strategies, problem solving techniques, and behavioral exchange strategies may also be utilized.	Practice communication patterns discussed in sessions. Engage in more shared activities and socially with others. Good faith contracts involving doing something for each other without keeping score.
Three to four months of intensive couples treatment. If this were to be successful, then another 3 to 4 months weekly, then biweekly. Individual sessions if a stalemate develops.	At least 6 months of weekly sessions and approximately 2 months of sessions being every 10 to 14 days. After the last session, a follow-up session about two months later would be scheduled. This could be conducted by phone or in the office.	Determined from one session to the next. In general, 25 weekly sessions lasting 6 to 7 months. As acceptance and tolerance techniques are mastered, sessions may be spread further apart until a mutually determined termination time is scheduled.	Frequency would be negotiated with Jan and Mike. Individual sessions to take sexual histories. Any individual issues would not be referred out. Consultation with a vocational specialist might be considered for Mike.

At termination, Jan and Mike would be able to discuss their problems with greater ease and less defensiveness. They would recover from conflicts quicker without separating. There would be more shared activities, including sex and more socializing with friends. Future sessions available as needed.	Termination is discussed early in treatment and focuses on identifying ways to avoid slipping back in to old patterns of thinking or behaving. Reviewing new strategies learned and brainstorming possible problem scenarios in the future and how Jan and Mike would manage them would all be part of relapse prevention. Booster sessions are also always available and encouraged.	Termination is mutually determined. In the last session, feedback from the therapist and couple is discussed. There is a review of the formulation, how they have achieved unified detachment, which will provide objectivity in discussing conflicts and empathic joining regarding their conflicts, which will be less intense due to the empathic joining. Relapse prevention is built in by identifying the themes and differences that lead to the conflicts. Future sessions are available as needed.	If planned, termination would involve a review of the "Five C's." Each would have achieved a greater differentiation from family-of-origin issues. Anxiety would be lower and trust would be greater. Each would report feeling that their psychological and emotional needs were being met satisfactorily. Relapse prevention would be addressed by discussing plans of how they might handle future problems as well as growth.

(continued)

TABLE E1 *(continued)*

Treatment Model

Object Relations	Adlerian	Narrative	Imago
Central focus is on understanding and interpreting the mutual projective and introjective identificatory system of the marriage. Patterns of interaction, related to family of origin, are identified and reworked.	A systems theory that is holistic, purposive, cognitive, and social, which focuses on the relationship or the patterns of interaction between the two. The communication and movement (cooperative or resistant) between the partners represents the expression of intentions and goals of each individual. How each thinks and feels influences their choices and how they behave, which creates the organization and pattern of the relationship or system.	Stories shape our lives and are our lives. Change occurs by changing the couple's stories. The dominant stories in a society are interconnected by the networks of language, beliefs, institutions, customs, and laws. These networks are referred to as discourses. Problems are the result of limiting and unsatisfying stories of oneself, others, and the world, and of invisible, or taken for granted, discourses.	Utilizes "couples dialogue" to enhance understanding of self and their partner without defensiveness. Empathy is deepened to "reimage" the other as an ally vs. an enemy. Frustrations are converted into desires, which are turned into Behavior Change Requests. Couples are encouraged to engage in caring behaviors, belly laughs, and to develop a vision for the marriage.

Primary skill is setting the frame. Must be able to identify repeated patterns of interaction and determine what protective purpose they serve. Maintain a neutral position of impartiality to create a psychological space for sharing of thoughts and feelings. Interpret defenses, anxiety, fantasy and inner object relations and be able to work with transferences and countertransferences.	Must establish a mutual and collaborative relationship. Be able to encourage and empower the couple. Focus on what they do rather then what they say. Recognize movement that is cooperative or resistant. Guide communication toward positive interaction. Help them understand the meaning they are giving to their experiences.	Maintain a worldview, which leads to improvisation and creativity. Confront the discourses that limit people while they pursue their preferred directions in life. Use the language of the couple. Create a sense of community and collaboration.	A belief in the healing aspects of relationships, self-growth and in attaining wholeness. IRT therapists meet educational and experience requirements, participate in an Imago couples weekend, and continue in supervision with a more experienced Imago therapist.
Clinical interview, which would assess how they deal with the therapist, enter the treatment process and how the therapist responds to Jan and Mike. Sexual history would be addressed through interview or through questionnaire.	Assessment is a process that starts immediately. A lifestyle analysis of each individual, which explores family-of-origin issues, early recollections, and the influence of birth order. The lifestyle formulation provides the therapist and couple with an overall pattern of relating. MCMI would also be utilized as well as "the question."	Standardized instruments and testing are usually not used. Questions aimed at inviting Jan and Mike to tell more satisfying and useful stories are used. Questions that help them locate the problems in their discourses and allow them to decide where they want their relationship to be, in spite of such discourses.	Imago work-up, which asks about early childhood caretakers. The clinical lecture/interview, which educates Jan and Mike on developmental stages of childhood from an IRT perspective. This also addresses the role of their developmental wounding as it relates to their choice of mate.

(continued)

TABLE E1 *(continued)*

Treatment Model

Object Relations	Adlerian	Narrative	Imago
Jan projects her needy part of herself into Mike, which she did previously with her younger brother. Mike projects into Jan the critical controlling part of his mother, with whom he is still attached. Jan feels abandoned by Mike, as she does by her parents. Jan resembles a nagging mother who frets and fusses over her troubled boy (Mike), who in response tries to avoid and tune out this nagging mother figure (Jan).	Jan was a parentified child. She tends to exert control over circumstances, is hard working and decisive, and critical and suspicious of other's motives. Mike is more of a loner with avoidant traits. He seems to suffer from inferiority feelings. He avoids conflicts, negates in emotional stonewalling, and passively expresses anger and rage. Each has married a parental figure.	No conceptualization in terms of healthy or unhealthy behavior or rational or irrational cognitions. Instead, the material presented are expressions of Jan and Mike's experiences.	Jan and Mike are almost emotionally bankrupt and have poor problem-solving skills. Mike underestimates his abilities and self-worth. Jan was parentified growing up. She has learned to overfunction and responds to Mike's inadequacy with criticism. Their relationship has developed into resentment and isolation. They avoid being together in order to avoid the chance of confrontations.

382

Short-term goals would involve restabilizing their social support network and rebuilding their context of shared activities. Learning how to face and analyze their conflicts as well as reversing their sexual withdrawal would be medium ranged goals. A long-term goal would be rebuilding intimacy. Goals are not geared toward symptom resolution but rather being able to face their conflicts, re-evaluate their choice of partner, and decide whether to recommit to the relationship or to separate.

Techniques consist of maintaining a listening attitude, being able to follow and recognize patterns, observing your own feelings, and making interpretations. The primary intervention is being able to use the countertransference to interpret the transference. Countertransference is used to create an understanding as to what it is like to be Jan and Mike.

Long-term goals would involve Mike adopting a healthier view of women and increase his ability to handle tension, as well as reduce Jan's tendency to be critical and be able to express softer emotions. Short-term goals, increase the amount of positive time together and type and amount of appreciation for each other, continue to point out the strengths and for Mike to maintain his sobriety.

Techniques focus on therapeutic questions. Focus would also be on solutions instead of problems. Teaching congruent communication, encouragement, and problem-solving, as well as psychoeducational strategies to address learning deficits related to family-of-origin issues would also be pursued.

To help Jan and Mike experience themselves as living out preferred stories of themselves individually and as a couple. Goals are considered projects. Instead of a problem of conflict-avoidance, a project of closeness would be pursued.

Techniques are referred to as practices. Questions, transparency, helping Jan and Mike externalize the problem by engaging them in externalizing conversations, writing letters, and having others present as witnesses to the couple's new and preferred story.

Long-term goal would include learning to maintain contact, encouraging each other in their personal and self-development and having fun with each other spontaneously. Short-term goals would include learning to dialogue to improve communication skills. Other short-term goals would be to develop problem-solving skills, adding positive behaviors in their daily lives, and to learn to use their relationship to heal childhood wounds.

A reconnection ritual when they come home each day. Learning the couples dialogue process. Convert frustrations into specific and positive Behavior Change Requests.

(continued)

TABLE E1 (continued)

Treatment Model

Object Relations	Adlerian	Narrative	Imago
Any unrecognized transference would be a potential pitfall.	Mike's inability to follow through on treatment objectives. Jan might be critical of the treatment process.	No pitfalls would be anticipated.	The biggest pitfall may be that treatment is too late. Another pitfall would be that each view their way as the "right way." Another would be that they do not buy into the IRT model.
No areas would be off limits. However, any sensitive topic would be addressed tactfully. Timing is important and a comfortable atmosphere must be established in order to address the trigger points to any sensitive area.	Mike's feelings of inferiority would be avoided, as well as their decision to not have children.	No areas would be avoided.	Topics come from the couple. However, issues such as Jan's cancer, her hysterectomy, the decision to not have children, Jan's feelings about Mike's past substance abuse and the fears of relapse would not be brought up until the relationship was stronger.
No other family members or friends would be included. There would be collaboration with any other treating professional involved.	No one else would be included in treatment.	Community is valued. Others would be included through inquiries about how they might view Jan and Mike, asking others to write letters of how they experience them, as well as inviting them into sessions.	Others are generally not included in IRT. If Mike really had ADD testing medications would be recommended. If Jan showed signs of depression, other treatment methods might be pursued.

Homework or special assignments would not be part of treatment unless sex therapy exercises were indicated.

Homework tasks would include controlled dialogue, encouragement meetings to increase positive exchanges, taking turns dating, and business meetings regarding their relationship, and attendance at Narcotics Anonymous meetings.

Writing letters to Jan and Mike summarizing their preferred stories and asking questions that could enhance further development of those stories.

Practicing the IRT couples dialogue. Writing out frustrations and convert them into desires and then into BCRs. Together they would write out what their perfect relationship would look like. List positive behaviors they would like each other to do and do it.

Sessions would be once a week or twice a week for 45 minutes. Individual sessions would only be pursued if an issue could not yet be raised with the other partner. If one individual's problems dominated the treatment, a referral would be made for individual treatment.

Treatment would last approximately 6 months involving 10 to 14 sessions. One individual session for each one would be part of treatment. Additional individual sessions would be scheduled as needed.

The frequency and length of treatment would be up to Jan and Mike. Individual sessions would be provided if requested. The idea of referring to an outside therapist would be discussed.

Typically, treatment is 10 to 12 sessions one and one half-hour every other week. A weekend couples workshop would also be recommended. Individual sessions would not be necessary.

(continued)

TABLE E1 *(continued)*

Treatment Model

Object Relations	Adlerian	Narrative	Imago
When unconscious projective identifications have been recognized, owned and taken back by each partner, love has been restored, sexual relationship is mutually gratifying, and when each other's needs can be differentiated and met termination would be pursued. Follow-up sessions would not be scheduled, but would be available if they would feel the need. Relapse prevention would involve Jan and Mike practicing the lessons learned in treatment, i.e., expressing their feelings, listening respectfully, and owning their own contributions.	Termination would involve a gradual increase in time between sessions. Relapse prevention would involve being able to engage them in the homework tasks, matching treatment strategies to their unique needs, and developing planned ways to handle external stressors. Booster sessions would be scheduled at 3 months and then at 6 months for the next 2 years, and then yearly.	Termination would be up to Jan and Mike. They could return any time. When Jan and Mike are living out their preferred stories, termination would be successful.	The couple generally determines termination. Therapy would be complete when they have more knowledge of each other's likes and dislikes, increase their fondness and admiration behaviors, build up their emotional bank account, and have good problem-solving skills. They would also be more involved in each other's personal and career goals. Relapse would be addressed by scheduling appointments every 3 to 6 months for at least a couple of years.

Treatment Model

Feminist Couples Therapy	Client-Directed, Outcome-Informed	Emotionally Focused Couples Therapy	Relationship Enhancement
An approach that is sensitive to the distribution of power, privilege, and responsibilities between men and women and is addressed in assessment and treatment. The change process addresses the here-and-now issues at the behavioral level first. If unsuccessful, treatment must focus on the domain of belief or meaning. If still unsuccessful, treatment should focus more directly on the feelings of the couple. Problems are examined based on 6 metaframeworks: internal process, sequences, organization, development, culture, and gender.	Identifies and expands on client resources, worldview, and experiences. Clients are seen as the stars of the therapy. This approach intertwines what the clients bring to treatment—client factor, the creation of a positive therapeutic alliance—relationship factor, a belief in the restorative powers of treatment—expectancy factor, and treatment techniques—model factor.	EFT looks at and understands adult love relationships based on attachment theory, which parallels feminist ideology in validating the desire for emotional responsiveness and is also compatible to systems theory. Distressed couples struggle for a secure attachment and become stuck in the factors characteristic of separation. EFT is based in the humanistic movement and holds strongly to the power of validating clients and respecting their reality.	An educational skill-training model, which teaches couples how to feel attached and emotionally engaged with one another. This engagement is based on interpersonal reflexes. Stress and conflict act as opportunities to deepen the engagement. Constructive relationship skills, precepts of non-judgment and acceptance are taught. RE is based on 3 skills: expressive (owning), empathic responder (receptive), and conversive (discussion-negotiation).

(continued)

TABLE E1 *(continued)*

Treatment Model

Feminist Couples Therapy	Client-Directed, Outcome-Informed	Emotionally Focused Couples Therapy	Relationship Enhancement
Must be comfortable working within an egalitarian relationship structure. The therapist must minimize the power and expertise differences between him or herself and the couple. Must be attuned to his/her own beliefs about the meaning of gender and make gender a part of treatment that is not shaming, aggressive, naïve, or polemical.	Must maximize client resources, form a strong alliance, and structure treatment around the clients goals and expectations. Must believe in the client's ability to know what is best and how to achieve that. Must be able to connect, listen, and demonstrate an understanding of others. Must be able to adapt the clients' values and expectations. Above all, must have an unwavering belief in human potential.	Must be able to create safety and to be empathetically attuned to both partners. S/he needs to be comfortable with the strong emotions that unfold in sessions. Needs to reflect and validate particular responses, heighten particular responses, and restructure interactions based on expanding emotional responses.	Must be able to engage couples during conflict and high arousal states. Other qualities include: empathy, genuineness, acceptance, and humility of one's own limitations. There are also 10 leadership/therapist skills: administering, structuring, demonstrating, reinforcing, modeling, prompting, supervising home tasks, doubling, and troubleshooting for self and for couple.
Clinical interviews, which would inquire about how the problem gets in the way of their relationship and what stops them from solving it. The problem would be explored from each metaframework. Individual sessions would be conducted to assess for partner violence.	Clinical interview utilizing "checking-out questions." Questionnaires such as the Session Rating Scale and the Outcome Questionnaire 45 are given each session and reviewed with the clients. The focus is on collaborating with the clients in order to determine the process of treatment.	The primary tools used are the Dyadic Adjustment Scale and clinical interview with the couple and each partner. An attachment history of each partner is elicited to learn how and to what degree each partner is sought and received comfort from attachment figures in family of origin.	Problems are formulated based on a collaborative process and the notion of equivalence. The clinical interview is the primary assessment tool. Inventories/questionnaires, such as Prepare/Enrich and the Interpersonal Checklist, which focus on the reflexive nature of human functioning are sometimes used.

Mike underfunctions and withdraws when Jan reacts angrily and confronts him. Jan acts as the relationship leader, from which she feels burdened. Mike feels that his needs/wishes are seen as unimportant. Jan may have a mild chronic depression, is severely undernurtured and unsure how to have such emotional needs met. Mike may be the "forgotten child" in his family and was sexually abused, which was probably traumatic. He has used drugs to numb out most of his life and has had little experience managing his affect. Mike has learned to expect criticism/hostility from women.

Conceptualization is based on direct observation of the interaction between clients and therapist, while being aware of the "lens" the therapist is using to view their clients. Conceptualization is based on the positives and the strengths of the clients: i.e., mutual interests, job stability, personal outside interests, desire to stay together.

Jan presents with an anxious or preoccupied attachment style and will need help in discussing her loneliness on weekends. Mike is fearful and avoidant and will need help in reframing his attachment needs.

Mike has used substances to deal with anxiety and unhappiness. An endogenous depression may be present. He has issues of abandonment from his father and dependency on his mother. Jan often functioned as a co-parent. She continues to take care of others, which is safer than depending on them. They have a dependent relationship. Both engage in rigid coping styles and have inefficient communication skills.

(continued)

TABLE E1 (continued)

Treatment Model

Feminist Couples Therapy	Client-Directed, Outcome-Informed	Emotionally Focused Couples Therapy	Relationship Enhancement
Mike's sobriety would be the first goal. Another goal would be to increase the number of caregiving and attachment behaviors. Fights would be left for the office as much as possible. Long-term goal would be to develop an idea of what kind of marriage each of them want and how intimate they want to be. Self-report would be the primary outcome measure. When Jan and Mike are able to solve problems together and enjoy each other, therapy would be considered successful.	Mike wants to not feel like he is under a microscope and Jan wants to feel that Mike is really listening. Developing trust would be a primary goal. Treatment goals would be constantly clarified. The steps to achieve the goals and measure progress would make up the treatment plan.	One goal would be to help them de-escalate the pattern of criticizing and distancing. Another goal would be to help them create more emotional engagement and to expand their interactional positions (i.e., Mike to be actively involved and Jan to soften). Short-term goals would follow the 9 steps to change. Success would be when both can unlatch from their negative interactive cycle, are less reactive, more engaged emotionally, and more responsive to each other. Progress would be measured through various scales (DAS, MSIS, RTS, and CTAS).	Goals would be mutually agreed upon and realistic. Specifically they would involve increasing emotional intimacy, decreasing conflicts, and increasing resolution to differences.

390

Increase the frequency and awareness of small, positive changes between each other. Caring Days exercise based on each other's list of what they would consider the other could do to show caring. Conflict resolution management would be taught, specifically Notarius and Markman's (1994) method.

There are 3 pitfalls to working with Mike and Jan.
1. Minimizing Mike's addiction and therefore his risk of relapse;
2. Focusing too much on the addiction issue, which would make Mike the problem and discourage him;
3. Due to Mike's use of substances to manage strong affect, exposing him to such circumstances may threaten his sobriety.

Amplifying the positive interactions already occurring (i.e., talking in the barn) and expand these into other settings. Focus on times that things are going well and think of the future. Interventions are collaboratively fashioned with Jan and Mike and must fit their worldview and expectations. They must create hope and strengthen the alliance and trust and further their involvement in treatment.

"Attribution creep"—the therapist believing that Mike's alcoholism is "the" problem. Another pitfall would be repeated use of an ineffective strategy. Another pitfall would be ignoring or dismissing Jan and Mike's beliefs of how change can occur. Neglecting their motivations and perceptions will inevitably lead to "resistance."

Tracking (i.e., of Mike's experiences of feeling dumb or criticized by Jan). Heightening (i.e., to clarify Jan's attachment fears). Evocative questioning (i.e., to help Jan articulate Jan's hurts). Disquisition to address the couple's dance. Structure interactions (i.e., to help Jan ask for what she needs).

A primary pitfall would center on Mike's abuse history. A concern would be how this has affected his ability to trust Jan or if it keeps him feeling unworthy, shameful or degraded. Need to check out if certain interactions trigger memories of Mike's abuse.

Draw upon the therapist/leadership skills. Structure interactions to practice the speaker-listener-conversive skill.

One pitfall would involve family-of-origin issues. Other pitfalls could be egocentrism of either partner, subtle conflicts that the therapist is unaware of, regression once treatment becomes less frequent, possibility of Mike relapsing or any physiological effects from use, and any unresolved anger in Jan regarding having to take care of her brother.

(continued)

TABLE E1 (continued)

Treatment Model

Feminist Couples Therapy	Client-Directed, Outcome-Informed	Emotionally Focused Couples Therapy	Relationship Enhancement
Areas would not be avoided, but rather approached cautiously, such as pushing for too much intimacy until there is a stronger foundation of caring behaviors. Another area would be focusing on Mike's substance use history without making it clear to him that that is not the whole problem. Lengthy discussion of what is wrong with their sexual relationship would be another area. Unless family-of-origin issues was constraining their relationship currently, this would not be addressed.	Areas addressed in treatment are based on the clients' worldviews and expectations. Jan and Mike would determine the direction and destination of treatment. The challenge for the therapist is to be able to attend to each individual's view while staying connected and respectful to both.	No areas would be avoided; however, the primary focus would be Mike and Jan's relationship.	The "speaker" is responsible for any topics they wish to address. The therapist would not limit treatment by judging what topics could or could not be addressed. If any area outside the expertise of the RE therapist were brought up, an appropriate referral would be made (i.e., major mental illness needing to be stabilized).
Others would be included only if family-of-origin issues were to become a focus. Individual therapy would be referred to another therapist and phone contact with that person would be important.	Any resource to the couple may be included. For example, a member of their support network may be invited into sessions, or Jan and Mike may be referred to community resources (i.e., self-help groups).	No others would be included in treating Mike and Jan. Consultations would be made with any individual therapists involved (i.e., if Mike saw someone about his abuse).	Including family members is very much a part of RE. If family-of-origin issues were to arise, an intensive, usually one-time extended session (6–18 hr.) would be pursued.

Homework would consist more of suggestions such as experiments or data collection, something that would be worth noticing.

Homework would focus on the positives (i.e., record times you notice the other doing or being like the person you fell in love with). Any homework is "checked out" to see if it "fits" for Jan and Mike. This is done to stay on track with the therapeutic alliance.

Homework focuses on the couple developing more awareness (i.e., experiments of discussing how each experienced a session) vs. practicing certain behaviors.

Homework would involve giving out the Client Guidelines and Goal Hierarchy List, which they are to modify and bring in to each session. They would be asked to arrange special time to practice the RE skills. These conversations would be audio-taped and later reviewed in sessions.

Weekly sessions including an individual session with each of them as part of the assessment process. Once a reasonably strong alliance was formed, sessions would become bi-weekly. Individual treatment would be recommended if progress was being constrained by one or both partners' intrapsychic issues.

As with all aspects of treatment, the timeline would be determined by the clients. Individual sessions would be offered if requested by either Jan or Mike. Self-report and assessments that portray the client's experience of progress and satisfaction would also be used.

About 15 weekly sessions depending on how much of an impact the abuse had and how responsive they were to the therapy process. Individual sessions may be pursued if an impasse occurs.

Generally 10 sessions over 3 to 6 months. The intake and early stage of treatment can be extended if need be. Booster sessions are also available. Individual sessions can be part of the couples treatment. If individual issues were overriding the couples work, a referral would be made.

(continued)

Treatment Model

Feminist Couples Therapy	Client-Directed, Outcome-Informed	Emotionally Focused Couples Therapy	Relationship Enhancement
Termination would involve stretching out the time between sessions until Jan and Mike felt comfortable not meeting for a month at a time. Sessions during termination would focus on continued refinement of the solutions they have been using, a review of what they have learned about themselves and each other, and how to maintain the relationship. Each person would also offer feedback on the treatment experience. When they have learned how to establish new thoughts and actions regarding what it means to be a couple, when they can recognize their needs and ask each other for what they want, and when they are able to collaborate and manage conflicts effectively, they would be ready for termination.	Jan and Mike's assessment of progress is seen as a sign of their resourcefulness. The therapist would help them to determine the degree to which their goals for treatment have been reached. At termination, sessions would focus on reviewing the newly acquired skills and relapse prevention would involve discussing plans of how to handle problems when they re-emerge. The pros and cons of ending would also be discussed. Jan and Mike would be thanked for teaching the therapist how couples can overcome hurdles and asked if the solutions they have used could be shared with other couples. This would empower Jan and Mike and transition them from helped to helper.	Once a secure attachment develops, new solutions to old problems can be discussed. Relapse prevention would be addressed by reviewing the gains from treatment and heightening the new interactional patterns learned. At termination, both would be able to regulate their fears and insecurities resulting in having less negative affect between them. They would be able to stay more engaged emotionally, resulting in more intimacy. They would be able to solve problems more effectively. They would also have expanded their ability to care and confide in each other, which would expand how they comfort each other.	Termination is discussed in the first sessions when treatment is explained to be structured, systematic, and time-designated. The training aspects of treatment, the home practice with supervision of audiotapes, and regularly scheduled booster sessions all address termination. Relapse prevention is addressed through the reviewing of progress made, the RE learned in treatment, and in preparing Jan and Mike to request a booster session when feeling a regression in the relationship.

TABLE E1 (continued)

	Conflict Resolution and Conflict-Focused Therapy
Summary of Model	Conflict produces tensions; conflict resolution yields relief of tensions. Unresolved conflicts create emotional distress. Conflicts occur on an intra-psychic level, between people, and between people and life circumstances. The interaction between people are reflective of their attachment bond. Conflict resolution treatment focuses on removing symptoms, resolving current sources of tension, and teaching conflict dialogue skills.
Therapist Skills and Attributes	Must be able to listen closely and accurately, convey warmth, be tactful, and show optimism and conviction in that conflicts can be resolved.
Assessment Instruments	Symptom checklist to identify areas for clinical questioning. Have the couple create a laundry list of the issues producing tension. Clinical observation and evaluation of the couple's conflict resolution skills. A key life events history would also be obtained.
Conceptualization	Neither were fortunate to develop a secure attachment with their parents. As adults, this poor attachment pattern has continued and evolved into a circular pattern of Mike avoiding or being "undependable" and Jan "nagging." Mike's drug use was another way to avoid. Mike shows depressive resignation, and his withdrawal agitates Jan, who resorts to attacking. This pattern of avoidance and ineffective communication keeps them from discussing serious matters.
Goals	Long-term goals include having better communication (cooperative dialogue skills) and conflict resolution. Goals would be measured by self-report of Jan and Mike feeling more connected, intimate, able to discuss upsets and turn them into shared learning experiences and be able to dialogue without the therapist's help. Anger, depression, and tension will turn into affection, laughter and emotional well being.

(continued)

TABLE E1 *(continued)*

Conflict Resolution and Conflict-Focused Therapy

Techniques and Interventions	Elicit laundry list. The couple will pick what to address at the start of each session. Conflict resolution skills. Visualize a stop sign when feeling anger. Encourage mutual empowerment through cooperative dialogue. Identify core concerns and utilize depth dives to guide resolution to specific conflicts. Coach listening skills and to use "I" statements while focusing on behaviors. Use role-plays to practice a disengagement-reengagement routine.
Possible Pitfalls	Mike's history of quitting activities increases the risk of him quitting treatment. Both will need consistent feedback on their progress. Refocusing Jan's stance of blaming may backfire. Threats of divorce and loud arguments will need to cease.
Areas to Avoid	Whether or not Mike had an affair at Jennifer's party and Mike's sexual molestation would be the two areas avoided, unless Mike or Jan brought it up.
Who Else to Include	Families of origin may be included from time to time, but only if Jan and Mike wanted to add this to their treatment.
Homework	Read a chapter a week from *The Power of Two: Secrets to a Strong and Loving Marriage* or the audiotape *Conflict Resolution for Couples*. Review the audiotapes of each session to consolidate learning.
Timeline for Treatment? Individual vs. Couple?	Approximately 3 to 6 months in 12 to 25 sessions. Medication may be pursued to ease depressive physiology or if Mike's Attention Deficit Disorder was complicating his functioning. Individual sessions would not be referred out. Confidentiality would be held for each individual.
Termination and Relapse Prevention	Can range from a summary session or two to a tapering off. Future sessions could be arranged anytime either one requested them. Prevention would be addressed by specifying the signs that would indicate slippage into old patterns and identifying strengths and skills learned in treatment.

It is evident that the approaches discussed in this text have many similarities in terms of conceptualization, assessment, and treatment of Mike and Jan. As we stated earlier however, no model can be all things to all people. It was our intention, and our recommendation, that this book serve as an example of the vast richness available in the treatment of couples. Hopefully, what has been highlighted in each chapter is the best that each approach has to offer. What is most striking is that each approach has distinct and unique characteristics of its own. We hope that you have been able to identify with certain aspects of each model in order to develop your own integrative approach to treating couples, and to find a path of effectiveness that fits your own individual style of treatment.

Index

Page numbers in *italics* indicate figures. Page numbers followed by "t" indicate tables.

AAMC. *See* American Association of Marriage Counselors

AAMFC. *See* American Association of Marriage and Family Counselors

AAMFT. *See* American Association of Marriage and Family Therapy

Abstractions, selective, cognitive-behavioral therapy and, 139

Absurdity, in directives, strategic therapy, 62

Acceptance, integrative behavioral couple therapy and, 186, 187, 188

Ackerman Institute, 6

Actions, of therapist, in Adlerian therapy, 106–108

Adler, Alfred. *See also* Adlerian therapy contribution of, 2

Adlerian therapy, 102–115, 380–386
actions, of therapist, 106–108
attributes, of therapist, 106–108
belief systems of couple, 104
constructivist therapy, 102
cooperation between partners, problems of, 102
couple system, 105
creative capacity, perceptions, meaning and, 104
Dreikurs, R., 103
lifestyles of partners, fitting together, 104
"masculine protest," concept of, 108
Milton Clinical Multi-Axial Inventory, 108

miracle question, 108
model, 102–105
patterns, of interaction partners, focuses on, 102
phenomenology, 106
purpose, of actions, 103
purposes of behavior, 105
relational conflict, attraction and, 103
relationship system, created by couple, 105
responsibility to decide, 104
sample case study, 108–114
assessment, 108–109, 109–110
conceptualization, 108–109, 110–114
homework, 113
relapse prevention, 113–114
termination, 113–114
timeline, 113
self-esteem, couple happiness, 104
skills, of therapist, 106–108
social interest, couple happiness, 104
subjective perceptions, 104
therapeutic questioning, 108
treatment model, 102–105

Affiliation, religious, of client, addressing, 46

Agreement, requirement for, in Imago relationship therapy, 117

American Association of Marriage and Counseling, 4

American Association of Marriage and Family Counselors, 5

American Association of Marriage and Family Therapy, 5

American Association of Marriage Counselors, formation of, 4

American Psychiatric Association, 1

Anger, dealing with, in Imago relationship therapy, 119

Anxiety
interpretation of, in object relations therapy, 85
in relationship field, differentiation of self and, 3–43
suppression of, 25

Anxiety field, ability to manage self in, 25

Attachment
need for, infant, 82
struggle for, 165

Attachment theory, 164

Attraction, relational conflict and, 103

Attributions, in relationship interactions, 139

Automatic thoughts
cognitive-behavioral therapy and, 139
identifying, 150–152

Bateson, Gregory, contribution of, 5

Bateson Project, 5

BCR. *See* Behavior Change Request

"Because" clause, use of, in object relations therapy, 85

Behavior change agreements, in cognitive-behavioral therapy, 149–150

Behavior Change Request, restructuring frustrations through, 118

Behavioral contract, in cognitive-behavioral therapy, 138

Behavioral marital therapy, 9

Behaviorism, synthesis of in Imago relationship therapy, 116

Belief systems of couple, in Adlerian therapy, 104

Beliefs, dominant story of society and, 342

Berman, E., 229

Biased explanations, cognitive-behavioral therapy and, 140

Bion, Wilfred, study of groups, 84

Boszormenyi-Nagy, Ivan, contribution of, 7

Bowen, Murray, contribution of, 25

Bowen family systems theory, 25–44, 367–371
anxiety
field, ability to manage self in, 25
in relationship field, differentiation of self and, 3–43
attributes, of therapist, 31–32
Bowen, Murray, contribution of, 25
catecholamines, flooding frontal lobes with, 25
coach, therapist as, 31
consultant, therapist as, 31
decisions, differentiated individual, 26
differentiated individuals, behavioral characteristics of, 26
differentiation
abilities with, 25
oppositional pressures toward, 26
of self, 3–43
digestive functions, suppression of, with anxiety, 25
emotional reactivity, of clinician, management of, 32
expansion of two-person system, into three-person system, 27
family diagram, 33
growth, anxiety suppression of, 25
hypothalamic-pituitary-adrenal axis, activation of, 25
immune functions, suppression of, with anxiety, 25
importance of therapist, reduction of, 31
limbic system, behavior coordination, 25
lower brain processes, coordination of behavior, 25
nature of relationships, differentiation and, 26
reactivity, emotional, of clinician, management of, 32
relationship
differences among participants in, 26
nature of, differentiation and, 26

reproductive functions, suppression of, with anxiety, 25
sample case study, 32–44
  areas to avoid, 40–41
  assessment, 32–35, *33*
  conceptualization, 35–37
  family members, inclusion of, 41
  homework, 41–42
  interventions, 38–40
  relapse prevention, 43
  techniques, 38–40
  termination, 43
  timeline, 33
  timeline for therapy, 42
  treatment goals, 37–38
self, differentiation, 25
  anxiety in relationship field, 3–43
skills, of therapist, 31–32
"solid self," 30
sympathetic nervous system, activation of, 25
togetherness, pressures toward, 26
"togetherness force," 26
treatment model, 25–31
triangling process, 27
two-person system, problems in, 28
Brief family therapy center, 6
Bruner, Jerome, 342

Calming, to listen without defensiveness, 116
Caring, integrative marital therapy and, 212
Carter, Betty, 8
Case study, 21–22
  overview, 13–14
Catecholamines, fontal lobe and, 25
CBMT. *See* Cognitive-behavioral marital therapy
Centering, to listen without defensiveness, 116
Change
  momentum of, strategic therapy and, 63
  promotion of, integrative behavioral couple therapy and, 187
  stages of, 165–166

Child abuse, 18
Church communities, support of, via religion, 47
Circular questioning, use of, 6
Client-directed, outcome-informed approach, 301–324, 387–394
  attributes, of therapist, 304
  expectancy, 303
  hope, 303
  Outcome Questionnaire 45, 305
  Session Rating Scale, 305
Coach, therapist as
  in Bowen family systems theory, 31
  in conflict resolution therapy, 252
Coaching of negotiation, strategic therapy, 62
Cognitive-behavioral approach, 372–379
Cognitive-behavioral marital therapy, 9
Cognitive-behavioral theory, 135–160
Cognitive-behavioral therapy, 135–160, 372–379
  analytic perspective, 141
  arbitrary inference, 139
  assessment, 142–144
  attributes, of therapist, 141–142
  attributions, in relationship interactions, 139
  automatic thoughts, 139
  biased explanations, 140
  cognitive distortions, found among couples, 139
  cognitive restructuring techniques, 138
  contract, behavioral, 138
  deductive reasoning, 141
  defensiveness, patterns of, 138
  dichotomous thinking, 139
  Dyadic Adjustment Scale, 143
  dysfunctional beliefs, about relationships, 139
  interventions, 148–152
  inventory, 141
  Inventory of Specific Relationships Standards, 143
  labeling, 140
  magnification, 140
  Marital Happiness Scale, 143
  Marital Satisfaction Inventory, 143

Standards *(continued)*
mind reading, 140
minimization, 140
mislabeling, 140
Model Attitude Survey, 143
overgeneralization, 139
personalization, 139
pleasing *vs.* aversive behavior, between partners, exchange of, 137
questionnaires, 141
Relationship Belief Inventory, 143
sample case study
automatic thoughts, identifying, 150–152
behavior change agreements, 149–150
behavioral interventions, 148
cognitive interventions, 150
communication training, 149
conceptualization, 144–156
family members, inclusion of, 153
homework, 153–154
pitfalls, 152–153
problem-solving training, 149
relapse prevention, 155–156
techniques, 148–152
termination, 155–156
timeline for therapy, 154–155
treatment goals, 146–147
selective abstractions, 139
self-instructional procedures, to decrease destructive interaction, 139
skills, of therapist, 141–142
social exchange theory, 138
treatment model, 137–141
tunnel vision, 140
unrealistic expectations in relationship, 139
withdrawal, patterns of, 138
Cognitive distortions, found among couples, 139
Cognitive restructuring techniques, 138
Collaborative problem solving, steps of, 248
Commitment, integrative marital therapy and, 211

Communication
among schizophrenics, 5
integrative marital therapy and, 212
Communication training
in cognitive-behavioral therapy, 149
integrative behavioral couple therapy and, 188
Comparative psychological treatment of couples, overview, 21
Complementarity, focus on, integrative marital therapy and, 211
Compromise, integrative marital therapy and, 212
Conflict, defined, 247-248
Conflict resolution, defined, 247–248
Conflict resolution therapy, 247–272, 395
attributes, of therapist, 251–252
coach, therapist as, 252
collaborative problem solving, steps of, 248
conflict, defined, 247–248
conflict resolution patterns, consequences, 249
conflict resolution theory, 248–249, 249t, 250
dysfunctional, *vs.* emotionally skillful individuals, 249
emotional distress, conflict theory of, 249t, 249–250
guide, therapist as, 252
healer, therapist as, 252
intrapsychic realm, conflicts within, 247
other treatment philosophies, relationship of, 250–251
sample case study, 252–271
anger, treating, 262
anxiety, treating, 263
avoidance, treating, 263
conceptualization, 254–260
depression, treating, 262–263
family members, inclusion of, 268–269
homework, 269
pitfalls, 267–268
relapse prevention, 271
techniques, 261–267

termination, 271
timeline, 269–271
treatment goals, 260–261
traffic police, therapist as, 252
treatment model, 247–251
"win-win waltz," 248
Conflict Tactics Scale, 182
Constructions, therapist's, strategic therapy, 59
Constructivist therapy, in Adlerian therapy, 102
Constructs, of presenting problem, development of, strategic therapy, 58
Consultant, therapist as, in Bowen family systems theory, 31
Contact with family of patient, Freud, 1
Container process, in Imago relationship therapy, 119
Contextual therapy, 7
Contract, behavioral, in cognitive-behavioral therapy, 138
Cooperation between partners, problems of, in Adlerian therapy, 102
Countertransference, in object relations therapy, 85
Couples dialogue, in Imago relationship therapy, 116
Couples therapy, overview, 1–12
Creative capacity, perceptions, meaning and, in Adlerian therapy, 104
Criminal history, 18
Critical life events timeline, overview, 20
Cross-generational coalitions, 62
Culture
  in feminist couples therapy, 327
  social factors such as, inclusion of, 46
Customs, dominant story of society and, 342
Cycle
  of human sexual response, stages, 3
  of interaction, emotionally focused couples therapy and, 163

DAS. *See* Dyadic Adjustment Scale
Dearborn, Lester, 4
Decisionmaking, by differentiated individual, 26

Deductive reasoning, cognitive-behavioral therapy, 141
Defense, interpretation of, in object relations therapy, 85
Defensiveness
  patterns of, 138
  reptilian portion of brain and, 116
Deity, relationship with, support of, via religion, 47
Delinquency among juveniles, increase, inception of couples therapy, 2
Dichotomous thinking, cognitive-behavioral therapy and, 139
Dickerson, Robert L., contribution of, 4
Dicks, Harry, 7, 84, 210
Differentiated individual, decisionmaking by, 26
Differentiation
  abilities with, 25
  behavioral characteristics with, 26
  oppositional pressures toward, 26
  of self, 3–43
Digestive functions, suppression of, with anxiety, 25
Directive, in strategic therapy, 58, 62
  categories, 62
Discourses, narrative therapy with couples, 342
Divorce rates, inception of couples therapy, 2
Double-bind theory, 5
Dreikurs, R., 103
Dyadic Adjustment Scale, 143, 168, 192
Dysfunctional beliefs, about relationships, 139

EFT. *See* Emotionally focused couples therapy; Emotionally focused therapy
Ego capability, of infant, 82
Ellis, Havelock, contribution of, 3
Embodied expressions, narrative therapy with couples, 344
Emotion
  as organizing force, 163
  showing of, by therapist, strategic therapy, 63

Emotional attachment, integrative marital
    therapy and, type of, 212
Emotional distress, conflict theory of,
    249t, 249–250
Emotional reactivity, of clinician, manage-
    ment of, 32
Emotionally focused couples therapy,
    163–185, 387–394
  attachment, struggle for, 165
  attachment theory, 164
  change, stages of, 165–166
  cycles of interaction, 163
  Dyadic Adjustment Scale, 168
  emotion, 165
    as organizing force, 163
  Gottman, John, 163
  helplessness, client's sense of, 165
  Kierkegaard, S., 164
  sample case study, 168–183
    areas to avoid, 179–180
    conceptualization, 171–173
    homework, 180
    instruments, 168–171
    pitfalls, 178–179
    techniques, 176–178
    termination, 181–183
    timeline for therapy, 180–181
    treatment goals, 174–176
  skills, of therapist, 166–168
  treatment model, 163–166
Emotionally focused therapy, 8
Emotionally skillful individual, *vs.* dys-
    functional individual, 249
Empathic joining, integrative behavioral
    couple therapy and, 187–188
Empathy
  defined, 117
  derivation of, 117
Encouragement, as intervention, strategic
    therapy, 58
Entitlement, indebtedness and, belief of, 7
Epston, David, 342
Erickson, Milton, 58
  contribution of, 6
Ethical sensitivity, integrative marital ther-
    apy and, 212
Ethnicity considerations, integrative mari-
    tal therapy and, 213

Evaluation of client, structural family the-
    ory, 51–52
Expansion of two-person system, into
    three-person system, 27
Expectancy, in client-directed, outcome-in-
    formed approach, 303
Expectation
  of others, past and, object relations ther-
    apy, 81
  in relationship, unrealistic, 139
Experiential therapies, 7
Explanations, biased
  cognitive-behavioral therapy and, 140

Fairbairn, Ronald, 7, 82
Families of Slums, publication of, 45
Family Institute model, 325–341
Family life cycle theory, 60
Family Life Education Movement, 4
Family-of-origin
  figures in, object relations therapy, 82
  sessions, integrative marital therapy
    and, 221
Family of patient, contact with, Freud, 1
Family relationships, restructuring of, 45
Fantasy, interpretation of, object relations
    therapy, 85
Feldman, Larry, 8, 210
Feminist couples therapy, 8, 325–341,
    387–394
  attributes, of therapist, 328
  culture, 327
  Family Institute model, 325–341
  gender, 325–341
  imbalance, of power, 325
  power, between men, women, 325
  privilege, between men, women, 325
  responsibilities, between men, women,
    325
  sample case study, 328–340
    areas to avoid, 336–337
    assessment tools, 328–330
    conceptualization, sample case study,
      330–333
    family members, inclusion of, 337
    homework, 337–338
    pitfalls, 336

relapse prevention, 339–340
techniques, 335–336
termination, 339–340
timeline for therapy, 338–339
treatment goals, 333–335
treatment model, 325–328
Fetus, pregnant mother, somatic partnership, 83
Focused thinking, in structural therapy, 47
Formulation, conceptualization of, integrative behavioral couple therapy and, 186
Foucault, Michel, 342
Fragmentation of family, with social hardship, 45
Framo, James, contribution of, 7
Freud, S.
psychoanalysis, as dominant ideology, 2
psychoanalytic principles, 81
Fromm, Erich, emphasis on individuality, 3
Frontal lobes, catecholamines and, 25
Frustration, personal growth via, 119

Gender, 8, 325–341. *See also* Feminist couples therapy
integrative marital therapy and, 213
Genograms, family, integrative marital therapy and, 220–221
German Marriage Consultation Bureau, development of, 3
Gesture, unconscious themes in, 81
Getting Love You Want: A Guide for Couples, 120
Global Distress Scale, 192
Gottman, John, 163, 274
Greenberg, Leslie, contribution of, 8
Groups, study of, by Wilfren Bion, 84
Groves, Ernest, 4
Growth, anxiety suppression of, 25
Guerney, Bernard, 9, 273
Guide, therapist as, in conflict resolution therapy, 252
Gynecologist, couples therapy by, 2

Haley, Jay, 58
contribution of, 5
Hare-Mustin, Rachel, 347
Healer, therapist as, in conflict resolution therapy, 252
Healing aspect of relationship, belief in, in Imago relationship therapy, 119
Helplessness, client's sense of, emotionally focused couples therapy and, 165
Hendrix, Harville, 9
Hirschfeld, Magnus, 3
History of presenting problem, overview, 19–20
Holding exercise, 118
Hope, in client-directed, outcome-informed approach, 303
Human sexual response cycle, stages of, 3
Humor, in directives, 62
Hypothalamic-pituitary-adrenal axis, activation of, 25

IBCT. *See* Integrative behavioral couples therapy
Identification, projective, in marital relationship, 84
Image processes, defined, 117
Imago processes, derivation of, 117
Imago relationship therapy, 8, 9, 116–134, 380–386
agreement, requirement for, 117
anger, dealing with, 119
assessment tools, 120–121
attraction, relational conflict and, 103
attributes, of therapist, 119
Behavior Change Request, restructuring frustrations through, 118
behaviorism, synthesis of in, 116
calming, to listen without defensiveness, 116
centering, to listen without defensiveness, 116
container process, 119
couples dialogue, 116
defensiveness, reptilian portion of brain and, 116

Imago relationship therapy *(continued)*
empathy
defined, 117
derivation of, 117
frustration, personal growth via, 119
Getting Love You Want: A Guide for Couples, 120
healing aspect of relationship, belief in, 119
holding exercise, 118
image processes, defined, 117
Imago processes, derivation, 117
Institute for Imago Relationship Therapy, 119
interventions, 124–126
limits, 126–127
listening to partner, 117
parent/child dialogue, 118
physics, synthesis of in, 116
psychoanalysis, synthesis of in, 116
"re-romanticizing," process of, 118
relapse prevention, 131–133
sample case study, 120–133
areas to avoid, 127–128
conceptualization, 121–123
family members, inclusion of, 128–129
homework, 129–130
instruments, 120–121
pitfalls, 126–127
techniques, 124–126
termination, 131–133
timeline for therapy, 130–131
treatment goals, 123–124
schools of thought, synthesis of in IRT, 116
sense of self, through dialogue, 116
skills, of therapist, 119
spiritual traditions, synthesis of in, 116
therapist, on path toward relational growth, 119
treatment model, 116–119
vision for marriage, development of, 118
Western spiritual traditions, synthesis of in, 116
Imbalance, of power, feminist couples therapy and, 325

Immune functions, suppression of, with anxiety, 25
Impartiality, object relations therapy, 85
Importance of therapist, reduction of, in Bowen family system theory, 31
IMT. *See* Integrative marital therapy
Indebtedness, entitlement and, belief of, 7
Individual psychology. *See* Adlerian therapy
Individuality, Erich Fromm's emphasis on, 3
Infantile fantasy, about earliest relationship, 83
Inference, arbitrary, cognitive-behavioral therapy and, 139
Inferiority, feelings of, power to overcome, 3
Inner object relations, interpretation of, object relations therapy, 85
Institute for Imago Relationship Therapy, 119
Institute of Sexual Science, founding of, 3
Institutions, dominant story of society and, 342
Integrating Sex and Marital Therapy: A Clinical Guide, 229
Integrative behavioral couple therapy, 9, 186–209, 372–379
acceptance, 188
of partner's behavior, 186
promotion of, 187
attributes, of therapist, 189–192
behavior exchange, 188
change, promotion of, 187
communication training, 188
Conflict Tactics Scale, 182
Dyadic Adjustment Scale, 192
empathic joining, 187–188
formulation, conceptualization of, 186
Global Distress Scale, 192
Marital Satisfaction Inventory-Revised, 193
Marital Status Inventory, 192
problem-solving training, 188
sample case study, 192–208

areas to avoid, 201–202
assessment tools, 192–194
conceptualization, 194–195
family members, inclusion of, 202
homework, 202–205
instruments, 192–194
interventions, 197–201
pitfalls, 201
relapse prevention, 207–208
techniques, 197–201
termination, 207–208
timeline for therapy, 205–207
treatment goals, 196–197
skills, of therapist, 189–192
theme, of couple, 187
tolerance, 188
treatment model, 186–189
Integrative marital therapy, 8, 210–228,
    372–379
attributes, of therapist, 212–214
caring, 212
commitment, 211
communication, 212
complementarity, focus on, 211
compromise, 212
emotional attachment, type of, 212
ethical sensitivity, 212
ethnicity considerations, dealing with,
    213
gender considerations, dealing with,
    213
interventions, 219–221
kindness, 212
meanings, manner in which conveyed,
    212
negative reactions, to therapist, 213
patterns of therapy, tailored to clients,
    211
sample case study, 214–226
areas to avoid, 222
assessment, 214
clinical interviews, 214
formal assessment devices, 215
observation, 214–215
conceptualization, 215–217
family members, inclusion of,
    222–223

homework, 223
potential pitfalls, 221–222
relapse prevention, 224–226
techniques, 219–221
family genograms, 220–221
family-of-origin sessions, 221
sexual histories, 220
termination, 224–226
timeline for therapy, 224
treatment goals, 217–219
seductive reactions, to therapist, deal-
    ing with, 213
self-determination, right to, 213
skills, of therapist, 212–214
treatment model, 210–212
trust, ability to establish relationship
    of, 212
trustworthiness, 212
Integrative theory, 161–298
conflict resolution therapy, 247–272
emotionally focused therapy, 163–185
integrative behavioral therapy, 186–209
integrative marital therapy, 210–228
intersystem model, 229–246
relationship enhancement therapy,
    273–298
Interactional system, intersystem model
    and, 230
Interactions, solutions as, in strategic ther-
    apy, 61
Intergenerational system, intersystem
    model and, 230
Interpersonal Check List, 281
Interstate road map, comparison of strate-
    gic therapy to, 59
Intersystem model, 229–246, 372–379
interactional system, 230
intergenerational system, 230
object-relations theory, in intersystem
    model, 229
PENN Council for Relationships, 229
sample case study, 231–245
areas to avoid, 240–241
assessment, 231–232
conceptualization, 232–235
family members, inclusion of,
    241–242

Intersystem model *(continued)*
  homework, 242–243
  interventions, 237–239
  pitfalls, 239–240
  relapse prevention, 244–245
  techniques, 237–239
  termination, 244–245
  timeline for therapy, 243–244
  treatment goals, 235–237
  skills, of therapist, 230–231
  treatment model, 229–230
Intrapsychic realm, conflicts within, 247
Introjection, psychic structure, object relations therapy, 82
Inventory of Specific Relationships Standards, 143
Invisible loyalties, impact of, 7
IRT. *See* Imago relationship therapy
ISRS. *See* Inventory of Specific Relationships Standards

Jackson, Don, 5, 58
Johnson
  Susan, 8
  Virginia, 3
Juveniles, delinquency among, increase,
  inception of couples therapy, 2

Kautsky, Karl, Center for Sexual Advice,
  establishment of, 3
Keith, David, contribution of, 8
Kierkegaard, S., 164
Kindness, integrative marital therapy and,
  212
Klein, Melanie, 7, 83

Labeling, cognitive-behavioral therapy
  and, 140
Laidlaw, Robert, contribution of, 4
Language, dominant story of society and,
  342
Laws, dominant story of society and, 342
Libidinal ego, 82
Lief, H., 229
Life events timeline, 20
Lifestyles of partners, fitting together,
  104

Limbic system, behavior coordination, 25
Listening to partner, in Imago relation-
  ship therapy, 117
Lower brain processes, coordination of be-
  havior, 25
Loyalties, invisible, impact of, 7

Mace, David, 4
Madanes, Cloe, 6, 58
Magnetic resource imaging, 58
Magnification, cognitive-behavioral ther-
  apy and, 140
Map, comparison of strategic therapy to,
  59
Marital Happiness Scale, 143
Marital hierarchy, strategic therapy, 62
Marital Satisfaction Inventory, 143
Marital Satisfaction Inventory-Revised,
  193
Marital Status Inventory, 192
Marriage and Family Relations course,
  first offering of for college
  credit, 4
Marriage Consultation Bureau, develop-
  ment of, 3
Marriage Council, 4. *See* PENN Council
  for Relationships
Marriage counseling. *See* Couples therapy
MAS. *See* Model Attitude Survey
"Masculine protest," concept of, in Adle-
  rian therapy, 108
Masters, William, contribution of, 3
MCMI. *See* Milton Clinical Multi-Axial
  Inventory
Meanings, manner in which conveyed, in-
  tegrative marital therapy and,
  212
Medical history, overview, 15
Menninger Clinic, 4
Mental Research Institute, founding of, 5
Merrill-Palmer School, 4
Meyerhoff, Barbara, 342
MHS. *See* Marital Happiness Scale
Milan Group, 6
Milton Clinical Multi-Axial Inventory,
  108
Milton Erickson, 6

Mind reading, cognitive-behavioral therapy and, 140
Minimization, cognitive-behavioral therapy and, 140
Minuchin, Salvador, contribution of, 6
Miracle question, in Adlerian therapy, 108
Mislabeling, cognitive-behavioral therapy and, 140
Mittleman, Bela, 1
Model, treatment, 21
Model Attitude Survey, 143
Montalvo, Braulio, contribution of, 6
Morals, of client, addressing, 46
Mother, functions of, object relations therapy, 83
Motivation, by therapist, strategic therapy, 63
MRI. *See* Magnetic resource imaging; Mental Research Institute
MSI. *See* Marital Satisfaction Inventory
Mudd, Emily, contribution of, 4
Multigenerational theory, in intersystem model, 229

Napier, Augustus, contribution of, 8
Narrative therapy with couples, 8, 342–361, 380–386
  attributes, of therapist, 345
  beliefs, dominant story of society and, 342
  customs, dominant story of society and, 342
  discourses, 342
  embodied expressions, 344
  institutions, dominant story of society and, 342
  language, dominant story of society and, 342
  laws, dominant story of society and, 342
  sample case study, 346–360
    areas to avoid, 355
    assessment, 346–347
    conceptualization, 347–350
    family members, inclusion of, 355–356

  homework, 356–358
  pitfalls, 354–355
  relapse prevention, 359–360
  techniques, 350–354
  termination, 359–360
  timeline for therapy, 358–359
  treatment goals, 350
  story, of client
    attitudes, interrelation of, 342
    changing, 342
  treatment model, 342–344
  values, attitudes, interrelation of, 342
  witness groups, 344
National Marriage Guidance Council of Great Britain, founding of, 4
Nature of relationships, differentiation and, 26
Nazi invasion, migration of analysts to U.S. during, 3
Negative reactions, to therapist, integrative marital therapy and, 213
Negotiation
  coaching of, strategic therapy, 62
  exercise, strategic therapy, 70–71
Neutral manner of questioning, by therapist, strategic therapy, 63
Nichols, William, 8, 210
Novelty, in directives, strategic therapy, 62

Oberdorf, Clarence, 1
Object Relations Model, 7
Object relations theory, in intersystem model, 229
Object relations therapy, 81–101, 380–386
  antilibidinal ego, 82
  anxiety, interpretation of, 85
  attributes, of therapist, 85t, 85–88
  "because" clause, use of, 85
  Bion, Wilfred, study of groups, 84
  countertransference, 85
  defense, interpretation of, 85
  Dicks, Henry, 84
  ego capability, of infant, 82
  expectation, of others, past and, 81
  Fairbairn, Ronald, 82

Object relations therapy *(continued)*
  family-of-origin, figures in, 82
  fantasy, interpretation of, 85
  gesture, unconscious themes in, 81
  impartiality, 85
  infantile fantasy, about earliest relation-
    ship, 83
  inner object relations, interpretation of,
    85
  introjection, psychic structure, 82
  Klein, Melanie, 83
  libidinal ego, 82
  model, 7, 81–82
  mother, functions of, 83
  need for attachment, infant, 82
  projective identification, in marital rela-
    tionship, 84
  psychic structure, 81
  psychoanalytic principles, basis in, 81
  psychological, creation of, 85
  relatedness, of infant, 82
  repression, psychic structure, 82
  sample case study, 88–100
    areas to avoid, 98
    assessment, 88–89
    conceptualization, 89–92
    family members, inclusion of, 98–99
    homework, 99
    interventions, 96–98
    pitfalls, 98
    relapse prevention, 99–100
    techniques, 96–98
    termination, 99–100
    timeline, 99
    treatment goals, 95–96, 96t
  "setting frame," 85
  silence, unconscious themes in, 81
  skills, of therapist, 85t, 85–88
  somatic partnership, between pregnant
    mother, fetus, 83
  splitting, psychic structure, 82
  termination, 85
    criteria for, 96
  therapist, use of self, 85
  transference, 85
  treatment model, 81–82
  unconscious themes, 81

Winnicott, Donald, 83
words, unconscious themes in, 81
Optimism, clinical, strategic therapy,
  59–60
Ordeal therapy, 6
Outcome Questionnaire 45, 305
Overgeneralization, cognitive-behavioral
  therapy and, 139
Oversimplifications, to solve problems,
  strategic therapy, 59

Papp, Peggy, contribution of, 8
Parent/child dialogue, in Imago relation-
  ship therapy, 118
Parker, Valerie, contribution of, 4
Patterns, of interaction partners, focuses
  on, in Adlerian therapy, 102
PENN Council for Relationships, 229
Personalization, cognitive-behavioral ther-
  apy and, 139
Phenomenology, in Adlerian therapy, 106
Philadelphia Child Guidance Clinic, 6
Physical growth, anxiety suppression of,
  25
Physics, synthesis of in Imago relation-
  ship therapy, 116
Pinsof, William M., 210
Pleasing *vs.* aversive behavior, between
  partners, exchange of, 137
Postmodern theory, 299–397
  client-directed, outcome-informed ap-
    proach, 301–324
  feminist couples therapy, 325–341
  narrative therapy, 342–361
Potential of client, focus on, strategic ther-
  apy, 59–60
Poverty of family, benefit of therapy, 45
Power, between men, women, feminist
  couples therapy and, 325
Pregnant mother, fetus, somatic partnership, 83
Prepare/Enrich Measure, 281
Presenting problem
  history of, 19–20
  overview, 18–19
Privilege, between men, women, feminist
  couples therapy and, 325

Problem behavior, as efforts at protection of loved ones, 60
Problem-solving training, integrative behavioral couple therapy and, 188
Projective identification, in marital relationship, 84
Protection, in strategic therapy, 60–61
Psychiatric history, overview, 14
Psychic structure, object relations therapy, 81
Psychoanalysis
  Freudian, as dominant ideology, 2
  synthesis of in Imago relationship therapy, 116
Psychoanalytic principles, basis of object relations therapy in, 81
Psychodynamic theory, 79–134
  Adlerian therapy, 102–115
  Imago relationship therapy, 116–134
  object relations therapy, 81–101
Psychological treatment of couples, comparative, 21
Purpose of actions, in Adlerian therapy, 103, 105
PUSH acronym, use of, in strategic therapy, 60–62

Questioning, neutral manner of, by therapist, strategic therapy, 63

Race, inclusion of in therapeutic approach, 46
Rachel Hare-Mustin, 8
Re-romanticizing, process of, in Imago relationship therapy, 118
Reactivity, emotional, of clinician, management of, 32
Relatedness, of infant, 82
Relational conflict, attraction and, 103
Relationship, differences among participants in, 26
Relationship Belief Inventory, 143
Relationship enhancement couples therapy, 9, 273–298, 387–394
  acceptance, 275
  accusations, 274

attributes, of therapist, 276–278
conflict, engagement deepening, 274
conversive skill, 275
empathic responding, 275
engagement, trust and, 273
generalization, 276
interpersonal reflexes, 273–298
intimacy, trust and, 273
judgment, 275
judgments, 274
maintenance, 276
quality of confrontation, 274
sample case study, 278–297
  areas to avoid, 291–292
  conceptualization, 278–280
  family members, inclusion of, 292–294
  homework, 294
  pitfalls, 289–291
  relapse prevention, 297
  techniques, 282–289
  termination, 297
  timeline for therapy, 295–296
  treatment goals, 282
softening, 274
stress, engagement deepening, 274
treatment model, 273–276
Relationship field, anxiety in, differentiation of self and, 3–43
Relationship system, created by couple, in Adlerian therapy, 105
Relationship with deity, support of, via religion, 47
Relationships, nature of, differentiation and, 26
Religion, supports offered by, 47
Repression, psychic structure, object relations therapy, 82
Reproductive functions, suppression of, with anxiety, 25
Responsibility
  to decide, in Adlerian therapy, 104
  between men, women, feminist couples therapy and, 325
Ritual, support of, via religion, 47
Road map, interstate, comparison of strategic therapy to, 59

Safran, Jeremy, contribution of, 8
Sample case study, 21–22
Satir, Virginia, contribution of, 7
Scharff
    David, contribution of, 7
    Jill, contribution of, 7
Schizophrenia
    communication with, 5
    Harry Stack Sullivan's work with, 3
Seagraves, Robert T., 210
Seductive reactions, to therapist, dealing
    with, integrative marital ther-
    apy and, 213
Selective abstractions, in cognitive-behav-
    ioral therapy, 139
Self
    active use of, 48
    differentiation, 25
        anxiety in relationship field, 3–43
    sense of, through dialogue, 116
Self-determination, right to, integrative
    marital therapy and, 213
Self-esteem, couple happiness, 104
Self-instructional procedures, to decrease
    destructive interaction, 139
Session Rating Scale, 305
"Setting frame," in object relations ther-
    apy, 85
Sexual response cycle, stages of, 3
SFT. See Structural family theory
Silence, unconscious themes in, 81
Silverstein, Olga, 8
Social exchange theory, in cognitive-be-
    havioral therapy, 138
Social factors, inclusion of, structural fam-
    ily theory, 46
Social history, overview, 15–17
Social interest, couple happiness, in Adle-
    rian therapy, 104
Social movements, inception of couples
    therapy and, 2
Social system, hierarchy, strategic ther-
    apy, 62
Socioeconomic status, inclusion of, struc-
    tural family theory, 46
Solid self, 30
Solution-focused therapy, 6

Somatic partnership, between pregnant
    mother, fetus, 83
Spiritual outlook on life, of client, ad-
    dressing, 46
Spiritual traditions, synthesis of in Imago
    relationship therapy, 116
SRS. See Session Rating Scale
Stages, human sexual response cycle, 3
Stone, Abraham, 4
Story, of client
    attitudes, interrelation of, narrative ther-
        apy with couples, 342
    changing, narrative therapy with cou-
        ples, 342
Strategic therapy, 58–78, 367–371
    absurdity, in directives, 62
    areas to avoid, 74
    change, momentum, 63
    coaching of negotiation, 62
    concerns of therapist, 69–70
    constructions, therapist's, 59
    constructivist view, 59
    constructs of presenting problem, devel-
        opment of, 58
    cross-generational coalitions, 62
    directive, 62
        categories, 62
        as means of intervention, 58
    encouragement, as intervention, 58
    Erickson, Milton, 58
    escalating sequence, into soothing se-
        quence, 61
    family life cycle theory, 60
    family members, inclusion of, 74
    Haley, Jay, 58
    homework, 74–75
    humor, in directives, 62
    interactional sequence of events, 61
    interactions, solutions as, 61
    interstate road map, comparison of the-
        ory to, 59
    intervention, 62–63
    interventions, 70–73
    Jackson, Don, 58
    Madanes, Cole, 58
    magnetic resource imaging, 58
    marital hierarchy, 62

motivation, by therapist, 63
novelty, in directives, 62
optimism, clinical, 59–60
oversimplifications, to solve problems, 59
pitfalls, 73–74
potential of client, focus on, 59–60
problem behavior, as efforts at protection of loved ones, 60
protection, 60–61
PUSH acronym, use of, 60–62
sample case study, 64–78
    assessment, 64
    conceptualization, 65–67
    treatment goals, 64–65
social system, hierarchy, 62
strengths of client, focus on, 59–60
success
    client's view of, 77
    therapist's view of, 76–77
techniques, 70–73
termination, 76
therapist
    attributes of, 63–64
    emotion, showing of, 63
    neutral manner of questioning, 63
    skills of, 63–64
timeline, 75–76
treatment model, 58
triangle, problems conceived of in, 61
Uncommon Therapy, publication of, 60
unit, coalition therapy, 61
Washington School diagnosis, 59
Washington School of Strategic Therapy, 58
win-win negotiation exercise, 70–71
Strengths of client, focus on, strategic therapy, 59–60
Structural family theory, 45–56, 367–371
    attributes, of therapist, 47–48
    church communities, support of, via religion, 47
    culture, social factors such as, inclusion of, 46
    Families of Slums, publication of, 45
    family relationships, restructuring of, 45

focused thinking, 47
fragmentation of family, with social hardship, 45
morals, of client, addressing, 46
poverty of family, therapy, benefit of, 45
race, social factors such as, inclusion of, 46
relationship with deity, support of, via religion, 47
religion
    addressing, 46
    supports offered by, 47
ritual, 47
sample case study, 48–56
    areas to avoid, 54–55
    assessment, 48–50
    conceptualization, 50–51
    evaluation of client, 51–52
    frequency, 55–56
    homework, 55
    interventions, 53–54
    other family members, inclusion of, 55
    pitfalls, 54
    relapse prevention, 56
    techniques, 53–54
    termination, 56
    timeline, 55–56
    treatment goals, 52–53
self, active use of, 48
skills, of therapist, 47–48
social factors, inclusion of, 46
socioeconomic status, social factors such as, inclusion of, 46
spiritual dimension, addressing, 46
therapist, as person, consideration of, 46
traditional view, 45–46
treatment model, 45–47
underorganization of family, with social hardship, 45
values, of client, addressing, 46
Stuart, Richard, 9
Subjective perceptions, in Adlerian therapy, 104
Substance abuse history, 17–18

Sullivan, Harry Stack, 3, 210
  contribution of, 5
Sympathetic nervous system, activation
  of, 25
Systems theory, 23–78
  Bowen family systems theory, 25–44
  strategic therapy, 58–78
  structural family theory, 45–56

Taboo, of contact with family of patient,
  in Freud, 1
Theme of couple, integrative behavioral
  couple therapy and, 187
Therapeutic double-bind, 5
Therapeutic questioning, in Adlerian ther-
  apy, 108
Therapist's skills, attributes, overview, 21
Timeline for therapy, Bowen family sys-
  tems theory, 42
Togetherness, pressures toward, 26
"Togetherness force," 26
Tolerance, integrative behavioral couple
  therapy and, 188
Traffic police, therapist as, in conflict res-
  olutions therapy, 252
Transference, object relations therapy, 85
*Treating Couples: The Intersystem Model
  of Marriage Council of Phila-
  delphia,* 229
Triangle, problems conceived of in, strate-
  gic therapy, 61
Triangling process, 27
Trustworthiness, integrative marital ther-
  apy and, 212
Tunnel vision, cognitive-behavioral ther-
  apy and, 140
Two-person system
  expansion of, into three-person system,
    27
  problems in, 28

Uncommon Therapy, publication of, 60
Unconscious themes, object relations ther-
  apy and, 81
Underorganization of family, with social
  hardship, 45
Unit, coalition therapy, 61

Values, of client, addressing, in structural
  family theory, 46
Vision for marriage, development of, in
  Imago relationship therapy,
  118

Walters, Marianne, 8
Washington School, 58, 59, 367–371
Weakland, John, contribution of, 5
Western spiritual traditions, synthesis of
  in Imago relationship therapy,
  116
Whitaker, Carl, contribution of, 7
White, Michael, 8, 342
Wile, Daniel, 210
Williams, A., 229
Win-win negotiation exercise, 70–71
"Win-win waltz," in conflict resolution
  therapy, 248
Winnicott, Donald, 7, 83
Withdrawal, patterns of, 138
Witness groups, narrative therapy with
  couples, 344
Words, unconscious themes in, 81
World War II, migration of analysts to
  U.S. during, 3